Task-Based Language Teaching

Task-based language teaching (TBLT) is an approach that differs from traditional approaches by emphasizing the importance of engaging learners' natural abilities for acquiring language incidentally through the performance of tasks that draw learners' attention to form. Drawing on the multiple perspectives and expertise of five leading authorities in the field, this book provides a comprehensive and balanced account of TBLT. Split into five parts, the book provides an historical account of the development of TBLT and introduces the key issues facing the area. A number of different theoretical perspectives that have informed TBLT are presented, followed by a discussion on key pedagogic aspects – syllabus design, the methodology of a task-based lesson and task-based assessment. The final parts consider the research that has investigated the effectiveness of TBLT, address critiques and suggest directions for future research. TBLT is now mandated by many educational authorities throughout the world and this book serves as a core source of information for researchers, teachers and students.

Rod Ellis is a research professor in the School of Education, Curtin University in Perth, Australia, as well as a visiting professor at Shanghai International Studies University and an emeritus distinguished professor of the University of Auckland. His most recent publication is *Reflections on Task-Based Language Teaching* (2018).

Peter Skehan is an honorary research fellow at Birkbeck College, University of London. His most recent publications include *Processing Perspectives on Task Performance* (2014) and *Second Language Task-Based Performance* (2018).

Shaofeng Li is an associate professor of second and foreign language education at Florida State University and an honorary professor at Zhengzhou University and Guangdong University of Foreign Studies. His main research interests include TBLT, language aptitude, working memory and form-focused instruction.

Natsuko Shintani is a professor in the Faculty of Foreign Language Studies, Kansai University. Her work has been published in leading journals and she is author of *Input-Based Tasks in Foreign Language Instruction for Young Learners* (2016).

Craig Lambert is an associate professor of applied linguistics and TESOL at Curtin University in Perth, Australia. His research on TBLT has appeared in leading journals and he is author of *Referent Similarity and Nominal Syntax in TBLT* (2019).

THE CAMBRIDGE APPLIED LINGUISTICS SERIES

The authority on cutting-edge Applied Linguistics research

Series Editors   2007–present: Carol A. Chapelle and Susan Hunston
                     1988–2007: Michael H. Long and Jack C. Richards

For a complete list of titles please visit: www.cambridge.org

Recent Titles in This Series:

Feedback in Second Language Writing
Contexts and Issues
Edited by Ken Hyland and Fiona Hyland

Language and Television Series
A Linguistic Approach to TV Dialogue
Monika Bednarek

Intelligibility, Oral Communication, and the Teaching of Pronunciation
John M. Levis

Multilingual Education
Between Language Learning and Translanguaging
Edited by Jasone Cenoz and Durk Gorter

Learning Vocabulary in Another Language
2nd Edition
I. S. P. Nation

Narrative Research in Applied Linguistics
Edited by Gary Barkhuizen

Teacher Research in Language Teaching
A Critical Analysis
Simon Borg

Figurative Language, Genre and Register
Alice Deignan, Jeannette Littlemore and Elena Semino

Exploring ELF
Academic English Shaped by Non-native Speakers
Anna Mauranen

Genres across the Disciplines
Student Writing in Higher Education
Hilary Nesi and Sheena Gardner

Disciplinary Identities
Individuality and Community in Academic Discourse
Ken Hyland

Replication Research in Applied Linguistics
Edited by Graeme Porte

The Language of Business Meetings
Michael Handford

Reading in a Second Language
Moving from Theory to Practice
William Grabe

Modelling and Assessing Vocabulary Knowledge
Edited by Helmut Daller, James Milton and Jeanine Treffers-Daller

Practice in a Second Language
Perspectives from Applied Linguistics and Cognitive Psychology
Edited by Robert M. DeKeyser

Task-Based Language Education
From Theory to Practice
Edited by Kris van den Branden

Second Language Needs Analysis
Edited by Michael H. Long

Insights into Second Language Reading
A Cross-Linguistic Approach
Keiko Koda

Research Genres
Exploration and Applications
John M. Swales

Critical Pedagogies and Language Learning
Edited by Bonny Norton and Kelleen Toohey

Exploring the Dynamics of Second Language Writing
Edited by Barbara Kroll

Understanding Expertise in Teaching
Case Studies of Second Language Teachers
Amy B. M. Tsui

Criterion-Referenced Language Testing
James Dean Brown and Thom Hudson

Corpora in Applied Linguistics
Susan Hunston

Pragmatics in Language Teaching
Edited by Kenneth R. Rose and Gabriele Kasper

Cognition and Second Language Instruction
Edited by Peter Robinson

Research Perspectives on English for Academic Purposes
Edited by John Flowerdew and Matthew Peacock

Computer Applications in Second Language Acquisition
Foundations for Teaching, Testing and Research
Carol A. Chapelle

Task-Based Language Teaching
Theory and Practice

Rod Ellis
Curtin University, Perth

Peter Skehan
Birckbeck, University of London

Shaofeng Li
Florida State University, Tallahassee

Natsuko Shintani
Kansai University, Osaka

Craig Lambert
Curtin University, Perth

CAMBRIDGE
UNIVERSITY PRESS

University Printing House, Cambridge CB2 8BS, United Kingdom

One Liberty Plaza, 20th Floor, New York, NY 10006, USA

477 Williamstown Road, Port Melbourne, VIC 3207, Australia

314–321, 3rd Floor, Plot 3, Splendor Forum, Jasola District Centre, New Delhi – 110025, India

79 Anson Road, #06–04/06, Singapore 079906

Cambridge University Press is part of the University of Cambridge.

It furthers the University's mission by disseminating knowledge in the pursuit of education, learning, and research at the highest international levels of excellence.

www.cambridge.org
Information on this title: www.cambridge.org/9781108494083
DOI: 10.1017/9781108643689

© Rod Ellis, Peter Skehan, Shaofeng Li, Natsuko Shintani and Craig Lambert 2020

This publication is in copyright. Subject to statutory exception and to the provisions of relevant collective licensing agreements, no reproduction of any part may take place without the written permission of Cambridge University Press.

First published 2020

A catalogue record for this publication is available from the British Library.

ISBN 978-1-108-49408-3 Hardback
ISBN 978-1-108-71389-4 Paperback

Cambridge University Press has no responsibility for the persistence or accuracy of URLs for external or third-party internet websites referred to in this publication and does not guarantee that any content on such websites is, or will remain, accurate or appropriate.

Contents

List of Figures	*page* vii
List of Tables	viii
Series Editors' Preface	xi
Authors' Preface	xiii

PART I	INTRODUCTION	1
1	The Pedagogic Background to Task-Based Language Teaching	3
PART II	THEORETICAL PERSPECTIVES	27
2	Cognitive-Interactionist Perspectives	29
3	Psycholinguistic Perspectives	64
4	Sociocultural Perspectives	103
5	Psychological Perspectives	129
6	Educational Perspectives	155
PART III	PEDAGOGICAL PERSPECTIVES	175
7	Task-Based Syllabus Design	179
8	Methodology of Task-Based Language Teaching	208
9	Task-Based Testing and Assessment	241
PART IV	INVESTIGATING TASK-BASED PROGRAMMES	281
10	Comparative Method Studies	283
11	Evaluating Task-Based Language Teaching	303

PART V	MOVING FORWARD	331
12	*Responding to the Critics of Task-Based Language Teaching*	333
13	*Questions, Challenges and the Future*	353
	Endnotes	371
	References	374
	Index	412

Figures

1.1	Outline of the task-based learning framework (based on Willis 1996, p. 52)	*page* 15
2.1	Cognitive-interactionist model informing TBLT	31
2.2	Model of non-understanding routines (Varonis and Gass 1985)	35
2.3	The explicit/implicit continuum (slightly modified from Lyster and Saito 2010, p. 278)	53
4.1	Activity theory model (Engeström 1999)	110
6.1	Maehr's theory of personal investment (from Lambert 1998)	161
9.1	An outline model for task-based testing	245
11.1	Types of evaluation	308

Tables

1.1	A typology of task types (based on Prabhu 1987, pp. 46–7)	page 8
1.2	Criteria for defining a task-as-workplan (based on Ellis and Shintani 2014)	10
1.3	Features of different tasks	11
1.4	TBLT and CLT/CLIL compared (based on Ortega 2015, p. 104)	18
2.1	Indicator types in corrective feedback (based on Lyster and Ranta 1997)	36
2.2	Task design and implementation variables investigated in interaction studies	40
3.1	Potential sequences in the SSARC model	83
3.2	A comparison between the LAC approach and the CH/SSARC model	87
3.3	Malicka and Sasayama's analysis of CH-linked variables	92
4.1	Basic constructs in sociocultural SLA	106
6.1	Instruction task discourse based on LGC	165
6.2	Narrative task discourse based on LGC	166
6.3	Opinion task discourse based on LGC	166
6.4	Strengths of LGC and TGC tasks within the L2 curriculum	168
7.1	Prabhu's criteria for task sequencing	183
7.2	Ellis' criteria for task sequencing (Ellis 2003)	198
8.1	Summary of pre-task methodological options	211
8.2	Summary of within-task methodological options	223
8.3	Summary of post-task methodological options	229
8.4	Participatory structure of task-based interaction	236
9.1	Overview of meta-analytic results	248
9.2	Level of difficulty linked to Conceptualizer and Formulator influences	263
10.1	'Need', 'search' and 'evaluation' in PPP and TBLT (Shintani 2015, p. 58)	294

10.2	General programme comparisons between TBLT and PPP	296
10.3	Focused comparison studies	298
11.1	Factors determining the success of innovations (from Ellis 1997, p. 29)	305
11.2	A selection of evaluations of TBLT programmes	310
12.1	The characteristics of TBLT according to Swan (2005a)	334
12.2	Critiques of TBLT	352

Series Editors' Preface

Task-based language teaching (TBLT) has been enormously influential since the 1980s, when it inspired a generation of language teachers seeking to engage productively with Communicative Language Teaching. Since then it has developed as an approach to methodology, assessment and syllabus design. As TBLT has grown in popularity it has also diversified, incorporating a number of theoretical stances towards how languages are learnt.

This book provides a substantial overview of the current position of TBLT in the language-teaching world. It covers both pedagogic and research perspectives, arguing that the two activities are complementary and mutually supportive. In terms of research, the book provides a detailed account of the theoretical approaches that underpin TBLT. Those theories relate to a number of perspectives: cognitive, psycholinguistic, sociocultural, psychological and educational. Under those headings, the book includes comprehensive and authoritative assessments of research into such issues as: the roles of interaction and feedback; measures of complexity, accuracy and fluency; the importance of classroom phenomena such as scaffolding and individual variables such as motivation; the relation between psychological variables and language learning; and the intersection between educational practice in general and language teaching in particular.

The pedagogic chapters are more practically oriented, but also draw extensively on research into the effectiveness of TBLT. They provide a wealth of information on how to design a task-based course, what methods are used in such courses and why, and how task-based learning can and should be assessed. What comes across strongly is the degree of variation within TBLT: there is no one syllabus design and no one methodology that takes precedence over others. The authors argue convincingly that this is a positive feature of TBLT, in that it can be adapted to suit a variety of contexts and learning styles. In short, the authors do not present TBLT as an approach wherein a centre imposes action on a periphery. Rather, the principles that lie behind TBLT are an inspiration for many kinds of classroom and assessment contexts.

The final part of the book presents an honest appraisal of task-based language teaching in relation to language teaching more generally. Research that addresses this issue is summarized and a balanced conclusion presented. TBLT is not a 'magic bullet', and research still needs to be undertaken to establish the extent of its efficacy. The chapters in this part indicate how this research can be done, and what challenges are involved in carrying it out. To date, the effectiveness of TBLT is apparent in situations in which it is the dominant paradigm and also in those where it exerts an influence on teaching and assessment approaches that prioritize attention to meaning and interaction.

The authors present TBLT as a major development in language teaching, and a crucial part of current pedagogic practice. The message of this book is that in TBLT research and practice form a continuous whole. It is a welcome addition to the series.

Authors' Preface

Interest in task-based language teaching (TBLT) has burgeoned over the last thirty years. It can now be considered one of the mainstream approaches to teaching second/foreign languages as reflected in the growing number of publications intended for teachers (e.g. Willis 1996; Willis and Willis 2007; Ellis 2018a) and an expansive body of research that has investigated the effect of task design and implementation variables on the performance of tasks and on L2 acquisition (e.g. Ellis 2003; Van den Branden, Bygate and Norris 2009; Robinson 2011; Long 2015; Skehan 2018).

This book aims to provide a comprehensive survey of the pedagogic and the research literature. It has three aims:

1. The general aim is to provide a broad-based and accessible state-of-the art account of TBLT by considering the pedagogical aspects of this approach and by reviewing relevant theories and research that have informed the design and implementation of task-based courses. While these two perspectives are inter-related they have led to somewhat different justifications for designing and implementing task-based courses.
2. The second aim is to examine the effectiveness of TBLT in relation to other mainstream approaches to language teaching. One of the criticisms levelled at TBLT is that there is insufficient evidence to demonstrate that TBLT is more effective in developing L2 learners' communicative abilities than other more traditional approaches. A number of comparative method and evaluation studies enable us to examine the validity of this criticism and to demonstrate that TBLT is effective.
3. The third aim is to examine the criticisms of TBLT that have been advanced by advocates of traditional language teaching and then to identify a number of 'real' issues that need to be addressed. To this end, we will consider the problems that teachers face in introducing TBLT into their classrooms and how these problems can be addressed.

There are two general principles that inform the positions we have taken in the book:

1. Task-based pedagogy and task-based research are complementary. There is perhaps no area of language teaching where pedagogy and research have been so closely intertwined. The practice of TBLT in real classrooms has raised questions that are not just important for teachers but also of interest to researchers. For example, teachers have expressed concern about learners' use of their first language (L1) when they are performing speaking tasks while researchers have investigated specific ways in which the use of L1 can facilitate both the performance of a task and second language (L2) learning. Research-directed activity has also fed into the practice of teaching. For example, the usefulness of having learners plan before they perform a task has been clearly established through the research that has investigated pre-task planning. As Pica (1997) noted teachers, methodologists and researchers have a shared interest in the use communication tasks. This shared interest is what informs the book.
2. We view TBLT as an approach, not a method. That is, TBLT is based on a set of general principles that inform how a language is best taught and learned but it is not prescriptive of either how to design a task-based course or how to implement tasks in the classroom. Nor is the approach monolithic. There are different versions of the approach. We acknowledge these differences and consider how TBLT can be adapted to take account of the needs of teachers and learners in different instructional contexts. This acknowledgement of the diversity in TBLT is a key feature of the book that distinguishes it from the narrower, more circumscribed view of TBLT found in some other publications.

Each part of the book approaches TBLT from a different angle while always maintaining the interface between pedagogical concerns and research and acknowledging the diversity within TBLT. Part I provides the general background to TBLT and serves as a foundation for subsequent parts. Part II focuses on the theories and research that have informed task-based research. It examines a number of different perspectives by addressing the theoretical constructs that underlie each perspective and the research methodologies that have been utilized in investigating them. In Part III the focus switches to pedagogy, drawing on relevant research and emphasizing the diversity in TBLT. It addresses the principles that inform the selection and sequencing of tasks in a task-based course, the methodological principles that underlie proposals for implementing a task in the classroom, and the kinds of assessment that are compatible with TBLT. Part IV looks at the research that has investigated complete TBLT courses. It considers whether the claim that TBLT is more effective than traditional, structural approaches to language teaching is justified and reports on evaluation studies that have examined the viability of introducing TBLT in different instructional contexts. Part V concludes the book by first examining the criticisms of TBLT that have been made and suggesting the lines of research needed to further understanding of the relationship between tasks and learning. Finally, we return to considering how task-based research and task-based teaching can most profitably interface.

The primary readers of this book will be researchers, postgraduate students and teachers who are interested in using TBLT in their classrooms. It seeks to be accessible to readers who are not familiar with the research and theory that inform TBLT but it is not a 'how-to-do-it' book. Our aim is to survey the field in order to provide a wealth of information that can inform the design of task-based courses, the planning of task-based lessons, the assessment of learning and the evaluation of courses.

Part I
Introduction

Task-based language teaching (TBLT) constitutes an approach to language teaching that prioritizes meaning but does not neglect form. It emphasizes the importance of engaging learners' natural abilities for acquiring language incidentally as they engage with language as a meaning-making tool; it thus contrasts with structural approaches that emphasize language as an object to be systematically taught and intentionally learned.

The purpose of the chapter in Part I of the book is to provide a general introduction by outlining a number of key issues that will be addressed more fully in subsequent parts. We begin by providing a historical sketch of TBLT, showing its pedagogic origins in communicative language teaching (CLT) and its theoretical foundations in second language acquisition (SLA) research and principles of sound education. We then trace the development of TBLT from its early days, pointing to the multiple influences that have helped to shape its evolution. We address key issues such as how to define 'task', how tasks have been classified, how they can be sequenced into a syllabus, how a complete lesson can be built around a task, the use of tasks in computer-mediated (CM) language teaching, and task-based assessment. We introduce the key construct of 'focus on form' and explain its importance in TBLT and consider the difference between 'task-based' and 'task-supported' language teaching.

TBLT constitutes a major innovation in those instructional contexts where language has been taught through a structural syllabus. For this reason, the evaluation of task-based courses plays an important role in understanding how TBLT can be made to work efficiently and effectively in different contexts. TBLT has not always been welcomed by members of the language teaching profession. We are aware of the critiques that have been mounted against TBLT and briefly address them. We point out that these are often based on misunderstandings of

TBLT, but we also acknowledge the need to demonstrate that TBLT is in fact more effective than traditional approaches.

As noted in the Preface, the position we have taken in this book is that TBLT is not a monolithic, tightly defined approach but quite diverse. There are many issues relating to the design and implementation of task-based courses that continue to be debated. It is appropriate, therefore, that the chapter ends with a set of questions rather than a summative statement about TBLT. These questions are addressed in subsequent chapters of the book.

1 The Pedagogic Background to Task-Based Language Teaching

The overall purpose of the chapter is to introduce key issues in task-based language teaching (TBLT), which will be taken up in subsequent chapters. We first consider initial proposals for a task-based approach in the 1980s. We then examine how TBLT subsequently developed, focusing on the design of a task-based syllabus and the methodology for implementing tasks. We briefly consider how TBLT has been adapted to computer-mediated (CM) environments and also look at task-based assessment. We discuss what evaluation studies have shown about the effectiveness of TBLT and the problems that teachers face in implementing it. The chapter concludes with a brief discussion of the criticisms that have been levelled at TBLT.

Starting Points

The importance of including tasks in a language curriculum was established in the communicative language teaching (CLT) movement of the 1970s and 1980s. TBLT grew out of this movement, with further input from early research in second language acquisition (SLA), which led to a questioning of the structural approach to teaching languages where a language is broken down into bits to be taught sequentially one at a time.

CLT

CLT drew on theories of language that emphasized communicative competence (Hymes, 1971) and that viewed language as functional in nature (Halliday, 1973). These theories led to the recognition that 'there is more to the business of communicating than the ability to produce grammatically correct utterances' (Johnson, 1982) and to the idea of replacing a traditional structural syllabus with a notional syllabus (Wilkins, 1976). In other words, there was a move away from a 'synthetic' way of teaching founded on an inventory of grammatical structures to an 'analytic' approach based on language functions such as 'expressing agreement or disagreement' and semantic notions such as 'time' and 'space'. However, the language teaching materials based on a notional syllabus (e.g. Abbs and Freebairn, 1982) did not differ greatly from those based on a structural syllabus. That is, the linguistic forms for expressing each notion were mainly presented in situations and then practised in controlled exercises. Thus, while the organizational framework of a language course had changed, the methodology had not.

There was, however, a growing recognition of the need for a communicative methodology. Johnson (1982), for example, advocated what he called the deep-end strategy, where 'the student is placed in a situation where he may need to use language not yet taught' so as to activate 'the ability to search for circumlocutions when the appropriate language item is not known' (p. 193). This called for communicative tasks where the learner' use of language was judged not in terms of whether it was grammatically correct but in terms of whether the communicative outcome of the task was achieved.

CLT never developed into well-defined 'method'. Howatt (1984) distinguished a weak version, where teaching content was defined in terms of the linguistic realizations of notions and functions, but the methodology remained essentially the same as in the traditional structural approach, and a strong version, where the content of a language programme was specified in terms of communicative tasks and the methodological focus was on fluency. TBLT grew out of the strong CLT approach.

SLA Research

The SLA research that started in the 1960s and 1970s fed into the emergence of TBLT. Cross-sectional studies of learners acquiring a second language (L2) naturalistically (e.g. Dulay and Burt, 1973) provided evidence that there was an acquisition order that was common to all learners irrespective of their first languages (L1) or their age. Furthermore, a very similar order was found in classroom learners, suggesting that instruction did not have a major impact on the developmental route learners followed. Longitudinal studies (e.g. Cancino, Rosansky and Schumann, 1978) showed that learners passed through a series of stages involving 'transitional constructions' en route to the target form. Progress was gradual and often very slow, and at any one stage of development considerable variability was evident in those constructions that had been acquired up to that point.

Furthermore, it was clear that learners did not set about achieving target-like use of grammatical structures in linear fashion. Rather, they worked on several structures concurrently. This research led to the claim that there was a 'natural route' for mastering the grammar of a language and that learners had their own 'built-in syllabus' for learning it (Corder, 1967).

Drawing on this research, Krashen (1985) argued that true proficiency in an L2 depends on 'acquisition', defined as 'the subconscious process identical in all important ways to the process children utilize in acquiring their first language' and not on 'learning', defined as 'the conscious process that results in "knowing about" language' (p. 1). *The Natural Approach* (Krashen and Terrell, 1983) constituted an attempt to apply Krashen's ideas about how languages were 'acquired' to pedagogic practice. It emphasizes activities that focus learners' primary attention on meaning and caters to incidental acquisition. TBLT is based on the same principle.

Early TBLT Proposals

'Tasks' figured in both early CLT and *the Natural Approach* but in neither were they conceived of as the units around which a complete language course could be built. It was not until the mid- to late 1980s that the first proposals for a task-based approach appeared. These early proposals (Long, 1985; Candlin, 1987; Breen, 1989) were largely programmatic in nature. They focused on the rationale for a task-based syllabus and outlined how to design and evaluate a task-based curriculum. Prabhu (1987) provided the first complete account of a task-based course while Nunan (1989) gave practical advice about how to design tasks.[1]

Rationale for TBLT

These early proposals were based on:

- research in SLA (Long, 1985);
- general educational principles (Candlin and Breen);
- dissatisfaction with structural-based teaching and the intuition that the development of grammatical competence was best achieved through the effort to cope with communication (Prabhu);
- the utility of 'task' as a unit that integrates *what* learners will learn (i.e. the syllabus) with *how* they learn (i.e. methodology) (Nunan).

From the start, therefore, there were multiple inputs into the rationale for TBLT.

- Drawing on research in SLA, Long (1985) argued that 'there is no reason to assume that presenting the target language as a series of discrete linguistic or sociolinguistic teaching points is the best, or even *a* way to get learners to synthesize the parts into a coherent whole' (p. 79). He saw an approach based on tasks as providing an 'integrated solution to both syllabus and methodological issues' (p. 89).
- Candlin (1987) critiqued traditional approaches from an educational standpoint. He argued that they failed to 'emphasize educational goals ... in their pursuit of cost-effective training' (p. 16). Along with Breen (1989), he emphasized the importance of teachers and students jointly negotiating the content of a course and argued that tasks provided the best means for achieving this. Candlin claimed that an approach based on tasks would enable learners 'to become more aware of their own personalities and social roles' (p. 17), foster self-realization and self-fulfilment and enhance their self-confidence.
- Prabhu's (1987) starting point was dissatisfaction with the Structural-Oral Situational Method which was dominant in his particular teaching context (India) at that time. He argued that 'the development of competence in a second language requires not systematization of language input or maximation of planned practice, but rather the creation of conditions in which learners engage in an effort to cope with communication' (p. 1) and that this could be best achieved by having students perform tasks.
- Nunan (1989) sought to provide teachers with a practical introduction to the design and use of tasks. He claimed that basing teaching on tasks avoided the traditional distinction between syllabus and methodology. Traditional syllabuses did have a role, but as checklists rather than as directives about what to teach. Thus the starting point was the selection of the task(s) for a particular lesson.

Defining 'Task'

The early proposals for task-based teaching all provided definitions of a 'task' but these varied in a number of ways. Breen's (1989) definition was the most encompassing. A task is 'a structured plan for the provision of opportunities for the refinement of knowledge and capabilities entailed in a new language and its use during communication'. According to this definition, a task could be both a brief practice exercise and 'a more complex workplan that requires spontaneous communication'. Other definitions emphasized four important aspects of a task:

- A task is a meaning-focused activity. It requires learners to focus on meaning rather than form (Nunan, 1989).
- A task does not specify the exact meaning-content to be addressed as this will be subject to modification when it is performed. The language needed to perform a task is negotiable as the task is performed.
- A task should bear some resemblance to a task that people perform in real life. Long (1985) defined tasks as 'the hundred and one things people do in everyday life, at work, at play and in between' (p. 89).
- A task should have 'a sense of completeness' and 'stand alone as a communicative act in its own right' (Nunan, 1989, p. 10).

One of the problems with these early definitions is that they conflated two senses of 'task' – task-as-workplan and task-as-process (Breen, 1989). It was the failure to make this crucial distinction that led to the claim that the traditional distinction between 'syllabus' and 'methodology' loses relevance. We will argue later, however, that this distinction is very relevant to TBLT and that it is best to define task as a workplan.

Classifying Tasks

We find a mixed bag of suggestions for distinguishing different types of task in these early proposals. Candlin commented that it is not possible to 'offer anything other than implicit suggestions that tasks might be catalogued under several distinct types' (1987, p. 14) and that as a result 'a typology is bound to be fuzzy-edged and at most a managerial convenience' (p. 15). Long distinguished 'target tasks' (i.e. real-life tasks such as 'selling an airline ticket'), 'task types' (i.e. general tasks such as 'selling an item'), and 'pedagogic tasks' (i.e. the actual tasks that teachers and students work with). Nunan presented a number of task typologies drawn from different sources, the most useful of which is Prabhu's (see Table 1.1). This is based on how the information in a task is handled by the participants.

Grading and Sequencing Tasks

The early proposals for TBLT identified a number of criteria for determining the difficulty of pedagogical tasks:

- The linguistic complexity of the input provided by a task.
- The amount of input provided in the task.
- The number of steps involved in the execution of a task.
- The degree of structure in the information presented or required by the task.

Table 1.1 A typology of task types

Type of task	Definition
Information gap	This type involves 'a transfer of given information from one person to another – or from one form to another, or from one place to another'.
Reasoning gap	This type involves 'deriving some new information from given information through the processes of inference, deduction, practical reasoning, or a perception of relationships or patterns'.
Opinion gap	This type involves 'identifying and articulating a personal preference, feeling, or attitude in response to a given situation'.

Source: Based on Prabhu (1987, pp. 46–7).

- The number of objects, events or people that need to be distinguished when performing the task.
- The extent to which the task requires reference to present or past/future events.
- The extent to which reasons for actions or decisions need to be given.
- The intellectual challenge posed.
- The learners' familiarity with the topic of the task.

It should be immediately apparent that while such factors can clearly influence the difficulty of individual tasks, they cannot be easily used to grade tasks. It is not evident, for example, how one factor should be balanced against others. Prabhu found that the grading and sequencing tasks in the Communicational Teaching Project was more a matter of intuition than precise measurement and therefore largely a matter of trial and error.[2]

Evaluating Tasks

The importance of evaluating tasks was also recognized in these early proposals for TBLT. Long made the point that the success of a task needs to be judged in terms of task accomplishment rather than target-like linguistic production. He suggested that specialists should assess whether learners had mastered the ability to perform a 'target task'. Candlin proposed three general areas to be considered in evaluating the utility of a task – its diagnostic value, its implementability in the classroom and the extent to which it fits in with and leads to other tasks. Nunan offered the most detailed proposal in the form of a checklist of questions to be asked about a task (see pp. 135–7). This list includes questions relating to the design of the task (e.g. 'Is there an information-gap?'), its implementation (e.g. 'What type of language is stimulated by the task?'), and the learners' affective response to the task (e.g. 'Does the task engage the learners' interests?'). As with the other aspects of TBLT, these suggestions were insightful but clearly programmatic.

Subsequent Developments

Over time, the issues raised in the early proposals were built on and new issues emerged. The rationale for TBLT was further expanded to incorporate general educational principles. The thorny issue of the definition of a task was revisited. The assumption that the traditional distinction between syllabus and methodology was no longer applicable in TBLT was challenged as it became clear that the issues relating to the design and implementation of tasks remain distinct and thus warrant separate consideration.

Broadening the Rationale for TBLT

We have seen that the underpinnings of TBLT lay in CLT (the 'strong version') and in SLA research and theory. With the exception of Candlin (1987), little attention was initially paid to broader educational principles. One of the major developments that followed was an attempt to align TBLT with general theories of education. Samuda and Bygate (2008) drew on Dewey's (1938) critique of the traditional classroom with its view of learning as the mastery of ready-made products and his emphasis on the importance of learning that connects with experience of the real world. They pointed to Bruner's (1960) emphasis on 'learning for use' where the learner is positioned not just as a 'student' but as a 'practitioner'. TBLT is highly compatible with the holistic, experience-driven pedagogies advocated by these prominent educationalists.

Defining 'Task'

Definitions of tasks have proliferated over the years. Van den Branden (2006) reviewed a total of seventeen different definitions which he divided into two groups, depending on whether they were viewed as tasks in terms of language learning goals or educational activity. We do not find this proliferation of definitions helpful and argue that there is a need for a definition that is applicable across contexts and purposes.

The problem in arriving at such a definition originates in the failure to distinguish task-as-workplan and task-as-process. This is evident in the meaning attached to the word 'activity', which figures in many of the definitions. This term is ambiguous as it can refer to both the actual materials that constitute a task (i.e. the workplan) or to the language use resulting from the performance of the task (i.e. the process). We argue that a task cannot be defined in terms of process as this is, to some extent, unpredictable. Moreover, from the perspective of course design as well as language testing and research, the starting point needs to be the task-as-workplan, namely the design materials that will create a context for the communicative use of the L2. Whether this is in fact achieved (i.e. whether the task-as-workplan results in the activity intended) is an important question which can only be answered by investigating the task-as-process.

We propose, therefore, a definition based on criteria that can be used to distinguish whether a given workplan is a task or not a task (i.e. an 'exercise'). We nevertheless acknowledge that some workplans may satisfy some but not all the criteria and therefore can be more or less 'task-like'. The criteria are listed in Table 1.2.

Table 1.2 Criteria for defining a task-as-workplan

Criteria	Description
The primary focus is on meaning	The workplan is intended to ensure that learners are primarily concerned with comprehending or/and producing messages for a communicative purpose (i.e. there is primary focus on meaning-making).
There is some kind of gap	The workplan is designed in such a way as to incorporate a gap which creates a need to convey information, to reason or to express an opinion.
Learners rely mainly on their own linguistic and non-linguistic resources	Learners need to draw on their existing linguistic resources (potentially both L1 and L2) and their non-linguistic resources (e.g. gesture; facial expressions) for comprehension and production. There is therefore no explicit presentation of language.
There is a clearly defined communicative outcome	The workplan specifies the communicative outcome of the task. Thus task accomplishment is to be assessed not in terms of whether learners use language correctly but in terms of whether the communicative outcome is achieved.

Source: Based on Ellis and Shintani (2014).

Issues Relating to Task Design

TASK TYPES

There is still no generally accepted way of classifying tasks. By and large, pedagogical accounts have continued to distinguish tasks in terms of the operations learners are required to carry out when they perform them. Willis (1996), for example, distinguished six types – listing, ordering and sequencing, comparing, problem solving, sharing personal experiences and creative. Other ways of classifying tasks have emerged from research that has investigated the communicative and cognitive processes involved in performing different tasks leading to a set of features (see Table 1.3) that may impact on the language a task elicits. Any particular task can be described in terms of the specific features it incorporates. For example, an information-gap task that requires one learner to provide detailed descriptions of a set of pictures

Table 1.3 Features of different tasks

Task type	Description
One way versus two way	In a one-way information-gap task, one participant holds all the information that needs to be communicated and thus functions as the information-provider while the other functions primarily as the receiver of the information but may interact if communication becomes problematic. In a two-way task, the information is split between the participants so both need to function as the providers and receivers of the information.
Monologic versus dialogic	A monologic task places the burden of performing the task entirely on a single speaker and therefore involves a long, uninterrupted turn. A dialogic task is interactive and thus necessitates interaction between the participants and typically results in shorter turns.
Closed versus open	In a closed task there is single (or very limited set of) possible outcomes (i.e. solutions). In an open task there are a number of possible outcomes. A closed task is typically an information-gap task whereas an open task is typically an opinion-gap task.
Convergent versus divergent	Opinion-gap tasks can require learners to converge on an agreed solution to the task or can allow learners to arrive at their own individual solutions.
Rhetorical mode	The task can involve describing, narrating, instructing, reporting or arguing.

in order for another learner to identify the objects referred to is one-way, monologic, closed, convergent and descriptive. An opinion-gap task where learners are given information about four people who need a heart transplant and have to decide which person will be given the one heart available is two-way, dialogic, open, potentially divergent and argumentative.

Another important distinction is between *real-world* and *pedagogic tasks*. The former are based on target tasks and so have situational authenticity. An example might be a task where two students take on the roles of hotel receptionist and prospective guest where the latter has to make a booking for a room based on the information provided by the former. A pedagogic task lacks situational authenticity but must still display interactional authenticity (i.e. result in the kind of natural language use found in the world outside the classroom). An example is the picture-description task described in the previous paragraph. An issue of some debate (considered below) is whether a task-based course should consist only of real-world tasks or whether pedagogic tasks also have a place.

A task can be *input-based*, requiring learners to simply process the oral or written information provided and demonstrate their understanding of it (for example by drawing a picture or making a model), or it can be *output-based*, requiring the learner to speak or write to achieve the task outcome. This distinction is important because, as Prabhu (1987) noted, beginner learners cannot be expected to use the L2 productively so task-based learning must initially be input-driven.

Tasks can also be unfocused or focused (Ellis, 2003). An *unfocused task* is intended to elicit general samples of language. In the early proposals for TBLT it was generally assumed that tasks would be unfocused. A *focused task* must satisfy the general criteria for a task but is designed to orientate learners to the use of a particular linguistic feature – typically but not necessarily a grammatical structure. This possibility was explored in an important article by Loschky and Bley-Vroman (1993). They suggested that a task could be designed in such a way that it made the processing of a particular grammatical structure:

1. 'natural' (i.e. the task lends itself, in some natural way, to the frequent use of the structure (p. 132),
2. 'useful' (i.e. the use of the structure is very helpful for performing the task) or
3. 'essential' (i.e. successful performance of the task is only possible if the structure is used).[3]

The incorporation of focused tasks into a task-based curriculum need not result in a return to a structural approach if there is no attempt to teach the target structure directly, only to create a communicative context for its use. Some proponents of TBLT (e.g. Skehan, 1998; Long, 2015), however, favour a curriculum consisting only of unfocused tasks. Focused tasks, though, have a role in directing attention at those specific linguistic features that learners have shown they have difficulty in using accurately. Also focused tasks have been used frequently in researching tasks.

TASK SELECTION

Long (1985) proposed that the tasks to be included in a course should be needs-based, that is, the starting point is the target tasks that a specific group of learners need to 'function adequately in a particular target domain' (p. 91). Once identified these target tasks can be grouped into task types. The obvious advantage of such an approach that it ensures the relevance of a task-based course. However, it may prove very difficult to identify the target task needs of some groups of learners (e.g. learners in foreign language settings). Cameron (2001), for example, argued that for young foreign language learners a needs-based syllabus is not feasible.[4] Van Avermaet and Gysen (2006) also questioned whether any transfer of learning from the performance of one task to another task of the same type can be expected. It does not follow, for example, that because learners can 'buy a railway ticket' then can also 'buy an airline ticket' even though both belong to the same task type (i.e. 'buying a ticket').

Arguably, what is needed for general purpose learners are pedagogic tasks that draw on interesting and familiar content. Estaire and Zanon (1994), in one of the earliest attempts to provide practical guidance in how to plan a task-based course, suggested that task selection should be based on 'themes', which they classified in terms of how close or remote these are to the lives of the learners – the students themselves, their homes, their school, the world around them and fantasy and imagination.[5] They suggested that those themes closer to their everyday lives would be more appropriate for beginner-level learners and more remote themes for more advanced learners. However, there are dangers in materials writers or teachers deciding what their students will find familiar, relevant or interesting. Park (2015), for example, reported a marked gap between the topics that Korean middle school teachers considered ideal and the topics preferred by their students.

TASK COMPLEXITY

The early TBLT proposals identified a number of factors that influence the complexity of a task but gave no guidance as to how these factors could be applied in the practical business of grading tasks. In Chapter 3 we will examine what light theories of task complexity and the research they have generated shed on the problem of grading tasks. There is, however, little evidence that these theories have had much influence on the design of task-based courses. Willis and Willis (2007), for example, offered a list of variables for assessing task difficulty but then, like Prabhu, concluded that teachers have to rely on their own intuition. They suggested that teachers will in general have an idea about whether a particular task is suitable for their students but that referring to a list of variables can help to sharpen their intuitions.

However, there have been attempts to develop explicit guidelines for determining task complexity. Duran and Ramant's (2006) 'complexity scale' for input-based tasks distinguishes three categories of task complexity: (1) the world represented in the task, (2) the processing demands required for task performance and (3) the linguistic input features. Parameters relating to each of these categories are identified and arranged on a three-point scale (from simple to complex). For example, for (1), the parameters are 'level of abstraction' (i.e. whether the topic is concrete or abstract), 'degree of visual support' (i.e. whether visual support is provided and supports task performance) and 'linguistic context' (i.e. whether the linguistic context is available and supports task performance). There have also been attempts to investigate the effects of specific variables predicted to influence the complexity of a task on both learners' actual performance of a task and on their subjective appraisal of its difficulty. We will consider this research in Chapters 3 and 7.

Research may lead to a theory of task complexity that can inform the grading and sequencing of tasks. However, tasks are conglomerates of variables and complexity is therefore influenced by the intersection of countless variables in ways that may make codification difficult if not impossible. Also, complexity depends on how the task is implemented (e.g. whether there is opportunity for learners to plan before they perform the task) as much if not more than on the design of the workplan. The grading and sequencing tasks remain a major challenge in TBLT. Perhaps the best that can be done, as Prabhu and Willis and Willis have suggested, is for teachers and course designers to rely on their experience and intuition while loosely guided by what research and theory has shown can affect task complexity.

Methodological Issues

The early proposals had little to say about how a task should be implemented and, with the exception of Prahbu, even less about how to plan a task-based lesson. Subsequently, however, greater attention has been paid to methodological issues in TBLT.

THE TASK-BASED LESSON

In the Communicational Language Project, a task-based lesson consisted of a pre-task, which served as a preparation for a main task of the same kind. The pre-task was performed in a whole-class context while the main task was completed by the students working individually. In other words, there was no small group work. In the pre-task the teachers guided learners' performance of the task by simplifying, repeating and paraphrasing their input to make it comprehensible and, where necessary, by reformulating the learners' own attempts to use the L2 in a target-like way. Prabhu rejected group work on the grounds that it would expose learners to poor models of English.

Willis (1996) proposed a very different framework for a task-based lesson, one that prioritized learner–learner interaction. This framework is shown in outline in Figure 1.1 and an example of a lesson plan based on it can be found in the Appendix to this chapter. It established the standard format for a task-based lesson, namely a pre-task stage, a main-task stage and a post-task stage. Willis prioritized small group work in the main task phase (called the 'task cycle') but allowed for teacher-centred activity in the pre-task and language focus stages.

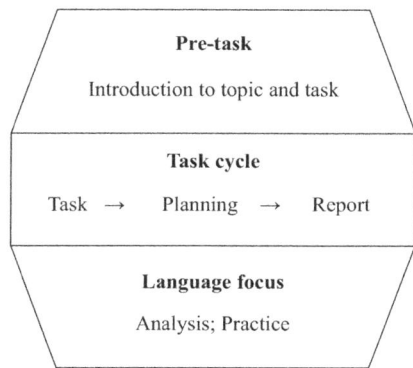

Figure 1.1 Outline of the task-based learning framework
Source: Based on Willis (1996, p. 52).

FOCUS ON FORM

Willis (1996) advised teachers to 'stand back and let the learners get on with the task on their own' (p. 54) and argued they should resist the temptation to provide language support or correct learners' production while they are performing a task. She suggested that a concern for accuracy would arise naturally in the reporting stage of task cycle and could be addressed directly in the language focus stage. Long (1991), however, argued that there was a need to draw learners' attention to form *during* the performance of a task. He coined the term 'focus on form' to refer to a teaching strategy that 'overtly draws students attention to linguistic elements as they arise incidentally in lessons whose overriding focus is on meaning or communication' (pp. 45–6).

Long (2015) saw focus on form as essentially reactive but in fact it can take place both pre-emptively (e.g. when a teacher or student anticipates the need for a specific linguistic item as they perform the task) and reactively in response to students' comprehension or production problems. It can also be very implicit, as when the teacher quickly recasts a learner utterance, or very explicit, as when the teacher points out an error and corrects it. In other words there are a variety of strategies available to teachers to attract learners' attention to form while they are performing the task (see Ellis, Basturkmen and Loewen, 2002).

The recognition that task-based teaching does not necessitate an exclusive focus on meaning but also allows for (indeed requires in the opinion of many commentators) attention to form during the performance of a task constitutes one of the major developments in TBLT. Nevertheless, the belief that teachers should not intervene either pre-emptively or reactively in a 'fluency' activity still holds sway in popular teacher guides. Hedge (2000), for example, observed that the teacher notes accompanying course books frequently instruct teachers to avoid correcting learners until the end of a fluency activity. There is, however, growing evidence that focus on form facilitates acquisition (see Ellis, 2015a).

According to Willis (1996), the point of the pre-task stage of a lesson 'is not to teach large amounts of new language and certainly not to teach one particular grammatical structure' (p. 43). Tomlinson (2015) took an even stronger stance, arguing against the pre-teaching of any language on the grounds that it 'risks changing the task into a language activity' (p. 329). These commentators adhere to the general principle of task-based teaching, namely that there should be no direct teaching of the language needed to perform a task. However, opportunities for introducing a focus on form in the pre-task phase are available. One possibility is to give learners the opportunity to plan before they perform a task. This will involve them in both conceptualizing what they wish to communicate and formulating the language they will need. Pre-task planning places the burden of working out how to perform the task squarely on the learner and thus is compatible with a key principle of TBLT, namely that the learners should be free to choose from their own linguistic repertoires. See Chapters 3 and 8 for research on planning in TBLT.

The post-task stage offers the clearest opportunities for form-focused activities including traditional ones. Willis and Willis (2007) suggested that when the task cycle is complete the teacher is free to isolate specific linguistic forms for study and work on these forms outside the context of the communicative activity. Selection of the linguistic forms for instruction can be based either on the task workplan – for example, by identifying specific items from the texts included in a workplan and preparing activities to practise or develop awareness of the use of them – or on linguistic features the learners experienced actual difficulty with when they performed the task.

The methodology of TBLT is now well articulated but there is no consensus about which methodological procedures are appropriate. There is a growing consensus that attention to linguistic form is needed as long as the primary focus remains on meaning. There are differences in opinion, however, regarding whether a focus on form is desirable during the performance of the task and also what strategies should be used to draw attention to form.

Content-Based Language Teaching and TBLT

Content-based instruction (CBI) and content-integrated language learning (CLIL) share with TBLT the assumption that a language is best learned when learners are primarily focused on using language. In CBI and CLIL learners learn language through the process of mastering the content of (typically) academic subjects (e.g. history, science, mathematics) and this can include completing subject-relevant tasks. It might seem, then, that CBI/CLIL and TBLT are just versions of the same overall approach. Ortega (2015), however, points out that 'the two fields are pre-occupied with quite distinct issues' (p. 103). Table 1.4 summarizes the differences Ortega identified. These differences are by and large contextual in nature, reflecting the importance of context and pedagogic purpose in shaping meaning-oriented approaches to language teaching. However, the differences are historical, reflecting how the two fields have evolved, rather than

Table 1.4 TBLT and CLT/CLIL compared

Task-based language teaching	Content-integrated language learning
Emphasis on college-level learners	Mainly implemented with school-level learners
Easier to implement in second language contexts	Common in foreign language contexts
Experimental research carried out in laboratories	Descriptive research of intact classrooms
Emphasis on transfer of learning from pedagogic tasks to real-life (target) tasks.	Emphasis on demonstrating balanced gains in language learning and content learning

Source: Based on Ortega (2015, p. 104).

fundamental. For example, there is growing recognition that TBLT is highly relevant for foreign language contexts and for young children.

Lyster (2007) provides an example of the kind of task that figures in a CBI. Students were asked 'to create a continent, identifying its name and illustrating its geographical features on a map, which they then presented to their teacher and classmates with a detailed explanation of how the various geographical features influence the continent's overall climatic conditions' (p. 74). This task illustrates one advantage that CBI has over TBLT: the choice of topics is determined by the need to follow the syllabus for a particular academic subject. However, CBI/CLIL do not rely exclusively on tasks to provide language-rich content. Teachers may engage in types of classroom interaction (e.g. initiate-response exchanges) that TBLT is designed to replace. This reflects the final point in Table 1.4, namely that in CBI/CLIL content learning is of equal importance to language learning and that tasks are not the only (or in some cases perhaps not even the best) way of teaching content.

Technology-Mediated TBLT

One of the major developments in the last thirty or so years has been the use of technology in language teaching – micro-computers in particular, but also mobile phones, telecommunication systems and social media sites. Computer-mediated language learning (CALL) appeared on the scene in the 1980s at much the same time as the early proposals for TBLT. While the initial proposals for TBLT had the face-to-face classroom very much in mind, it was not long before suggestions appeared for CM task-based teaching. Developments in

CALL mirrored those in language pedagogy in general. There was a structural/behaviourist phase that gave way to a communicative phase and finally to a more integrative stage with the 'centrality of task-based authentic learning moving increasingly into the foreground' (Thomas and Reinders, 2010, p. 6).

Technology-mediated TBLT has a number of advantages. Lai and Li (2011) emphasized the natural synergy of technology and TBLT:

> On the one hand, technology facilitates and enhances TBLT both in terms of its effectiveness and its contribution to our understanding of TBLT; on the other hand, TBLT serves as a useful pedagogical framework and set of principles that can enrich and maximize the use of technology for language learning. (p. 499)

Technology affords multi-modal opportunities for presenting complex workplans (aural, written and visual) and for performing them synchronously and/or asynchronously. Appel and Gilabert (2002) describe a task that involved planning a route and budget for a one-night trip that required email exchanges, the use of web pages and synchronous communication. Technology allows the input materials for a task to be fed into the performance of the task in steps. This is also possible in the face-to-face classroom but is much easier in a technologically mediated environment. In short, technology makes tasks that require complex outcomes possible and it can make rich, multilayered input available for achieving them. It not only enriches learners' opportunities for language learning but also helps to foster electronic literacy and increase learners' ability to handle multi-modal communication.

By and large the model of TBLT presented in the previous sections of this chapter is premised on a set of more or less disconnected tasks which provide the basis for individual lessons – as, for example, in the Communicational Language Project. Ortega (2009) suggested that technologically driven TBLT should be reconceptualized as project-based, where there is a series of interlocking tasks relating to the overall goal of the project. Again, this is possible in a face-to-face environment – in fact Skehan (1998) proposed just this – but it is arguably easier to organize with the assistance of technology.

The increasing interest in technology-mediated TBLT is reflected in the growing literature on the subject (e.g. González-Lloret and Ortega, 2015; Thomas and Reinders, 2015) and in the appearance of online TBLT courses (e.g. Duran and Ramault, 2006). There are also problems and challenges. Learners may lack the necessary technical skills to exploit the multi-modal resources made available to them. Teachers often lack training in how to handle tasks in a technologically mediated environment while the emphasis on learner-centredness can leave them uncertain of their own role.

Task-Based Language Assessment

The development of TBLT ran in parallel with 'a general move away from discrete-point, indirect testing, and towards more integrated, direct performance assessments' (Norris et al., 1998, p. 54) based on tasks. In fact, though, as Bachman (2002) pointed out, the use of tasks for assessment purposes had figured in direct language testing for some time. What was new was the idea of using tasks not as a means of eliciting learner performances as basis for assessing learners' general abilities (i.e. their language proficiency) but for determining whether they were capable of performing specific target tasks. When tasks are used to assess L2 general proficiency, the assessor makes a judgement of the learner's performance of a task based on a rating scale that specifies the different abilities being assessed and the level achieved. Popular tests such as TOEFL (Test of English as a Foreign Language) and IELTS (International English Language Testing System) assess proficiency in this way. In task-based language assessment, however, task performance is assessed in terms of task accomplishment.

The basic principle of task-based assessment was clearly stated by Long and Norris (2000):

> Task-based assessment does not simply utilize the real-world task as a means for eliciting particular components of the language system, which are then measured or evaluated; instead the construct of interest is performance of the task itself. (p. 600)

For Long and Norris – in line with Long's (1985) views about TBLT – the tasks used for assessment should reflect target tasks (i.e. real-life tasks). They proposed using needs analysis to identify the specific target tasks relevant to a particular group of learners and deriving authentic assessment tasks from these. Douglas (2000) developed a framework for analysing target tasks as communicative events with the aim of achieving a high level of correspondence between the target task and the assessment task.

There are, however, problems with such an approach (see Bachman, 2002). As we have already pointed out, a needs-based approach is not appropriate for all learners. *Situational authenticity* is clearly important if the purpose of the test is to assess learners' ability to perform the tasks in a specific target domain but it is less relevant when the purpose is to assess the communicative abilities of general purpose learners for whom there is no clearly defined target domain. For such learners a more realistic aim is *interactional authenticity* in the assessment tasks. However, guaranteeing interactional authenticity is not easy. The very fact that learners know they are being assessed encourages them to display what they know rather than to interact in a natural way.

Teachers, however, are more likely to be concerned with formative rather than summative assessment. Formative assessment is an essential part of TBLT and involves obtaining information about how learners perform tasks. The information needed relates to both the product of the task (i.e. did the students succeed in achieving the outcome of the task?) and its actual performance (i.e. did the students engage actively when they performed the task?). Van Gorp and Deygers (2014) provide a detailed account of a formative assessment of a reading task designed for primary school students in Belgium. It was based on a set of key questions that addressed whether (1) the students' reading of the task-based material was goal oriented, (2) they could find the information they were looking for, (3) the teacher could identify and address any problems the students experienced and, more generally, whether (4) the students demonstrated self-reliance, positive attitudes to the task and reflective ability. Such a formative assessment can shed light not just on the students' abilities and the teacher's contribution to their development but also on how the task itself might be improved for future use. There is a strong case for student self-assessment. After completing a task, learners can be guided to self-assess their own performance of it. Butler (2017a) was able to show that not only are quite young children capable of this but that their self-assessment correlates well with more objective assessment.

Task-based assessment is discussed in Chapter 9.

Evaluating TBLT

We have seen that TBLT grew out of CLT but developed into a distinct approach to language teaching. By rejecting the premise that a language can be taught piecemeal in linear fashion and by proposing instead an approach catering to the learner's natural propensity for learning a language, TBLT can be seen as a radical alternative to traditional forms of language teaching – what Long (1991a) called 'focus on forms'.

There is plenty of evidence of the uptake of TBLT. Starting in 2005, there has been a biennial TBLT conference where task-based educational ideas and research are presented and discussed. A number of countries have officially mandated the use of TBLT. In 1999 the Education Department of Hong Kong launched the Target Oriented Curriculum, which was underwritten by a task-based approach. In Belgium task-based syllabuses and materials were developed for teaching Dutch both as a first and second language at the primary, secondary and adult education levels (see Van den Branden 2006). The new English curriculum in China does not specify any particular teaching approach but recommends the use of task-based teaching as the means for achieving integrated skills development, problem-solving abilities and cooperative learning (Wang, 2007). There have also been countless small-scale implementations of TBLT in contexts where teachers are free to choose their own approach (see, for example, Leaver and Willis, 2004 and Edwards and Willis, 2005). TBLT has progressed well beyond theory into actual practice but it is clearly important to evaluate to what extent TBLT has been successfully implemented in different instructional contexts.

There have been a number of evaluations of TBLT programmes. One of the first was Beretta and Davies' (1985) evaluation of Prabhu's Communicational Teaching Project. This reported results that lent support to the effectiveness of task-based teaching. Beretta and Davies concluded that task-based instruction produces significantly different learning from traditional form-focused instruction. In a follow-up evaluation, however, Beretta (1990) questioned whether the methodological innovations required by the project were actually implemented by the teachers involved. He concluded that the principles and methodology of task-based instruction had not been fully assimilated by the regular classroom teachers involved in the project.

Later evaluations of TBLT carried out in different teaching contexts pointed to a number of difficulties in implementing it:

- teachers' misunderstanding about the nature of a 'task'
- problems with oral use of the target language in the case of teachers for the whom the target language was also an L2
- overuse of the L1 by the students when performing tasks
- difficulty in adjusting tasks to the students' level of proficiency
- difficulty in implementing tasks in large classes
- lack of task-based teaching resources and limited time for teachers to develop their own resources
- uncertainty about how grammar was to be handled in TBLT
- the need to prepare students for formal examinations
- lack of training in TBLT.

This list paints a bleak picture of the viability of implementing TBLT. However, many of the same problems are likely to arise whenever teachers are faced with an innovation of any kind and are addressable by ensuring that the appropriate conditions for innovation have been established – in particular through teacher training programmes.

Also, there are cases showing the successful uptake of TBLT. González-Lloret and Nielson (2015), for example, report a carefully planned evaluation of a TBLT course for agents in the US Border Patrol Academy who needed to use Spanish in their daily work. The students in the task-based course outperformed students in a traditional grammar-based course in terms of fluency and also achieved an equivalent level of grammatical accuracy. They all passed the performance-based assessments. The students also reported finding the course useful and relevant to their work. In Chapter 10 we examine a number of experimental studies that have compared TBLT and other approaches, while in Chapter 11 we look at evaluation studies that have examined how TBLT has been implemented in a range of different instructional contexts.

Critiques of TBLT

The advocacy of TBLT has to a large extent been driven from the top down by teacher educators with a background in applied linguistics, in particular SLA. For this reason, perhaps, TBLT has met with considerable resistance and is the subject of a number of critiques (e.g. Sheen, 1994, 2006; Swan, 2005a). Many of these critiques, however, derive from a misunderstanding of TBLT (Ellis, 2009a; Long, 2016). For example, some critics have wrongly assumed that it necessarily involves learners working in groups to perform speaking tasks. Often critics have failed to recognize that TBLT is not monolithic but incorporates a range of possibilities which share the central idea that a language is best learned *through* the effort to use it communicatively. The critiques have also been directed at TBLT for general language teaching and ignore the obvious suitability of TBLT for specific-purpose language teaching.

However, some criticisms deserve serious consideration. One of the main criticisms is that there is no evidence that TBLT is more effective than a traditional focus-on-forms approach. Sheen, in particular, has argued the need for comparative studies that investigate the relative effectiveness of the two approaches and attempted such a study himself (R. Sheen, 2006). Sheen is right in demanding evidence but his own study was methodologically flawed in several ways and demonstrates the difficulty in designing comparative method studies. In fact, though, there is evidence from both evaluation studies and from experimental studies (e.g. Shintani, 2015) that TBLT can deliver on its promise to foster the development of both linguistic and communicative competence in an L2 more effectively than traditional 'focus-on-forms' instruction.

Another criticism worthy of serious consideration is that TBLT is incompatible with cultures of learning that are different from those in

Western settings. Littlewood (2014), for example, argued that CLT (including TBLT) is ill-suited to the traditional Chinese culture of learning, where 'education is conceived more as a process of knowledge accumulation than as a process of using knowledge for immediate purposes' (p. 653) and which therefore emphasizes knowledge transmission and teacher-centred instruction. Littlewood came out in favour of task-supported language teaching, where tasks are used to provide communicative practice for language items taught in accordance with a traditional structural syllabus – in other words, presentation, practice, production (PPP).

This last criticism leads to an important question. To what extent should the choice of teaching approach be determined by psycholinguistic or cultural factors? To a very considerable extent the advocacy of TBLT has been based on the former. Opposition to TBLT has been based on the need to acknowledge the cultural realities of classroom life. If the goal is to achieve the ability to use an L2 for real-life purposes then traditional approaches do not have a good record of success. If, however, the alternative to these approaches – TBLT – proves difficult to implement, then, it too is unlikely to be successful. There is no easy resolution to this conundrum except to note that a modular language curriculum makes room for both a traditional approach and for TBLT.[6]

Conclusion

We have seen that TBLT grew out disillusionment with the structural approach. It was informed by CLT and recognition of the need to develop fluency in an L2, by theory and research in SLA that pointed to the difficulty of intervening directly in the process of L2 acquisition, and by educational theories that challenged traditional transmission-style teaching and emphasized the need for holistic, experiential instructional activities. From its starting point in the 1980s fully-fledged proposals for using tasks as the basic unit for teaching and assessment have been developed and there are now accounts and evaluations of complete task-based programmes. There are books that detail how teachers can set about implementing TBLT in their classrooms. Not surprisingly there are also critiques that have raised a number of issues relating to both the rationale for TBLT and its implementation.

We conclude with a list of questions arising from the account of TBLT in this chapter:

1. How should the central unit of task-based teaching – the task – be defined?

2. What kinds of tasks are appropriate for different groups of learners? Is a needs-based approach for identifying target tasks appropriate for all learners?
3. How can the problems of determining the complexity of tasks be resolved to ensure that learners of different levels of proficiency are faced with tasks that pose a reasonable challenge?
4. How can task-based teaching be made to work for beginner learners who have no or very little knowledge of the L2?
5. Is there a role for focused as well as unfocused tasks and, if so, how should focused tasks be incorporated into a task-based syllabus?
6. Is there merit in a modular curriculum that includes both a task-based component and a traditional structural component? How should such a curriculum be organized?
7. What alternatives are there for the organization of a task-based lesson? Is the lesson format proposed by Willis (1996), which has proved very influential, the only way?
8. How can a focus on form be best incorporated into a task-based lesson?
9. How can teachers carry out formative assessments of task-based lessons to gather evidence of whether learning is taking place and what changes may be needed to the task?
10. What problems do teachers face in implementing task-based teaching and how can these be addressed?

This chapter has offered provisional answers to these questions based on our own views about TBLT but, as we have also pointed out, there are alternative positions. These questions are revisited throughout the book and in particular in the concluding chapter.

Appendix: Example of a task-based lesson plan (based on material developed by Tom Marchand – see http://willi-elt.co.uk/wp-content/uploads/2015/03/1StrictParents.pdf

Talking about Families—How Strict Are/Were Your Parents?

1 *Introductory questionnaire:*
When you were a child:
a) Do you think your parents were strict or easy-going?
b) Did they allow you to stay out late at night?

c) Did they let you go on holiday on your own?
d) When you went out did you always have to tell them where you were going?
e) Did you always have to do your homework before supper?
f) Did your parents make you help about the house?
g) What jobs did they make you do?
h) Did you have to wash the car?

PREPARATION: Teacher makes sure that learners understand the questionnaire.

TASK: Learners work in groups to answer the questions.

PLANNING: Teacher tells learners that a spokesperson from each group will be asked to report the results of their discussion to the class as a whole. Learners are given time to help the spokesperson plan the report.

REPORT: Spokespersons for two or three of the groups deliver their reports. The other groups listen and make notes comparing the report with their own results. Teacher leads a round-up discussion which will include contributions from groups which did not report.

2 Discussion: *Whose parents were the strictest?*

TASK: Learners work in groups to decide which of them had the strictest parents.

PLANNING: Teacher tells learners that a spokesperson from each group will be asked to report the results of their discussion to the class as a whole. Learners are given time to help the spokesperson plan the report.

REPORT: Spokespersons for two or three of the groups deliver their reports. The other groups listen and decide which parents were the strictest. Teacher leads a round-up discussion which will include contributions from groups which did not report.

3 **Listening:** Tim made recordings of some of his friends talking about how strict their parents were. For example:

> *My Dad is a quiet man really, so he didn't really make me do much at home. He sometimes asked me to wash his car or cut the grass, but I was never forced to do it, and I could usually get some pocket money for it as well. I think my Mum was also pretty easy-going; she let me stay out late with my friends. As long as she knew where I was, she wouldn't mind so much what I did.*

4 **Language practice:**

For the form-focused work, the final stage in a task-based cycle, activities focusing on expressions of permission and compulsion were devised.

Part II
Theoretical Perspectives

This section focuses on the theories and research that afford different perspectives on task-based research. It aims to address the following questions:

1. What theoretical view of language performance and learning underlies each of these perspectives?
2. What key theoretical constructs inform the investigation of tasks in the different perspectives?
3. What research methodology is used to investigate tasks in each perspective?
4. What differences are there in the way acquisition/language use is conceptualized and operationalized in these perspectives?

Chapter 2 presents the theory and research related to the cognitive-interactionist perspective, which was introduced in Chapter 1. It examines how different kinds of tasks create opportunities for interaction that foster the processes involved in second language (L2) and thereby highlights the importance of social interaction for task-based language teaching (TBLT). It addresses the role that the negotiation of meaning and form play in the implementation of tasks and how negotiation is achieved through interaction, especially when there is corrective feedback (CF). This chapter also examines to what extent and how interaction fosters acquisition when tasks are performed. It concludes with an evaluation of this approach to investigating tasks, pointing out both its strengths and weaknesses.

Chapter 3 presents theory and research that examine tasks in relation to the cognitive processes involved in second language (L2) production in what we have called the psycholinguistic perspective. The chapter explores and critiques two models of task-based performance – the Limited Attention Capacity Hypothesis (LACH) and the Cognition Hypothesis (CH) – which have informed a large body of research. The chapter reviews studies that investigated how task design and implementation variables impact on task performance in terms of the complexity, accuracy, lexis and fluency of the learners' production. The chapter also considers a key issue for TBLT, namely the relationship between task performance and L2 acquisition.

Chapter 4 offers a *sociocultural perspective* on tasks. In sociocultural theory a 'task' is viewed an artefact for mediating learning through interaction. It views 'task' as always interpreted by the participants so that what the task is intended to achieve (i.e. the task-as-workplan) may well not match what the task actually achieves when it is performed (i.e. the task-as-process). Like the cognitive-interactionist perspective, the sociocultural perspective views tasks in terms of the interactions to which they give rise, emphasizing the importance of the collaborative nature of the interaction for 'learning' (defined as other-regulation) and for 'development' (defined as self-regulation). It reviews a range of research that has investigated tasks from a sociocultural perspective, including studies involving 'languaging', dynamic assessment and concept-based language instruction.

Individual learner factors play an important role in how a task is performed. This requires a perspective that draws on the theory and research that addresses the psychology of the learner – what we call the psychological perspective on TBLT. Chapter 5 surveys the large body of research on the role of cognitive aptitudes (including working memory) in mediating the effects of different instructional tasks on language performance and acquisition. The chapter will also discuss the influence of affective factors such as motivation and language anxiety on task performance and outcome. A key focus of this chapter is how these psychological variables mediate the performance of a task and the learning that results.

In Chapter 6, the final chapter in this section, we adopt and educational perspective on TBLT. The chapter begins by summarizing general educational theories that support an approach to learning that emphasizes experience and 'doing' over knowing and 'telling' – such as those of Dewey (1938) and recent work on complex skill acquisition and training. It then considers research that draws on educational accounts of the role of 'engagement' in task performance and learning and the importance of investigating learners' perceptions of the tasks they perform as well as their actual performance.

2 Cognitive-Interactionist Perspectives

Introduction

According to the Interaction Hypothesis (IH) 'negotiation for meaning, and especially negotiation work that triggers interactional adjustments by the NS or more competent interlocutor, facilitates acquisition because it connects input, internal learner capacities, particularly selective attention, and output in productive ways' (Long, 1996, pp. 451–2). In this way, Long captured the symbiotic relationship between interaction and cognition; that is, interaction activates the mental mechanisms involved in processing input and output in ways that result in acquisition. The IH was subsequently broadened into what Gass and Mackey (2007) called the *interaction approach*, which concerns what happens 'when learners encounter input, are involved in interaction, receive feedback and produce output' (p. 176). According to this perspective, tasks will prove effective to the extent to which they provide input and promote interaction of the kinds that activate the mental mechanisms involved in acquisition.

We begin this chapter with the 'cognitive side' by examining the role of *attention* in second language (L2) acquisition and *implicit/incidental acquisition*, which proponents of task-based language teaching (TBLT) such as Long (2015) and Ellis (2003) see as central cognitive processes. This is followed by an account of interaction and how researchers have analysed it. The next sections, which constitute the core of this chapter, consider how cognitive-interactionist perspectives have informed the design and implementation of tasks, how tasks induce noticing, how the interactions they afford result in acquisition, and how interaction takes place in small group work. In the concluding section of the chapter we consider the strengths and limitations of cognitive-interactionist accounts of TBLT.

Cognitive Processes: Implicit Learning, Incidental Learning and the Role of Attention

For Long (2015), the essential empirical problem in second language acquisition (SLA) that needs an explanation is why children are entirely successfully in acquiring their mother tongue implicitly while adults are largely unsuccessful. According to Long (1990, 2015), L2 acquisition is maturationally constrained because adults no longer have full access to the mechanisms involved in implicit learning and thus are 'partially disabled language learners' (Long, 2015, p. 41). Long maintains, however, that 'implicit learning is still the default learning mechanism' (p. 43) for adults and cites as evidence studies (e.g. Rebuschat and Williams, 2009; Leung and Williams, 2011) that demonstrate implicit learning is still possible in adults for some aspects of grammar such as simple form-meaning mappings and basic word order. Long also recognizes the need for explicit learning to help overcome the limitations of adult implicit learning. However, he rejects the view that explicit, intentional learning constitutes an alternative to implicit learning as claimed by skill-learning theory and as manifested in the language teaching approaches based on that theory. For Long, explicit learning has a more limited role – to prompt initial perception of L2 forms in the input and thereby to help learners to overcome entrenched first language (L1) routines. That is, he sees the explicit knowledge that results from intentional learning as changing how learners attend to input and as tuning the implicit processes involved in acquisition (N. Ellis, 2005). In other words, TBLT, when supported by strategies that focus learners' attention on form, promotes implicit learning.

Cognitive models of L2 acquisition also draw heavily on Schmidt's (1990, 1994) views about the importance of *attention* in L2 acquisition. Schmidt distinguishes two levels of attention – a low level which he calls 'noticing' and a deeper level involving 'understanding'. For example, a learner may 'notice' the plural-s on a noun and register that this signals 'more than one' or the learner may go a step further and consciously construct a rule for expressing plurality (i.e. add 's' to a noun to signal 'more than one'). According to this view, completely implicit learning is not possible as 'noticing' involves consciousness which is a prerequisite for acquisition to take place. However, Schmidt (2001) later modified this position. While continuing to emphasize the importance of 'noticing', he acknowledged that *detection* or what Gass (1988) called *apperception* can take place subconsciously as claimed by Tomlin and Villa (1994). Williams (2013, p. 39) similarly claimed that 'whilst attention does appear to be necessary for learning,

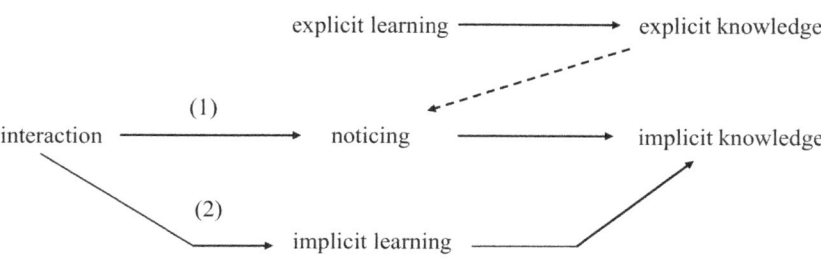

Figure 2.1 Cognitive-interactionist model informing TBLT

awareness might not be'. Schmidt was ambivalent about the role of 'understanding', viewing it as potentially helpful for acquisition but not necessary.

Drawing on these key constructs, we can outline the cognitive-interactionist model that underscores TBLT (see Figure 2.1). Learners are exposed to input through interaction. Implicit learning can occur when learners learn without conscious attention to linguistic forms in the input (i.e. there is an absence of 'noticing') and this results in implicit knowledge – the kind of knowledge required for easy and fluent communicative language use. However, adult L2 learners are limited in their ability to learn in this way but, fortunately, there is another route to implicit knowledge which can compensate for their reduced capacity for implicit learning.[1] This involves the explicit knowledge they have gained from intentional language learning, which serves as an activator of noticing and, in this way, facilitates the development of implicit knowledge. In Figure 2.1 the line linking explicit knowledge and 'noticing' (i.e. the conscious awareness of linguistic features) is dotted. This is intended to show that this link is variable, depending on both external factors such as interactive strategies that attract attention to form and internal factors such as learners' propensity and ability to attend to form. The model posits no direct relationship between explicit and implicit knowledge. In other words, there is no substitute for implicit learning or noticing as the means for achieving implicit knowledge of a language.

There remain a number of issues that require clarification. First, *implicit* and *incidental* learning are often treated as synonymous but they are not.[2] Whereas the latter is defined as learning without consciousness and involves only detection, the former involves 'noticing', i.e. focal attention and conscious awareness of specific linguistic forms. The route labelled (1) in Figure 2.1 represents incidental learning and the route labelled (2) implicit learning. Incidental acquisition can occur in all kinds of instruction, including explicit instruction. For example, learners may incidentally acquire features y and z even when the instruction is explicitly directed at feature x. This possibility has been little investigated, however, and is perhaps unlikely given that the focal attention directed at the target structure may inhibit attention to other features. Loewen, Erlam and Ellis (2009), for example, found that learners failed to acquire third person-s incidentally when the explicit instruction directed attention at the indefinite article. Incidental acquisition is more likely when learners are primarily focused on meaning-making and take time out to attend to form when occasion calls for this. This is what TBLT caters to through various strategies that attract learners' attention to form while they are communicating (as discussed later in this chapter). TBLT aims to foster implicit learning through the apperception that takes place as learners engage in the communication needed to achieve the task outcome. However, for adults at least, it is incidental rather than implicit learning that is central in TBLT.

A second issue concerns the role of output in cognitive-interactionist theories. Long tends to emphasize input but also acknowledges the role of *pushed output* in facilitating noticing. Skehan (1998), drawing on and extending Swain's (1985, 1995) arguments in support of *comprehensible output*, lists six roles for production: (1) It serves to generate better input through the feedback that learners' efforts at production elicit. (2) It forces syntactic processing (i.e. it obliges learners to pay attention to grammar). (3) It allows learners to test out hypotheses about the target language grammar. (4) It helps to develop automaticity of existing L2 knowledge. (5) It provides opportunities for learners to develop discourse skills, for example by producing 'long turns'. (6) It helps learners to develop a 'personal voice' by steering conversations onto topics they are interested in contributing to. We would add that production also provides the learner with 'auto-input' (Schmidt and Frota, 1986) as learners can benefit from the 'input' that their own output provides them with. Output is part of interaction but it can also occur when learners are not interacting. In Chapter 3 we examine in detail how learner production contributes to L2 development.

The third issue is controversial. It concerns the nature of the 'explicit learning' in Figure 2.1. For Long (2015), explicit learning is of value when it is embedded in the communicative interactions that result from the performance of a task. That is, it involves only 'brief episodes of selective learner attention to critical segments of input (*focus on form*)' (p. 53). In other words, Long rejects providing for explicit learning separately. Ellis (1994, 2018a), however, suggests that the knowledge that learners gain from explicit language lessons facilitates the 'noticing' of linguistic forms in the input – as indicated in Figure 2.1 – and is also of value for monitoring output. In other words, Ellis argues that an explicit focus on form does not always have to be contiguous with the performance of a task. While 'brief episodes of selective attention' (Long, 2015) may be desirable,[3] some explicit lessons may help learners to acquire those linguistic 'fragile' features which are often not learned even when focus on form accompanies the performance of a task. From this perspective the ideal is a modular curriculum involving a primary task-based component with a secondary structural component, a possibility discussed in Chapter 7.

Analysing Interaction

Interaction occurs when two or more people engage in communication. Prototypically it occurs face to face but there is growing interest in the interaction that arises when tasks are technologically mediated (e.g. González-Lloret and Ortega, 2015; Granena, 2016). Interaction can be two-way (i.e. all the participants contribute actively) or one-way (i.e. one person does all the speaking and the other(s) just listens as in a lecture). In two-way communication, learners have the opportunity to both receive input and produce output. In one-way communication, the speaker produces output and the other(s) receives input. This is an important distinction for task-based instruction because it underscores a key difference in tasks; as noted in Chapter 1, output-based tasks aim to provide opportunities for two-way interaction whereas input-based tasks are essentially one-way.[4]

However, the input that arises when an input-based task is performed in an interactive situation is not fixed.[5] Speakers adjust their choice of language in accordance with their assessment of the listeners' abilities to comprehend. In other words, input is continuously modified; often it is simplified but sometimes it can be elaborated, which Long and Ross (1993) suggest is more facilitative of acquisition. There is a rich literature documenting the characteristics of the 'foreigner talk' that occurs when native speakers talk to L2 learners (see Gass, 1997; Ellis, 2008) and of the 'teacher talk' found in classrooms (Henzl, 1979). Such talk helps to provide learners with the comprehensible input that Krashen (1985) argued is essential for acquisition. When teachers perform input-based tasks, they naturally modify their speech to ensure comprehension. Shintani (2012), for example, showed how repeating the same input-based tasks with young L2 learners resulted in changes in the teacher's input. The teacher gradually reduced her use of the L1 (Japanese) while increasing the length of her utterances by elaborating the commands she gave to the children. If it is a learner who performs a one-way task (e.g. when a learner is describing where to locate places on a map), the resulting output is monologic. Nevertheless, when this takes place in an interactive context, learners will still need to make efforts to ensure they are comprehensible and this involves *discourse management* (i.e. deciding how much information to provide, checking comprehension, repeating, paraphrasing etc.).

In the classroom context, discourse management is evident in the pre-emptive strategies that both teachers and learners use to anticipate and prevent problems arising during interaction. Teachers, for example, pre-empt by asking questions (e.g. Do you know what 'economy' means?) or by warning learners to take care (e.g. Remember – you need to use the past tense when telling the story). Learners too pre-empt by asking questions (e.g. 'Do I need past or present tense here?'). Some researchers (e.g. Long, 2015) have argued that what is important is the *discourse repair* work that activates the internal mechanisms involved in acquisition. That is, interaction works for acquisition when interlocutors *react* to problems – communicative or linguistic – that arise as a task is performed. Other researchers (e.g. Ellis, 2017a), however, have argued that interaction involving pre-emptive moves aimed at preventing problems is also facilitative of acquisition. Arguably, both reactive and pre-emptive interactive strategies can activate the cognitive processes involved in acquisition.

In accordance with the IH, research on two-way tasks has focused on the *discourse repair* that occurs when communication problems arise and negotiation takes place. Varonis and Gass (1985) developed a model of 'non-understanding routines' (see Figure 2.2 and the example below). This distinguishes the turn that triggers non-understanding and the subsequent turns where there is an attempt to resolve the problem. This model allows for the identification of specific discourse strategies for resolving communication problems. Foremost among these strategies is corrective feedback (CF).

Example:

S1: Einstein's scientific work helped Americans make the nuclear bomb. (T)
S2: Clear bomb? (I)
S1: No nuclear, nuclear, nuclear bomb. (R)
S2: Nuclear bomb. I see. (RR)

(Aubrey, unpublished data)

Table 2.1, based on Lyster and Ranta (1997), defines the principal types of indicator moves, along with comments on whether they are input-providing or output-prompting and whether they are implicit or explicit in nature, although this latter distinction is not clear cut as it depends more on context and on how an indicator is delivered than on the type of indicator – an important point which we consider later in

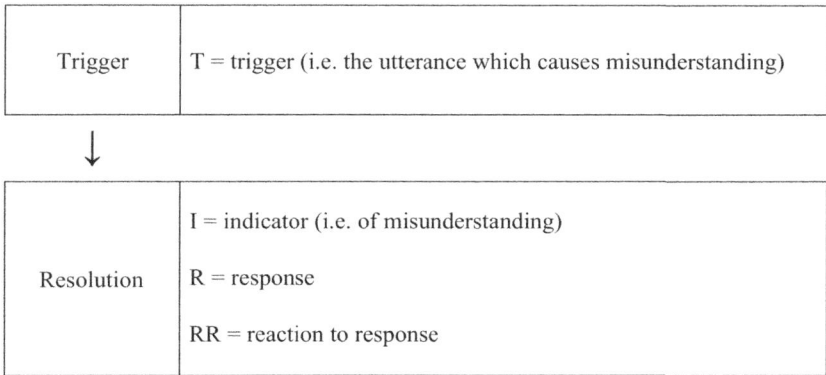

Figure 2.2 Model of non-understanding routines
Source: Varonis and Gass (1985)

this chapter. These indicators also differ in the nature of the problem they are typically used to tackle. Some signal that there is a communication problem and thus relate to the *negotiation of meaning* while others just signal that the problem is linguistic in nature and thus involve the *negotiation of form* (Lyster, 2001). The indicator types constitute the different ways of conducting CF and doing 'focus on form', a major area of interest in the interaction approach. They connect with cognitive mechanisms in different ways and have different implications for language acquisition – see Table 2.1.

Not all indicators require a response. Input-providing indicators such as recasts place no obligation on the addressee to respond. In contrast, output-prompting indicators do require a response in accordance with Grice's (1975) Cooperative Principle, but even in this case learners may sometimes opt not to respond if, for example, their linguistic resources prevent them from doing so. The first response option, therefore, is *no response*. Other indicators – a confirmation check for example – require no more than an *acknowledgement*. This often takes the form of simply saying 'yes' followed by a topic-continuing move, as in this example:

S: I was in pub
   (2.0).
S: I was in pub.
T: In the pub?
S: *Yeah* and I was drinking beer with my friend.
                    (Ellis, Basturkmen and Loewen, 2001).

Table 2.1 Indicator types in corrective feedback

Type	Definition	Example	Comment
Repetition	The addressee repeats the speaker's utterance to signal that there is a comprehension problem	L1: I felt really chuffed with the results of my exam. L2: *Chuffed*. L1: Yes, I did better than I expected.	This is implicit and output-prompting. Lyster (1998) pointed out that repetitions are ambiguous as they can also signal understanding. Thus, they may lead to a resolution of the problem or they may not.
Confirmation check	Any expressions 'immediately following an utterance by the interlocutor which are designed to elicit confirmation that the utterance has been correctly heard or understood by the speaker' (Long, 1983, p. 137)	Learner 1: Ok it's in the it's in the corner the building Learner 2: *In the corner?* Learner 1: yeah (Gilabert, Baron and Llanes, 2009, p. 377)	Like a repetition, a confirmation check simply repeats the problematic utterance or part of an utterance but the rising intonation more clearly signals there is a problem (i.e. makes the move more explicit) and thus may be more likely to lead to a successful resolution.
Clarification request	Any expression that elicits clarification of the preceding utterance	Learner 1: Go walking it's two apples further two streets more it looks. Learner 2: *Two what?* Learner 1: Two streets further. (Gilabert et al., 2009, p. 376)	Clarification requests are output-prompting. They place the burden of resolving the problem on the speaker who created it. They are often viewed as implicit as they occur naturally in everyday conversation but they are in fact quite explicit in signalling that there is a communication problem.
Metalinguistic clue	A move that provides a comment or questions some aspect of the preceding	S: There are influence person who T: *Influential is an adjective* S: Influential person	Metalinguistic clues are output-prompting (i.e. they do not provide the learner with the remedy of the problem) and they are clearly very explicit as they respond to the

	utterance, signalling a linguistic problem		form of the preceding utterance rather than its meaning. This type of indicator is more likely to be used by a teacher than by a learner.
Explicit correction	A move that indicates an utterance is problematic and at the same time provides the solution to the problem	(unintelligible) because of his power. (Sheen, 2004, p. 278).	This type of indicator is explicit and input-providing. Like metalinguistic clues it is more likely to be performed by a teacher although learners have also been observed to correct each other explicitly.
Elicitation	A move aimed at extracting the correct linguistic form from a speaker.	S1: And three pear (sounds like 'beer'). S2: Three beer. T: *Not beer. Pear.*	It is output-prompting and explicitly corrective. It negotiates form rather than meaning and is used more or less exclusively by teachers.
Recast	An utterance that rephrases an utterance 'by changing one or more of its sentence components (subject, verb or object) while still referring to its central meanings' – Long, 1996, p. 436). Various types and characteristics of recasts have been identified (e.g. partial; versus full) – see Y. Sheen (2006).	An elicitation can take the form of a question (e.g. How do we say x in English?), a statement requiring completion (e.g. You ___) or a request to reformulate (e.g. Can you say it another way?) – Sheen (2004, p. 278). S: I stand in the first row. T: You stood in the first row. S: Yes. (Y. Sheen, 2006, p. 35)	Recasts are input-providing and are generally considered implicit. However, they can also be made more explicit, especially if intonation is used to highlight the part of the utterance that has been reformulated.

Source: Based on Lyster and Ranta (1997).

Learners may respond to an indicator such as a recast by echoing it or by modifying their initial output in what is called *uptake*. Lyster and Ranta (1997) pointed that uptake can be of two kinds depending on whether the problem is or is not repaired. In *uptake-with-repair*, the learner either repeats the indicator move if this is input-providing, as in this example:

S: I got up late today morning.
T: Today morning? This morning.
S: This morning.

Or, if the indicator consists of a prompt, the learner may self-repair the utterance that triggered the negotiation. Uptake-with-repair constitutes one kind of *modified output*. However, this construct is broader as it includes occasions when learners attempt to modify output without being prompted to do so by feedback. Sometimes, as in the example that follows, the learner may attempt to repair following feedback but fail to do so, resulting in what Lyster and Ranta called *uptake-needs-repair*.

S: I have an ali [bi].
T: You have what?
S: an ali [bi] (i.e. S continues to mispronounce 'alibi').

Uptake-needs-repair can involve a complete failure to address the problem or, in some cases, partial repair (i.e. the learner corrects part of an erroneous utterance).

The various strategies involved in discourse management and repair constitute the means for conducting *focus on form* while a task is being performed (see Ellis et al., 2001). Focus on form is a necessary feature of Long's (2015) definition of TBLT. It constitutes the means for drawing learners' attention to linguistic features when problems arise in the communication resulting from the performance of a task. The linguistic problems that are addressed can be wide-ranging and unpredictable or they can be pre-determined and therefore predictable. This will depend on whether the task is unfocused or focused – a distinction introduced in Chapter 1 (see p. 12). If the task is unfocused the linguistic features addressed will be whatever happened to cause a problem. The resulting focus on form will be extensive (i.e. many different forms will be addressed). There is evidence to show that problems relating to vocabulary receive more attention than grammatical problems when the negotiation involves meaning (Pica, 1996) because the wrong or mispronounced word is more likely to lead to communication breakdown than a missing grammatical morpheme.

However, when it is form (rather than meaning) that is negotiated all forms – phonological, lexical and grammatical – are likely to receive attention. If the task is focused, the focus on form will be directed at whatever is the target feature of the task with the same feature addressed repeatedly (i.e. it will be intensive). As we noted in Chapter 1, some proponents of TBLT favour unfocused tasks. However, many researchers investigating the effects of CF (e.g. Lyster, 2004; Ellis, Loewen and Erlam, 2006) have elected to investigate focused tasks because these make pre-testing and post-testing of the targeted feature possible and thus allow for the effect that focus on form has on acquisition to be investigated.

Early research in the cognitive-interactionist paradigm focused on the negotiation of meaning and reactive focus on form but increasingly researchers have broadened the frame of reference to examine how learners and their interlocutors attend to form when purely linguistic problems arise. In particular, language-related episodes (LREs),[6] defined as 'any part of dialogue where the students talk about the language they are producing, question their language use, or correct themselves or others' (Swain and Lapkin, 1998, p. 326), have proved a popular way of investigating task-based interaction. Plonsky and Kim (2016), for example, found that 25 per cent of all the interactional features examined in the studies included in their meta-analysis were LREs. Studies examining tasks from a sociocultural perspective, which have increased in number over time, favour LREs. These studies will be considered in detail in Chapter 4. There have also been attempts to investigate how tasks impact on other aspects of interaction. Gilabert and Baron (2013), for example, examined how task type and task complexity affected learners' use of pragmatic features (requests and suggestions). Sato (2017) focused on 'collaborative sentence completion', where one learner helps another learner to complete an utterance.

Task-based interaction studies are of two basic kinds. There are what Plonsky and Kim (2016) call 'task-based learner performance studies' (p. 74). These are studies that manipulate various dimensions of task design and implementation conditions in order to investigate what effect they have on interaction. This type of study was dominant in early research and is viewed by Plonsky and Gass (2011) as the first phase of interactionist research. The second kind is 'task-as-treatment studies', where the aim is to investigate what effect a particular task design or implementation condition has on either the processes involved in acquisition (e.g. noticing) or on L2 acquisition. These studies figure in the second phase of interactionist task-based research. We will begin by looking at task-based performance studies and then move on to task-as-treatment studies.

Task-Based Learner Performance Studies

A major research strand in the Interaction Approach has focused on what kinds of tasks are most likely to result in the types of interaction that foster language acquisition. Much of the early research, reviewed in Ellis (2003, 2012) examined how different design features and implementation strategies impacted on the negotiation of meaning. Table 2.2 shows the variables investigated.

This research typically involved laboratory-based studies so the findings may not be applicable to classroom contexts (see Ellis, 2012) but it provides a clear indication that task design and implementation influence the level and kinds of interaction that take place. Regarding task design variables, Ellis concluded that negotiation of meaning was more likely to occur with tasks that required information exchange (i.e. information-gap tasks) than with tasks where information exchange was optional (i.e. opinion-gap tasks) (Long, 1980; Foster, 1998) and also more likely when a task was two-way (i.e. the information to be exchanged was split among participants) than when it was one-way (i.e. one learner held all the information to be exchanged) (Long, 1989). Closed tasks also led to more negotiation of meaning than open tasks (Long, 1989). Learners also negotiate more in tasks with unfamiliar topics than in those with familiar topics (Gass and Varonis, 1984) and more in tasks with human-ethical content than in tasks with objective-spatial content (Berwick, 1990). Regarding task implementation variables, the participant role, task repetition, and interlocutor proficiency were all found to impact on the level of

Table 2.2 Task design and implementation variables investigated in interaction studies

Design variables	Implementation variables
1. required vs. optional information exchange	1. participant role (e.g. listener vs. active participant)
2. information gap: one-way vs. two-way	2. task repetition
3. task outcome: open vs. closed tasks	3. interlocutor familiarity (i.e. participants familiar with each other vs. not familiar)
4. topic (e.g. topic familiarity)	4. interlocutor proficiency
5. discourse mode (e.g. narrative vs. description)	
6. cognitive complexity (e.g. context-embedded vs. context-reduced)	

negotiation. Learners negotiate more when their role requires them to speak as well as listen (Gass and Varonis, 1994) in the first performance of a task than in a repeated performance (Gass and Varonis, 1985), and when the less proficient learner is put in charge of the interaction (Yule and McDonald, 1990). Pica, Kanagy and Faludan (1993) attempted to consolidate the findings of these studies into a general framework that could account for the differential effect that tasks have on interaction.

More recently, researchers have drawn on Robinson's (2007b) Cognition Hypothesis (CH) to investigate how task complexity affects interaction, measured in terms of LREs. Robinson argued that more complex tasks result in more acquisition-rich interaction than less complex tasks. [7] Task complexity was operationalized in terms of the presence or absence of specific task features (e.g. +/− there and now; +/− reasoning; +/− few elements) with simpler tasks being those with - features. A number of studies (e.g. Gilabert et al., 2009; Kim, 2009; Révész, 2011; Baralt, 2014; Kim and Taguchi, 2015) lend support to Robinson's claim. For example, more complex tasks lead to more LREs than simple tasks.

Solon, Long and Gurzynska-Weiss (2017) is a good example of this kind of study but it also illustrates the danger of over-generalizing the effect of task complexity on interaction. They investigated seventeen dyads of intermediate L2 Spanish proficiency performing focused tasks that were designed to contextualize the pronunciation of Spanish phonemes built into street names (e.g. Calle Copa vs. Calle Capa). The tasks were designed to differ in complexity according to the number of elements they contained. To establish whether this task feature did in fact distinguish the complexity of the tasks, the actual time and the learners' retrospective estimate of the time they had spent on the tasks were recorded. The learners performed the map tasks in pairs; one learner held a version of the map showing the route but minus place names and the other a version with the place names but minus the route. LREs were identified in all the interactions. Overall, there were more LREs in the complex task, as predicted. However, pronunciation-focused LREs were highest in the simple task. Solon et al. (2017) suggested that whereas learners may be used to consciously reflecting on grammar they lack experience in reflecting on pronunciation features and thus are less likely to engage in LREs focused on pronunciation. In other words, the extent to which task design affects LREs may differ according to the linguistic features being investigated.

Somewhat surprisingly, there has been very little research that has investigated tasks in relation to pragmatic aspects of language use. Gilabert and Baron (2013) compared university-level English as a Foreign Language (EFL) learners' performance of two tasks which differed in type (one was a two-way split information task with a convergent goal and the other a two-way shared information task with a divergent goal) and in complexity (there was a simple and complex form of both tasks). They found that the divergent task produced more overall moves and also a greater variety of moves. The complexity of the tasks affected the number of overall moves but had no effect on the variety of moves. Given that pragmatic competence is a key feature of language proficiency, there is an obvious need for more studies that shed light on how task selection and task design impact pragmatic aspects of language production.

There has been increasing interest in how computer-mediated (CM) tasks affect interaction (see, for example, Ziegler, 2016). Studies have sought to compare the similarities and differences between tasks performed face to face and in a CM context. Ziegler, drawing in particular on Smith (2003), points out that one difference is that whereas the response to a communication problem usually occurs immediately after the trigger in face-to-face interaction, it is often delayed in CM tasks, especially if these involve text chat. There are also differences in the effect that different CM modalities (i.e. text chat, audio, or video) have on negotiation. For example, Jepson (2015) found that repair moves were more frequent when tasks were performed in voice than in text chat. Researchers have also been interested in whether the type of task affects negotiation in CM interaction. Blake (2000) reported that one-way tasks where the information was split resulted in more negotiation than decision-making tasks where the information was shared, thus replicating one of the main findings for face-to-face tasks. Ziegler calls for more research investigating all the issues.

These studies afford a general picture of how task variables can impact on interaction. But they need to be viewed with circumspection. Each task involves a cluster of variables that are likely to interact in the effect they have on interaction. Studies have typically manipulated task types in terms of pairs of variables (e.g. one-way versus two-way; familiar versus unfamiliar topics; closed versus open; +/− reasoning; +/− here and now; +/− number of elements) but the tasks used in these studies inevitably involved a cluster of variables. This makes it difficult to generalize the research findings. We cannot be sure, for example, that unfamiliar tasks will lead to more negotiation of meaning than familiar tasks in all cases as other variables – such as the number of elements involved in the task – may counteract this general tendency. Furthermore, how a task is implemented will also affect the interaction that results. A one-way task may not result in less negotiation than a two-way task if the learners are instructed to interact actively and if the information to be exchanged is held by the less proficient learner.

The combinations of design and implementation variables are multitudinous. Thus, while it may be possible to design studies that investigate how two or three variables impact jointly on interaction, taking into account all the potentially influential variables that make up a task will prove impossible. At best, then, the research provides only clues as to how task design and implementation can affect interaction.

Task-as-Treatment Studies

When tasks are used as the means for intervening in the process of L2 acquisition researchers have addressed three key questions: (1) What do learners pay attention to (i.e. notice) when they perform a task? (2) What is the relationship between noticing and learning? (3) What learning occurs when interactive tasks are performed? We will consider studies that have investigated these three questions.

Tasks and Noticing

Researchers interested in whether noticing occurs when a task is performed have investigated both pre-modified input (i.e. input that has been specially designed to facilitate comprehension) and interactionally modified input (i.e. input that is modified when a learner signals a comprehension problem).

NOTICING IN PRE-MODIFIED INPUT

In the case of pre-modified input, efforts are made to draw learners' attention to specific linguistic features either through (1) 'flooding' the input with exemplars of a specific feature, or (2) highlighting a specific form in the input. By and large input enhancement of this kind has been undertaken with written input in reading tasks but it is also possible with oral tasks. One obvious way in which this can happen is by repeating the key lexical or grammatical items, using intonation and stress to highlight them, or by providing additional clues, such as gesture, to help learners decode their meanings. The input modifications found in pre-modified oral input are very similar to features found in teacher-talk (Ellis, 2015b). Overall, the research shows that input enhancement does facilitate noticing but, as Lee and Huang's (2008) meta-analysis showed, its effect is often quite limited. Han, Park and Combs (2008, p. 600) noted that 'there are numerous methodological idiosyncrasies characterizing the individual studies' – such as the number of times a specific feature was highlighted, the number of texts involved, and whether learners received explicit instruction on the targeted feature(s) prior to exposure to the input – all of which can impact on noticing.

NOTICING IN INTERACTIONALLY MODIFIED INPUT

Noticing is arguably more likely to occur in the pre-emptive and reactive focus on form episodes that arise when interactive tasks are performed than in pre-modified input. One measure of whether noticing occurs in such episodes is whether there is learner uptake. Ellis et al. (2001) investigated the frequency of focus-on-form episodes (FFEs) when experienced teachers performed communicative tasks with adult English as a second language (ESL) learners, reporting that there was an FFE approximately every one and a half minutes. They investigated whether the different kinds of FFEs resulted in uptake and whether this uptake was 'successful' (e.g. resulted in learners repairing their own errors).[8] Learner-initiated pre-emptive focus on form – for example, when a learner posed an explicit question about a linguistic form – resulted in a high level of successful uptake. Reactive focus on form (where the teacher responded to a learner utterance containing an error) also regularly led to successful uptake. In contrast, teacher-initiated pre-emptive focus on form , where it was the teacher who made a linguistic form the topic of the interaction, was much less likely to result in successful uptake. This study suggests that noticing can occur frequently in task-based interactions but that this may depend on what kind of focus on form learners experience.

Other noticing studies have focused solely on reactive focus on form – in particular, recasts. Recasts, which juxtapose a learner utterance containing an error with a target-like reformulation of the utterance, provide what Long (1996) considered the ideal context for the learner to not just notice the target form but also to compare their erroneous form with it – what Schmidt and Frota (1986), called *noticing-the-gap*. In the exchange that follows, for example, the learner overgeneralizes the use of the regular past tense (*doed*) – a common error – and the teacher immediately recasts the erroneous part of the utterance. The learner uptakes the correction, repairing the error. The learner then continues, making another tense error, but this time he corrects himself without the teacher's intervention.

L: When he 18 years old he m– if he doed it.
T: Did it.
L: Uh did it.
T: Yeah.
L: Must go to the prison? went to the prison.

Prompts can also result in noticing by inducing learners to attend to the linguistic problems in their utterances. Prompts in fact are more likely to result in uptake-with-repair than recasts as they require a response from the learner (Lyster and Ranta, 1997).

To investigate whether noticing occurs following CF researchers have either investigated uptake-with-repair as in Ellis, Basturkmen and Loewen (2001) or elicited retrospective self-report from learners, for example using stimulated recall (Gass and Mackey, 2000). An example of the first approach is Ellis and Mifka-Provozic (2013). They reported that 84.5 per cent of the recasts were followed by uptake-with-repair, suggesting that in the context of a foreign language classroom recasts were highly salient to the learners and that the teacher's corrections were consistently noticed. However, as Sheen (2004) showed, the level of uptake-with-repair following recasts varies considerably depending on the instructional context. It is much more likely to occur in contexts that encourage a focus on form (e.g. foreign language classrooms) than in contexts where meaning remains primary (e.g. immersion classrooms).

Egi's (2007) study is a good example of the use of stimulated recall. She investigated whether learners paid attention to specific linguistic forms in the recasts they received by replaying extracts from their conversations that contained recasts and inviting them to comment on them. She distinguished comments where (1) they showed awareness that an error had been made but no awareness of the target-like form in the recast, (2) awareness of the target-like model but no awareness that their original utterance was problematic and (3) awareness of both the error and the target-like model in the recast. No noticing was reported most of the time for morphosyntactical features. However, Egi reported that 18.7 per cent of the learners' comments demonstrated awareness in terms of (2) and a further 26.05 per cent awareness in terms of (3).

NOTICING IN ORAL, WRITTEN AND CM INPUT

Learners' ability to engage in noticing and subsequent form-meaning mapping when the task involves processing oral input may be limited. The ephemeral nature of input does not allow them time for internal processing. In contrast, written input 'may encourage learners to move beyond simple registration of new forms items and engage in intake processing' (Gilabert, Manchon and Vasylets, 2016, p. 125). These authors point out that many tasks typically combine oral and written input in an 'interweaving of modes' (p. 129). Many decision-making tasks, for example, include substantial written input to prompt group discussion. There is a need to investigate how hybrid tasks involving both oral and written modes affect key processes such as noticing but, as Gilabert et al. noted, little has been done to date.

This mingling of oral and written modes is also evident in tasks involving synchronous text-based communication where interaction unfolds in real time but affords a visible record in writing (Smith, 2003). CM tasks performed via text chat seem ideal for promoting noticing as learners can inspect a written record of their interactions. Text chat also affords an opportunity to use eye-tracking technology to identify when learners attend to specific forms – an opportunity that is not possible for face-to-face interaction. Smith (2012) used this method, reporting that learners regularly attended to the specific words that had been reformulated in the recasts that followed utterances containing an error. Yuksal and Inan (2014) used stimulated recall to compare noticing in CM and face-to-face interaction; they found that while negotiation occurred more frequently in face-to-face contexts, noticing was more likely to occur in synchronous CM communication. Other studies (e.g. Gurzynski-Weiss and Baralt, 2014), however, failed to find any clear advantage for noticing in CM interaction in comparison to face-to-face interaction.

Noticing and Acquisition in Task-Based Interaction

Cognitive-interactionist theories distinguish intake (i.e. the initial registration of linguistic forms in working memory) from acquisition (i.e. the modification of the learner's interlanguage system in long-term memory) – see, for example, Leow (2015). Intake is likely to involve noticing (i.e. the conscious registration of linguistic forms). But noticing does not guarantee acquisition. Evidence for this comes from Mackey (2006). She found that the level of noticing following recasts or clarification requests varied according to target structure, with higher levels evident for question forms, much lower levels for past tense and intermediate levels for plurals. Eighty-three per cent of the learners who reported noticing question forms demonstrated acquisition (i.e. they improved in their ability to form questions in a post-test). However, the relationship between noticing and the other two target features was not established. Other studies (Mackey and Philp, 1998; Ellis and Mifka-Provozic, 2013) also cast doubt on whether uptake-with-repair (the clearest sign that noticing has occurred) is important for acquisition.

These studies all involved focused tasks. In contrast, Loewen (2005) investigated the pre-emptive and reactive FFEs that arose incidentally in lessons based on unfocused tasks. As in Ellis et al. (2001), he first identified the FFEs and then devised tailor-made tests to assess the linguistic features addressed in these episodes. He administered the tests to the particular learners who had participated in the episodes one day later and also two weeks later to see if participation in the form-focused episode had led to learning. Out of the 473 FFEs that were tested, 47.6 per cent of the responses were correct in the immediate test and 39.3 per cent in the delayed test. Loewen noted that these results were roughly comparable to other studies (e.g. Williams, 1999; Nabei and Swain, 2001) and felt they were 'encouraging, given the incidental and generally brief nature of the FFEs' (Loewen, 2005, p. 381). Loewen also investigated whether particular features of the FFEs were more likely to result in correct test responses. The feature most likely to predict learners' correct responses to tests items was successful uptake, suggesting that when noticing had taken place learning also occurred. However, successful uptake was only predictive of correct responses to the grammar and vocabulary items in the test. For pronunciation the key features of the FFEs were complexity (i.e. long FFEs were associated with more correct responses than brief ones) and source (i.e. FFEs involving the negotiation of meaning led to more correct responses than FFEs involving the negotiation of form). However, while successful uptake can be seen as evidence of noticing, its absence does not preclude the possibility of noticing having occurred. Arguably, long FFEs and the negotiation of meaning are exactly those features of interaction likely to induce noticing. Loewen acknowledged a limitation of his study, namely that the tests he used most probably measured the learners' declarative rather than their procedural knowledge.

Tasks and Acquisition

The bulk of the task-based research based on cognitive-interactionist theories has been entirely product-oriented. That is, it has investigated whether focus on form results in acquisition without also investigating what happens when learners perform tasks. A typical study involves the use of focused tasks. Learners are first tested on the linguistic feature (typically grammatical) that is targeted by the task, perform one or more tasks during which they receive some type of focus on form, and then complete an immediate post-test and, some time later, a delayed post-test. We begin by considering studies that have investigated input-based tasks followed by a detailed look at research that has investigated output-based tasks and CF.

INPUT-BASED TASKS

TBLT has generally been seen as involving production-based tasks. However, as noted in Chapter 1, tasks can also be 'input-based'.

An input-based task aims to promote interlanguage development by directing learners' attention to L2 input through listening or reading. One of the key definitional features of a task is that learners are required to use their own linguistic and non-linguistic resources to communicate. In the case of input-based tasks, this means that they have to use their knowledge of the L2 in conjunction with contextual clues provided by the task to process the input they are exposed to where 'process' refers both to comprehending the meaning of the input and, potentially, attending to linguistic form (i.e. noticing). It is important that the outcome of the task can only be achieved if the learners are successful in comprehending the input. Although input-based tasks do not require leaners to produce in the L2, learners may elect to respond to the input they receive using their L1 or, if they are able, their L2. In other words, production is not ruled out and in fact has been shown to occur (e.g. Shintani, 2015).

An input-based task often takes the form of a listen-and-do task, which requires learners to listen to commands or descriptions and then perform actions (e.g. a physical action or pointing to a picture) to show they have understood. Early studies of listen-and-do tasks (e.g. Ellis, Tanaka, and Yamazaki, 1994; Loschky, 1994; Ellis and He, 1999; Ellis and Heimbach, 1997) showed that they can lead to learning vocabulary. These studies, motivated by the IH, investigated the effect of exposure to different kinds of input (unmodified, pre-modified and interactionally modified) on acquisition. They reported somewhat mixed results, reflecting differences in the design of the studies. In Loschky's (1994) study the target items were first presented to the learners before they listened which may explain why he found no differential effect for types of input. In Ellis et al. (1994) there was no prior presentation of the target words. Learners in the interactionally modified condition were encouraged to signal their non-understanding if they did not understand the input. The study reported a clear advantage for modified input, especially interactionally modified input. However, the interactionally modified input typically took longer to complete than tasks involving pre-modified input. In Ellis and He (1999), the time taken for the pre-modified and interactionally modified conditions was the same and in this study there was no difference in their effectiveness. These studies suggest one reason why interactionally modified input has been found to assist acquisition – it gives learners additional time to process the input. If pre-modified input allows adequate processing time it can be just as effective.

These early studies investigated the effect of performing input-based tasks on vocabulary acquisition. Later studies included grammatical features as well as vocabulary in their design. The tasks were designed to force attention to the target grammatical features. For example, in Shintani and Ellis (2010) and Shintani (2015), the learners (six-year-old Japanese children) needed to attend closely to the input to distinguish English singular and plural nouns and could only complete the tasks successfully if they did so. In Erlam and Ellis (2018) the learners were required to distinguish L2 French singular and plural forms. These studies, like the earlier ones, showed that performing input-based tasks results in the acquisition of vocabulary. They also showed that they can help grammar acquisition. They were clearly effective in developing learners' receptive knowledge of the target grammatical features but less so in developing productive knowledge, possibly because the tasks did not provide the amount of exposure needed to develop productive use of the grammatical forms.[9]

For input-based tasks to work for acquisition they must create a functional need for learners to attend to the target items and to engage in form-meaning mapping. It is relatively easy to ensure that this happens in the case of lexical items as learners will only be able to do the tasks if they understand the vocabulary in the input. It is more difficult in the case of grammar. Some grammatical features, for example, convey no meaning. Shintani (2015) investigated whether the input-based tasks she designed helped learners attend to English copula-*be* as well as plural-*s*. The input exposed the learners to numerous exemplars of copula-*be* but they did not acquire it, which Shintani suggested was because it is a non-meaning bearing feature so they could understand the directions without having to process it. This is, of course, a limitation of focused production-based tasks as well and, in fact, as Loschky and Bley-Vroman (1993) pointed out, it is a lot easier to design input-based tasks that make the processing of specific grammatical features 'necessary' (as opposed to 'natural' or 'useful') than production-based tasks.

Considerable skill on the part of the teacher is required to ensure that input tasks are effective. Learners need instant feedback on whether their efforts to understand have been successful. The teacher needs to utilize a variety of strategies to help learners to understand – using repetition, highlighting key items intonationally, utilizing contextual clues etc. The extract from Shintani (2016) that follows illustrates the skills involved. The teacher is instructing learners to find the picture cards representing different animals and to take them to the 'zoo' (depicted in a frieze on the wall of the classroom). To select the right card the learners need to be able to distinguish 'squirrels' from 'squirrel' (for which there was a separate card). The teacher first ensures the learners' attention, then gives the direction, repeating the key item ('squirrels') three times. When a learner uses Japanese (his L1) to check understanding, the teacher immediately confirms. When the students mention colours to help them identify the correct animal, she corrects them and provides a contextual clue by pointing at a brown object in the classroom. The learners performed the task successfully, demonstrating their ability to process plural-*s*.

T: Okay the next. Okay, listen. please take the squirrels, squirrels to the zoo. Squirrels.
S2: Doubutsuen [the zoo]?
T: Zoo, that's right.
S5: Green? Blue?
S1: White?
T: No, no, no, not white. Not green. Not blue. Brown (pointing to a brown item in the classroom)
S2: Brown.
S3: (Showing 'two' with his fingers) two?
T: Two, yes. Three (.) two (.) one (.) go.
Ss: (All the students showing the correct cards)
T: Yes everyone is correct.

Input-based tasks have an important role to play in TBLT. In the case of beginner-level learners they are essential as learners cannot be expected to produce in the L2 until they have built up a linguistic repertoire receptively. But they also have an important role to play in later stages of L2 development. Apart from their contribution to acquisition, they facilitate what might be called 'input-processing fluency' – the ability to rapidly and effortlessly segment input and derive meaning from it. This is an essential element of L2 proficiency.

OUTPUT-BASED TASKS AND CORRECTIVE FEEDBACK

The bulk of the research investigating the effect that performing output-based tasks has on acquisition has focused on the implementation rather than the design of the tasks – in particular, the role of CF. The research has been experimental in design and has almost invariably involved focused tasks and reactive focus on form (i.e. CF). Sato and Loewen (2018) refer to 'the burgeoning body of research investigating variables that moderate the effectiveness of corrective feedback' (p. 536). These variables include:

- Feedback versus no feedback
- Extensive versus intensive feedback

- Type of CF (e.g. input-providing versus output-prompting; explicit versus implicit)
- Immediate versus delayed
- The target structure
- Effect of pre-teaching the target structure
- Moderating role of learner factors (e.g. working memory).

We will briefly consider each of these variables but will leave the moderating role of learner factors to Chapter 5.

Feedback versus No Feedback
Several of the studies involved a task-control group – i.e. a group that performed the task(s) but without receiving any CF. These studies enable us to address whether CF has any additional value for acquisition. This is an important question and one clearly relevant to theory-building. According to theories that reject a role of negative evidence in acquisition and view acquisition as driven entirely by positive evidence (see, for example, Schwartz, 1993), performing tasks without CF will be as effective as performing them with it. In contrast, cognitive-interactionist theories predict that CF will enhance the effectiveness of tasks by facilitating noticing and modified output. As already noted, for Long (2015) reactive focus on form is necessary to help adult learners overcome their limited capacity for incidental/implicit language learning especially if the grammatical features lack saliency and/or acquisition is blocked by their L1.

The research indicates that acquisition can sometimes take place simply as a result of performing tasks. As we will see in Chapter 3, this is an underlying assumption of the cognitive theories of Skehan (1998) and Robinson (2007b). High-proficiency learners in particular may benefit just as much from just performing tasks as performing them with feedback (e.g. Ammar and Spada, 2006). However, some studies (e.g. Lyster, 2004) have found that performing tasks without CF does not lead to acquisition. The most general finding is that CF results in greater acquisition than no CF. Meta-analyses of CF studies, for example, report a clear effect for CF. Lyster and Saito's (2010) meta-analysis – arguably the most relevant here as it was restricted to classroom-based studies – reported a medium-sized mean effect size ($d = 0.74$) for comparisons involving groups that received and did not receive feedback. The research, then, lends clear support for CF when learners perform tasks.

Extensive versus Intensive Corrective Feedback
As we have noted, intensive CF is possible when the task is a focused one because it makes it possible for the teacher to focus correction on

the features targeted by the task. In contrast, CF is extensive when the task is an unfocused one and the teacher corrects whatever errors learners happen to make as they perform the task. Researchers have opted to investigate focused tasks and intensive CF. Pre-testing is possible if there is a pre-selected target but problematic if there is not.

In an interesting study, Nassaji (2017) compared the relative effectiveness of intensive and extensive CF. Three groups of intermediate-level ESL learners completed two tasks. One group received intensive recasts directed at article errors, a second group received extensive recasts directed at a range of errors, and a third group performed the tasks with no CF. The main finding was, somewhat surprisingly, that the extensive recasts were more effective than the intensive recasts in enabling acquisition of English articles. It should be noted, however, that both experimental groups received almost the same number of corrections of their article errors. The difference lay in the fact that the extensive group received an additional 122 recasts directed at other errors. Nassaji suggested that the advantage found for extensive CF might have been because its sheer frequency oriented the learners to pay greater attention to the corrections. This study, then, is not a good test of the relative effectiveness of extensive and intensive CF. For a grammatical feature such as articles, extensive feedback is likely to be effective because it is in fact intensive. But this will not be the case for grammatical structures that occur infrequently with unfocused tasks. There is an obvious need to investigate whether extensive feedback is effective and this will call for longitudinal studies.

Type of Corrective Feedback

We have noted that CF strategies can be distinguished in terms of two dimensions – input-providing versus output-prompting and implicit versus explicit. We also noted that in fact strategies can vary in terms of how implicit/explicit they are. Figure 2.3 shows how the two dimensions intersect. Researchers initially focused on these two dimensions but more recently have begun to examine how varied execution of the same strategy can affect acquisition.

Both input-providing (typically recasts) and output-prompting CF have been found to be effective but overall output-prompting CF has a stronger impact on acquisition than input-providing (Lyster, 2004; Ammar and Spada, 2006; Ellis et al., 2006; Mackey, 2006; Loewen and Nabei, 2007; Yang and Lyster, 2010; Sato and Loewen, 2018). Lyster and Saito's meta-analysis of classroom-based CF studies reported a large effect size for comparison of prompts and control

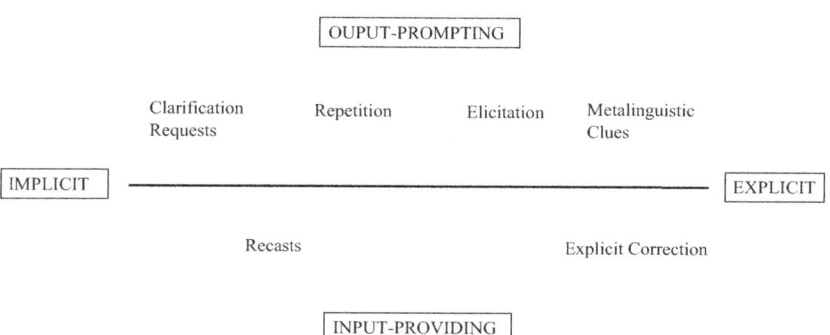

Figure 2.3 The explicit/implicit continuum
Source: Slightly modified from Lyster and Saito, 2010, p. 278.

group (d = 0.83) and a medium effect size for the same comparison for recasts (d = 0.53). However, Lyster and Saito also pointed out that the standard deviations and confidence levels for these contrasts varied widely, which they suggested was because of the difficulty of implementing these CF strategies consistently in a classroom setting. In fact, the comparison between recasts and prompts is conflated with that between implicit and explicit CF. While recasts might be considered generally implicit (but see later in this section), prompts vary considerably, with some (e.g. clarification requests) implicit and others (e.g. elicitation) much more explicit. Thus the superiority of prompts may be due to their explicitness rather than to the fact that they lead to learners modifying their output. Some recent studies, however, have attempted to address these design problems by comparing a single, implicit input providing strategy with a single output-prompting strategy. Mifka-Profozic (2013) compared recasts with an implicit type of prompt (clarification requests) and found the former more effective in enabling high school learners of L2 French to improve accuracy in the use of *passé composé* and *imparfait*. Sato and Loewen (2018) investigated the same two implicit corrective strategies on Chilean university students' acquisition of English third person-s and possessive determiners (*his/her*), reporting that the output-prompting strategy proved more effective but only for possessive determiners. To my mind the jury is still out regarding the relative efficacy of input-providing and output-prompting CF and is unlikely to be resolved quickly given the multitude of learner and contextual factors that can impact on how these two types of CF are implemented and how they are perceived and responded to by learners.

The distinction between implicit and explicit types of CF is also problematic. Li (2013a) noted that it is important to distinguish the perspective of the instructor/researcher from that of the learner. From the perspective of instructor, the difference depends on whether the feedback *directs* or just *attracts* attention to the linguistic form that is the focus of the feedback. From the perspective of the learner, it depends on whether or not the learner perceives the feedback as corrective. Li argued that the explicit/implicit distinction should be viewed from the perspective of instruction. CF is implicit if it is implemented in such a way that it does not aim to make learners aware they are being corrected (irrespective of whether they do in fact become aware); it is explicit if it is implemented in a way that overtly signals a correction is being made. In other words, the difference lies in how the CF is implemented.

There are two ways of investigating the relative effectiveness of implicit and explicit CF. One way is to compare different types of CF that are generally accepted to be either implicit or explicit. The other way is to compare the same CF type when it implemented in an implicit and explicit way. Most of the studies to date have adopted the first approach. Ellis et al. (2006) reviewed a number of early comparative studies of explicit and implicit feedback. The implicit feedback typically consisted of recasts in these studies. Explicit feedback was operationalized by means of explicit correction or metalinguistic clues. Ellis et al. concluded that overall the studies pointed to an advantage for explicit feedback. Their own study also reported that explicit CF was superior. Ellis (2019) reviewed a number of later studies (e.g. Varnosfadrani and Basturkmen, 2009; Li, 2010; Yilmaz, 2013a, 2013b) and confirmed the superiority of explicit CF, which is evident in both immediate and delayed post-tests and in also in tests that require controlled and more automatic processing. Not all the studies reported in favour of explicit CF. For example, Goo (2012) found no difference between the effects of metalinguistic feedback and recasts. Li (2014) also reported that implicit CF (recasts) were more beneficial for low-proficiency learners of a complex Chinese structure.

Arguably, the more interesting comparisons of implicit and explicit CF are those where the comparison involved the same CF strategy implemented in different ways. Nakatsukasa (2016), compared a group that received recasts with a group that received recasts accompanied by gestures. Nakatsukasa was interested in whether gestures enhanced the effect of recasts but her study can also be seen as investigating the relative effects of implicit-type recasts and recasts made more explicit through gestures. She reported that only the group that was exposed to recasts with gestures outperformed the control group on the delayed post-test. Nassaji (2009) distinguished implicit and explicit variants of both recasts and prompts in the interactions that arose in a task-based lesson. Learning was measured in terms of the learners' ability to correct their errors in a written task that they had completed prior to interacting with the teacher. The more explicit forms of recasts and prompts led to higher rates of correction than the more implicit forms of both strategy types. Both these studies suggest that explicit CF is more effective than implicit. Zhao (2015), however, reported that implicit and explicit recasts were equally effective for Chinese university students' acquisition of English third person-s and argued that this may have been because the sheer frequency of the implicit recasts, along with the students' predisposition to attend to form, made them perceptually salient to the students.

It is important to recognize that all these studies reported that CF helped acquisition. But it is not easy to come to clear conclusions about the relative effectiveness of different types of CF or of different ways of implementing the same CF strategy. This is not so surprising given differences in the participants, the context and the design of the studies. Attempts to compare their results runs into the apples-and-oranges problem. Recasts may be less effective than prompts in immersion classrooms, for example, but very effective in classrooms where learners are focused on form (Lyster and Mori, 2006; Zhao, 2015). It may be desirable from a theoretical perspective to tease out the relative contributions of different types of CF, but from the pedagogic perspective (which is must be the primary concern in a book about TBLT) it is sufficient to acknowledge that all types can be effective and that the best advice that can be given to teachers is to opt for a variety of strategies as Lyster and Ranta (2013) proposed.

Immediate versus Delayed CF
Some proponents of TBLT (e.g. Willis and Willis, 2007) recommend delaying correction until learners have completed a task. Cognitive theories of L2 acquisition suggest that CF will work best when it is offered in a 'window of opportunity' (Doughty, 2001) (i.e. immediately after an error has been committed). However, there are grounds for believing that delayed CF can foster metalinguistic understanding by encouraging learners to reflect on the corrections they receive. One clear advantage of delayed feedback is that makes it much easier for the teacher to select which type of CF to implement. Delayed feedback is, of course, inherently explicit even if it involves recasting learners' errors.

Despite the theoretical and pedagogic relevance of this issue, there has been relatively little attention paid to it by researchers. Rolin-Ianzati's (2010) study of delayed CF distinguished two different approaches corresponding to the input-providing and output-prompting types of feedback found in immediate CF. In one approach the teacher provided the corrections while in the other the teacher elicited corrections from the students. Drawing on sociocultural theory, Rolin-Ianzati suggested that eliciting correction will be more effective but she did not investigate this. In a laboratory-based study (Quinn, 2014), ninety intermediate-level adult ESL learners were randomly assigned to immediate, delayed or no CF conditions. The grammatical target was English passive constructions. The immediate and delayed feedback consisted of a prompt that pushed the learners to self-correct followed by a recast if needed. There were statistically significant improvements resulting from both feedback conditions but no differences between them. The task-only condition (no CF) was just as effective as the CF conditions. Li, Zhu and Ellis (2016) compared the effects of immediate and delayed CF involving prompts followed by recasts on Chinese high school learners' acquisition of past passive constructions. Both types of CF resulted in gains on a grammaticality judgement test (GJT) but no effect for either type of CF was found on an elicited imitation test (EIT). A slight advantage was found for immediate feedback on the GJT, which was explained in terms of the learners using the feedback progressively in the production of new past passive sentences as they performed the tasks. These studies do not allow any clear conclusion to be reached about the relative effects of immediate and delayed CF and point to the need for further research.

Target Structure

Another variable potentially affecting the learning that results from CF when learners perform tasks is the linguistic feature(s) targeted by the CF. In the case of grammatical targets, it is quite likely that CF will vary in how effective it is. Studies that have investigated this have compared the effect that CF has on grammatical structures hypothesized to differ in terms of their difficulty.

Several studies suggest that the difficulty of the target structure is a factor influencing how effective CF is. Ellis (2007) compared the effects of two types of CF (recasts and metalinguistic comments) on two grammatical structures – comparative adjectives and past tense (-ed). He evaluated the learning difficulty of these two structures using a variety of criteria (e.g. input frequency, processability, reliability of the explicit rule) and concluded that overall the comparative was likely to pose a greater learning burden than past tense (-ed). The effect of the recasts on the acquisition of these two structures did not differ but the effect of metalinguistic comments was more evident on the comparative structure. Li (2014) also compared the effect of recasts and metalinguistic corrections. The target structures were Chinese classifiers and perfective aspect markers with the former deemed more salient and therefore the more easily learned. Results for the two structures only differed for recasts. In the immediate post-test recasts had stronger effect than metalinguistic comments on the more salient structure in the delayed post-test for low-proficiency learners. In the post-test, however, recasts had a greater effect on the less salient structure for high-proficiency learners. Yang and Lyster (2010) compared the effects of recasts and prompts on regular and irregular past tense forms in English. Prompts were more effective for regular -ed but there was no difference for irregular forms. Finally, Sato and Loewen (2018) compared the effects of two implicit types of CF (recasts and clarification requests) on the acquisition of third person-s (considered non-salient) and possessive determiners (considered salient). They reported that the group that received clarification requests outperformed the group receiving recasts but only for possessive determiners.

Perhaps the only clear conclusion that can be reached from these studies is that the nature of the grammatical structure does indeed mediate the effect of CF as Long (2007) claimed would be the case. However, the results of these studies do not allow for any firm conclusions about the interaction between CF type and grammatical structure. Again, this is perhaps not surprising given that the grammatical targets in these studies varied greatly and there is a lack of an agreed set of criteria for evaluating their difficulty. Li's (2014) study also suggests that the learners' proficiency level moderates the interaction between CF types and grammatical structure. From a practical point of view, it is difficult to see how teachers should take account of the grammatical target in deciding what type of CF to provide. At best, all they can do in intensive CF is select a structure that they deem is within the developmental level of their students, e.g. a structure that students have started to deploy but often erroneously.

Effect of Pre-teaching the Grammatical Target
An important issue for TBLT is whether teachers should explicitly teach the grammatical target of a task in the pre-task phase of a lesson (see Chapter 1). Long (2015) is adamantly opposed to this on the grounds that it constitutes a return to focus on forms. However, in many CF studies (e.g. Lyster, 2004; Sato and Loewen, 2018) explicit instruction was included in the pre-task phase.[10] Two questions

arise. First, does pre-teaching the grammatical structure have an impact on how the task is performed? Second, does pre-teaching the grammatical structure enhance the effect of the CF?

The first question is of interest because of the claims made for how task performance assists acquisition. This is dealt with in Chapter 3, where the effect of task design and conditions on the complexity, accuracy and fluency (CAF) of learners' production is considered. Does pre-teaching a grammatical structure affect CAF? Again, there is little research that has addressed this. In Mochizuki and Ortega (2008) there were three treatment conditions – a no-planning condition, an unguided planning condition and the condition of greatest interest here – a guided planning condition, where the participants (first-year high school students in Japan) were given a handout about English relative clauses, listened to a pre-recording of the task performance, and then had five minutes to plan before they performed the task. The performance of the task, which was designed to elicit use of relative clauses, was analysed in terms of amount of relative clause use, the accuracy of relative clause use, and the global complexity and global fluency of the language produced. The guided planning group produced more than twice as many relative clauses as the other two groups and their relative clauses were also more target-like. However, there was no difference in global complexity and fluency in the three conditions. This study, then, suggests that pre-teaching does not impact negatively on how a task is performed and in fact can have a positive effect on production of the target feature.

Another study, however, suggests otherwise. In Ellis, Li and Zhu (2018) one group of Chinese high school learners received a brief grammar lesson on the English passive voice followed by five minutes of practice activities prior to performing two dictogloss tasks while another performed the same task but with no pre-task instruction or practice. The learners' task performance was coded in terms of their production of the target structure and on global measures of CAF. The results showed that the pre-task instruction led to more frequent but not more accurate use of the target structure, but that it had detrimental effects on CAF.

The second question was addressed by Li et al. (2016). Using the same learners as in Ellis et al. (2018), they compared the effects of performing the tasks (1) without pre-task explicit instruction, (2) with pre-task explicit instruction, (3) with CF but no explicit instruction and (4) with both explicit instruction and CF on acquisition of past passive constructions, as measured by means of a GJT and an EIT. On the GJT, conditions (2), (3) and (4) led to significant gains with explicit instruction plus feedback showing the largest effects. On the EIT, there was no effect for any of the three treatment groups when the data were analysed for the whole cohort. However, when the learners were subdivided into those with zero and some prior knowledge based on their pre-test EIT scores, condition (4) was more effective than the others.

It would be premature to advise teachers about whether to include explicit instruction in the pre-task phase of a lesson but the evidence suggests that it is likely to result in more attempts to use the target structure and may sometimes be beneficial for learning. It may, however, interfere with the general performance of a task. There are, of course, other ways of providing explicit instruction – during the performance of the task if learners fail to use the target structure (as in Samuda, 2001) or after the task has been completed in the post-task stage (as suggested by Ellis, 2003). These are considered in Chapter 8.

Task-Based Interaction in Small Group Work

All the research we have considered to date has examined interaction in tasks performed in a teacher–class participatory structure. In some ways this runs contrary to a general understanding of what TBLT entails. Mainstream accounts of TBLT assume that tasks will be largely carried out in small group work. We need to ask, therefore, whether the interactions that arise in small groups when tasks are performed manifest focus on form similar to that found in teacher-led lessons and whether learning results.

Group work is generally seen as advantageous for language learning. In an early study, Long et al. (1976) reported that students working in small groups produced a greater quantity of language and also better quality language than students in a teacher-fronted, lockstep classroom setting. Small group work provided more opportunities for language production and greater variety of language use in initiating discussion, asking for clarification, interrupting, competing for the floor and joking.

Group work has been found to result in more interactional adjustments than in teacher–class interaction but only if the task is of the required information exchange type (Pica and Doughty, 1985a, 1985b). In an often-cited article, Long and Porter (1985) pointed to a number of advantages of group work:

1. Quantity of practice (i.e. there is more opportunity for language practice in group work than in lockstep lessons).

2. Variety of practice (i.e. in group work learners can perform a wide range of language functions).
3. Accuracy of student production (i.e. learners have been shown to use the L2 just as accurately in group work as in lockstep lessons).
4. Correction (i.e. students engage in self- and other corrections to a greater extent in group work than in lockstep teaching).
5. Negotiation (i.e. students engage in more negotiation of meaning sequences when performing communicative tasks in group work than in teacher-led lessons).
6. Task (i.e. group work lends itself to the performance of two-way tasks that elicit negotiation of meaning sequences).

Nassaji (2009) also found a clear advantage for group work. He compared the interactions occurring in three participatory structures – whole class, group work, one-on-one (all involving a teacher). The study involved fifty-four hours of communicative lessons in seven intact classes. Overall 1,986 FFEs were identified – 1,325 in whole class, 511 in group work, 150 in one-on-one interactions. He found that reactive FFEs are more likely to occur in individual and small group interactions than in the whole class context but pre-emptive FFEs, which were more frequent overall, were more likely in a whole class context. FFEs in small group work and in one-on-one interactions are more likely to lead to correct responses in tailor-made tests administered after class than FFEs in a whole class context (69% and 66% vs. 48%). Nassaji concluded that focus on form is a socially mediated process.

However, not all researchers provide such a favourable account of group work. Researchers have noted that learners sometimes overuse their L1 when performing tasks in groups (Carless, 2004). Adams, Nuevo and Egi (2011) observed that the studies vary in how frequently CF occurs in learner–learner interactions, with some showing that it is very infrequent. Toth (2008) noted that learners in groups tend to use a limited range of feedback strategies and, in contrast to teachers, they tend to focus on a wide range of linguistic features.

Few studies have actually investigated whether group work interaction results in acquisition. Adams et al. (2011) investigated whether the implicit and explicit feedback in learner–learner interactions was related to acquisition. Learners in high-intermediate classes in an adult ESL school in the United States worked in pairs to complete tasks designed to elicit the use of past tense and locatives. They were not instructed to provide CF. The interactions were coded for all instances of feedback, whether the feedback was implicit or explicit, and whether the learners modified their output when they were corrected. Acquisition was measured by means of a GJT and an oral production test.

Adams et al. reported that a third of the feedback was non-target-like and that there was relatively little output-prompting feedback. There was no evidence that either implicit or explicit corrections promoted acquisition of past tense but recasts were related to scores for the locative in the delayed post-test. They concluded 'it seems likely that feedback may not play as important role in learner–learner interactions as it plays in NS–learner interactions [native speaker–learner interactions]' (p. 56). They suggested that the widely focused nature of the feedback may have made it less salient and that the learners may have been hesitant in accepting that the feedback they received was correct.

The difference in the accounts of group work interaction found in these studies is not so surprising as its effectiveness must surely depend on the particular learners involved. What may be crucial is the mindset of the learners. Sato (2017) defined mindset as 'a disposition toward the task and/or interlocutor prior to and/or during the interaction' (p. 255). His study indicated that learners with a positive mindset engaged in more correction, language-related collaboration and collaborative sentence completion than learners with a more negative mindset. One way of inducing a positive mindset is through training. Sato and Lyster (2012) reported that training Japanese university students to make use of CF during group work led to them providing both more and more effective CF (prompts) and also to more repair work. For group work to deliver on its promises in TBLT, then, learners may require guidance in the behaviours that are needed to ensure that it is effective for acquisition.

Conclusion

Cognitive-interactionist theories support TBLT by emphasizing that (1) acquisition of an L2 occurs incidentally/implicitly when learners are focused on meaning as they perform tasks, but that (2) focus on form is needed to ensure that learners attend to the linguistic forms they are exposed to in the input. Interaction facilitates learning when it promotes noticing and noticing-the-gap. To examine whether and to what extent this happens, researchers have utilized discourse analysis to identify those features of interaction that theory predicts will facilitate acquisition. Key overlapping constructs are negotiation of meaning, negotiation of form, and pre-emptive and reactive focus on form. Interaction works for acquisition when it enables learners to map form onto meaning in a context where they are communicating purposively as they perform tasks.

We distinguished two strands of research – (1) task-based learner performance studies and (2) task-as-treatment studies. The former sheds light on how task design and implementation features affect the kinds of interaction that result from a task. The latter shows how performing tasks can induce noticing and facilitate acquisition. A major focus of research that has drawn on cognitive-interactionist theories is CF. We discussed various aspects of this research – whether CF has add-on value to performing a task, extensive versus intensive feedback, type of feedback, immediate versus delayed, choice of target structure and the effect of explicit instruction in the pre-task phase. We also considered interaction in group work.

What then do we know?

- Closed tasks of the required information exchange type are best for promoting negotiation of meaning.
- Interactionally modified input (including in text chat) is more likely to induce noticing of linguistic forms than pre-modified input but this may be because it affords learners more time to process input.
- Participating in FFEs helps acquisition especially if learners have opportunities to repair their errors.
- Input-based tasks work for acquisition providing that they create a functional need for learners to map forms onto their meanings. This is more likely to occur if learners have an opportunity to interact when they do not understand the input.
- Intensive CF facilitates acquisition.
- On balance, explicit feedback is more effective than implicit feedback and, in the eyes of some researchers, output-prompting feedback is more effective than input-providing.
- CF can work for acquisition even when it is delayed until the post-task stage of a lesson.
- The effectiveness of feedback depends on the grammatical targets to which the correction is directed.
- Explicit instruction in the pre-task phase may help to elicit use of the target structure when the task is performed and assist acquisition but may also impact on the overall quality of learners' production.
- While group work may be generally beneficial, learners may not always engage in much correction unless they are trained to do so.

Many of these conclusions are necessarily tentative – partly because in some cases the research is still very limited and partly because the available research findings are not always consistent. Also, as we have noted, the complexity of interactional phenomena such as CF makes it difficult to arrive at clear conclusions based on studies that investigate just one or two variables at a time and cannot take account of the intertwined relationships among a host of variables.

There are some obvious limitations in the research we have reported. One concerns how learning is measured. Uptake-with-repair may serve as a measure of noticing (intake) but it cannot be used as a measure of learning, which requires administering tests. A great variety of tests have been used. In some studies (e.g. Ellis et al., 2006; Li, 2013a) care was taken to include tests that measured both declarative and procedural knowledge of the target structures. This is important as the aim of TBLT is to develop learners' procedural L2 ability so GJTs or tests that tap into controlled language cannot be used to assess whether tasks have worked as they are intended to. We are still a long way off knowing whether TBLT enables learners to develop the implicit knowledge of an L2 that Long (2015) saw as the goal.

Interaction is a complex phenomenon with many facets. In this chapter we have focused quite narrowly on those constructs that SLA researchers have deemed theoretically important for understanding how interaction 'connects input (what learners hear and read); internal learner capacities, particularly selective attention; and output (what learners produce) in productive ways' (Long, 1996, pp. 451–2). It should be noted, however, that the acquisition potential of interaction does not rest solely in the fairly narrow set of constructs that we have considered. Other aspects of interaction – for example, the extent to which learners have the opportunity to play an initiating as well as a responding role in interaction (see Ellis, 1999) or the extent to which learners have the opportunity to produce long turns – are also important. Some researchers are moving away from the narrow approach we have adopted to consider how 'engagement' is evident in interaction. This more encompassing approach is considered in Chapter 6.

Another limitation of the research that the cognitive-interactionist perspective has spawned is that it has focused almost entirely on the short-term effects of performing interactive tasks. Thus we know almost nothing about how interaction feeds acquisition over time. There is an urgent need for longitudinal studies that investigate how patterns of interaction change and what the accumulative effects of engaging in interaction over time are. More studies, such as those of Shintani's (2016) five-week classroom-based study of TBLT and Saito and Akiyama's (2017) one-semester study of video-based interaction, are needed. These studies revealed that task-based interaction does help acquisition in the long term but also point to possible limitations. Shintani's young learners demonstrated little productive ability. Saito and Akiyama's adult learners demonstrated no improvement in aspects of language that only develop slowly and gradually (e.g. pronunciation), leading these researchers to suggest that explicit instruction may be needed to complement interaction.

3 Psycholinguistic Perspectives

Introduction

The focus in this chapter is on the work that has been done, both theoretical and empirical, to understand what happens in task performance from a psycholinguistic perspective. This does not, in any way, conflict with the more socially oriented chapters in Part II of the book, but it does reflect the considerable work with a more purely cognitive perspective that has been done. First, typical methods of measuring task performance are described, essentially because these become the touchstone for the more substantive discussions which follow. Then two approaches are covered which account for a considerable amount of the recent research: the Limited Attentional Capacity (LAC) approach (Skehan, 2014c) and the Cognition Hypothesis (CH)/Stabilize, Simplify, Automatize, Restructure, Complexify (SSARC) model (Robinson, 2015), focusing on tasks themselves – task design, task characteristics and so on. The discussion attempts to address six questions:

- What is the main focus of the approach, and correspondingly, what is de-emphasized?
- What is the role of acquisition?
- How important are performance issues?
- What theoretical accounts are provided?
- What is the research base?
- What research methods are typical for the approach?

The following section compares the two approaches and explores strengths and weakness with each. Then the final section of the chapter focuses on current issues with psycholinguistic approaches.

Measuring Task-Based Performance

It may seem odd to start the chapter with a concern for the rather 'technical' area of measurement, but there are issues to be resolved in this area, and these have an impact on the more substantive discussions which follow. So the section is necessary, but only to prepare the ground for what comes later.

Cognitively oriented task research has been remarkably focused on a limited number of performance areas. Initially (Ellis, 1987; Crookes, 1989) these were complexity, accuracy and fluency (CAF). More recently the area of lexis has been added to this list, and so, strictly speaking, we should now be concerned with structural complexity and lexical complexity separately, although the acronyms CAF (Housen and Kuiken, 2009) and CALF (Skehan, 2009a) are common in referring to this approach to measurement. There are several justifications for this approach:

- Statistically, the four areas have distinctness as shown by factor analyses of datasets that generate separate factors (Skehan and Foster, 1997; Tavakoli and Skehan, 2005). In other words, it is quite possible that someone will obtain high scores in one dimension of performance and not in others: there is no guaranteed proficiency effect leading to even performance in each area.
- The four areas, as will be shown in more detail throughout this chapter, can be influenced by different variables, so that what raises one (e.g. complexity), may not generalize to other areas, and may even lower it (e.g. fluency).
- It has been argued (Skehan, 1998, 2014c) that there is an acquisitional sequence consistent with the four areas, with complexity (structural or lexical) coming first, as an interlanguage system is destabilized and grows, followed by greater control, first through the reduction and even elimination of error and then followed in turn by the development of fluency, as not only is accuracy increased, but this is done at reasonable speed of production.
- There is some evidence of the four areas reflecting different priorities, of personal styles, with some learners emphasizing accuracy or fluency, and others complexity (Skehan and Shum, 2017).

Given this background, it is worth exploring each of the areas, and the progress that has been made in measurement in recent years.

Structural Complexity

Early research in this area focused on two approaches. These were to explore the range of structures that were used in a task, on the one hand, and to compute a measure of subordination, on the other. The former emphasizes structural variety, assuming that this reflects a greater underlying structural repertoire. The latter takes subordination to be an effective surrogate for general complexity, on the assumption that the more speakers can pack more information into what they say or write through this linguistic device the greater the underlying structural system that they have available. Although the former, range, has generated considerable interest, it has not been used nearly as widely as subordination-linked measures. These have become fairly routine in task-based research. There is even a journal article (Foster, Tonkyn and Wigglesworth, 2000) which has been very influential in the field in the attempt to standardize the measures used to facilitate cross-study comparisons.

As operationalizations of complexity, the subordination-based measures have been very useful in task research. More recently an alternative approach has been proposed. Norris and Ortega (2009) suggest that, for more advanced levels, the subordination-based measures do not discriminate so well, and they propose such measures should be supplemented by indices based on the average number of words per clause. Since this proposal such measures have been used in many research studies, so it is interesting to explore what the relationship is between these two types of measure. Inoue (2013), Pang and Skehan (2014), Skehan and Shum (2017), and Wang and Skehan (2014) all report correlations on this issue: the typical correlation from this range of studies, over different proficiency levels and with different research designs, is less than 0.20. In other words, the two measures are clearly concerned with different constructs, and so research studies need to include both. Reviewing this area, Skehan (2018) also proposes that there are indications of systematic influences. Narrative (vs. interactive) tasks and planned conditions raise both subordination and words-per-clause. Structured tasks and there-and-then conditions raise subordination only. Low proficiency (possibly surprisingly), native-speaker status, a here-and-now condition and less structure raise words-per-clause only. This is clearly an area where more research is needed to account for these emerging generalizations. But for now, it is clear that both types of measure are independently essential.

Accuracy

As with complexity, there are also some alternative choices with regard to measures of accuracy. Prominent amongst these are: (1) the proportion of error-free clauses, (2) errors per (usually) 100 words and, more recently, (3) error gravity (Foster and Wigglesworth, 2016). The use of each of these can be defended on theoretical and/or practical grounds. Perhaps the first has accumulated most findings in existing research, and so one can have confidence in it on that basis. The second has been advocated as more appropriate for some languages, such as German (Mehnert, 1998). The third has been proposed as having more construct validity, since it is argued that treating all errors as equal is inappropriate since some impact on communication more than others (Foster and Wigglesworth, 2016). In an examination of the functioning of all of these measures, through the examination of a number of datasets, Skehan (2018) proposes that, empirically, it does not matter which is used: unlike the structural complexity measures, which do not intercorrelate highly, all the accuracy measures show very high correlational levels – almost always above 0.80, and often clearly above that. So in this case, we appear to have simplicity of measurement – the choice that is made does not seem to have a severe impact on results.

Lexical Complexity

Two measures of lexical complexity have been widely used in task research. *Lexical diversity* measures are based on type-token ratios. Given the well-established and strong relationship between text length and type-token ratios (correlations of -0.70 are typical – Foster and Skehan (2012) – demonstrating that the longer the text, other things being equal, the lower the type-token ratio), there needs to be a correction made to compensate for text length. Typical, but by no means the only alternatives, would be the mean segmental type-token ratio, and D, computed by the Child Language Analysis (CLAN) suite of programmes (Macwhinney, 2000). *Lexical sophistication* aims more at the construct of lexical richness, and is based on the proportion of words that are used in a spoken or written performance which are deemed difficult. Difficulty is usually defined in terms of frequency, and so the claim is that 'penetration' of a text by more difficult words is reflective of a more extensive mental lexicon.

As with the structural complexity measures, it is interesting that the different lexical measures do not intercorrelate highly (Skehan, 2009b). Each appears to be doing something different. High lexical diversity reflects speakers or writers who do not reuse the same words so much in a text, and this seems distinct from second language (L2) users who draw upon less 'obvious' words, the target of lexical sophistication. There is no literature yet on what influences each of these measures selectively (in contrast, as we have seen, to the different structural complexity measures). Lexical diversity, though, does distinguish very clearly between native and non-native speakers (Skehan and Shum, 2017), whereas lexical sophistication does not. The former seems to be a capacity of the speaker, whereas the latter seems more task-influenced (Skehan and Shum, 2017).

Fluency

In some ways this is the most complex sub-dimension of performance. It has been argued that fluency can be subdivided into breakdown-linked fluency, repair-linked fluency and speed (Tavakoli and Skehan, 2005). The first is typically measured through pausing, the second through behaviours such as reformulation, replacement, repetition and false starts. Speed is typically measured through words or syllables per minute, but De Jong et al. (2013) advocated the use of mean syllable duration, i.e. inverse articulation rate, since it is more normally distributed. There are also composite measures such as length of run and phonation time, as well as, possibly, double occurrences, e.g. the number of times that pauses and repair coincide (Kahng, 2014).

The sub-dimensions of fluency intercorrelate at a level between the correlations reported for accuracy and structural complexity. In other words, the relationships are positive, but not necessarily strong. In addition, there are several emerging issues in fluency measurement. First, there is the issue of pause or repair location. Skehan (2009b, 2018) argued that end-of-clause dysfluencies should be considered to be distinct from mid-clause dysfluencies, and indeed it may be the case that mid-clause pausing is similar to repair, more generally. Second, there are also concerns about surrogate measures, as, for example, with mid-clause filled pauses being taken as a surrogate (easier to measure) for unfilled mid-clause pauses (notoriously more difficult to measure). Lambert, Kormos and Minn (2016) use them in this way whereas Skehan (2018) reports quite low intercorrelations between filled and unfilled mid-clause pauses. Most challenging and exciting of all, linkages have been proposed between different types of dysfluency and the detail of psycholinguistic speech production processes (Lambert et al., 2016) from Levelt's model of speaking, and we will return to this in the section on the Limited Attentional Capacity Approach.

General vs. Specific Measures

All the measures we have considered so far have been generalized in nature, taking an entire speech sample and then measuring the various sub-dimensions of performance while drawing on the entire sample. Specific error types, e.g. of aspect or agreement, do not figure in this analysis. Such generalized approaches have the advantage that they are based on the largest amount of data possible. They also enable the sub-dimensions of performance to be measured separately. As a result they are, perhaps, the most effective way of detecting differences between experimental conditions that affect task performance.

But they are also crude, and so there is a strong case for using more specific measures. R. Ellis (1987), for example, used the different forms of the English past tense (regular, irregular, copula) to try to capture differences between rule-based and lexical forms. Using specific measures of this type connect more naturally with acquisitional processes, and, perhaps, patterns of development of different interlanguage subsystems. They also enable more precise hypotheses to be framed. Robinson (2015), for example, makes linkages between specific measures which derive from cognitive linguistic analyses of performance, linked to different experimental conditions. But the major disadvantage here is that the use of specific measures risks reducing the amount of data that can be analysed. Specific hypotheses, while desirable, mean that particular tokens have to be generated, and in sufficient quantities to confirm or disconfirm the hypotheses. Engineering research designs which do this are not at all easy and there is the danger that such a design may compromise the 'taskness' or naturalness of the data collection by constraining too narrowly what needs to be done. As a result, the researcher has a considerable dilemma. Both types of measure, generalized and specific, have their uses, and so where possible, using both is desirable. It is simply that, for much of the time, specialized measures will not be feasible to enable effective statistical testing. Where it can be done, however, it is highly desirable.

Models of Task-Based Performance

This, the main section of the chapter, will consider first Skehan's LAC approach, followed by Robinson's CH, and in its most recent form the SSARC model.

Part One: The LAC Approach

Skehan's LAC approach arose out of a series of studies conducted with Pauline Foster (Foster and Skehan, 1996, 1999; Skehan and Foster, 1997, 1999). The results of these studies suggested (bearing mind that they used measures of structural CAF) that there was often a trade-off between the performance areas, particularly between accuracy and complexity. For example, in one study (Foster and Skehan, 1996) exploring planning, a group simply given planning time produced the highest level of accuracy, whereas a group given planning time and instructions which emphasized ideas to be expressed, produced the highest levels of structural complexity and lower accuracy. A factor analysis conducted in Skehan and Foster (1997) confirmed this separation between complexity and accuracy. These findings contributed to the development of the importance of trade-off, against the background of limited attentional resources and working memory. In other words, given such limitations, if one is performing close to one's limit (as these tasks were designed to provoke) there is the strong possibility that prioritizing one performance area may well be at the expense of another. Since this start, a wide range of studies that are consistent with this interpretation have appeared (Foster and Skehan, 1999, 2013; Skehan and Foster, 1999, 2005, 2007).

This general approach is still actively pursued, as in Tavakoli and Foster (2008), Foster and Tavakoli (2009), Foster and Skehan (2012, 2013) and the chapters in Skehan (2014a). But it has changed over the years, not least since the emphasis has moved away from trade-off, since this term implies inevitability, and that there will always be a tension between accuracy and complexity. Now it is more appropriate to refer to the LAC approach, since this emphasizes the importance of attention and working memory constraints, but not that these constraints cannot be overcome. The approach is characterized through a series of principles (Skehan, 2015, 2018). These are:

Principle 1: *Working memory and attention are limited*. The working memory literature is huge, and demonstrates quite clearly that this aspect of memory, effectively current consciousness, has limited size and that this limitation has an impact on attention (Wen, 2015; Skehan, 2016). In working memory research there may be dispute about the exact size of the memory, but the disagreements are so slight that this does not really change the impact this limitation has on the field of L2 acquisition and performance (Cowan, 2015). LAC also assumes limited attentional availability, and while it is accepted there may be variation in how much attention is available (e.g. for motivational reasons, more, or less, attention may be mobilized at a particular time), there is still a maximum and this maximum is assumed to represent a significant functional constraint for the L2 user.

Principle 2: *The CALF framework is useful*. Essentially this is a restatement of the first section of the chapter. The claim is simply that viewing performance in this way, with these sub-dimensions, is revealing about the different influences, e.g. task characteristics, task conditions and the effects they have on performance. The areas are particularly important in capturing the effects of different independent variables, and of tensions between them.

Principle 3: *Tasks are analysable, but difficult to work with*. Much research with tasks explores broad task types (e.g. personal information exchange, narrative, interactive) or more specific characteristics (structured or not; requiring information transformation versus simple retrieval). The aim is to establish generalizations about performance on such tasks which would be useful to predict future performance or to understand development and acquisition. These analytic schemes have been productive, and have contained considerable promise, delivering a number of very useful results, practically and theoretically. But tasks are also difficult to work with, since there may be a fundamental distinction between the intended task and the actual task (Breen, 1984; see also the discussion in Chapter 1). In other words, individuals doing tasks can take the task in different directions to those anticipated, and so one of the fundamental problems in working with tasks is that analytic schemes do not always transfer into actual task performance in straightforward ways. This is discussed more extensively in the Issues part of the chapter, particularly the section on Task Conditions, where it is also argued that task conditions are more dependable sources of influence (Skehan, 2016).

Principle 4: *Linking task performance (as well as notions of attentional limitations, CALF-measured performance and task characteristics) to the Levelt model of speaking is productive and a potential basis for effective predictions.* Levelt (1989, 1999) distinguishes between three major stages of speaking. These are intended to account for the case of first language (L1) speaking, but they are generalizable, with modification, to the L2 case (De Bot, 1992; Kormos, 2006; Skehan, 2014c). The three stages are conceptualization, formulation and articulation. The first is concerned with developing the ideas to be expressed, working out, in a conversational context, what needs and is appropriate to be said. This stage ends with the development of the pre-verbal message. Formulation is concerned with clothing the pre-verbal message (propositional rather than linguistic in nature) with language. The first sub-stage is to retrieve appropriate lemmas from the second language mental lexicon (SLML), the second is to use the rich information contained in the lemmas as the basis for syntax-building, and the third is to take the semi-assembled message and to access relevant phonological information, again from the lemmas. This information is then fed to the final stage, Articulation, which converts the phonological outline into actual speech. In addition, the process of speaking is also accompanied by the capacity to monitor (and therefore modify) what is being assembled, although according to the Levelt model this can only be done at particular points in the speech production process. It is also important to clarify that the different components in this model, conceptualization, formulation, articulation, are encapsulated and modular. What this means is that each gets on with its job, operating simultaneously to the other modules within the system. Each module is working on something different. The Conceptualizer delivers the pre-verbal message to the Formulator, and then gets on with the next communicative cycle at the very same time as the Formulator is operating upon the input it has received from the pre-verbal message. The same applies to the Articulator, which also gets on with its job in parallel fashion. This simultaneous operation of each stage is vital for the smooth capacity we have to use our L1.

The LAC approach, though, is concerned with L2 speaking. Crucial for this is the SLML. This is smaller, slower, less well organized and, importantly, often not as rich in the information that is held in a lemma (information such as appropriate syntactic frames, multiple potential meanings, phonological information, collocates, discourse functioning and so on). As a result, during speaking (or writing, come to that), the Conceptualizer may make demands upon the SLML to underpin Formulation, but these demands cannot be met at all, or only partially, or cannot be met quickly enough. As a result, parallel functioning, the norm in L1 language, cannot be sustained, and effortful, attention-consuming serial-processing results, as problems at one stage of the speech production process divert attention from the others, until the problem is solved. Then the thread of discourse has to be (painfully) retrieved.

A final point in this regard is that there are connections between CALF and the stages within the Levelt model. Conceptualization does map reasonably on to structural and possibly lexical complexity, and Formulation has stronger links with accuracy and fluency. These mappings are not, by any means, exact. Conceptualization, for example, is likely to link with fluency also, when it underpins a more macro approach to discourse, spanning several clauses or sentences (Skehan, 2018). It may also, as when Conceptualization is assisted by planning opportunities (Pang and Skehan, 2014), help accuracy by avoiding more difficult language. But in the main, there is something of a connection between CALF and the Leveltian stages.

Principle 5: *Task characteristics and task conditions influence performance separately and in combination.* This may seem simply a statement of the obvious, but in the LAC approach it does have some theoretical importance! Recall the claim that attentional limitations are a constraint, not an inevitability. The point is that allocating attention to one area may have a negative impact on other dimensions of performance (a statement, in itself, consistent with a trade-off interpretation). But essentially this represents a challenge – the need to overcome attentional limitations by judicious task design/choice and implementation through task conditions. A task 'event' is a bundle of things: a combination of task characteristics (because tasks are not characterized by one feature only) and combinations of task conditions as well. Task and task condition research has delivered a range of generalizations. Briefly and incompletely, but relevant to the present argument, these are:

- structured tasks raise accuracy
- tasks requiring information transformation or integration raise complexity
- tasks based on familiar and concrete information increase fluency
- pre-task or strategic planning raises complexity and fluency and to a lesser extent, accuracy
- online planning, if there is room for conceptualizer use, raises accuracy
- repetition raises CAF
- post-task conditions raise accuracy.

These generalizations relate to the point, just made, that task characteristics and conditions influence performance separately. In themselves, they could be consistent with a trade-off interpretation (with the exception of task repetition, to which we return later in this section). But the important point is to consider combinations of task characteristics and conditions. Careful combinations can lead to increases in more than one dimension of task performance. For example, Tavakoli and Skehan (2005) and Tavakoli and Foster (2008) report that structured tasks which also require information integration (in both these cases linking background and foreground information) raise accuracy *and* complexity. The push to accuracy comes from the structured nature of the task while complexity is induced by information organization. Foster and Skehan (2013) report that a complex (interactive decision-making) task allied to a post-task condition raises complexity and accuracy. The decision-making nature of the task raises complexity, and the post-task is important for accuracy. Such results suggest that attention allocation can be manipulated, and that, within the constraints of the total amount of attention available, more than one performance area can be raised. The central claim (and this is important in relation to the CH discussion below) is that the LAC approach contends that careful combinations of tasks and conditions are all that is needed to produce the joint raising of accuracy and complexity, and that it is the separate but interacting influences that produce this effect.

Repetition is an interesting part of the task literature (Bygate, 2001). Wang (2014) shows how it raises all aspects of performance. Lambert et al. (2016), in a study with multiple repetitions, also report positive effects. It appears that repetition is a technique which enables more effective conceptualization and formulation and that these translate into raised structural CAF. Lambert et al. (2016) link successive repetitions with different Leveltian stages. Wang (2014), in slight contrast, suggests that one repetition, provided that it is immediate, allows all performance areas to benefit. Her argument is that the first performance engages the Conceptualizer, the Formulator *and* the Articulator, and this underpins raised CAF. So this task condition, in itself, seems to contain all the ingredients needed to raise three performance areas.

Principle 6: *Task difficulty needs to be analysed distinctly for the Conceptualizer and the Formulator*. The LAC approach does use the concept of difficulty (cf. the different approach taken by the CH below), and regards this as inherent within the task. Obviously people will respond to this difficulty differently, but it is contended that it is useful to regard tasks as more or less difficult than one another. But the major complication is that what makes a task difficult in terms of the Conceptualizer may not be the same as what makes a task difficult in terms of the Formulator. The first is likely to emphasize the ideas within a task, their accessibility, their need for manipulation and so on. The second is concerned with how the SLML is accessed, is adequate and can respond to the demands that are made upon it by the Conceptualizer. Obviously this also links with the conditions under which a task is done, e.g. time pressure, so it is not simply the task itself. But the task itself is central and influences how the speaker or writer has the SLML resources to respond to the demands of the task. Potentially, therefore, there are separate variations in difficulty for the Conceptualizer and the Formulator. This is developed further in Chapter 9, when task-based assessment is considered.

Acquisition

LAC addresses this in two ways (Skehan, 2007, 2012, 2013). First, it is assumed that the CALF categories can represent an acquisitional sequence, and so tasks which promote greater complexity are pushing for new language, while tasks which promote accuracy or fluency are supporting control of an existing interlanguage level. In this view, first there is destabilization, and then there is a concern for control (eliminating inaccuracy first, and then achieving fluency second).

But second, and more fundamentally, LAC regards the task itself as having the important function of making some aspect (or aspects) of language salient. It is assumed that the teacher records what language has been made salient in this way, as when some language has been noticed (Schmidt, 1994), or a gap has been noticed through the creation of 'a need to mean' (Samuda, 2001). Then it is assumed that important acquisitional work takes place *at a post-task stage*, where the teacher can react to the language which has emerged in this way, and use pedagogic techniques to bring understanding, or extension, or integration or consolidation, as appropriate. The important point is that this language is what has emerged when the learner has transacted a task. The language is not pre-selected, but comes into focus because of the needs of the learner.

The Research Base

The research base for the LAC approach is not enormous and its claims focus on consistency with the underlying principles, rather than on predictions followed by confirmation through controlled experimentation. The initial impetus for the approach, as mentioned, came from a series of studies done by Skehan and collaborators. A first set of studies explored issues of task type (personal information exchange, narrative retelling, decision-making[interactive] tasks) and task characteristics (e.g. task structure, information organization), as well as task conditions such as planning and post-task conditions. The results of the studies were interpreted as suggestive of limited attentional capacities. In addition, various generalizations were apparent, such as familiarity of information and task structure being associated with raised accuracy; interactive tasks associated with raised complexity; information distribution being associated with raised complexity also; and a series of influences (familiar information and structure again) with greater fluency. But beyond these generalizations, there seemed to be tensions such that different performance areas might be associated with different influences, and if one was raised, others were often lowered. A major competition for resources, evident in these studies, was between accuracy and complexity (Foster and Skehan, 1996; Skehan and Foster, 1997), but competition between fluency and other areas, usually accuracy, also occurred. (Lexis did not come into sharp focus in this earlier set of studies, and so does not figure in any of these claims.) Hence the notion of trade-off at that time, and more recently the notion of LAC.

The same research team also reported occasions when accuracy and complexity were jointly raised, which might appear to challenge a limited attention account. Two studies by Foster and Skehan (1999, 2013) showed this pattern. Skehan (2014c) provides an interpretation of these results, in effect what is covered as Principle 5: that separate influences on accuracy and complexity combine to raise each of these areas. In Foster and Skehan (1999), with several planning conditions, it was the teacher-led planning which produced the joint raising, and it was argued that teachers pushed learners to engage with both accuracy and complexity. In Foster and Skehan (2013) it was the conjoint influence of a decision-making format (which led to raised complexity) linked with a post-task condition (which raised accuracy). There is one important additional point to make here. Skehan (2014c) argues that to establish that accuracy and complexity are jointly raised in a way that questions the relevance of limited attention being relevant, one has to report the correlation coefficient between accuracy and complexity and this needs to be at least reasonably high. This would indicate that the same individuals can sustain higher accuracy and complexity. In the studies in question, despite the joint accuracy-complexity effect evident through group mean scores and inferential statistics, the accuracy-complexity correlations were either very low or low. In other words, it appears as though some participants prioritized accuracy while others prioritized complexity, but not often both. In a way, this is indirect evidence of a trade-off effect.

More recently there have begun to be studies which explore the LAC approach from a more prediction-oriented standpoint, exemplifying Principle 4 – the connection with the Levelt model. Typical here is Wang and Skehan (2014). They manipulated the two variables of task structure and time perspective. The former was operationalized and interpreted as a general problem-solution structure in a video narrative retelling compared to non-structured narrative stories. The latter was operationalized broadly as in the Cognition Hypothesis (CH), through video-based narrative retellings, simultaneously or delayed, to achieve time perspective difference. But the interpretation of the two time perspective conditions was very different to the CH proposals. The here-and-now condition was interpreted as low in longer-term memory demands but higher in working memory and general pressuring demands through less negotiability of content. The there-and-then condition was interpreted as higher in long-term memory demands but lower in working memory demands. It was also regarded as much more negotiable. Predictions were therefore made that structure and time perspective (there-and-then) would have positive influences on accuracy and complexity and that they would interact. These predictions were clearly upheld for complexity. Accuracy was more mixed in that main effects were not evident but there was an interaction, with the least error in the there-and-then structured condition. So in this case, the LAC approach led to testable predictions, and reasonable, if not total confirmation.

An Evaluation of the LAC Approach

The LAC approach is essentially bottom-up in nature. It attempts to account for task characteristic and task condition effects as they emerge from research studies. Tasks are not seen as the result of overarching conceptual categories but rather accumulate from a range of sources. Foster and Skehan (1996), for example, based the three task types they used (personal information exchange, narrative retelling, problem-linked decision-making) on a survey of language teaching materials. The previous literature is also important in identifying researchable tasks – as in the impact of R. Ellis (1987) and Crookes (1989), whose findings on planning were suggestive of the fertility of this research area. Similarly, post hoc analyses of research results may be suggestive of important patterns which need to be confirmed and extended. Typical examples here would be a focus on structured tasks, as well as the importance of information integration, since these variables were apparent only after reflection on research results. Any general analysis of task types then is based on the pattern of studies and results which accumulate, interpreted through the six principles that have described.

Inevitably, as results accumulate, and confirm or disconfirm or modify, so generalizations may change. This, clearly, is a post hoc approach, which can be criticized as such (Robinson, 2007b). In other words, the LAC has not been strong on predictions, and accordingly is weakened in face of the criterion of falsifiability. Indeed, one of the central concepts, limited attention leading to trade-offs in performance, is rather elastic. If a particular set of results occurs indicating trade-offs in performance, a ready-made account is available, just as, if they do not occur, one can say that attentional limitations were not relevant and trade-offs did not occur. At the very least, therefore, replication becomes more important to at least demonstrate that any effects of trade-off are consistent, even if they are not strongly motivated by any particular theory.

It is important, therefore, to consider whether the LAC approach could make predictions and be falsifiable. There are, perhaps, two responses that can be made in this regard. First, there is the possibility of what might be termed mini-theories. The range of generalizations that has emerged from task research may be disappointingly small (see discussion below), but we do now have several. The various generalizations can then be the basis for predictions. For example, structure has been reported as raising accuracy and fluency. Skehan (2018) offers an analysis as to why this is so, involving the connection between wider discourse functioning (macro processes) and detailed focus on the surface of language at the clause level (micro processes). All of this is based on a particular interpretation, specifically problem-solution, of task structure (Winter, 1976; Hoey, 1983). But this is only one way of structuring a task. The prediction could then be that other forms of structure will produce a similar impact on performance. The same approach could be taken with other generalizations which have emerged in the task literature, such as the role of information integration and transformation. Other tasks could be analysed through these concepts, exploring other forms of information integration and transformation, and the predictions made for the new contexts which are based on existing findings.

This is rather opportunistic and particular, though. More relevant would be a wider framework within which to locate the different sorts of tasks and conditions which have been used. It is here, once again (see Principle 4), that the use of the Levelt model (1989), applied to the L2 case (Kormos, 2006), is vital. The model proposes three stages in speech production, as we have seen, and it suggests a structure for the Formulator which makes the SLML central. Already this suggests ways in which predictions can be made regarding tasks and task conditions. The mini-theories mentioned, regarding structure and information organization, fit in nicely. The former, task structure, unites Conceptualizer work (to develop a macrostructure to the task) with Formulator work (as attention is more available for SLML operations, given the easing effect on attention of a broader macrostructure). The latter, information organization and transformation, makes it clear that Conceptualizer work is going to be more intensive, as information is manipulated, leading to higher structural complexity.

Drawing on the Levelt model in this way enables predictions regarding more than task characteristics and task conditions. The SLML is, as we have seen, central to the LAC. One implication of this is that, as proficiency develops, it is likely that the SLML will also grow, in size, organization, richness and speed. This development has the potential to recast the relationship between the Conceptualizer and the Formulator for the L2 speaker. A more effective SLML means that Conceptualizer demands can be greater and still be met, and Formulation can proceed more effectively. This, in turn, allows an interesting connection with the CH, which, amongst other predictions, argues that complexity and accuracy of performance can be jointly raised.

The LAC approach, too, could predict that accuracy and complexity could be more easily jointly raised – but only at higher proficiency levels. Indeed, this possibility has confirmation in Malicka and Levkina (2012), who report that the accuracy–complexity relationship is higher in precisely this way.

Part Two: The CH and the SSARC Model

The CH was developed by Peter Robinson to account for task performance, again broadly using a CAF framework. In addition, the CH makes proposals regarding pedagogic issues, such as task sequencing and syllabus design, as well as the role of tasks in catalysing feedback and acquisitional processes (Robinson, 2011). The basic CH approach underwent significant change with the development of the SSARC model (Robinson, 2015), and so the present account will first deal with the earlier phase, which only implicated the CH, before going on to explicate the newer approach, incorporating SSARC.

The CH has a more prominent foundation in linguistic analysis than the LAC. In earlier formulations the main influence was Givon (1985) and functional linguistics. More recently there has been greater emphasis on cognitive linguistics (Ellis and Robinson, 2008). With both, the assumption is that communication is meaning-driven and that linguistic exponents respond to the functional/cognitive demands placed upon them. In addition, Robinson (2011) takes a radically different view of attentional functioning to the LAC. While limitations in working memory are accepted, the same is not so true for attentional resources. Following Wickens (2007) and Sanders (1998), Robinson proposes that attention can expand to meet the demands placed upon it and that it is more appropriate to speak of 'resource pools' which can be drawn on provided that they do not compete for exactly the same resources. Hence, for example, separate demands on different modalities should not compete for resources. Thus, the trade-off aspect of the LAC does not function as a constraint in the same way.

As one moves to detail, Robinson proposes a triadic componential framework, subsuming task complexity, task conditions and task difficulty. The first of these focuses on the task itself, and its complexity: this is the central feature of the CH (and see below). Then task conditions are concerned with participation variables, while task difficulty involves what the speaker (or writer) brings to the task, a set of characteristics which may change how the task is approached, given that some people may have more relevant abilities than others. Each of these will now be described in more detail. Chapter 5 focuses narrowly on the learner factors involved in task difficulty.

Task complexity is concerned with the cognitive demands of a task and how these connect with actual performance. First of all, there is a major distinction between resource-directing variables and resource-dispersing variables. Resource-directing variables are hypothesized to push the speaker towards engagement with language itself. The consequences of this are that accuracy and complexity are *both* raised, with this linking with the way attention expands to meet functional needs. One performance area does not have a negative influence on the other because each is a reflection of the engagement with language. Another consequence is that it is hypothesized that there is greater likelihood of noticing, and of generating, interactional feedback and negotiation for meaning. Resource-directing variables are exemplified by:

1. time perspective (here-and-now vs. there-and-then)
2. intentional reasoning
3. spatial reasoning
4. causal reasoning
5. number of elements
6. perspective-taking.

In contrast, there are resource-dispersing variables. These do not push the speaker towards language engagement, but they do affect the general dispersal of resources. They do not connect with predictions such as the accuracy–complexity relationship. Their impact on performance is consequently not linked to language itself. Typical resource-dispersing variables are:

1. planning time, or not
2. single vs. dual task
3. task structure, or not
4. number of steps
5. independence of steps
6. prior knowledge.

The discussion so far is, then, in terms of task complexity and its impact on language performance. Task conditions, in Robinson's model, in contrast, are concerned with the interactional demands of tasks. These are of two general sorts: participation variables and participant variables. The former are concerned with the nature of the task outcome, the number and relationship of the participants in the task, and the scope for negotiation within the task. The latter are concerned with how the participants relate to one another, in terms of things like proficiency level, gender, degree of familiarity with one another and the relevant world knowledge that each of them has.

Task difficulty, finally, is concerned with learner factors. Note here that difficulty is not seen as a quality of a task (since it is complexity that is emphasized in that regard). Instead task difficulty involves the qualities (both ability and affective) that the participant brings to the task. Ability factors concern things like working memory, capacity to switch attention, reasoning ability, mind/intention reading, aptitude and field independence. Affective variables consist of task motivation, anxiety, willingness to communicate, openness to experience, control of emotion and self-efficacy. The difficulty of an actual task is then a result of the interaction between task complexity and task difficulty factors.

The heart of the CH is task complexity, but it is clear that the enumeration of task condition and task difficulty variables contains massive potential for a research programme. Each of the condition or difficulty variables represents a hypothesis as to what influence they will have, e.g. the effect on performance of a task with an open solution, or a convergent solution and so on (and see discussion in Chapter 2). Largely, this potential research programme is embryonic rather than realized, but there are many interesting possibilities here. In the SSARC model, the task difficulty variables are discussed a little more extensively than before, and linked to different ways that task complexity resource-directing variables might function. Several of the resource-directing variables involve reasoning, and the task difficulty reasoning-ability variable is related to these, with the suggestion that tasks which require different sorts of reasoning might function more effectively with participants higher in reasoning ability. This is, as yet, untested.

The CH model has generated a considerable amount of research (see below). It has lent itself to predictions and to research designs which probe, particularly, the impact of resource-directing variables. But there are pedagogic implications of the CH also and, more recently (Robinson, 2015), the CH has been extended in this direction. Two principles pave the way for this, and each is concerned with task sequencing:

Task Sequencing Principle 1: Only the cognitive demands of tasks relating to intrinsic conceptual and cognitive-processing complexity (i.e. resource-directing and resource-dispersing variables) are involved in task sequencing. Task condition and task difficulty variables, while important, do not influence sequencing itself.

Task Sequencing Principle 2: In sequencing tasks, resource-dispersing variables should be increased first, and only then should resource-directing variables be increased. The intention here is to guide learners from the known, through the development of automaticity, to the need to develop new form-function mappings and to restructure-complexify.

This leads to the SSARC model, expressed in three equations, as in Robinson (2015, p. 94):

Step 1, SS (stabilize, simplify) = i x e [('s'rdisp) + ('s'rdir)]^n
Step 2, A (automatize) = i x e [('c'rdisp) + ('s'rdir)]^n
Step 3, RC (restructure, complexify) = i x e [('c'rdisp) + ('c'rdir)]^n

where i = current interlanguage state, e = mental effort, 's'= simple task demands, 'c' = complex task demands, rdisp = resource-dispersing tasks, rdir = resource-directing tasks and ^{n} = potential number of practice opportunities on tasks.

To expand on these equations:

SS (Simple, stable): This level involves the use of current interlanguage. Demands from the task are kept low so there are low resource-dispersing demands and low resource-directing demands.
A (Automatization): The point here is to increase resource-dispersing demands. This in turn is seen as promoting speedier access to resources and also automatization.
RC (Restructuring, complexifying): At this stage, the increase in resource-directing demands is hypothesized to promote restructuring and lead to new form-function mappings. Increasing complexity then is intended to destabilize interlanguage.

The development of the SSARC model is, then, intended to expand the CH and make it relevant to pedagogic decision-making regarding syllabus design.

Acquisition

The CH offers two basic influences on acquisition. First, there is a performance-supporting role. Task complexity pushes for raised complexity and accuracy as attention responds to functional needs. In this way the learner is pushed to develop abilities to use language, and possibly, through the greater complexity of language, to restructure and become a more effective communicator. Second, tasks of greater complexity are seen as more likely to generate negotiation of meaning and noticing. In other words, they are seen as nurturing the sort of personalized, timely feedback that the Interaction Hypothesis (IH) advocates, as described in Chapter 2.

The development of the SSARC model extends this picture. Recall that the sequence embodied in this acronym is:

Table 3.1 Potential sequences in the SSARC model

	Possible sequence 1	Possible sequence 2	Possible sequence 3
Low res. dis., low res. dir.	Structured, here-and-now	Planned, few elements	Few steps, no reasoning
High res. dis., high res. dir.	Unstructured, here-and-now	Unplanned, few elements	More steps, no reasoning
High res. dis., high res. dir.	Unstructured, there-and-then	Unplanned, more elements	More steps, reasoning

1. stabilize, simplify
2. automatize
3. restructure, complexify.

These stages, portrayed through equations, also have terms in the equations for the amount of potential effort, and the number of practice opportunities at each stage. This system is then consistent with the sorts of sequences exemplified in Table 3.1.

The Research Base

It is too early to draw on a research base for the SSARC model so the focus here is on the CH. The CH is more straightforward to deal with in this regard. This is because it makes some predictions which are much clearer than the LAC approach, principally that task complexity will raise *both* accuracy and complexity.

There are two major strands to the research base: individual research studies and meta-analyses. Regarding individual studies, the CH has generated a very large number of examples. Typically the research design is to manipulate one or more of the resource-directing variables to explore whether the more complex task (judged on this basis) generates raised accuracy and complexity. Sometimes a resource-directing variable is combined with a resource-dispersing variable, although this can be a difficult design to manage because the two types of variables can make conflicting predictions (Inoue, 2016). Typical studies of this sort (and there are many more, but essentially more of the same) are Niwa (2000: cited in D. Ellis, 2011), where task complexity only influenced lexical density; Robinson (2001), where accuracy and fluency were affected by task complexity, but not structural complexity; Kuiken and Vedder (2008), where accuracy was affected but structural and lexical complexity were not; Gilabert, Barron and Levkina (2011), where again accuracy was affected but complexity was not; and Michel (2011), where no effects were found. The generalization which emerges from these (and many other studies) is that there is a link between task complexity and accuracy, but that is all, and finding studies which report increases in both is very difficult to do, although Ishikawa (2007) does report such results, albeit for a writing-based study. This consistency of results is important, since a central and innovative claim of the CH is that accuracy and complexity can be raised simultaneously.

There have been two major meta-analyses of the CH. These will be developed at greater length in the first of the Issues sections (on Tasks and Conditions), and will only be summarized here. Jackson and Suethanapornkul (2013) report results which essentially focus on resource-directing variables, and even within these, largely the variable of time perspective. They report average effect sizes of −0.16 for fluency, 0.28 for accuracy and −0.02 for complexity as well as 0.03 for lexis (all Cohen's d). This confirms the pattern given. There is no joint raising and the one effect size of note has to be regarded as small. A much larger meta-analysis, with more studies and a wider range of variables, is provided by Malicka and Sasayama (2017). They analysed enough studies to be able to provide average effect sizes for two resource-directing variables. With time perspective they report values of −0.03 for fluency, 0.15 for accuracy and 0.41 for complexity. Lexis gives an average effect size of 0.12. With reasoning demands, the values are −0.12, fluency; 0.12, accuracy; 0.09, complexity; and 0.34, lexis. Again the typical result is a close-to-zero effect size, with the exceptions of 0.41 for complexity, time perspective, and 0.34 for lexis, reasoning demands. There is also the point that the pattern here does not totally agree with Jackson and Suethanapornkul's (2013) findings: they found their higher value for accuracy (principally based on time perspective) whereas Malicka and Sasayama (2017) report their highest value for complexity, also for time perspective. The general conclusion has to be that resource-directing variables do not generate high values, that there is inconsistency in the results. Basically there is little evidence of joint raising of accuracy and complexity.

An Evaluation of the CH/SSARC Model

The first point to make is that the CH has been extremely successful in generating research. The number of CH-oriented studies is now more than a hundred. Connected to this, a considerable strength of the hypothesis is that it makes predictions, particularly that of task complexity raising accuracy and complexity together. The main hypothesis also has interesting supporting hypotheses, such as the functioning of attentional resources. All of these features have to be evaluated positively.

But there are also some problems with the CH, both logical and empirical. First, the distinction made between resource-directing and resource-dispersing variables, central to the hypothesis, is not entirely clear. There are resource-directing variables which do not seem to sit comfortably with the others. Time perspective, for example, which contrasts the (less complex) here-and-now condition with the (more complex) there-and-then condition, on the basis of memory demands, could be viewed quite differently to the CH interpretation. The former condition may also have greater and less avoidable input-processing problems, through the presence of visual material, with all its detail. The latter, although requiring memory, enables considerable negotiability in how to select and organize material. Different performances might be down to these non-resource-directing influences.

More generally, there is scope to clarify the unity that is intended to link the various resource-directing variables. There is an obvious connection between the different reasoning-based variables (intentional, causal, spatial). But the relationship of these to perspective-taking and number of other elements would benefit from greater clarification, as would how all these variables impact upon language involvement. Conversely, it could be argued (Skehan, 2015, 2018) that the resource-dispersing variables of planning and task structure could lead to language involvement akin to resource-directing variables. Qualitative research with planning (Pang and Skehan, 2014) suggests that some people use the time to engage with ideas (which have language implications) or even language itself. Structure may push speakers to engage with the language required to do justice to this design feature. The problem-solution structure, a key feature of LACH research studies (Tavakoli and Skehan, 2005) is fundamentally concerned with causal reasoning. So in these cases it is difficult to argue that a resource-dispersing variable is only concerned with processing. One has to conclude that there is potential for realignment of what should be considered resource-directing and resource-dispersing.

There is also the issue of evidence. As we saw in the section 'The Research Base', the clear majority of studies report a resource-directing variable impact on *either* complexity *or* accuracy, usually accuracy. This applies when one examines individual studies. It also applies to the meta-analyses which are available; there is a slight contradiction between Jackson and Suethanapornkul (2013) and Malicka and Sasayama (2017) in that the former reports a small accuracy effect but no complexity effect, while the latter larger meta-analysis reports the reverse. This is damaging for the CH since the hypothesis predicts joint raising as central to the hypothesis. To discover that only one area is raised suggests little more than the proposition that tasks and task condition can influence performance, which is, really, the starting point for all task research.

It is too early to offer much of an evaluation of the extension to the SSARC model. The model seems largely a set of proposals which need fleshing out. For example, the formulae which are used are currently rather opaque, without any detail regarding terms such as 'e' for mental effort and 'n' for number of practice opportunities. In addition, while the model clarifies how one might sequence particular combinations of resource-directing and resource-dispersing variables (e.g. time perspective and planning), it does not clarify how particular combinations like this would fit into a longer sequence as one would expect from a practical syllabus. Finally, the sequence of stabilize – simplify – automatize – restructure – complexify seems unclear, and possibly conflicts with some theories of learning. It seems to propose automatization *before* restructuring-complexifying, rather than the other way around. Perhaps connected with this, it lacks clarity as to what happens after the restructuring-complexification has taken place. One wonders if there is need for consolidation or practice at this point.

Comparing the Two Approaches

As a first view of the comparison between the two approaches, Table 3.2 presents a series of categories drawn from questions raised in the introduction to this chapter, and then a capsule description of the LAC approach and the CH/SSARC model in each case. The table will be the basis for the subsequent discussion.

The first two categories in the table bring out clear differences between the two approaches. What comes across is that the LAC approach is firmly rooted in psycholinguistic approaches to L1 production applied to the L2 case while the CH emphasizes more linguistic approaches of a functional/cognitive persuasion, and then does not elaborate any particular model of speaking as relevant (though see Kormos, 2011). The hinterland for each approach, in other words, is a long way apart.

The different performance influences similarly show marked differences. The LAC approach is somewhat opportunistic and accumulates influences through research findings. There are some more general categories (complexifying, pressuring, easing, focusing: see Skehan, 2009c) and these are relatable to the extension of the Levelt model but there is no subsystem of influences. In contrast the CH has, as

Table 3.2 A comparison between the LAC approach and the CH/SSARC model

Area of similarity/difference	LAC	CH/SSARC
Linguistic underpinning/model of speaking	• Levelt model is central • No specific linguistic analysis	• Cognitive linguistics • Little emphasis on a psycholinguistic model of speaking (but see Kormos, 2011)
Analysis of memory and attention	• Both working memory and attention are limited • They are a constraint that has to be worked around	• Expandable attention • Resource pools
Performance and influences upon it	• Task and task condition are individual influences which then combine • Influences largely emerge through research • The constraint of limited attention pervasive	• Fundamental role for resource-directing and resource-dispersing variables • Prediction of accuracy–complexity relationship influenced by task complexity
Measuring performance	• Generalized measures of CALF	• General and specific measures, usually of CAF • Some importance for noticing, feedback and interactional moves
Acquisition	• Transacting tasks makes language salient. This language needs to be recorded and worked on at the post-task stage	• Resource-directing tasks push for greater interaction and uptake of task-relevant input. SSARC sequence to promote interlanguage development
Pedagogy	• Methodology influenced by above view on acquisition • No suggestions on syllabus design	• Clear SSARC sequence advocated in focused areas within syllabus design, but little on a general syllabus

central, the contrast between resource-directing and resource-dispersing variables. There are three aspects to this. First, there is the different functioning of the two classes of variable, one claimed to have language implications, and the other claimed to have processing implications. Second, there is the issue that the different variables within the resource-directing heading are seen as similar, just as the variables within the resource-dispersing heading are seen as similar to one another, but obviously different from the resource-directing variables. The third CH aspect in relation to performance concerns general vs. specific measures. LAC, as we have seen, focuses on general measures. These are an important component for the CH/SSARC model, but, in addition, there are proposals that particular measures should also be used. So it is proposed that a resource-directing variable like complex reasoning links with cognitive state terms, or spatial reasoning with expression of motion events, or time perspective to tense and aspect in the present (here-and-now) compared to events happening elsewhere in time and space (there-and-then).

The two approaches have fairly distinct approaches to the process of acquisition. LAC addresses this in two ways (Skehan, 2007, 2012, 2013). First, it is assumed that the CALF categories can represent an acquisitional sequence, and so tasks which promote greater complexity are pushing for new language, while tasks which promote accuracy or fluency are supporting control of an existing interlanguage level. In this view, first there is destabilization, and then there is a concern for control (eliminating inaccuracy first, and then achieving fluency second). But second, and more fundamentally, LAC regards the task itself as having the important function of making some aspect (or aspects) of language salient (Willis and Willis, 2007). It is assumed that there will be a record of what language has been made salient in this way, as some language has been noticed (Schmidt, 1994) or a gap has been noticed through the creation of a need to mean (Swain, 1995; Samuda, 2001). Then it is assumed that important acquisitional work takes place *at a post-task stage*, where the teacher can react to the language which has emerged in this way and use pedagogic techniques to bring understanding, or extension, or integration or consolidation, as appropriate. The important point is that this language is what has emerged when the learner has transacted a task. The language is not pre-selected but has emerged because of the needs of the learner. In contrast, the major emphasis within the CH/SSARC is towards the use of interaction leading to feedback and noticing. It is assumed that greater task complexity through resource-directing tasks leads to a greater engagement with language and that part of this will mean that learners will be more likely to negotiate, more likely to provoke and process relevant feedback, more likely to notice and, therefore, following the IH (see Chapter 2), more likely to make progress.

Linked to this is what can be said about syllabus, and the sequencing of pedagogic activities. Essentially, the LAC has very little to say here. There is a broad commitment to tasks varying in difficulty (note: not Robinson's analysis of difficulty – more his analysis of complexity), and the suggestion that simple tasks should come first and lead subsequently to greater difficulty. In this respect, the range of task characteristics and task conditions would come into play here. One interesting point is that LAC proposes that difficulty is different for the Conceptualizer and Formulator, and this would then have an impact on how pedagogic tasks might be sequenced. Complexification and destabilization would come first, and this would be followed by the development of control. In contrast, the CH/SSARC has more to say about sequencing. This is particularly so in the SSARC model, as described, with the move from low resource-directing and dispersing to low resource-directing but high resource-dispersing, to high resource-directing and dispersing. This is linked to the engagement of existing interlanguage at the first stage, then the development of automatization, followed by a push for restructuring and complexification and a challenge to the existing interlanguage system.

There are, then, many points of difference between the two approaches. They differ clearly in their connections with linguistics, psycholinguistics and attentional functioning. They also contrast in their views of acquisition (provoking and using feedback compared to counterpunching at the post-task stage). But there are other areas where, although differences are clear, there might be scope to argue that the differences may not be as great as first sight would suggest. Both, for example, are committed to basing claims about tasks on research evidence. Both, also, are committed to understanding how tasks have an impact on performance, and also how they might be used in pedagogic contexts.

An interesting way of bringing them closer together is to relate them to proficiency level, as we have seen, and also modality. LAC essentially offers a view of language production where Conceptualization makes demands upon the Formulator which are met, or not, through the operation of the SLML. The impact of attentional limitations is clearest at this point. If the SLML is not large enough, or rich enough, or fast enough, processing difficulties will occur. When this happens, parallel performance is derailed, and the speaker (or writer) has to deal with the problem which has arisen (need to find alternative expression because a needed lemma does not exist; repair because an existing lemma does not contain enough information, e.g. syntactic frame, collocation; or repair because the Formulator does not handle its work in time). These problems, first of all, are not so acute when writing is involved. One of the central claims of the CH is that accuracy and complexity are jointly raised, in response to (resource-directing) language demands. When less communicative pressure is involved, as in writing, or online planning, this may be more achievable. Exactly the same would apply at higher proficiency levels. As the SLML grows (as proficiency grows) the sorts of problems that the speaker has when Conceptualizer demands create pressure for the Formulator, will be lessened and so parallel function (and perhaps jointly raised complexity and accuracy) is more likely. One could even add to this a task difficulty factor from the CH: if working memory is greater, this too might ease the functioning of Formulator use during communication. Indirect evidence for this comes from studies (reviewed in Skehan, 2018) that working memory has an impact with online planning but not with strategic planning. So one can conclude that the two approaches may not be so far apart on the accuracy-complexity issue, depending on the proficiency level, modality and relevant individual differences.

Issues in Psycholinguistic Analyses of Tasks

So far the discussion has been very much through the lenses of the LAC approach and the CH/SSARC model, considered separately and also together. The two approaches have been influential and generated a lot of research, generally from one perspective or another. But a good deal of research has been conducted from more neutral standpoints, and interesting issues have emerged. Five such issues will be considered in this last section.

Tasks and Conditions: Perspectives from Meta-Analysis

It is useful, at the outset, to explore the general evidence relating to the effects of tasks on L2 performance. Malicka and Sasayama (2017) report on a meta-analysis of task-related studies. The motivation for this research was to gain greater understanding of task complexity, the central part of the CH. But the analysis makes important contributions, beyond its specific focus on the CH, because it includes a wide range of variables, including resource-dispersing variables (in contrast to Jackson and Suethanapornkul (2013) who focused only on resource-directing variables in their meta-analysis). Malicka and Sasayama's (2017) results are shown in Table 3.3. The table shows the results arranged by CALF area, in columns, and then resource-directing and resource-dispersing variables, in rows. The values shown in the table are effect sizes, using Cohen's d. The data represents the most comprehensive analysis presently available of general task effects on performance. By way of clarification, with resource-directing variables, a negative sign means that the variable in question reduces the level of performance. With resource-dispersing variables, a negative value indicates that the 'simpler' condition (planning, a repeated task, a structured task, a task with familiar information, a task with support) produced the higher level of performance.

Several generalizations emerge from Table 3.3. The analysis which follows takes effect sizes greater than 0.30 as worth commenting on.

1. Resource-dispersing variables clearly have stronger and more consistent relationships with performance than do resource-directing variables.
2. None of the variables, resource-directing or resource-dispersing, raise all performance areas. Resource-dispersing variables, in general, raise three areas (CAF) as do the specific resource-dispersing variables of repetition (CAF) and task structure (C, L, F).
3. No resource-directing variables have large effect sizes for accuracy whereas two resource-dispersing variables (planning, repetition) do.
4. Resource-directing variables are rather inconsistent in their effects, with reasoning raising lexis, and time perspective (i.e. the there-and-then condition) raising structural complexity.
5. In general, modality (i.e. oral vs. written performances) suggests that written performances respond more positively to the range of variables for complexity; that accuracy shows lower response, and that fluency is more affected by resource-dispersing variables. (However, it is important to point out that the measurement of fluency is most altered when one moves from oral to written modes.)

The results broadly agree with the existing literature but with some points where additional claims might be made. After all, Malicka and Sasayama's (2017) work derives from a meta-analysis and this means that a sufficiently large number of studies on a particular task feature have to be available to enable any sort of effect-size-based generalization. There is room, in other words, to draw on other studies as well, which probe variables not investigated sufficiently widely to be included in the meta-analyses. So, based on such a wider reading, and on a synthetic basis, one might add:

- tasks based on more concrete information tend to raise fluency
- tasks which require integration of information tend to raise complexity

Table 3.3 Malicka and Sasayama's analysis of CH-linked variables

Task feature	Complexity		Accuracy		Lexis		Fluency	
Resource-directing	0.13		0.13		0.28		−0.09	
Reasoning	0.09		0.12		0.34		−0.12	
HnN/TnT	0.41		0.15		0.12		−0.03	
Referential demand							0.08	
Resource-dispersing	−0.77		−0.73		−0.27		−0.34	
Planning	−0.88		−0.87		−0.21		−0.25	
Repetition	−0.57		−0.61		−0.11		−0.59	
Structure	−0.53		−0.16		−0.5		−0.62	
Familiarity	−0.12		−0.19				−0.22	
Support					−0.56		−0.66	
	All Oral Tasks	All Written Tasks	All Oral Tasks	All Written Tasks	All Oral Tasks	All Written Tasks	All Oral Tasks	All Written Tasks
Resource-directing (all combined)	.02	.26	.17	.06	.34	.19	−.10	−.07
Resource-dispersing (all combined)	−.75	−.91	−.80	−.47	−.24	−.33	−.27	−.83

Note: HnN/TnT = Here-and-now/There-and-then.

- tasks which require transformation of material also tend to raise complexity
- post-task conditions raise accuracy, and sometimes complexity.

In addition, there are some inconsistencies between other research and the findings reported in Table 3.3. Jackson and Suethanapornkul (2013, p. 15), in their meta-analysis, also motivated by the CH, and based only on resource-directing variables, focused mainly on time perspective. They reported mean effect sizes of complexity: -0.02; accuracy: 0.28; lexis: 0.03; and fluency: -0.16. The accuracy effect here may not be large but does contrast with the smaller finding in Malicka and Sasayama. In a reverse direction this is also true for complexity, but here Malicka and Sasayama (2017) report the higher value, at 0.41. Even so, the prevailing impression from Jackson and Suethanapornkul (2013) is of quite low mean effect-size values.

The most important conclusion one can draw from Table 3.3 is that the resource-dispersing variables generally are associated with consistently higher effect sizes: planning (strategic and online) and repetition are very clearly involved here, as are task support and task structure. In fact, though, three of these resource-dispersing variables are task conditions, and so it may be more appropriate to think of them as more clearly defined by this aspect. This leads to the possible claim that task conditions are more consistent influences on performance – a point developed in Skehan (2016). Correspondingly, and more contentiously, task characteristics themselves, with exceptions, such as structure, have been something of a disappointment. It is to examining why that might be so that we now turn. First we will re-analyse the notions of tasks and task characteristics. Then we will explore the nature of task conditions more generally.

The Feasibility of Analysing Tasks

In a study of the impact of the resource-directing variable concerning the number of participants, Sasayama (2015) used narrative picture series to compare performance with the four values of one, two, four and nine participants. She argued that most studies with this variable typically only use two values, and with possibly no great difference in the number of participants. Using a range from one to nine was then a response to this – a greater overall range plus the inclusion of intermediate numbers of participants. Although she did find a broad effect for the number of participants, this general finding was complicated by the issue of clarity. For the manipulation to work, the number of participants in a picture series has to be interpreted in the way that was intended. This was not the case in her study, with the result that there was confusion as to the roles and relationships involved in some of the picture series. The largest number of participants did make a difference, but the intermediate values presented much less clear a picture, since misinterpretation (given the time available for the task) occurred.

Another issue emerges from work by Inoue (2016). She explored, in a testing context, whether two picture narrative retellings could be established to be equivalent. Despite careful attention to task design, she found that although in many ways the picture series did seem to be equivalent, the performances that they elicited differed in significant ways (and this would have implications for their satisfactoriness in a testing context). It turned out that in one case the amount of inference was greater, while in the other, in addition to greater clarity of how the story developed (cf. Sasayama, 2015), one could analyse the story as being structured (i.e. there was a disguised variable involved). These unforeseen aspects of the two narratives led to different methods of using complex language. The 'structured' narrative led to more subordination while the higher-inference narrative elicited higher words-per-clause measures. So once again, two initially well-analysed narratives produced different results through unforeseen design factors, and these were only revealed clearly by careful data analysis.

The studies by Sasayama (2015, 2016) and Inoue (2013, 2016) provide particular examples of how tasks may not produce the performances that were intended. The Sasayama (2015) study provides another insight because she also used qualitative techniques to probe why her participants did not respond in the predicted way to the one, two, four and nine participants in the picture-based narratives they were given. This data was very revealing. In general, the participants, if they saw clarity in the narrative, got on with telling the story. If they did not, they simply made the best of things, and developed hypotheses about the characters in the stories, their relationships and their motivations. If something did not seem to fit in to their interpretation, the participant ignored it. The question then arises as to whether these two studies, each very careful investigations of task functioning, were simply untypical in the unforeseen results they obtained, or whether they connect with more general and fundamental issues in the use of tasks.

There is a link here with a major generalization that comes out of contemporary cognitive psychology. Kahneman (2011) offers a general analysis of problem-solving and typical cognitive behaviour. He distinguishes between two systems. System 1 is intuitive, fast and does not require much effort. System 2 is logical, slower and requires conscious effort and thought. System 2 is, of course, fundamentally superior (if slower), but human beings are lazy. The result is that we default to System 1 even when this is not appropriate. Worse, when we are confronted by a difficult problem, a typical response is not to engage System 2 and solve the difficult problem in a logical way. Instead we change the problem to make it easier, and best of all, easy enough for System 1 to (appear to) work. Kahneman (2011) reviews a massive literature in cognitive psychology which supports these claims. In L2 task-based performance, we need to take this literature seriously. Its implication is clear, and entirely consistent with Inoue's (2013) and Sasayama's (2016) findings – the more a research design introduces more difficult tasks, especially ones based on cognitive analysis and rather subtle differences between conditions, the more likely it is that their will not be a focus on the full range of the details of the task (since this would require System 2), and instead System 1 will be brought into play. This is not to say, remotely, that these designs are wrong. It is, fundamentally, the problem that the predictability of tasks is by no means an exact science. This difficulty can be overcome, to some extent. Piloting may give some confidence if it can demonstrate that the intended task and the actual task coincide sufficiently. Gathering qualitative data can also help in this regard, and even give indications as to how a task can be modified to achieve the intended goals. But for now, the possible lack of convergence of intended and actual tasks remains a nagging worry.

There are still two troublesome aspects of task research that need to be considered. The first of these concerns the importance of negotiability. There is always the paradox that the essence of taskness is that participants are expressing meanings, and if this is the case, there is the likelihood that they will want to express their own meanings! But in doing this, they may take a task away from what the task designer intended. But also, if a task participant is able to exert some personal control and direction when they are doing a task, in addition to introducing a lack of standardization in the language the task elicits, there is also the major factor that the speaker can nudge the task into areas where they feel more comfortable, or more knowledgeable, or have relevant linguistic resources. They may not be so 'imprisoned', that is, within the tight designs of a particular task (e.g. a narrative picture series). This may not be so important within a study based on only one task type, but where different task types are compared, if one task type has potential for negotiability while the other does not (or less so), this has a problematic effect on comparisons. Consider, for example, a here-and-now task, where the stimuli are clearly present, and have to be attended to, with a there-and-then task, where the stimuli are no longer present, but there is the potential to shape the discourse more freely. The contrast may then not simply be time perspective, but also the speaker's capacity to shape the discourse.

But it gets worse! A sociocultural account of tasks (see Chapter 4) would argue that a task, through the interactions of the participants, has a life of its own, and can be reinterpreted in whatever direction the participants want to develop. We are back to the point that if a task is an opportunity to express meanings, then the meanings which are expressed cannot be preordained or constrained. As just discussed, the point about negotiation concerned freedom to use whatever language elements are preferred. But it was assumed that the broad parameters of the task were accepted. Here, in contrast, we are concerned with ways in which the task itself is modified, transformed, ignored or subverted (Coughlan and Duff, 1994). Participants might simply redefine the task. It can be argued that, if a task is worthwhile, this is inevitable!

In summary, we see that:

- tasks may be unclear;
- tasks may contain hidden variables other than those under investigation;
- participants may approach a task from a very different perspective to the task designer;
- tasks which enable participants to shape the language that they use may be easier to do, and more richly done, than tasks which constrain tightly;
- tasks themselves may be changed, subverted and even ignored.

If we reflect upon the findings reported in Table 3.3, one can come up with the generalization that tasks are a perilous area within which to research! Effects have been found, with some consistency, but perhaps less often than one would wish, given the amount of theorizing that has gone into task design linked to task performance. This is a major challenge for the future of task research.

Task Conditions

In contrast to task characteristics, the task condition variables in Table 3.3 (planning, repetition, support) showed appreciable effect sizes with more than one aspect of performance (taking appreciable to mean an effect size of 0.30 or more). The exception with task characteristics, which we will return to at the end of this section, is task structure, which showed medium effect sizes with three areas (complexity, lexis and fluency). This raises the interesting question as to why these conditions-linked variables should have such consistent and appreciable effects.

Skehan (2016, 2018) makes two general suggestions as to why this is so. The first has already been touched upon: the flexibility that is associated with conditions regarding the content of what is said or written. Generally, with planning or repetition, the task concerned is likely to allow the speaker (or writer) to make choices and select the emphasis or stance to be used, as well as the content to be included. In turn, there is the possibility that where language itself is concerned, there is greater opportunity to shape what is said so that it fits areas of strength, whether these be organized and possibly previously used ideas, or the specifics of language, of lexis and so on. The result is that planning or repetition provide greater opportunity to polish what is said and to achieve higher levels of performance.

The second point is that condition-type research is more likely to link naturally with models of speaking. Given the stages of Conceptualization, Formulation (syntactic encoding, lemma retrieval) and Articulation, and the associated process of monitoring (Levelt, 1989, 1999), one can quickly sketch out possible linkages. Strategic planning enables more effective Conceptualization, as the ideas in the task are wrestled with and developed. It also facilitates processes of retrieval and rehearsal (Ortega, 2005), which, if retained, will advantage the lemma retrieval and syntactic encoding components of the Formulator, as well, possibly, as the Articulator. Online planning can then ease the operations of the Formulator, as lemma retrieval has a little more time to function as a deeper and more extensive process, and also, possibly, as the speaker has time to adapt the message to avoid difficulties. Repetition has all the advantages of strategic planning (organization of ideas and rehearsal). But in addition the first performance (or earlier performances if they are multiple) pushes the speaker to confront the limitations of shallower lemma retrieval, and possibly leave traces which are undeveloped in the first performance but can be exploited subsequently. The repeated performance can then be based more firmly on more native-like lemma retrieval and more efficient Formulator operation. In addition, and very distinct from strategic planning, the first performance will have engaged the Articulator and sensitized the speaker to problems that occur at that stage of speech production (Wang, 2009).

One other condition in task-based research, not covered in Malicka and Sasayama (2017) because of the small number of studies, fits this analysis quite neatly. It is to explore the effects on task performance itself of anticipation of a post-task. In a series of relevant studies

Skehan and Foster (1997), Foster and Skehan (2013) and Li (2014) have shown that if speakers doing a task know that there will be a post-task (needing to engage in a public performance; being expected to transcribe a recording of their own performance doing the task) they are likely to be more accurate in the actual task performance, and with decision-making, interactive tasks, more complex also. Again, in Leveltian terms, one can relate the higher accuracy (and complexity) to the process of monitoring where participants have been induced to focus on form to a greater degree than they otherwise would have done. Anticipation of what is to come changes the focus of attention during the actual task performance. Once more, a standard model of speaking illuminates the way a task condition can have an effect on performance.

Interestingly, the task characteristic highlighted here as being consistently successful – task structure – is analysable in Leveltian terms. The very fact of structure pushes the speaker to be concerned with the connection between elements (indicating relationships, expressing causality), essentially describable in resource-directing terms, as argued earlier in this chapter. This is not particularly Leveltian. But also important is the complementary influence on macro and micro processes. The broad macrostructure of a task provides an organizing framework for the speaker which guides overall structure. This then allows the speaker to see a clearer relationship between the overall message and the details of what are being said at any particular time. This enables more attention to be directed at the surface of language – essentially a Formulator operation. It also enables the speaker to recover from any glitches in speaking (e.g. because of lemma retrieval difficulties) and make links between Conceptualizer and Formulator (and regain parallel processing after it has been knocked off course). So a large part of the advantage of structured tasks can be related to a model of speaking also.

The Challenge of Calibrating Task Complexity

Both the LAC and the CH indicate important roles for task complexity. The LAC is concerned with difficulty, and distinguishes between Conceptualizer-linked difficulty and Formulator-linked difficulty. But in each case, task demands are seen as having an impact on the structural and lexical complexity of the language which is induced by a task. The CH/SSARC approach makes task complexity central and the driving force for language development and syllabus design, with resource-directing influences central for interlanguage change.

It has to be admitted, though, that in both cases the approach has been to analyse tasks from what might be euphemistically called a 'logical' perspective and then make inferences about their complexity. The optimistic hope has been that research results would confirm the analyses which were the starting point for research studies. Clearly the pattern of research results in the literature has been rather disappointing in this regard. There are successes but there are a fairly extensive list of failures, as the meta-analyses and more narrative accounts of research are beginning to show. This, in turn, raises the obvious question as to why the starting point for these enquiries might not have been better if, first, task complexity had been researched, and then, once tasks of different complexity have been empirically established, more theory-based research studies could have been conducted more effectively.

More recently a range of research studies have indeed taken this more foundational approach. Central here is the need to have some method of establishing task difficulty/complexity that is independent of initial theorizing, and a key component of this is the concept of cognitive load (Sweller, 1988, 1994). This concept originated in cognitive psychology, and proposes that different tasks can exert a different load on the cognitive and psycholinguistic processes that underpin speech. If greater cognitive load can be identified for a task, then we have an independent means of making claims about task difficulty/complexity. In that respect a range of secondary measures have been proposed which could function as indices of cognitive load. These include:

- self-report of, for example, mental effort required by a task, or of the difficulty of the task
- expert analysis
- time estimation
  - where participants are told ahead of time they will be asked to estimate how much time a task has taken
  - where participants are not warned they will be asked to estimate time, but are indeed asked to do so after task completion
- secondary tasks, where participants need to monitor some additional task, such as detecting some sort of colour change. Reaction time and accuracy in doing so are the major indices
- eye-tracking
- pupillary response, for example where the amount of pupillary change is measured.

Such techniques are being used more frequently in psycholinguistically based task research. The approach is little more than ten years old, but now an increasing number of studies is beginning to convert the original promise of such measures into more dependable results. So it may be possible to make substantial claims of task difficulty/complexity other than general theory or inferences made only after research results are obtained. The result of this is that it may be possible to evaluate competing claims, e.g. the LAC approach, or the CH/SSARC model, in a more defensible manner.

At present it is too early to offer any major conclusions because, although research using such techniques is growing, we are not yet to be able to offer wide-ranging generalizations. A few points are worth making, though. First, there is broad congruence, and therefore encouragement, in the way different measures do show some convergent validity. Révész, Michel and Gilabert (2016), for example, report that accuracy in a colour-change secondary task, self-ratings and expert ratings give similar results across a series of tasks. We need more studies to demonstrate such congruence of results. Second, even so, there are some less consistent results. Révész et al. (2016) report that accuracy in colour-change detection worked as intended, but reaction time in the same secondary task did not. Interestingly, Sasayama (2015) also used a colour-change secondary task (which differed in some details) and she found that reaction times did reflect proposed task complexity, but accuracy did not. There is some way to go here. Third, many researchers have focused on one secondary measure, and then compared it to general task analysis and self-rating measures, of mental effort and/or task difficulty. But there is also scope to explore how the different secondary measures interrelate, and whether, for example, time estimation, secondary tasks and physiological measures such as eye-tracking, deliver consistent results. There is little evidence so far on this point. Fourth, it is possible, at present, that the intervals that have been used between simple and complex are rather large. It may be more challenging to explore whether smaller intervals, or stepped intervals, can generate consistent results also. Sasayama (2015), for example, found that when she used a narrative retelling with one, two, four or nine participants, the secondary measures confirmed the largest difference but were not so effective with the intermediate values. Finally, there may be scope to broaden the types of task which have been investigated. So far, entirely reasonably, the impetus for tasks that are researched has been the CH. But we also saw that Skehan (2018) proposes that one needs to distinguish between difficulty (his term) as perceived in the Conceptualizer and in the Formulator stages. It might be useful therefore to explore whether the range of secondary measures is equally effective when tasks independently vary these two speaking stages.

Native-Speaker Baseline Data

One final area is worth mentioning in terms of psycholinguistically motivated task research. It is to argue for the relevance of native-speaker baseline data (D. Ellis, 2011). In general, it is not typical of task studies to gather such data. This is understandable because to gather such data would introduce a significant complication in any research study. Researchers want to get on with investigating the variables, the tasks, the conditions that are important to them, rather than find ways of complicating life. But nonetheless to have some baseline data is very important if we are to make solid judgements about tasks.

The chapter has provided many examples of variables which have been studied and linked to different aspects of performance. Similarly, theoretical accounts also propose that certain tasks, or categories of task, such as resource-directing or resource-dispersing, will have consistent influence on performance. Claims are then made that some tasks are more likely to foster acquisition, or to help L2 learners to achieve higher levels of performance. But one has to consider the question as to whether the same tasks or the same conditions would produce the same effects with native speakers. Accuracy is a bit of a complication here. The point of using native-speaker baseline data is that native speakers, by definition, have complete language systems. As a result, one can expect that they will simply be accurate, and so comparing them with non-native speakers for accuracy will simply demonstrate that the non-native speakers are non-native speakers. But the situation is more instructive with structural or lexical complexity and different aspects of fluency. If a task does not produce change in performance with native speakers in these areas, then we have to question what we are doing if the task is used with non-native speakers. There may be good reasons for using the task, but they are certainly not so obvious in these cases. Equally, if a task or a task condition does produce a different level of performance with native speakers, then we have a touchstone against which to judge the performance of non-native speakers. Is performance affected in the same direction? To the same extent? Or even, possibly, to a greater extent? Without this information, it is difficult to disentangle the effects of tasks and task conditions, on the one hand, and the effects of speaker status, on the other.

There are some studies comparing native and non-native performance. Foster (2001) showed that native speakers use formulaic language differently to non-native speakers. They rely on such language more in unplanned speech, and less in planned speech. Being given planning opportunities seems to enable them to produce more creative language. Non-native speakers are the reverse and use planning opportunities to access formulaic speech more effectively. Skehan (2009b) reports that there are very large lexical differences, for lexical sophistication and for lexical diversity, between these two groups, with the difference being largest for lexical sophistication with a narrative task and for lexical diversity with an interactive, decision-making task. He also reports that planning has little effect for native or non-native speakers regarding lexical diversity, whereas it does have an effect for lexical sophistication, for a personal information exchange task and a decision-making task for non-native speakers, but a narrative for native speakers. Skehan and Shum (2017), based on four video-based narrative retellings, which vary in degree of structure, confirm these results of a native to non-native difference for lexical diversity but less so for lexical sophistication. There are slight differences between the two groups for structural complexity, with native speakers producing higher subordination scores on two tasks, but the non-natives having a significantly higher value for words-per-clause on one of the four tasks (and arithmetically higher scores on the other three). There are also clear differences between the two groups for fluency, with the native speakers consistently pausing less, repairing less and speaking faster. As a final point, there is also interesting evidence of prevailing styles of speaking. Both groups show strong cross-task consistency for lexical diversity, pausing (both clause boundary and mid-clause) and repetition. Lexical sophistication has clear style involvement for the native speakers but not for the non-natives. Finally, structural complexity scores show much less evidence of style.

It would be helpful if more research is reported which shows native and non-native speaker performance of this sort. This should give us a clearer understanding of how tasks have a contribution to make, specifically in influencing non-native-speaker performance.

4 Sociocultural Perspectives

Introduction

As Zuengler and Miller (2006) noted, the first twenty years (i.e. 1970–1980) of second language acquisition (SLA) research were dominated by a cognitive view of how a second language (L2) is acquired (i.e. the mental processes involved in the conversion of input into intake and the role of L2 production in acquisition). This view informed the previous two chapters. Chapter 2 examined how task-based language teaching (TBLT) has drawn heavily on the cognitive-interactionist theories of Long, Gass and Mackey (among others). Chapter 3 drew on cognitive models of speaking to show how task design and implementation features impact on the complexity, accuracy, lexis and fluency (CALF) of learners' production. Zuengler and Miller went on to point out that, starting around 1990, an alternative paradigm emerged in SLA – one that emphasized the social nature of L2 acquisition. They reviewed a number of social theories – sociocultural theory (SCT), language socialization, community of practice, Bakhtin's dialogic perspective and critical theory – all of which emphasize the importance of the social context and the centrality of participation in explaining how learners use and acquire – or fail to acquire – an L2. From this perspective, the development of an L2 was not a question of taking possession of knowledge but of taking part in social activity (Sfard, 1998). It rejects the distinction between 'use' and 'acquisition', which lies at the heart of cognitive theories of L2 acquisition, and prefers the metaphor of 'appropriation' over that of 'acquisition'. Of the social theories mentioned by Zuengler and Miller the one that has been the most fully developed and has the greatest relevance to TBLT is SCT.

The advent of this 'social turn' (Block, 2003) in SLA was not welcomed by some advocates of cognitive SLA (e.g. Gass, 1998; Long, 1998) and, arguably, its impact on TBLT has been much less than that of cognitive SLA. Ellis (2003) included a chapter on sociocultural SLA and tasks in his book *Task-Based Language Learning and Teaching* but Long (2015) gives it no space at all in his *Second Language Acquisition and Task-Based Language Teaching*. Neither 'social' not 'sociocultural' appear in the index of his book. Clearly, though, there is a social dimension to tasks. Also, as proponents of sociocultural SLA (e.g. Lantolf, 2000; Swain, 2000) take pains to point out, SCT is not just a social theory; it aims to explain how the social use of a language serves as both the source and context of the development of higher-order abilities. In other words, there is an important cognitive element to sociocultural SLA. Nevertheless, as we will see, not all proponents see sociocultural SLA as providing a theoretical basis for TBLT. Lantolf (see Lantolf and Thorne, 2006; Lantolf and Poehner, 2014), for example, sees SCT as supporting the development of declarative knowledge through the explicit teaching of linguistic forms in an approach that Long would doubtlessly dismiss as 'focus on forms' and therefore as antithetical to TBLT.

This chapter begins with a brief account of sociocultural SLA and of activity theory. It then reconsiders the incidental-intentional learning distinction (so central to an understanding of TBLT) from the perspective of sociocultural SLA. The next two sections address what insights SCT has to offer for the design and the implementation of tasks. The chapter ends with a reconsideration of the role of explicit instruction in L2 acquisition in the light of the evidence provided by research based on SCT.

Sociocultural SLA

Sociocultural SLA draws heavily on the work of Vygotsky (1978, 1986), Leontiev (1981) and Wertsch (1985), among others. There are now a number of accounts of the theory, as applied to SLA (e.g. Lantolf, 2000; Lantolf and Thorne, 2006; Lantolf and Poehner, 2014; Storch, 2017). We will draw on the account provided by Swain, Kinnear and Steinman (2014). Their unique book offers readers a set of narratives told by L2 learners and their teachers and uses episodes from these narratives to illustrate and discuss the key concepts. For readers interested in developing an understanding of sociocultural SLA, this book is highly recommended.

Swain et al. explain that the most basic concept of Vygotsky's work is that 'the individual cannot be understood in isolation but only as part of a history, a culture and a society' (2014, p. x). It follows that in order to understand how an individual's mental development takes place it is necessary to examine how this individual engages with people in social activities. They point to Vygotsky's basic premise, namely that individuals' minds develop through the guidance of a more experienced and knowledgeable person. Vygotsky's method for investigating development involved observing individuals performing tasks that they could not do by themselves,[1] providing them with help and noting how these individuals made use of the guidance provided.

Basic Concepts

Swain et al. acknowledge that it is not easy to explain SCT because the interconnectedness of its concepts make it difficult to know where to start. Their approach is to distinguish a set of basic concepts that constitute the core of the theory and a number of related concepts that figure strongly in sociocultural SLA. Table 4.1 provides a brief description of these basic concepts along with examples taken from Swain, Kinnear and Steinman (2011).

Sociocultural SLA explains L2 development in terms of the inter-relatedness of these concepts. It views learning an L2 as like any other kind of learning. That is, it is mediated; learning occurs when a learner has the chance to interact with cultural artefacts, with social interaction (one type of cultural artefact) serving as the primary means of mediation. Learning commences *within* an interaction between an expert (a teacher or a more advanced learner) and a learner, resulting in the co-construction of a ZPD. It is through participating in ZPDs the learner comes to understand scientific concepts, which are crucial for higher-order thinking. Non-ZPD interactions also contribute to learning, but only of everyday concepts. What the learner manifests in a ZPD may be internalized, allowing the learner to achieve self-regulation. In other words, there is a progression from intermental behaviour to an intramental state. The routines and patterns that figure in social interaction are also internalized and can re-emerge in private speech (talking to oneself), which serves as means for self-regulating when a problem cannot be immediately solved. Mediation and the construction of ZPDs generally occur when the learner experiences positive emotions.

Scaffolding, Languaging and Imitation

An issue of both theoretical interest and of obvious relevance to TBLT is how social interaction facilitates the construction of a ZPD. In other words, what does an expert and a learner have to do when interacting to create a ZPD? This is analogous to the question we addressed in Chapter 2 when we considered cognitive-interactionist perspectives on

Table 4.1 Basic constructs in sociocultural SLA

Concept	Description	Example
Mediation	The material and symbolic tools that organize or regulate our behaviour. Generally speaking material tools (e.g. a hammer) are directed towards the environment whereas symbolic tools (e.g. language) are directed towards changing our psychological selves (Swain et al., 2011, p. 152).	Mona tells how her father gave her a grammar book and how Mona's use of the grammar book was mediated through interaction with her father.
Zone of proximal development (ZPD)	An interaction during mediation enables an individual to achieve more than he/she could have achieved working alone. The ZPD is co-constructed by the learner working with an expert.[a]	A student (Brock) accidentally runs into his teacher, who expects him to apologize. At first Brock does not do so but when prompted he apologizes in English (his L1) rather than French (the L2). He is reprimanded by his teacher. Another student (Sarah) then helps Brock out by whispering *Je m'excuse*, which Brock repeats.
Private speech	Speech that is social (intermental) in origin and form but psychological (intramental) in function. It is speech addressed to oneself and is used by individuals to mediate their own behaviour when they experience a cognitively complex problem. L2 learners typically use their first language (L1) for private speech.	Jody was about to catch a bus when a stranger asked her which direction the bus was going to in Chinese. She replied *sei* (west). On the bus she begins to question herself in English to try to decide whether *sei* was correct. She rehearses the ingrained sequence *dong, lam, sei, bach* to herself until she realizes that it corresponds to *east, south, west, north* and that she had given the man the wrong information. *Sei* actually means 'west' and the bus was going east.

Concept	Definition	Example
Intermental; intramental; other-regulation; self-regulation; internalization	Intermental refers to processes that occur between individuals. Intramental refers to processes that occur within one individual. Other-regulation is behaviour that is regulated (i.e. mediated) by another person; self-regulation is behaviour where an individual exercises control over him/herself. Internalization refers to how a social (i.e. intermental) process is transformed into a psychological (i.e. intramental) process. It captures the progression from other-regulation to self-regulation.	Sarah helped Brock with *je m'excuse* when Brock was unable to say it himself. This constitutes an example of intermental, other-regulated behaviour in a ZPD. Brock was then able to apologize in French to his teacher. However, we do not know whether he internalized *je m'excuse* and thus can use it to apologize in French in the future. Further evidence would be needed to demonstrate self-regulation (internalization).
Everyday concepts; scientific concepts	Everyday concepts are 'understandings individuals develop from their experiences to solve various cognitive/emotional problems' (p. 150). They do not constitute part of a system, are context-dependent and are applied without consciousness. Scientific concepts are systematic, hierarchical, context-free and subject to conscious manipulation. They are acquired through mediation.	Thaya read a story he had translated from Tamil (his L1) into English to a group of postgraduate students who commented on the story. In their discussion of Thaya's story, the students drew on a variety of scientific concepts (i.e. rhetorical devices and literary strategies) which they had appropriated from their readings and presentations in the postgraduate course they were taking.
Cognition and emotion	Emotions, like cognition, are socially constructed. The emotional experience arising from a situation determines what effect it has on a person's mental development. Thus cognition and emotion are interrelated and cannot be considered separately.	Grace recounted her experience as a bilingual (Greek-English) when living in Greece and in Canada. She reported that her sense of a lack of competence in Greek (a negative emotion) when living in Greece led her to keep silent. In contrast, feeling embarrassed in elementary school in Canada when she inadvertently used a Greek word led her to learn the equivalent English word.

---

[a]. The Zone of Proximal Development (ZPD) is not the same as Krashen's (1981a) i+ 1 concept, which tied to the notion of a fixed order of acquisition. See Dunn and Lantolf (1998).

TBLT, namely what kinds of interaction trigger the internal processes (such as noticing) involved in L2 acquisition? SCT emphasizes the joint interactional behaviour of the expert and the learner (or between learners) as a ZPD is always co-constructed. It defines interactional behaviour much more broadly than in the cognitive-interactionist approach. A key construct is scaffolding.

Scaffolding refers to the interactional work by which one speaker (usually the expert) assists another speaker (usually the novice) to perform a skill or a linguistic feature that he/she cannot perform by him/herself. Storch (2017), in her summary of L2 classroom research based on SCT, emphasizes the importance of scaffolding. She traces interest in it to Aljaafreh and Lantolf's (1994) study of the feedback that a tutor provided on a L2 learner's writing. The tutor systematically (and without training) utilized a variety of feedback strategies, commencing with very implicit strategies and then moving to more explicit to help the student self-correct his/her errors. The importance of this study is that it established the necessity – from a sociocultural perspective – of providing the minimal amount of scaffolding needed to construct a ZPD. It also indicated that learning could be measured not just in terms of whether a learner had achieved self-regulation but also in terms of whether there was a change in the amount and level of scaffolding needed to mediate the correct production of a specific feature. The role played by an expert has been further developed in *dynamic assessment*, which integrates assessment and instruction by identifying a learner's potential for learning in scaffolded conversations. This is considered in the section 'Dynamic Assessment'. Other researchers have focused on how L2 learners scaffold each other when performing a task. Storch's work on effective collaboration is a notable contribution here and will also be discussed later.

A second concept is related to scaffolding but offers a broader perspective on how the use of language can mediate the learning of a language. Swain (2006) coined the term *languaging*, which she defined as 'the process of making *meaning* and shaping knowledge and experience through *language*' (p. 98). Languaging can occur in social interaction or in the individual learner when it takes the form of private speech. In a whole series of studies – see Ellis (2012) for a review – Swain and her co-researchers explored how L2 learners used language (both their L1 and the L2) to address linguistic problems that arose when they were performing tasks. Learners engaged in language-related episodes (LREs), defined as any part of a dialogue where they 'talk about the *language* they are producing, question their *language* use, or correct themselves or others' (Swain and Lapkin, 1998, p. 326).

In LREs linguistic features become the topic of talk and the focus of explicit attention. In this respect, SCT differs from the psycholinguistic and cognitive-interactionist perspectives by placing a premium on explicit and intentional learning – a point we will pick up later in this chapter.

Vygotsky (1986) saw one way in which everyday concepts can be transformed into scientific concepts as through *imitation* – the means by which socially constructed forms of mediation are internalized. Imitation is not the same as the 'copying' that occurs when an individual mimics a stimulus, as in behaviourist learning theories. Rather it is a conscious, reflective activity on the part of the learner. A distinction can be made between 'simple imitation' and 'persistent imitation' (Lantolf and Thorne, 2006). The former involves the unreflective attempt to reproduce a model – as, for example, when a learner just repeats a recast that repairs an error. The latter is intentional and is related to the goal the learner has for performing an utterance. It is also cyclical, with each attempt at imitation based not on the original model but on the previous imitation. Crucially, too, imitation is transformative; it involves modification of the model. For example, to qualify as imitation a learner would have to not just repeat a recast but to build on it. Imitation can occur in both social interaction and in private speech.

These three concepts all relate to the central concept of mediation. Learners participate in social interaction, which scaffolds the production of utterances they are incapable of producing independently, offers opportunities for learners to 'language', and creates contexts where learners can modify and extend the models they are exposed to by means of imitation. For mediation to be effective, however, it has to be goal-directed. This takes us to Activity Theory.

Activity Theory

Activity Theory was a development of Vygotsky's ideas by Leontiev (1978). It was extended further by Engeström (1999). The core of the theory is represented in Figure 4.1. For our purposes the 'subject' is a language learner. The 'goal' can be construed narrowly as the performance of a single utterance designed to achieve some purpose (e.g. politely refuse an invitation or deploy a grammatical feature accurately) or more broadly as the achievement of the outcome of a task (in the sense of this term in TBLT). The 'mediational means' refer to the various artefacts (material and symbolic) that mediate an activity. The interior of the triangle represents the activity that takes place. Engeström's extended model incorporates three

110   *Theoretical Perspectives*

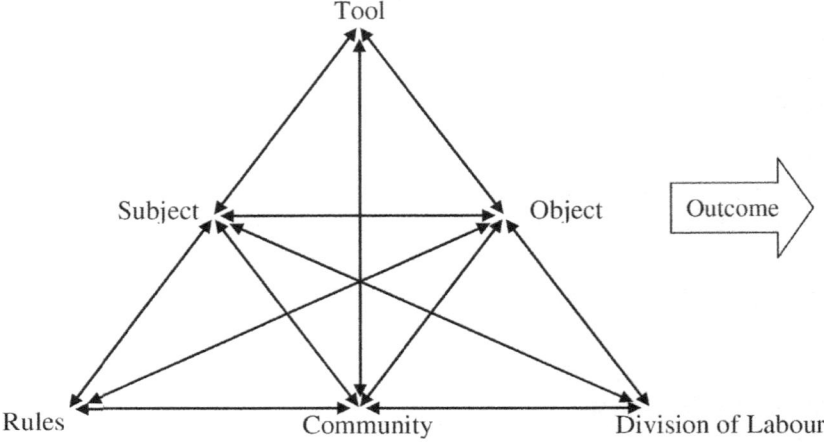

Figure 4.1 Activity theory model
Source: Engeström (1999)

contextual elements that impact on the activity that takes place: (1) rules (i.e. the norms that govern the use of language in a particular context, (2) community (i.e. the social group that a learner belongs to) and (3) division of labour (i.e. how the work done to achieve the goal is shared out among the participants in the activity). These components of an activity system interact among themselves in complex ways. Neither the components nor the relationships between them are static. It is this that gives Activity Theory its 'messiness and power' (Swain et al., 2011).

An activity has three levels: (1) motive, (2) action and (3) conditions (or operations). That is, a learner has a motive for performing an action that is directed at achieving the object (goal) and utilizes appropriate operations to achieve this. The motive determines the goal and also the operations that are used to achieve it. A good example is Wertsch, Minick and Arns' (1984) study. They compared how urban schoolteachers and rural mothers in Brazil mediated children's performance of a puzzle copying task. Although the task was the same for both the teachers and the mothers, the activity that resulted was very different. The teachers' motive for performing the task was educational (i.e. the children needed to learn how to function independently) and the goal was to help the children to carry out the actions themselves. Accordingly, they offered the children clues about what parts of the puzzle they needed to attend to. The rural mother's motive was to complete the task as quickly as possible and the goal was to prevent their children from making errors.[2] To this end they gave explicit instructions about how to build the puzzle. The fact that the same task can result in very different activities, involving different operations, has important implications for TBLT, which we will consider later in this chapter.

Incidental and Intentional Language Learning Revisited

One of the main differences between the cognitive theories that inform TBLT and sociocultural SLA lies in how they envisage the contributions of incidental and intentional language learning. Central to Long's (2015) cognitive-interactionist theory of instructed language acquisition is the notion of implicit/incidental learning. He cites Doughty (2003):

[T]he findings of a pervasive implicit mode of learning, and the limited role of explicit learning in improving performance in complex control tasks, point to a default mode for SLA that is fundamentally implicit, and to the need to avoid declarative knowledge when designing L2 pedagogical procedures.

(p. 298)

However, Long also acknowledged adults' reduced power for implicit language learning and thus accepted that there might be a need for 'facilitating *intentional initial perception* of new forms and form-meaning connections' (Long, 2015, p. 49; italics in original). For Long (and in mainstream views about TBLT) this is not to be achieved by explicit language teaching but through focus on form as learners perform tasks (see Chapter 2). Long rejects the explicit teaching of predetermined linguistic features (i.e. focus on forms). The justification for Long's position lies in the attested orders and sequences of acquisition of grammatical structures, which arise because of the way in which implicit L2 knowledge is acquired and which cannot be altered through instruction. The goal of instruction is to speed up progression through the natural route of acquisition by fostering incidental acquisition.

Sociocultural SLA takes a radically different stance on the role of incidental and intentional language learning. Social mediation is directed in helping learners form scientific concepts through both external guidance, imitation and private speech. In Swain's research, when learners perform tasks they engage in LREs, many of which involve quite explicit attention to linguistic forms and intentional language learning. Sociocultural theorists such as Lantolf and Swain focus on how learners develop their conscious understanding of the meanings encoded by specific linguistic forms and how mediation helps them to achieve this. The goal of instruction is not implicit knowledge (which is rarely referred to in the sociocultural literature) but declarative knowledge. In other words, they see instruction as helping learners to go well beyond the incidental perception of new forms, which result only in everyday concepts, to the conscious formation of scientific concepts about language through intentional learning.

In taking the position that explicit instruction and intentional language learning are not just desirable but necessary for developing an L2, Lantolf (2009) disputes the empirical basis for Long's position, namely the existence of a natural route of acquisition. His view is that any grammatical structure can be learned at any time provided that it is appropriately mediated. This claim, however, runs up against research that indicates instruction is powerless to alter the route learners follow. To counter this evidence Zhang and Lantolf (2015) conducted a study designed to test Pienemann's (1985) Teachability Hypothesis, according to which instruction directed at a specific grammatical feature will only be successful if that feature is next in line to be acquired in terms of the natural sequence of acquisition. Using an approach called concept-based language teaching, based on Vygotskian principles (discussed later in this chapter), they taught adult learners of Chinese an L2 grammatical structure that lay well ahead of their current developmental stage and concluded that 'it is possible to artificially construct a developmental route different from the one predicted by natural developmental sequences, in agreement with the claims of Vygotsky's developmental education' (Zhang and Lantolf, 2015, p. 152). Other studies also provide evidence of variable developmental routes (see Ellis, 2015b).

A key issue here, however, is whether instruction results in implicit knowledge, on which claims about developmental sequences are based. While Lantolf does not deny the existence of implicit knowledge, which he correlates with everyday concepts, he argues that the goal of instruction – for adults at least – is automatized declarative knowledge, i.e. explicit knowledge that is available for use without the need for conscious control. This is what Zhang and Lantolf claimed the instruction achieved in their study. In this way the objection that Long and others raise to focus on forms is circumvented. There is, however, a further problem. DeKeyser (1998) questions the viability of teaching complex grammatical rules. To overcome this objection to explicit instruction, Lantolf and Thorne (2006, pp. 298–302) argue that concept-based language teaching, where the focus is on mediating learners' conscious understanding of meaning-form mappings, can result in automatized explicit knowledge of even very complex structures.

In short, whereas mainstream TBLT – as reflected in Long (2015) – is founded on cognitive-interactionist theories that prioritize incidental acquisition and focus on form, sociocultural SLA supports explicit instruction – as long as it conforms to Vygotskian principles – and intentional language learning. In effect, sociocultural theorists such as Lantolf lend support to task-supported language instruction, where tasks provide opportunities to apply conscious linguistic knowledge that has been explicitly taught in meaning-focused activity.

Sociocultural SLA: Task Selection and Design

As we have seen in Chapters 2 and 3, both cognitive-interactionist and psycholinguistic perspectives afford insights about the selection and design of tasks in a task-based course. Skehan (2001), for example, draws on his earlier research to suggest how a number of design features (e.g. the familiarity of information, the degree of structure and the complexity of the outcome) affect the complexity, accuracy and fluency (CAF) of learners' production. He proposed that such information is useful because it enables course designers to select a variety of tasks to ensure balanced L2 development. Robinson (2001) also identified a number of factors (e.g. whether a task requires reasoning) that affect the complexity of a task. Researchers working in the psycholinguistic paradigm (e.g. Sasayama, 2016) have shown that task factors impact directly on the cognitive load imposed by the task and indirectly on how the task is performed. Cognitive-interactionist researchers (e.g. Pica, Kanagy and Falodun, 1993) have investigated how task design features influence the extent to which negotiation for meaning takes place. Designers of task-based courses are able to draw on this research to make informed decisions about the design of task-based syllabuses, although, as we have seen, neither the cognitive-interactionist nor the psycholinguistic approach has solved all the problems associated with task selection and sequencing.

SCT, however, offers no assistance to the course designer. According to Activity Theory, the same task can result in very different activities as a result of differences in the motives of the task participants and the goals they set for the performance of the task. Differences in how the same task is performed can also arise as a result in differences in the rules, community and division of labour. Several studies testify to the fact that the same task can be performed in very different ways. The most often cited is Coughlan and Duff (1994). They showed that the same task can be performed differently by different learners (Hungarian school students and an adult English as a Second Language [ESL] learner) and by the same learner (the adult ESL learner) at different times. Donato (2000) also provided evidence to show that 'tasks do not manipulate learners to act in certain ways because participants invest their own goals, actions, cultural background, and beliefs (i.e. their agency) into tasks, and thus transform them' (p. 44). A similar position can be found in Dynamic Systems Theory (de Bot and Larsen-Freeman, 2011). From the perspective of this theory, how learners perform a task cannot be predicted because of the interconnectedness of all the variables involved in the task itself, in the learner and in the situation and psychological context. The activity system created by the interactions among these variables is inherently dynamic and task performance unsystematic.

It would seem then that, from the perspective of sociocultural SLA and Dynamic Systems Theory, 'task' does not constitute a viable unit for designing a task-based course or for conducting research because how it is performed is unpredictable – a view argued strongly by Seedhouse (2005a). Nevertheless, teachers and researchers do have to make decisions about what tasks to select. There has to be a starting point and, in fact, some SCT researchers have made suggestions about what kinds of tasks are needed. Storch (2017), for example, commented 'what SCT implies for L2 learning/instruction is the need for two key ingredients: *challenge* and effective support' (p. 77; italics added). In other words, (1) there is no sense in asking learners to perform easy tasks because learners will draw on everyday concepts or the scientific concepts they have already internalized and thus do not require mediation, and (2) the co-construction of ZPDs requires tasks that challenge but are not so far beyond the learners' current abilities that they cannot be successfully performed through mediation. Bygate (2018) also suggested that predictability is a matter of degree and pointed out that Dynamic Systems Theory acknowledges the emergence of 'patterns' of behaviour. He suggested that tasks manifest 'pragmatic predictability' and that it would be possible to select tasks in terms of the trajectories of behaviour they elicit. He illustrated this idea by pointing out that there were predictable phases in the performance of a picture story task where learners work in groups, each holding one of the six pictures that make up the story, and pass through phases (e.g. description, comparison, interpretation, narration) to achieve the task outcome.

Research on dynamic assessment (not to be confused with Dynamic Systems Theory) implicitly acknowledges that there are inherent differences in the complexity of tasks. A key issue when investigating mediated assistance is the extent to which learners are able to transfer the learning that takes place in the performance of the mediated task to a new, *more complex* task (Poehner, 2008). Van Compernolle,

Weber and Gomez-Laich (2016), for example, investigated the effect of instruction motivated by SCT on learners' acquisition of the pragmatic uses of Spanish *tú* and *usted*. They deliberately included items of differing levels of complexity in an appropriate judgement task and a written discourse completion task in order to see whether the learners' understanding of these two linguistic forms was generalizable beyond the specific contexts that figured in the mediated test. Ableeva and Lantolf (2011) also reported a study in which they sought to demonstrate transfer from the mediated development of listening comprehension to a new, more difficult listening task. Notions of task complexity are inherent in 'transfer' and clearly sociocultural researchers do employ some intuitive sense of what constitutes complexity in a task.

By and large, however, SCT addresses the issue of what constitute a 'challenging' or 'complex' task in terms of the teacher's (or researcher's) experience of working with tasks with particular learners. In other words, what tasks to incorporate into a course are not decided *a priori* but as the course progresses through an inspection of how learners perform particular tasks and the teacher's developing understanding of what degree of difficulty is needed for the ongoing construction of ZPDs.

A good example of this approach can be found in Mochizuki's (2017) proposal for 'contingent needs analysis', which she suggested can help to identify the gap between the task-as-workplan and the activity that arises from it. Clearly, if there is no close correspondence between 'task' and 'activity' as SCT claims, a traditional needs analysis of the kind that Long (2005, 2015) recommends makes little sense. Mochizuki's idea is that an analysis of how learners perform a task can help to identify the contradictions and tensions that arise and this information can be fed back into what teachers need to do to ensure the effective mediation of subsequent tasks. Mochizuki's study used Activity Theory to examine how two different groups of learners participated in feedback sessions on doctoral students' writing. The 'needs' she identified included the importance of the facilitators equipping students with the strategies required for giving and receiving feedback and the need to address the power relations that suppress some students' participation in giving and receiving feedback.

It would seem then, a task-based course informed by SCT will, at best, just have a provisional syllabus, which is redeveloped as the course continues. The actual syllabus is the one the teacher ends up with. We accept that this is always the case but we will argue that in many instructional contexts there is a clear need for an *a priori* task-based syllabus.

Sociocultural SLA: Task Implementation

SCT has much more to say about how tasks should be implemented than about task design or selection. Indeed, the focus of SCT is more or less entirely on how tasks can be implemented in order to mediate learning effectively. It is in this respect, then, that SCT has the most to offer TBLT. For reasons of space, we will illustrate what SCT-inspired research has shown by focusing on three major areas of enquiry – *graduated feedback*, *collaborative dialogue* and *dynamic assessment*.

Graduated Feedback

In Chapter 2 we saw that cognitive-interactionist views of L2 acquisition have motivated a number of studies that have investigated whether one type of corrective feedback (CF) (e.g. explicit feedback) is more effective in promoting acquisition than another type (e.g. implicit feedback). We noted that the results of these studies do not enable a single type of feedback to be identified as the most effective. This is because there are differences in how learners react to feedback depending on individual learner factors (such as working memory) and contextual factors. Such differences are to be expected from the perspective of SCT and Activity Theory. SCT has taken a radically different approach to investigating CF, which is conceived of as a form of mediation aimed at learner development.

Aljaafreh and Lantolf (1994) (see also Lantolf, Kurtz and Kisselev, 2016), examined writing conferences where a tutor provided oral feedback on students' written work. They developed a 'regulatory scale' to reflect the extent to which the tutor's oral feedback was implicit or explicit. For example, asking learners to find and correct their own errors constitutes an implicit strategy while providing examples of the correct pattern is a highly explicit strategy. An intermediate level occurs when the tutor indicates the nature of an error without identifying it for the learner. This scale reflects a central claim of SCT, namely that for CF to be effective if must be fine-tuned to the learner's development (i.e. provide the minimal assistance needed to induce a self-correction).

In a study based on Aljaafreh and Lantolf's regulatory scale, Nassaji and Swain (2000) investigated two Korean learners of English. One learner was provided with graduated assistance (i.e. the tutor systematically worked through the regulatory scale to tailor the feedback supplied) while the other learner was given only random help (i.e. the tutor was supplied with a random list of correcting feedback strategies). Nassaji and Swain reported that systematic graduated feedback was more effective in assisting development than the random feedback. However, a limitation of this study is that random feedback is highly unnatural and unlikely to occur in actual teaching. A more interesting comparison would be one that compared graduated feedback with a specific type of feedback that cognitive-interactionist research has found to be effective.

Erlam, Ellis and Batstone (2013) conducted such a study. They compared the effects of graduated feedback and explicit correction on two grammatical structures – English past tense and articles. In contrast to Aljaafreh and Lantolf (1994), they found no evidence of any shift in the quality of graduated feedback over the two occasions that correction was provided on the students' writing. Evidence from a post-test showed that graduated feedback resulted in greater gains in accuracy than explicit correction for articles but not for past tense. It is possible, therefore, that when the form-meaning mapping is transparent (as is the case for English past tense), graduated feedback is not necessary. Responding to Erlam et al.'s (2013) study, Lantolf et al. (2016) argued that development, as measured by a graduated feedback index, is not linear, that unidirectional change from one week to the next is not to be expected and therefore investigating development by means of a pre- and post-test as in Erlam et al. is not appropriate.

A strength of the SCT research on CF is that it recognizes that feedback is contingent on the learner's response to it. In research based on cognitive-interactionist SLA, CF is typically construed as of the one-shot kind. That is, every time an error occurs it should be corrected by a pre-determined corrective strategy (e.g. recasts or prompts). In other words, CF is something done to a learner. In contrast, in SCT, CF is seen as co-constructed between an expert and novice and as continuing over several turns and times in the search for a ZPD.

Collaborative Dialogue

Following Swain (2000), we have elected to use the term 'collaborative dialogue' rather than 'scaffolding' because it more accurately captures how social interaction mediates development. The scaffolding metaphor implies a pre-planned architecture but, according to SCT, mediation is a jointly constructed activity and is thus flexible and collaborative. The research on graduated CF is one example of collaborative dialogue. In this section, we look at other ways in which it has been investigated in research involving tasks. We will not attempt an extensive review of the research but rather focus on a few representative studies.

Intersubjectivity

Swain et al. (2011) pointed out that for the co-construction of a ZPD 'there needs to be some level of intersubjectivity' (p. 24) in the sense of a shared understanding of the goal of performing a task. Ellis (2003) illustrated the importance of intersubjectivity in an exchange between a teacher and a beginning L2 learner. To begin with the teacher and learner have different goals. The teacher's goal was to help the learner to describe what is wrong in a picture of a bicycle with no pedals. This goal was beyond the learner's linguistic ability, who therefore established a simpler, different goal – identifying the colours of objects in the picture. As a result, in the early part of this sequence, the participants are functioning at cross-purposes. Eventually, intersubjectivity is achieved in turn (7) when the teacher accepts the learner's goal. As a result, a ZPD is constructed in turn (8) when the learner builds on the teacher's preceding utterance to produce what Ellis claimed was the first instance of a two-word utterance (*black taes*) in his data for this learner.

1. T. I want you to tell me what you can see in the picture or what's wrong with the picture
2.   L. A /paik/ (= bike)
3. T. A cycle, yes. But what's wrong?
4.   L. /ret/ (= red)
5. T. It's red yes. What's wrong with it?
6.   L. Black.
7. T. Black. Good. Black what?
8.   L. Black /taes/ (= tyres).
(From Ellis, 2003, p. 181)

The importance of shared goals is obvious. It should be noted, however, that the rubric for a task cannot guarantee shared goals – as was the case in this sequence – and as SCT predicts. When learners work in pairs or small groups, they may need to agree on the goal for a task before they start to perform it. This can involve meta-talk about the task, which in monolingual groups may well be carried out in the L1. Brooks and Donato (1994), for example, described how even though the teacher carefully explained the task goals, the learners often felt the need to discuss these between themselves. They argued that this constitutes a legitimate use of the L1 in task-based teaching.[3]

Talk in Group Work

According to SCT, development occurs when an expert mediates the novice's performance of a task. Accordingly, much of the research has investigated how ZPDs are constructed in teacher–learner interaction. But, in fact, learners can also successfully mediate each other's development. Thus, as in research in the cognitive-interactionist paradigm, many SCT-motivated studies have investigated how learners perform tasks in pairs or small groups.

In an early study, Donato (1994) investigated groups of university students of French performing an oral activity. In a detailed analysis of an exchange involving the negotiation of the form *tu t'es souvenu*, Donato showed how the students jointly managed components of this structure, compared what they produced with what they perceived as the ideal solution, and used their collective resources to minimize frustration and risk. This collaborative scaffolding enabled the joint construction of the correct form of the verb even though no single learner had demonstrated knowledge of it prior to the task. This study, therefore, demonstrated the central claim of SCT, namely that 'higher mental functioning is situated in the dialectal processes embedded in the social context' (p. 46). Donato also provided evidence of internalization by showing that the joint performance of new structures on one occasion was frequently followed by individual learners' self-regulated use of them on a later occasion.

One of the most complete studies of group work from a SCT perspective is Ohta's (2001) account of beginner learners in a Japanese foreign language classroom. Through the detailed analysis of sequences of talk by these learners, she identified the various scaffolding techniques they used to help construct ZPDs. For example, when a listener observed a partner struggling to produce an utterance he/she would wait to give the partner time to complete it, prompt him/her by repeating a syllable, co-construct the utterance by providing a syllable, word or phrase that contributed towards its completion, or sometimes, provide an explanation in the L1 (English). Ohta emphasized the reciprocal nature of assisted performance: 'This is the key to peer assistance – that both peers benefit, the one receiving assistance and the one who reaches out to provide it' (p. 125).

The quality of collaboration in group work varies, however, so a key question is what constitutes effective collaboration. Storch (2002) investigated this by analysing the patterns of dyadic interaction found in ESL students' performance of a range of tasks. She identified four basic patterns based on two intersecting dimensions involving (1) mutuality (i.e. 'the level of engagement with each other's contribution') and (2) equality (i.e. 'the degree of control or authority over a task') (p. 127). Storch investigated the extent to which 'learning', as evidenced in the interactions, led to 'development', as shown in the performance of subsequent tasks. She reported that the most collaborative dyad (i.e. the dyad manifesting high mutuality and high equality) achieved the most instances of transfer of knowledge.

SCT prioritizes social interaction as the primary means of mediation. However, SCT, also acknowledges that a learner can mediate him or herself by means of private speech. A question of some interest, therefore, is whether there is any advantage of a task being performed socially as opposed to individually. Storch (2007) compared ESL students completing a text-editing task in pairs and individually. She found no difference in the accuracy of their edited texts. Nevertheless, she argued that performing the task in pairs was advantageous because it afforded opportunities for using the L2 for a range of functions that would promote language learning. Other studies (e.g. Swain and Lapkin, 2007), have shown that interaction with the self (i.e. private speech) is effective in mediating development.

Languaging

The languaging that occurs when learners focus on linguistic problems as they perform tasks has been investigated in a series of studies by Swain and her co-researchers (e.g. Swain and Lapkin 1998, 2001, 2002; Watanabe and Swain, 2007; Swain et al., 2009). The typical design of these studies involved: (1) transcribing a recording of learners performing a task, (2) identifying LREs and coding them as successfully resolved, unsuccessfully resolved or unresolved, and (3) investigating whether the learners were subsequently able to use the features they had targeted in the LREs accurately. Swain often chose tasks that were likely to result in linguistic problems. Swain (1995), for example, reported a study by La Pierre involving a dictogloss task that resulted in 140 LREs being identified.

Languaging in Swain's studies is clearly a collaborative activity. The analyses of the talk generated by learners reveal the mental processes that mediated L2 learning (e.g. generating alternatives, assessing alternatives through hypothesis testing and applying rules to new L2 contexts). In some of the studies, Swain included pre- and post-tests in order to see whether the dialogic activity that occurred as learners performed the tasks enabled them to move from incorrect to correct responses. There was clear evidence of this happening (see, for example Swain and Lapkin, 1998).

However, the studies also demonstrated considerable variability in learners' ability or preparedness to 'language'. Watanabe and Swain (2007), drawing on Storch's (2002) research on collaboration in small group work, investigated the patterns of interaction that took place in pairs of learners and the relationship of these to learning. The pairs of learners differed in their L2 (English) proficiency. The learners wrote an essay in pairs (the pre-test), were given a reformulated version which together they compared with their own text, and then individually rewrote their essay (the post-test). Learning was operationalized in terms of whether the changes that the learners made to their original text were correct. Proficiency differences in the pairings made little difference in post-test performance but the extent to which the pairs engaged in collaborative patterns of interaction did. Swain et al. (2009) reported that 'high languagers' produced more and better quality LREs, demonstrated greater depth of understanding and had higher scores in tests than 'low languagers'.

These studies provide clear evidence of the power of languaging as a mediating tool. All of the studies involved learners grappling with language problems, working towards a conceptual understanding in order to solve them, and thereby learning to use linguistic forms in a target-like way.

The strength of Swain's research is that 'development' is not investigated solely in terms of the LREs that arise in social interaction or in the 'language units' observed in interaction with the self but also in transfer to subsequent tasks or tests. There are, however, some limitations. In general, the studies did not convincingly demonstrate full transfer of learning as they did not show that the learners were able to generalize their learning to *new* tasks and *new* contexts. Nor did they provide convincing evidence that the learners had automatized their linguistic knowledge. Many of the studies involved writing rather than speaking.

Dynamic Assessment

Dynamic assessment also involves mediation through collaborative talk. It aims to achieve 'the dialectic integration of instruction and assessment' (Lantolf, 2009), thereby overcoming the dualism evident in much of the applied linguistics literature. Drawing on the idea of graduated feedback, the tester aims to show both what learners can do independently and what they can achieve with assistance, the aim being to measure learners' potential for future learning as well as their actual learning.

Dynamic assessment has now become one of the major lines of research in sociocultural SLA (Poehner and Lantolf, 2005; Poehner, 2008; Lantolf, 2009; Poehner and Infante, 2017). It can be carried out in two ways – the interventionist and the interactionist. In the former the training provided by the tester is pre-planned. This makes it well suited to assessing large numbers of learners and also to the computerized delivery of mediation. In interactionist dynamic assessment the mediation provided is highly flexible and tailored to the individual learner and thus corresponds more closely to the original idea of graduated feedback. 'In interactionist DA, the priority that trumps all others is learner development' (Poehner, 2008, p. 66).

Interventionist Dynamic Assessment

Poehner (2008) discussed a number of interventionist models of dynamic assessment. Budoff's Learning Potential Measurement Approach pioneered the sandwich format (i.e. there was a pre-test and a post-test in order to identify to what extent different learners benefited from the training). Carlson and Widl's Testing-the-Limits Approach asked examinees to give reasons for both their correct and incorrect choices during the training. The resulting learner profiles included information about the learners' ability to verbalize their linguistic choices. In Brown's Graduated Prompt Approach, transfer tasks are included to see whether the improvement resulting from mediation transfers to both similar and dissimilar tasks from those used in the treatment. These possibilities have been incorporated into SLA studies involving dynamic assessment.

A good example of an interventionist study is van Compernolle and Zhang (2014).[4] They administered a version of the oral elicited imitation test (EIT) (Erlam, 2006). The test consisted of six sets of sentences with three pairs of sentences in each, one grammatical and one ungrammatical. Each sentence contained two exemplars of each target feature (plural -s; past-tense -ed; third person -s). If the learners were able to imitate a sentence correctly without assistance they scored four points. The researchers suggested that this indicated that they had implicit knowledge of the target structure. If they failed to imitate it correctly, they were given three clues ordered from implicit to explicit and awarded marks on a declining scale (three, two or one) depending on the level of assistance they needed to imitate a sentence correctly. Van Compernolle and Zhang suggested that these clues prompted learners to use their metalinguistic knowledge. If a learner ultimately failed to produce a sentence they scored zero. They reported detailed results for one learner. Interestingly, the unsupported accuracy level for the three structures was the same as for the natural order of acquisition (Krashen, 1981a). With assistance, however, the learner was able to produce all three structures accurately and needed less assistance as he moved through the sets of sentences in the test. This study, then, lends support to the central claim of sociocultural SLA. It demonstrated that the mediation enabled the learner to produce grammatical structures accurately when he was unable to do so independently.

Commenting on their study, Van Compernolle and Zhang noted 'one of the issues ... is whether, and to what extent, mediation in DA promotes greater control and speed of access to metalinguistic knowledge during performance, or if it supports the development of a learner's implicit (unconscious, procedural) competence' (p. 401). We will take up this important issue in the conclusion to this chapter.

Interactionist Dynamic Assessment

As Poehner (2008) pointed out, interactionist dynamic assessment owes much to Feuerstein's ideas. Feuerstein was concerned with helping children who were 'retarded performers' as a result of their impoverished social experiences. His work was premised on the assumption that 'the more a child is subjected to mediated learning experiences, the greater will be his capacity to benefit from direct exposure to learning' (Feuerstein, Falik and Rynders, 1988, p. 58). In other words, Feuerstein was not just concerned with helping children perform tasks but, crucially, with assisting their general cognitive development (i.e. their ability to learn). The value of Feuerstein's work for dynamic assessment with language learners lies, in particular, in the very detailed account he provides of how mediated language experiences can be distinguished from other types of interaction. He identified eleven attributes of effective mediation. These include the importance of reciprocity (i.e. the collaborative nature of the mediation), transcendence (i.e. true development manifests itself in a child's ability to perform increasingly complex tasks) and the mediation of meaning (i.e. the importance of engaging the child in cause-and-effect and inferential thinking).

Lantolf (2009) provides an example of interactionist dynamic assessment involving two interactions between a mediator and an advanced L2 learner of French. In the first interaction where the learner narrates a scene from a Hollywood movie, the learner experiences problems in deciding whether to use *passé composé* or *imparfait*. She initially opts for *imparfait* but is challenged by the mediator, which prompts the learner to try to justify her choice. As she launches into an explanation, she talks herself into the more appropriate option and settles on *passé composé*. In the second interaction a problem emerges with a complex negative construction. This time the mediator has to engage in more extensive assistance involving hints, explicit explanation and finally recasting the learner's attempt to produce the structure. Lantolf argued that whereas the choice of verb aspect lay well within this learner's ZPD, necessitating minimal assistance from the mediator, the complex negative construction was, at best, only in the very early stages of development and thus necessitated more overt mediation.

The Relevance of Dynamic Assessment to TBLT

Dynamic assessment studies provide some of the richest examples of how ZPDs can be scaffolded. They illustrate the kinds of strategies that teachers can use when implementing tasks. These studies also shed light on assessment involving tasks. Advocates of TBLT are clear that assessment, like teaching, must be task-based (Norris, 2009a). The kinds of assessment that have been proposed (see Chapter 9), however, are based on the unmediated performance of tasks. That is, the focus is on learners' solo performances. SCT questions the validity of such assessments. It proposes that a more valid assessment can be derived by examining learners' mediated performance of tasks in order to demonstrate their potential.

There are problems, however. Where teaching is concerned, interactionist dynamic assessment is not practical in instructional contexts involving large classes although computer-delivered interventionist dynamic assessment may be. Where assessment is involved, there needs to be a way of deriving scores from a dynamic assessment. Qin and van Compernolle (in press) suggest three scores are possible: (1) an actual score, (2) a mediated score and (3) a learning potential score. This, however, is only feasible in interventionist DA where there is a pre-determined number of mediational clues.

Concept-Based Language Instruction

We have seen that SCT emphasizes the importance of developing scientific concepts in the learner. Lantolf and Zhang (2017) argued that 'discovery learning' – of the kind that TBLT aims to foster - cannot ensure that L2 learners will develop the necessary scientific concepts. They therefore argued for the explicit teaching of grammatical concepts. However, Lantolf maintained that this cannot be achieved by teaching learners rules of thumb that figure in traditional grammar teaching. He commented 'rules of thumb are not necessarily wrong, but they generally describe concrete empirical occurrences of the relevant phenomenon in a fairly unsystematic fashion and, as a result, fail to reveal deeper systematic principles' (Lantolf, 2007, p. 36). Accordingly, he set out the case for presenting learners with conceptually organized grammatical knowledge where the links between semantic/functional concepts and linguistic form are specified in detail. To this end, he saw cognitive linguistics and systematic-functional grammar as providing the necessary bases for a 'developmental education' involving concept-based language instruction.

Concept-based language instruction is based on Gal'perin's (1989) proposal for systemic-theoretical instruction. Lantolf and Zhang (2017) identified five phases in this kind of instruction. In the orienting phase, a clear goal is specified and the means for achieving it established. The aim is to create a dissonance between the learner's existing everyday knowledge and the new scientific knowledge. In the second phase, the scientific knowledge is given a material or visual instantiation in the form of Schema for the Orienting Basis of Action (SCOBA). This can take the form of a diagram, a chart, a picture or physical objects (e.g. Lego pieces). The aim here is to discourage rote memorization of the new information and to facilitate its application in practical activity. The third phase connects the SCOBA to practical activity. This is where tasks can come in. In the fourth phase learners engage in overt verbalization by explaining their understanding of the new information to someone else or aloud to themselves. This is when 'languaging' occurs. In the final phase learners demonstrate fluent control of the new knowledge by performing additional communicative activities (i.e. tasks).

The study that provides the clearest account of concept-based language instruction is Negueruela and Lantolf (2006). This study investigated twelve students in a university Spanish as a foreign language class, which met three times a week for fifteen weeks. The explicit instruction involved a SCOBA for presenting grammatical aspect. It consisted of a flow chart that led the learners through a series of questions to help them understand when to use the preterite and imperfect tenses in Spanish. The students were asked to verbalize the Schema six times while carrying out a number of oral and written communicative activities. Finally, they completed a written communicative task. The students' verbal explanations of the grammatical structures were collected at the beginning and end of the course. Initially these were simplistic and incomplete, reflecting the rules of thumb in student textbooks with which the students were familiar. Their explanations at the end of the course, although not always complete, were generally more coherent and accurate, which Negueruela and Lantolf suggested demonstrated that internalization of the concepts was taking place. The study also provided evidence to show that the learners' improved conceptual understanding was reflected in improved accuracy in new production tasks.

By and large, concept-based language instruction studies have focused on the learning of grammatical features. In an interesting study, Kim and Lantolf (2018) investigated whether this kind of instruction was effective in enabling L2 learners to comprehend sarcasm. They noted that previous research has demonstrated that learners often fail to detect sarcasm and argued that to overcome this problem learners needed a full, scientific account of how sarcasm functions in English. They provided learners with a list of the linguistic, paralinguistic and contextual cues that signal sarcasm and asked them to view of series of video clips to decide whether they contained sarcastic utterances and if they did to verbalize the clues they had used to detect them. Eight out of nine learners increased their scores in the immediate post-test, maintained improvement in the delayed test and also were better able to identify relevant cues.

Concept-based language instruction can be seen as a version of task-supported language teaching. For this reason it will probably be rejected by proponents of task-based language instruction. Clearly it involves intentional learning, not the implicit/incidental learning that TBLT is primarily directed at fostering. The studies to date do not provide convincing evidence of full automatization of the target structures as they did not include free oral production tasks, but they do indicate that the learners were able to use them in activities that allow for controlled processing. The studies have also typically involved university-level students, so the suitability of this kind of instruction for younger learners or even adult learners with low language analytical ability, who might be less able to handle the very detailed information provided in SCOBAs, is doubtful.

Conclusion

SCT made a relatively late entry into SLA but since the 1990s it has become increasingly influential. There are numerous books devoted to it. Readers looking for a comprehensive account can refer to Lantolf and Thorne (2006) or Lantolf and Poehner (2014). There is also a journal (*Language and Sociocultural Theory*) devoted to the application of the theory to language, including L2 acquisition.

By claiming that learning originates *within* social activity, SCT offers an explanation for L2 development that is radically different from that of cognitive or cognitive-interactionist SLA, which views L2 acquisition as an essentially mental phenomenon. Not surprisingly, SCT has been largely ignored by cognitive SLA. Long (2015), for example, dismissed SCT (along with Piaget) on the grounds that the core constructs of SCT – inner speech, appropriation, mediation, self-regulation and the ZPD – are 'nebulous' and inadequate both theoretically and experimentally. While it is perhaps true that these concepts do not interconnect into a tightly woven theory, as Swain et al. (2011) acknowledged, Long's dismissal of sociocultural SLA is unwarranted. The central concept – mediation – provides a basis for investigating how participation in the social uses of language does not just facilitate learning – the cognitive perspective – but where it happens on the fly.

In what ways, then, does SCT constitute a theoretical framework for TBLT? We have argued that SCT has little to say about the design of task-based courses. It offers no obvious basis for selecting which tasks to use or how to sequence tasks to ensure they offer the right level of challenge to L2 learners. SCT proponents assume that teachers will use their experience of their students to gauge what tasks to use. In many instructional contexts such as foreign language classes in state schools, however, teachers need the support of a syllabus.

In contrast, we have shown that SCT has much to offer teachers when it comes to how tasks can be implemented to foster L2 learning. Research that has investigated graduated feedback, collaborative talk and dynamic assessment provides rich accounts of how learning can be mediated in both teacher–learner and in learner–learner interactions. It shows how learners can be talked and can talk themselves into using linguistic features that lie outside their independent control. This research, perhaps more clearly than any other, shows how participation *is* learning and thus feeds directly into our understanding of task-based language instruction. For example, it demonstrates convincingly that learners' use of their L1 has a positive role to play in task performance and as such supports the growing recognition that the L1 is a valuable resource in the L2 classroom (Hall and Cook, 2012). SCT, then, is of value when it comes to deciding how tasks can be effectively implemented. In Chapter 3 we noted that it is task implementation rather than task design that had emerged as important for creating the types of language use deemed important for acquisition. From this perspective, SCT has much to offer TBLT.

SCT also provides a theoretical basis for task-supported language teaching. By rejecting the existence of a universal route for L2 acquisition, proponents of SCT dismiss the principal objection to 'focus on forms'. Research on dynamic assessment has focused on how to mediate the development of specific grammatical features. Concept-based language instruction is based on key principles of SCT (i.e. the importance of scientific concepts and of verbal mediation). It has been found to help learners develop declarative knowledge of highly complex grammatical and socio-pragmatic features. However, to date both dynamic assessment and concept-based language instruction have only been tried on adult, university-level learners, who are adept at explicit, analytical language learning. Whether they are appropriate for younger, school-based learners, who are better equipped to engage in the implicit/incidental learning that task-based instruction caters to, remains to be shown. Also – potentially the main caveat – research based on SCT has not convincingly shown that learners can utilize the scientific concepts that instruction helps them to develop in the kind of language use that TBLT prioritizes – spontaneous, naturally occurring speech.[5]

The cognitive and sociocultural perspectives are often seen as incompatible and therefore incommensurate. It is unfortunate that proponents of each remain hostile to each other. The position adopted by Ellis (2000) was that pedagogy involving tasks can benefit from both perspectives. He cited van Lier's (1996) plea for a 'dual vision' – the need for teachers to keep in mind 'a long-term sense of direction and the need to make on-line decisions that take account of the exigencies of the moment' (p. 215). Cognitive perspectives arguably provide a long-term sense of direction for TBLT as they address head-on the need for a syllabus about which SCT has virtually nothing to say. SCT, however, offers rich insights as to how teachers can best handle online decision-making as they implement tasks.

5 *Psychological Perspectives*

The psychology of second language (L2) task performance refers to factors relating to 'the mental experiences, processes, thoughts, feelings, motives, and behaviours of individuals involved in language learning' (Mercer, Ryan and Williams, 2012, p. 2). The psychological dimension of task-based language teaching (TBLT) thus defined includes the learner characteristics that are, in Snow's (1991) terms, 'propaedeutic' ('required as preparation for a learning condition') (p. 205) to a learning goal, including affective (feelings and emotions), conative (motivation) and cognitive (reasoning and memory) variables. In this chapter, we discuss the role of these variables in affecting task performance and the effects of task-based instruction by elaborating the theoretical underpinnings for the role of psychological factors and synthesizing the research on these factors.

The factors are broadly divided into cognitive and affective factors, following Robinson (2011). In line with the current mainstream second language acquisition (SLA) literature (Dörnyei, 2005; Mercer et al., 2012; Ellis and Shintani, 2014) these variables are collectively referred to as individual difference variables. Special attention is given to language aptitude and working memory in the cognitive domain and motivation and anxiety in the affective domain, due to their importance for TBLT, the relatively clear definitions and operationalizations of the constructs, and the availability of a body of relevant empirical research. The synthetic review of each of these variables starts with an overview of the construct in L2 research in general, including, but not limited to, the conceptualization, operationalization and methods of the research, followed by a more specific discussion of the TBLT research.

Theoretical Issues

The theoretical basis of the role of individual differences in language learning can be found in Robinson's Cognition Hypothesis (CH)

(2001, 2011; see Chapter 2). Robinson's theory posits a three-component framework: task complexity, task conditions and task difficulty, which concern the conceptual/cognitive, interactional and perceptual demands of tasks, respectively. Among the three dimensions, task difficulty relates to individual difference variables, including affective (e.g. motivation and anxiety) and cognitive (e.g. language aptitude and working memory) variables, which account for interlearner variation in task performance. Individual differences constitute a key component of Robinson's triadic framework that interacts with the other two components in affecting learners' task performance.

The CH makes the following predictions about how individual difference variables interact with the other two groups of variables. First, individual differences in the affective domain are implicated when tasks are performed under different conditions leading to emotions and interpersonal relationships coming into play. For example, monologic tasks (e.g. narratives) that require public reporting may lead to more anxiety than dialogic tasks performed in pairs or small groups; tasks that require equal contribution from all participants are likely to be more motivating than those that only require some participants to contribute. Second, individual differences in cognitive abilities are related to performance along different dimensions of task complexity. For example, reasoning ability is important for successful performance in tasks that are complex along the resource-directing dimension which pose greater processing demands; attention control is predictive of performance in tasks manipulated along the resource-dispersing dimension. Third, the role of individual differences is more evident in complex tasks that are more demanding of cognitive abilities than simple tasks that require less mental effort and fewer cognitive resources.

It can be seen that the CH affords a theoretical basis for the role of individual difference factors in task *performance* involving learners' existing knowledge and skills, but it does not spell out how these variables impact L2 *development* or learning (gains in new knowledge and skills). However, as we will see, empirical studies have investigated both performance (e.g. Ahmadian, 2012) and learning (e.g. Li, 2013a, 2013b). Another caveat is that the matching of different types of individual difference variables on the one hand and variables relating to task condition and task complexity on the other may not be as transparent as predicted by the CH. For example, anxiety is an affective variable that is postulated to be drawn upon when tasks are performed under different conditions, but it is also possible to posit a logical link between anxiety and the procedural aspects of tasks, such as 'with or without planning time' (Mak, 2011) or 'with or without task structure' (Trebits, 2014). Nevertheless, the CH is the only theory that has attempted to map the complicated relationships among the three groups of task variables and foreground the importance of learner factors in accounting for variation of task performance in the triadic framework.

Language Aptitude

Overview

According to Carroll (1981), language aptitude is a componential construct that consists of three cognitive abilities, namely phonetic coding ability, language analytic ability (which entails grammatical sensitivity and inductive learning) and rote memory, which correspond to the learning of pronunciation, grammar and vocabulary respectively. Language aptitude is considered to be (1) domain specific in the sense that it is only important for learning a foreign language, (2) distinct from other individual difference variables such as motivation and anxiety, and (3) not subject to change. While some of these characteristics have been empirically confirmed, others remain controversial. Gardner and Lambert (1965) found that foreign language learners' scores on the subtests of the MLAT (Modern Language Aptitude Test) (Carroll and Sapon, 1959) loaded on different factors from their scores on the subtests of the PMA (Primary Mental Abilities) – a test of academic intelligence – suggesting that language aptitude involves distinct abilities for other academic subjects. However, in a meta-analysis on the construct validity of language aptitude (Li, 2016), aptitude was found to overlap with intelligence. The meta-analysis also found that aptitude was unrelated to motivation and negatively correlated with anxiety. Regarding whether aptitude is subject to change, there is no clear answer. While some studies found that learners with more language learning experience had higher aptitude scores than those with less experience (e.g. Einstein, 1980), it is possible that those learners with more experience may have had high aptitude to begin with. Therefore, there is a need for research to show (1) the higher scores of those with more experience are not due to their higher aptitude, and (2) the improvement in the same learners' aptitude scores is only attributable to study experience instead of maturation effects.

Language aptitude has been measured via test batteries consisting of multiple subtests that tap the three components, and the most influential test is the MLAT. The MLAT was validated with more than 5,000 foreign language learners and therefore has strong predictive validity, but it has been criticized on a number of accounts. First, it was validated in the 1950s using traditional audiolingual classes characterized by rote learning and mechanical practice. Thus, whether it is relevant to current meaning-oriented approaches that emphasize the importance of exposure to authentic linguistic materials and incidental learning is questionable. Second, it was developed based on observations of what happened in language classes, not on SLA theories, and therefore it lacks theoretical basis. Third, the five subtests do not correspond with the three hypothesized aptitude components, making it difficult to interpret the related findings. Fourth, these abilities are only important for learning the formal aspects of language and for learning language as discrete items and they do not account for how the pragmatic and contextual aspects of a language are learned (Skehan, 2002). Despite the criticisms levelled against the MLAT, it is still the most dominant aptitude test in current research. Recent developments include the Hi-LAB (High-Level Language Aptitude Battery Test) (Linck et al., 2014), which targets high-level learners, and tests of implicit aptitude (see Wen et al., in press).

Aptitude and TBLT

Aptitude research falls into two major categories: predictive and interactionist, and TBLT falls into the latter. Predictive research aims to investigate the associations between aptitude and learning rate regardless of learning conditions. Interactional studies, which are mainly based on Robinson's triadic framework (2011) and his Aptitude Complexes Hypothesis (2002), seek to ascertain whether the role of aptitude or different aptitude components varies as a function of different learning conditions such as the following four (see Robinson, 2002):

(1) short-term classroom treatments developed on the basis of a set of pedagogical constructs, such as deductive vs. inductive instruction (Hwu et al., 2014);
(2) laboratory-based treatments defined and operationalized in terms of the degree of explicitness such as explicit, implicit and incidental (de Graaf, 1997);
(3) instructional treatments involving interactional corrective feedback (CF) (Sheen, 2007);
(4) specific instructional approaches such as communicative teaching (Ranta, 2002) or immersion (Harley and Hart, 1997).

Among the four streams of research, (1) and (2) are not entirely conducted with instructional tasks; (3) concerns how focused tasks containing CF facilitates L2 development; and (4) caters to some of the fundamental principles of TBLT (Ellis, 2003): the primary focus is on meaning, the tasks relate to the real world and task outcomes are non-linguistic. The focus of this section is the studies in the third and fourth categories.

Aptitude and CF. As discussed in Chapter 2, there has been extensive research on the role of CF in SLA because feedback embedded within meaning-oriented tasks caters to an important principle of TBLT – focus on form (Ellis, 2003; Spada et al., 2014; Long, 2015). One line of feedback research concerns whether the effectiveness of feedback is constrained by individual differences in language aptitude. For example, Sheen (2007) conducted a classroom study where English as a Second Language (ESL) learners received recasts and metalinguistic feedback in learning English indefinite articles *a/an*. She reported that language analytic ability only predicted the effects of metalinguistic feedback, not those of recasts. Yilmaz (2013a) reported that explicit correction was more effective than recasts only when learners had high analytic ability. These two studies suggest that aptitude is more clearly relevant in explicit learning conditions.

However, two studies (Trofimovich, Ammar and Gatbonton, 2007; Sachs, 2010) that investigated computerized feedback reported that aptitude was also important in implicit learning conditions such as when no feedback or implicit feedback (recasts) was provided. However, the recasts in Trofimovich et al.'s study, which included a correct model regardless of whether the utterance was correct, are not really implicit. An explanation for Sachs' finding is that the instructional treatment required the learners to process the linguistic target to complete the task, which drew on their analytic ability.

The influence of aptitude in CF also depends on the nature of the linguistic target. Li (2013a, 2013b) investigated the three-way interaction between feedback type, language aptitude and the linguistic target. He found that in the learning of Chinese classifiers, analytic ability was correlated with the effects of recasts but not metalinguistic correction. In contrast, the data for perfective *-le* showed that the reverse was true: analytic ability predicted the effects of metalinguistic correction, but not recasts. Li attributed this discrepancy to the different linguistic properties of the two structures: the classifier is syntactically and semantically simple, so the provision of metalinguistic explanation levelled off the role of analytic ability. However, in the recast condition where metalinguistic explanation was unavailable, analytic ability came into play. The perfective *-le* is an opaque structure that involves complicated form-meaning mapping, and understanding the metalinguistic explanation poses challenges for analytic ability. When metalinguistic information was absent, the learners were unable to learn this complicated structure despite support in the form of recasts (which were not effective in learning the aspect marker). In this case, analytic ability did not play a role because learners were unable to learn the linguistic target by relying on their analytic and they were unable to benefit from the instruction.

Aptitude and meaning-focused language teaching. As mentioned, the MLAT – the most influential aptitude test – was validated in traditional audiolingual classes involving rote learning and mechanical drills, which led to questions regarding whether it is relevant in more meaning-oriented approaches such as communicative language teaching (CLT) or immersion. Ehrman and Oxford (1995) stated that the suspicion was unfounded because their study showed that aptitude was the strongest predictor of learning in foreign language classes which were 'heavily influenced by the communicative teaching trends' (p. 77). However, the classes that contributed the data were from state-funded intensive programmes that, as the researchers admitted, partly relied on drilling, and therefore the extent to which they were communicative is uncertain. Stronger support for the relevance of aptitude in CLT comes from Ranta's (2002) study, which showed that aptitude was significantly correlated with learning outcomes on multiple measures in classes judged to be communicative based on observations and interviews with the teachers. One caveat about Ranta's study is that aptitude was measured by means of a metalinguistic test, not a validated measure such as the MLAT, although first language (L1) metalinguistic knowledge has been shown to be related to language analytic ability (Alderson, Clapham and Stee, 1997).

Harley and Hart's studies (1997, 2002) show that aptitude was implicated in French immersion classes for young learners where the L2 was learned through exposure to the language. However, these studies reported an interaction between age and aptitude components, that is, the learners whose initial age of exposure was younger relied on memory and the later starters on analytic ability. Harley and Hart's findings demonstrate that (1) aptitude is not only important in form-based instruction but also in meaning-based instruction, (2) aptitude is drawn on by young learners (10th and 11th graders), and (3) learners of different age groups or at different stages of learning may draw on different aptitude components.

Summary

The three types of studies discussed allow us to reach the following tentative conclusions. First, the feedback research indicates that aptitude is more likely to be drawn on in tasks with an explicit focus on form, which disadvantages low-aptitude learners. However, because overall explicit feedback has proven more effective than implicit feedback (Ellis, Loewen and Erlam, 2006; Li, 2010), at least in the short term, it is advisable to make the corrective intention known to the learner when CF is used as a form-focusing device in TBLT. (See Chapter 2 for more detailed discussion of CF in TBLT.) Second, despite the need for more research, the findings to date suggest that aptitude is relevant in meaning-based instruction such as CLT and immersion classes. Furthermore, the finding that younger and older learners draw on memory and language analytic ability respectively suggests that a heavy dose of form-focused instruction is not ideal for young learners.

Working Memory

Overview

Working memory refers to the ability to simultaneously store and process incoming information. Baddeley (2007) proposed a componential model where working memory consists of a central executive and three slave systems – a phonological loop, a visuospatial sketchpad and an episodic buffer. The central executive coordinates different components, controls attentional shifts between meaning and form and between information retrieval and task performance, and inhibits irrelevant information (Miyake and Friedman, 1998; Juffs and Harrington, 2012). The phonological loop is responsible for storing and rehearsing verbal information. The visuospatial sketchpad deals with visuospatial information such as images, shapes and locations. The episodic buffer integrates information from the slave systems and long-term memory. Although working memory has been argued to be a component of language aptitude, research has shown that it is separate from aptitude (Li, 2017), probably because working memory is a domain-general cognitive device that is essential for learning in general, not just language learning.

Working memory has been measured in two ways – by using simple tasks that only tap the storage component and complex tasks that gauge both the storage and processing components (Conway et al., 2005). Simple tasks include the word span or digit span tests that require learners to repeat series of unrelated words, non-words or digits. A complex task typically consists of two parts: one that requires the learner to conduct some sort of information processing and one that requires the learner to recall an element of the item in question. For example, in a typical reading or listening span test, the learner reads or hears sentences divided into sets of two to seven sentences (called span sizes), judges their semantic or syntactic plausibility (e.g. 'The man standing in his office was bitten by a wall'), and at the end of each set, recalls the final word of each item in that set. In addition to listening or reading span tests, other measures of complex working memory that have been used in the literature include operation span tests that ask the learner to perform some mathematical computation and remember the letter or word that follows the equation in the item (e.g. '10/2 − 2 = 5 Q') and backward digit span tests where the learner is presented with sets of unrelated digits and asked to recall the digits in the reverse order. Forward digit span is considered a simple task and backward digit span a complex task.

Working Memory and TBLT

We will now consider the research that has investigated how working memory is implicated in task-based instruction. This research falls into two broad categories: studies examining the effects of working memory on task *performance* under different conditions and studies exploring how working memory mediates the *learning* that results from interactional feedback. These studies are based on three theoretical models of TBLT and SLA: the Limited Attention Capacity Hypothesis (LACH) (Chapter 3), the CH (Robinson, 2011) and the Interaction Hypothesis (IH) (Long, 1996, 2015) – see Chapters 2 and 3. The LACH posits a central role for working memory – a limited capacity device – in affecting learners' task performance, which is often assessed through measures of complexity, accuracy and fluency (CAF). The LACH draws on Levelt's (1989) theory of speech production, which holds that the production of spoken language undergoes three stages: conceptualizing the message, formulating the language representation (selecting the linguistic forms for the message) and articulating the message. In Levelt's model, the role of working memory is restricted to message conceptualization, and formulation and articulation are 'underground processes' (p. 22) that happen without awareness and that are beyond attention control. However, while it is perhaps true that formulation and articulation are automatic in L1 oral production, L2 oral production often relies heavily on attention control in all three phases, not only during message conceptualization. This suggests a more crucial role for working memory in L2 production.

The CH states that complex tasks involving resource-directing variables divert the learner's working memory resources to the 'input that complex tasks promote' (p. 19), and therefore the role of working memory should be more evident in complex tasks than simple tasks.

The theoretical justification for a mediating effect of working memory on the effects of interactional feedback can be found in the IH (Long, 1996, 2015). This emphasizes the role of selective attention when focusing on linguistic forms in meaning-oriented tasks as learners switch attention between form and meaning, necessitating a heavy reliance on working memory. In the case of CF, the learner must attend to and temporarily hold the information contained in the feedback and retrieve information from long-term memory in order to process the available negative and/or positive evidence. At the same time, the learner needs to maintain the continuation of the ongoing discourse. Some feedback types such as output-prompting feedback (Ellis, 2010) push the learner to modify their output, and this also requires working memory resources.

Working memory and task performance. Studies investigating the role of working memory in performing tasks have examined how it interacts with planning, learner proficiency, +/− task structure and task complexity. With regard to planning, researchers (R. Ellis, 2005) distinguish pre-task or strategic planning and within-task planning (i.e. whether learners are pressured to perform the task rapidly or are given time to think about the information to be communicated and the language needed).

Within-task planning, then, can be studied by determining the time learners are given to perform a task, as in Ellis and Yuan (2004). However, in many task-based studies within-task planning was either not controlled or there is a lack of information about whether or not it was controlled. Ahmadian (2012) is one of the few studies investigating the role of working memory in careful online planning. The study showed that working memory as measured through a listening span test was significantly correlated with accuracy and fluency but not complexity. Guará Tavares (2011) examined the effect of working memory in pre-task planning and found that in the planning condition, the learners with high working memory outperformed those with low working memory in terms of complexity and fluency but not accuracy. Working memory did not affect the task performance of the no-planning group. One problem with this study, however, is that the working memory was measured using a speaking span test where the learners were asked to create grammatically and semantically acceptable sentences with given words, which might be considered more like a speaking test than a memory test. Also, there was no information about whether and how online planning was restricted.

These findings are derived from separate studies conducted in different settings and using varying methods. One study that investigated both pre-task and unpressured within-task planning with learners from the same instructional context is Li and Fu (2018). The study found significant correlations between working memory (measured via an operation span test) and accuracy and fluency in the within-task planning condition, but no significant correlations were found for the pre-task planning condition. Also, the majority of the correlations for the within-task planners were positive while those for the pre-task planners were mostly negative, suggesting that larger working memory capacity did not help in pressured performance.

The role of working memory may also be constrained by learners' general L2 proficiency, as found by Gilabert and Munoz (2010). In this research, adult L2 English learners at a Spanish university were divided into high- and low-proficiency groups based on their scores on the Oxford Placement Test. They performed a video narrative task where they watched a video twice and retold the story with no pre-task planning and no time limit for task performance. Learners' working memory scores on a reading span test were found to be only predictive of lexical complexity for the high-proficiency learners' oral performance and there were no significant results for the low-proficiency group. One possible explanation is that at the lower-proficiency level it was the learners' linguistic proficiency rather than their working memory capacity that affected task performance.

Kormos and Trebits (2011) reported a study examining whether working memory had differential effects on structured vs. unstructured tasks. In the structured task, learners were asked to tell a story based on a set of cartoon pictures sequenced in the correct order. In the unstructured task, they had to invent a story based on a set of unrelated pictures. In both tasks, learners were allowed two minutes to plan before starting the narratives, but it is not clear whether there was a time limit for task performance. Significant effects for working memory were found for the structured task but not the unstructured task, but the relationship between working memory and task performance was non-linear. For example, learners with high working memory capacity outperformed those with lower memory abilities in terms of clause length, but the latter performed better in terms of subordination. The researchers speculated that although the structured task was assumed to be simpler, it may have turned out to be more cognitively demanding because the learners had no choice but to follow the provided storyline, which posed a greater challenge than in the unstructured task where they had more freedom to draw on their own linguistic resources. This might explain why working memory was only predictive of the performance under the structured task. The researchers further pointed out that working memory may not always be beneficial because those with higher working memory may try to attend to too many aspects of performance, which can have a detrimental effect on their performance.

Finally, there is one study (Crespo, 2011) that investigated the interaction between working memory and task complexity operationalized as +/− reasoning. Adult L1 Spanish EFL (English as a Foreign Language) learners performed two versions of the same decision-making task, the more complex version requiring learners to figure out the relationships between more elements, consider more factors when making decisions and have access to fewer resources. The study included measures of three aspects of working memory: phonological short-term memory, attention control – one function of the central executive – and working memory as a global construct. Surprisingly, neither working memory nor attention control showed strong correlations with performance in either of the two task conditions. Phonological short-term memory, however, was significantly correlated with a number of outcome measures for both the simple and complex tasks. The study failed to confirm Robinson's prediction that complex tasks are more likely to draw on working memory. It suggests that increasing task complexity along the resource-directing dimension may not increase the processing load. The study also suggests that despite the putative links between working memory and L2 task performance, phonological short-term memory, which has received little attention in task-based research, may prove to be critical in speech production.

To sum up, the studies on the impact of working memory on L2 task performance showed the following:

(1) Working memory seems to be implicated in unpressured performance during within-task planning, while its role during pressured performance after pre-task planning is inconclusive;
(2) the role of working memory is greater for advanced learners;
(3) tasks that provide a clear structure for performance may tax learners' working memory resources to a greater extent than tasks without a clear structure (contrary to what is commonly assumed);
(4) there may be a non-linear relationship between working memory and task performance and greater working memory capacity may have adverse effects in some task conditions;
(5) complex tasks along the resource-directing dimensions do not necessarily draw more on working memory than simple tasks;
(6) the role of phonological short-term memory in oral task performance may be of particular significance – see the section 'Working Memory and CF'.

Working Memory and CF

Mackey et al. (2002) was the first study to explore the role of working memory in noticing interactional feedback embedded in communicative tasks and facilitating L2 development. Thirty ESL learners whose L1 was Japanese were paired with native speakers of English and performed three communicative tasks during which the learners received recasts on errors relating to English question formation. The results showed that learners with high working memory capacities reported more noticing of feedback but that those with low working memory scores manifested greater development initially. However, those learners with high scores did better in the delayed post-test. Kim et al. (2015) confirmed Mackey et al.'s findings. Working memory was predictive of ESL learners' noticing of recasts and the effects of recasts on question formation in dyadic interaction. Kim et al. also examined the +/− reasoning variable, reporting that task complexity was not a significant predictor of the noticing of feedback or learning gains. However, more learners with high working memory in the complex task advanced to higher stages of question formation than in the simple task.

Révész (2012) reported a complex interface between working memory and outcome measures in a study of the effects of recasts on learning. The study included two measures of phonological short-term memory (digit span and non-word repetition) and one measure of working memory (reading span). The effects of the recasts were measured by means of an oral description task, a written production task and a grammaticality judgement task. It was found that phonological short-term memory was correlated with gains in accuracy in oral production and working memory with gains on the written tests. Révész argued that phonological short-term memory facilitates the acquisition of proceduralized/implicit knowledge whereas working memory is more useful for the development of declarative/explicit knowledge. The hypothesis about the differential roles of different types of working memory in facilitating the acquisition of different types of knowledge is important and needs to be investigated further.

Goo (2012) and Yilmaz (2013a) probed the interface between working memory and feedback type, both studies investigating both explicit feedback – metalinguistic feedback in Goo's study and explicit correction in Yilmaz's – and implicit feedback – recasts in both studies. However, they obtained different results. Goo found working memory to be a significant predictor of the effects of implicit feedback while Yilmaz reported it was correlated with the effects of the explicit feedback. Goo explained that the learners who received recasts utilized their working memory to notice the linguistic target, whereas the metalinguistic feedback did not pose attentional demands. Yilmaz also resorted to the concept of noticing when interpreting his results, arguing that the recasts in his study were not explicit enough to trigger the learners' working memory for conscious learning. However, an explanation is still needed for the conflicting findings for the explicit feedback types. One possibility is that the explicit feedback in Goo's study contained rule explanation, which does not require heavy use of the storage function, whereas the explicit feedback in Yilmaz's study took the form of explicit correction, necessitating storage of the corrections in order to induce the general rule.

Li (2013a, 2013b) investigated the interaction between working memory, feedback type and the nature of the linguistic target. Li reported that working memory was drawn upon when learners received metalinguistic feedback in learning both Chinese classifiers – a simple structure and the perfective *-le* – a complex structure, but not when they received recasts. However, one striking finding was that working memory was a positive predictor of the effects of the explicit feedback in the learning of classifiers but a negative predictor for the perfective *-le*. In other words, learners with high working memory capacity benefited less from metalinguistic feedback when learning a complex linguistic structure. Li referred to Newport's Less Is More Hypothesis (1990) when interpreting the results, that is, with high working memory capacities tend to store linguistic input as large chunks and ignore the detail, while those with smaller working capacities engage in deeper processing of the linguistic input. Li's studies again show the contingent relationship between cognitive resources and task conditions.

Summary

It seems that learners make heavy use of their memory resources when planning their speech during unpressured performance. Allowing pre-task planning may alleviate the burden on working memory. Furthermore, given the positive effect of unpressured online planning on task performance, allowing *both* pre-task planning and unpressured within-task planning can be expected to have even greater effects on task performance. One important implication from this line of research is that tasks that are assumed to be simple may turn out to be complex and consequently be more taxing on working memory resources. A further finding is that working memory is implicated in processing the online feedback embedded in communicative tasks. To date, however, there has been no study investigating the role of working memory in delayed, offline feedback.

Motivation

Overview

Motivation is considered a primary determinant of L2 success, which explains why it has been one of the most extensively studied individual difference factors. Dörnyei (2005) explained that the importance of motivation lies in that fact that it 'provides the primary impetus to initiate L2 learning and later the driving force to sustain the long and often tedious learning process' (p. 65). Motivation, according to Ellis' (2015b) synthesis, is a complex construct consisting of three components: (1) the reasons why a learner wants to learn an L2, (2) the effort one invests in the learning process and how it is influenced by the immediate context, and (3) the impact of the evaluation of the outcome and progress of learning on subsequent behaviour.

Of these three aspects of motivation, those in (1) constitute generalized, macro motives that relate to the general goal to be achieved and the general orientation towards the language, culture and speech community. These include the traditional integrative and instrumental motivation in Gardner's (1985) model, with the former referring to motives arising out of positive attitudes towards the speakers of the target language and the desire to integrate and identify with the community, and the latter to pragmatic motives such as getting a job or promotion. Those involved in (2) and (3) can be regarded as the specific, micro aspects of motivation that relate to the process of learning or the ongoing learning tasks.

The tripartite framework also incorporates the dynamic, situated model of motivation proposed by Dörnyei and his associates (Dörnyei and Ottó, 1998; Kormos and Dörnyei, 2004; Dörnyei, 2005; Dörnyei and Ushioda, 2009), which differs from the traditional static model, where motivation is viewed as a trait that correlates with the ultimate learning outcomes. In this model, motivation is (1) subject to temporal variation and (2) influenced by multiple contextual factors such as the school, the course, the class and the target language. Dörnyei's ideas are well represented in the so-called 'process model' (2005, p. 84) where different conglomerates of motives are drawn on at different stages of learning. At the pre-actional stage prior to the start of the learning process, learners' motivation is generated and the goal is set. This is called choice motivation, and it relates to learners' general dispositions or the macro factors in Gardner's model. During the actional stage or the learning process, the general motivation is influenced by various supporting factors as well as factors that inhibit distractions and supress unfavourable behaviours (e.g. off-task behaviours). These factors influence executive motivation. In the post-actional stage when the learning process/task is completed, the learner makes retrospective evaluations of what transpired during the learning process, and the results of the evaluation in turn affect subsequent actions. This concerns the attributional dimension of motivation.

One motivation theory proposed by Dörnyei (2005) that has had a profound influence on recent research is the L2 self system. This entails three dimensions of motivation: Ideal L2 self, ought-to L2 self and L2 learning experience. The Ideal L2 self refers to the motivation driven by the desire to reduce the discrepancy between one's current state and the future state to be reached (e.g. 'I often imagine myself speaking English fluently'). The ought-to L2 self concerns the motivation that prompts the learner to study an L2 to avoid the negative consequences (e.g. 'If I don't study English, others will be disappointed'). L2 Learning Experience relates to the motives associated with the immediate contexts of learning as determined by the curriculum, the course materials and the teacher (e.g. 'I always look forward to English classes'). Whereas the two types of self-related motives are associated with the macro dimensions of motivation drawn upon in the pre-actional stage, the motives relating to learning experience concern the micro aspects of motivation and are involved in the actional stage and the post-actional stage (although Dörnyei was not clear about which of the three types of motivation are important in the post-actional stage).

Motivation in TBLT

Task motivation encompasses all motives that may affect task performance or engagement at any of the three stages of a task cycle (pre-task, main task and post-task). It will be influenced by both general motives such as the Ideal Self and the Ought-to Self but in particular by the more specific motives relating to the task-as-workplan and task-as-process (see Chapter 1), such as attitudes towards the task, perceptions about the difficulty or complexity, how the task is implemented and the other participants, all of which are subsumed under the L2 Learning Experience component of the L2 Self System. In this section, we discuss what the little empirical research has shown about task motivation and how the concept of motivation has been investigated in relation to TBLT.

Dörnyei (2002) was one of the first to explore the multifaceted nature of task motivation in dyadic interaction. The study included measures of different levels of motivation, including generalized dispositions such as integrative and instrumental motivation, as well as motivation relating to the immediate contexts such as attitudes towards the course and the task. The outcome measure was task engagement, which was operationalized as the number of words and turns produced by the learners (forty-four Hungarian secondary school EFL students) in an argumentative task. It was found that all motivation variables except for integrative motivation were significantly correlated with task engagement. However, a different picture emerged when the learners were divided into two groups based on their task attitudes. Whereas both generalized and task-specific motives were predictive of high-task attitudes and learners' engagement, the engagement of learners with low-task attitudes was only predicted by course attitudes. This suggests that their lack of interest in the task was compensated for by their positive attitudes towards the course. The study also found that the task engagement of the learners with low-task attitudes was affected by their interlocutors' motivation. Taken together these results indicate that both task-specific and general motives contribute to task motivation and that task motivation is co-constructed.

Drawing on the same data as Dörnyei (2002), Kormos and Dörnyei (2004) found that although the learners' task attitudes predicted the quantity of their oral production (number of words and turns), this factor did not have a positive effect on the quality (the linguistic accuracy and complexity) of their production. Course attitudes were found to be significantly correlated with both quantitative and qualitative aspects of production. In a study by Al Khalil (2011), learners' general motivation measured by Gardner's Attitude/Motivation Test Battery (AMTB) (1985) was significantly correlated with the CAF of the oral production of forty-four L2 Arabic learners in the United States when engaged in dyadic communication with a native speaker. Integrative motivation was significantly correlated with the noticing of recasts, an index of task engagement. These two studies seem to indicate that task-specific motivation affects task engagement, and that more general types of motivation may affect both task engagement and the linguistic aspects of task performance. Following Dörnyei and Ushioda (2009), we can suggest motivation is best conceived as not directly related to achievement but as the antecedent of action that may have indirect effects on achievement. It would follow that measures of motivated behaviours such as task engagement are better measures of motivation.

Dembovskaya (2009) examined whether pre-task motivation-enhancing strategies lead to more positive perceptions of learners' task experience and whether pre-task cognitive strategy training improves students' task performance in terms of the CAF of their oral production. L2 French learners at a US university performed an information-gap task where they received a list of objects and clues found in the apartment of a crime suspect and were asked to work in groups to come up with a description of the suspect. To motivate one group of learners the teacher informed them about the value of the task (e.g. by telling them it would help them improve their communicative competence), enhanced their interest (e.g. by telling students that other students had performed the task and found it enjoyable) and promoted their self-confidence (e.g. by telling students that they could do it well). The students in the other group were equipped with the linguistic and strategic tools needed to complete the task, such as activating their schematic knowledge and informing them what information to look for to identify a suspect. The results showed that the group that received the pre-task motivational instruction perceived the task to be more interesting and valuable and themselves as more autonomous than the groups that did not receive motivational training, but the finding was only true of Year 2 students, not Year 3 students. Also, there was no difference in the two groups' performance of the task. Noteworthy is the fact that although the pre-task phase can be thought of as corresponding to the pre-actional stage in Dörnyei's process model as it relates to so-called 'choice motivation', the pre-actional stage in Dörnyei's conceptualization concerns L2 learning in general and therefore is seen as involving generalized motives. In this study, the pre-actional stage concerns a task and, consequently, the choice motivation that the learners received training for relates more clearly to task-specific motivation.

Jauregi et al. (2012) investigated whether learners' motivation can be improved through authentic, video-web communicative tasks. A group of L2 Dutch learners in Czech attended three 30-minute virtual interaction sessions with some Dutch pre-service language teachers. A thirteen-item questionnaire was utilized to measure different dimensions of motivation – attitudes towards interacting with native speakers, attitudes towards the course and attitudes towards the L2 culture. Significant effects were found and the effects were more prominent for the beginner group than the more advanced learners. What is unique about this study is that motivation was examined as a dependent variable that served as the 'effect' rather than 'cause', and it (both integrative motivation relating to the culture and speech community and more specific motivation relating to the course) was found to be improved through task-based interaction.

One commonality between these two studies is that learners' motivation seems to more easily influenced at the beginning stage of L2 learning than at more advanced stages. One possible explanation is that the attitudes and perceptions of more advanced learners about the learning process or tasks are entrenched and not easily swayed. It can also be speculated that learners that choose to proceed to higher stages of learning are more motivated to begin with. In any case, it would seem more important to enhance learners' motivation at the beginning stages of learning, so the interface between motivation and learner proficiency seems to be a promising area of research.

Summary

The few studies that have investigated task motivation show that it is a dynamic, complex and multi-componential construct. It consists of motives relating to different facets of the learning task, including general learning goals, course motivation and motives to do with the performance of the task per se. These motives have been found to be significant predictors of learners' task engagement and performance. Pre-task motivational strategies can enhance learners' motivation to perform a task while participation in meaning-oriented tasks can improve learners' course and integrative motivation. Finally, initiatives to increase learners' motivation seem to work better for low-level learners than high-level learners, suggesting that practitioners should make a special effort to stimulate and maintain beginning L2 learners' motivation when implementing TBLT.

Motivation is one of the most promising areas of TBLT research and Robinson's (2011) triadic framework provides a useful framework for so doing. For example, while increasing the cognitive demands of a task may enhance learners' task performance, increasing task complexity beyond a certain threshold may have a harmful effect on learners' motivation, which may in turn have adverse effects on their task performance and engagement. Second, with regard to the variables relating to task condition, research on whether and how factors pertaining to participatory structure and participant characteristics affect motivation may provide valuable insights for the implementation of TBLT. For example, Dörnyei's (2002) finding that learners' motivation was affected by their partners' motivation suggests that it is advisable to pair up learners' with different levels of motivation. However, Dörnyei and Kormos (2000) found that the relationship between task participants was predictive of task engagement when the task was performed in their L1 but not when the task was performed in the L2. This suggests that participants' relationships may not be as important as teachers have assumed but clearly more research is needed. Third, it is surely important to examine how motivation in contrast to and in combination with other individual difference factors affects task performance but to the best of our knowledge, there has been no research in this regard.

Anxiety

Overview

Horwitz, Horwitz and Cope (1986) defined anxiety as 'the subjective feeling of tension, apprehension, nervousness, and worry associated with an arousal of the autonomic nervous system' (p. 125). Three types of anxiety have been identified in the literature: trait anxiety, state anxiety and situation anxiety (Ellis, 2015b). Trait anxiety is a personality variable that refers to the general disposition, state anxiety relates to one's emotional condition at a particular moment and situation anxiety is associated with what one experiences in particular contexts. Trait anxiety accounts for interpersonal variation, that is, certain individuals are inherently more anxious than others. State and situation anxiety can be considered as intrapersonal variables in the sense that the same individual may experience different levels of anxiety at varying moments in a particular situation and in different situations. Language learning anxiety is a type of situation anxiety, and it occurs when a leaner produces or comprehends an L2. Horwitz et al. (1986) argued that language learning anxiety is principally derived from three sources: spontaneous communication, fear of negative evaluation and test anxiety. In L2 research, anxiety has been by default been associated with speaking, and measures of anxiety – typically questionnaires – primarily consist of speaking-related items (Phillips, 1992; Aida, 1994), although anxieties for other skills such as listening (Elkhafaifi, 2005), writing (Cheng, Horwitz and Schallert, 1999) or reading (Saito, Horwitz and Garza, 1999) have also been investigated. Furthermore, anxiety can be debilitative or facilitative, that is, while too much anxiety may have a negative influence on task performance or learning outcomes, a certain amount of anxiety may play a positive role. However, the distinction has not received much attention in empirical research.

In general, anxiety has been found to have negative effects on language learning (e.g. Ewald, 2007), which is in line with the harmful effect of anxiety on general academic performance ($r = -0.25$), according to a meta-analysis of 126 studies (Seipp, 1991). Tobias (1985) attributed the adverse effect of anxiety to cognitive interference, that is, anxiety-prone learners have to split their cognitive resources between task-relevant and task-irrelevant processes, thereby affecting their task performance. Drawing on Tobias's model,

MacIntyre and Gardner (1994) posited that anxiety causes interference at all three stages of learning: (1) when learners receive linguistic input, (2) when learners try to organize and store input, and (3) when learners are required to produce previously learned material. MacIntyre and Gardner developed the Input, Processing and Output Anxiety (IPOA) scale to measure the types of anxiety for the three stages of learning, with six items for each of the three stages. Theoretically sound as it might be, some of the items in the questionnaire do not seem to be clear measures of the three types of anxiety. For example, the items for input and processing are not clearly distinguishable, and one item in the output section is about test anxiety. Finally, while the mainstream view is that anxiety is a cause for low achievement, Sparks and Patton (2013) contended that it is the consequence of learning difficulties or lack of aptitude.

Anxiety and TBLT

The research on the role of anxiety in TBLT has revolved around three themes. One is the correlation between anxiety and task complexity. As discussed, the CH (Robinson, 2011) predicted that stronger correlations between anxiety and task performance can be expected when task complexity is increased along either resource-directing or resource-dispersing dimensions. Put in another way, as the processing demands of tasks increase, the negative impact of anxiety becomes more evident. A second line of research has focused on whether learners' anxiety levels vary as a function of the modality of interaction. For example, computer-mediated (CM) task-based instruction may alleviate learners' anxiety in the absence of the pressure and interaction demands that characterize face-to-face communication. A third stream of research focuses on the mediating effects of anxiety on the learning that results from CF provided in communicative tasks. In the following, we discuss these studies in more detail.

Task complexity. There have been two studies investigating the correlations between anxiety and the resource-directing variable of 'with or without reasoning demand'. In Robinson's (2007c) study, forty-two L1 Japanese university EFL students formed twenty-one dyads, each performing three narrative tasks at different levels of reasoning demand. Each dyad was given a set of jumbled pictures. One learner narrated the story based on the sequence he/she decided on and the other put the pictures in the sequence based on the speaker's narrative. Anxiety was measured using MacIntyre and Gardner's (1994) IPOA scale. Output anxiety was found to be negatively correlated with syntactic complexity, and with the increase of task complexity the correlations became stronger. However, one interesting finding that was not discussed in detail is that processing anxiety was significantly and positively correlated with the accuracy of the production under the simple task condition.

Kim and Tracy-Ventura (2011) examined the mediating role of anxiety in affecting the learning of the English past tense morphology under three task conditions that differed in terms of the presence of reasoning demand (simple vs. complex) and number of elements (complex vs. more complex). The study involved 128 Korean EFL learners who performed four dyadic interaction tasks within a two-week period. The researchers found that the learners with low anxiety (measured through a six-item questionnaire) outperformed their high-anxiety peers in all task conditions. They concluded that there was no interaction between anxiety and task complexity because the role of anxiety did not vary across task conditions.

Whereas these two studies concern a resource-directing variable that involves information manipulation, Trebits (2014) examined a resource-dispersing variable relating to the procedural dimension of task complexity: single vs. dual task. In this study, which is based on the same data as Kormos and Trebits (2011) (discussed in the section on 'Working Memory and TBLT'), the learners performed a cartoon description task where they told a story following a given sequence, and a picture description task where they told a story based on unrelated pictures that must be sequenced logically during the narrative. The cartoon task was easier in terms of content organization than the picture task – a dual task condition where the learners had to attend to both content organization and language formulation (selection of linguistic forms). However, the author argued that the cartoon task was more challenging in terms of language formulation than the picture task because the former required the learners to select linguistic forms to match the prescribed content while the latter allowed learners the flexibility of tailoring the content to match their linguistic repertoire. As in Robinson (2007c), anxiety was measured via the IPOA battery. It was found that: (1) in the cartoon task, processing anxiety correlated positively with lexical and syntactic complexity, and (2) in the picture task, output anxiety correlated negatively with accuracy.

As can be seen, it is difficult to draw unequivocal conclusions about the interface between anxiety and task complexity due to the conflicting findings, which in turn may have resulted from the methodological differences between the studies. However, these studies did show some interesting patterns. First, anxiety does have some negative effects on task performance and L2 development. As Robinson (2007a) and Trebits (2014) showed, it had a negative impact on task performance, particularly in complex tasks. Kim and Tracy-Ventura (2011) showed that low-anxiety learners consistently outperformed high-anxiety learners while learning the English past tense. Second, it would seem that anxiety may be facilitative of some aspects of oral production in simple tasks where the burden of content organization is alleviated and where anxiety may serve as an impetus for more attention to the linguistic aspects of their task performance. This is evidenced by the finding in both Robinson and Trebits's studies that significant, positive correlations were found for anxiety in the simple task conditions. Third, Kim and Tracy-Ventura found that low-anxiety learners outperformed high-anxiety learners in both simple and complex task conditions. However, the data also showed an advantage for complex tasks in comparison with simple tasks in enhancing L2 development regardless of anxiety – a finding that was not discussed due to the focus of the study. This raises the question of whether priority should be given to the effectiveness of instruction or the concern over the possible negative consequence of incurring more anxiety by using complex tasks.

Task modality. Computer-mediated (CM) communication in the form of text chat has been assumed to be effective in easing learners' anxiety in comparison with face-to-face communication because of the opportunity for more online planning and lack of requirement for public performance in the former mode. However, Baralt and Gurzynski-Weiss (2011) showed that there was no difference between the two modes of communication in terms of the amount of anxiety the learners experienced. What is unique about this study is that it examined state anxiety, that is, whether there was any change in learners' anxiety measured during and after task performance. Twenty-five fourth-semester Spanish learners from a large public university in the United States performed an information-gap task where they engaged in dyadic interaction with a native-speaker interlocutor in CM and face-to-face communication. The results revealed no difference in the learners' anxiety between the two modes of communication either during or after task performance. The researchers explained that this might be because the novelty of engaging in online chat in the foreign language led to anxiety levels comparable to face-to-face communication. While this stands to reason, an alternative speculation is that the study happened in a laboratory setting that did not require public performance, which is often the direct cause of anxiety.

In another study, Satar and Ozdener (2008) compared the effects of text and voice chat on the development of Turkish EFL learners' oral proficiency and on learners' anxiety. Ninety high school students were divided into three groups: text chat, voice chat and control.

The learners in the experimental groups were paired up and performed two tasks in each of four treatment sessions. The task types included information gap, problem-solving, jigsaw and decision-making. The control group followed the normal curriculum and did not receive any treatment. The learners also answered the Foreign Language Classroom Anxiety Scale (FLCAS) anxiety questionnaire (Horwitz et al., 1986) before and after performing the tasks. The results showed that (1) both chat groups outperformed the control group in their speaking performance as a result of the treatment, and (2) the text chat group showed significantly lower anxiety scores after the treatment, although the anxiety level of the voice chat group was also reduced (the change was non-significant). The researchers explained that online chat led to lower anxiety because it was a secure environment without peer pressure. However, surprisingly, the control group showed consistently higher anxiety scores than both experimental groups both before and after the study even though they did not participant in any chat sessions.

In these two studies, interaction happened either between a native-speaker interlocutor and a learner or between two learners. A recent study by Côté and Gaffney (2018) examined the impact of anxiety on learners' public performance in front of a large group. The researchers claimed that this setting is more representative of a real classroom and therefore the findings have higher ecological validity. The study involved sixty-one beginning learners of French at a Canadian university who completed a grammar and vocabulary lesson followed by two production activities in a face-to-face mode and a CMC (computer-mediated communication) mode. The learners also answered a revised version of the FLCAS questionnaire. The study revealed that the learners experienced significantly less anxiety and produced significantly more turns and words in the CMC mode than the face-to-face mode.

Overall, the limited research on the effects of modality of instruction delivery on learner anxiety show that learners indeed suffer from lower anxiety in the CMC mode compared with the face-to-face mode. However, the outcomes investigated in the studies relate primarily to the process aspects of task-based instruction, such as the number of words produced, and more research is necessary whether anxiety affects the product dimensions or learning gains in the two modes of instruction in different ways.

Task-based feedback. There have been two studies on the mediating role of anxiety in affecting the effectiveness of CF embedded in communicative tasks (Sheen, 2008; Rassaei, 2015). In Sheen's study, sixty-one learners from a large ESL programme in a US community college were divided into two groups: recast and control, each subdivided into high and low based on their anxiety, which was measured through a six-item questionnaire. The recast group performed two narrative tasks, each including a practice stage where they worked in groups, followed by a reporting stage where each student produced a few sentences before passing the speaker role to another group member. The teacher corrected their errors on English articles *a/the* by using recasts. The results revealed that low-anxiety learners not only benefited more from recasts in learning the target structure but also produced more modified output (responses after feedback) than high-anxiety learners.

Rassaei carried out a study with Iranian EFL learners from a private language teaching institute following Sheen's procedures, but the researcher included two types of feedback: recasts and metalinguistic correction, aiming to see whether anxiety has differential impacts on the effects of the two types of feedback. The study found that high-anxiety learners benefited more from recasts, and low-anxiety learners benefited from both recasts and metalinguistic feedback. However, a closer inspection of the results showed that in the recast group, high- and low-anxiety learners were similar in their scores across all three tests of treatment effects, but in the metalinguistic group, low-anxiety learners performed consistently better than high-anxiety learners. It would seem that anxiety did not play a role when recasts were provided – a finding that is different from Sheen's finding that anxiety played a negative role in affecting the effects of recasts. However, one piece of useful information to take away from this study seems to be that metalinguistic feedback – an explicit form of correction – does have an adverse effect on learning outcomes.

Summary

To conclude this section, we would like to point out that the amount of research on the role of anxiety is in disproportion to its importance given its putative connections with TBLT. The limited research seems to suggest that anxiety is unfavourable for speech performance under complex task conditions, and that there is a possibility that simple tasks favour anxious learners by freeing up their cognitive resources and diverting their attention to the linguistic aspects of their performance. In terms of its role in affecting the learning of new linguistic knowledge, anxiety seems to have a harmful effect, regardless of task complexity. The research on task modality suggests that in laboratory settings text-based CM interaction seems to lessen learners' anxiety compared with face-to-face interaction, and that within CMC, text chat has a positive effect in reducing anxiety compared with voice chat. The research on CF indicates that explicit feedback in the form of metalinguistic correction disadvantages highly anxious learners while mixed findings are obtained for whether anxiety affects the effects of recasts.

Final Comments

In general, the research on aptitude was conducted to ascertain whether aptitude mediates the effects of different instructional treatments or whether it is implicated in different learning conditions. The research has shown that traditional aptitude is a set of cognitive abilities that are most likely drawn on in tasks with an explicit focus on form. One promising area of research that has been recently initiated is identifying those abilities that are important in implicit or unconscious learning (Granena, 2013, 2015), which TBLT is claimed to facilitate. It would be interesting to ascertain whether a task-based approach draws more on implicit aptitude than traditional aptitude, which has been found to be relevant to explicit learning.

The research on working memory explored whether it affected learners' performance under different task conditions and how it mediated the effectiveness of interactional feedback. One general finding supported by several studies is that the role of working memory is more evident in unpressured performance where learners have opportunities to plan the content and language of their speech. The role of working memory in mediating the effects of CF has been attributed to its function in noticing the corrective force of feedback. One objective of this stream of research should be to identify tasks that facilitate task performance or L2 learning but do not pose heavy processing demands on working memory resources. For tasks that enhance task performance or learning outcomes but are taxing on working memory resources, it is important to find ways to support learners by alleviating the processing load.

The few studies of task motivation investigated the predictive power of generalized and task-specific motives for task engagement and performance and ways to improve task motivation. Unlike the research on the two cognitive variables, studies on motivation are less uniform and the findings are less robust, reflecting in part the lack of theorization about its role in L2 acquisition (Dörnyei, 2005; Ellis, 2015b) and the uncertainty over the nature, composition and measurement of the construct. However, as pointed out, the investigation of task motivation may provide important insights, given that students' lack of motivation has been considered a major hindrance to the implementation of TBLT in some contexts – for example, in foreign language as opposed to L2 settings (Ellis, 2003).

The research on anxiety affords a complex, interesting picture that to some extent undermines the commonly held beliefs about this affective factor. For example, while it did have some adverse effects under some task conditions, there was also evidence for a possible positive effect for anxiety. One principle that should be adhered to is to (1) prioritize task or instruction type when facing the choice between tasks that enhance learning and those that cause less anxiety, but (2) find ways to adapt the aspects of the task or instruction that disadvantages highly anxious learners. For example, if complex tasks consistently show larger effects than simple tasks in improving learners' L2 knowledge for both high- and low-anxiety learners, as Kim and Tracy-Ventura's (2011) data showed, then it would be advisable to use complex rather than simple tasks even though complex tasks may cause more anxiety. However, teachers then should take steps to reduce learners' anxiety by manipulating the procedural aspects of task, such as by allowing learners to plan before performing a task. However, to date, there has been no research on the role of anxiety in different planning conditions.

Finally, we would like to call for more research into the role of individual difference variables in affecting task performance and learning gains. It is a mistake in tacitly (and mostly) assuming that tasks work in the same way for all people, and this concern has been borne out by the limited research we synthesized in this chapter.

6 Educational Perspectives

Introduction

This chapter provides an overview of some key aspects of twentieth-century educational philosophy in relationship to contemporary task-based language teaching (TBLT) principles and practices. It constitutes a very different approach to the preceding chapters in Part II, which drew on theory and research in second language acquisition (SLA). As we noted in Chapter 1, the initial impetus for TBLT came from SLA but educational perspectives have increasingly informed developments, drawing attention to how general educational principles can shape TBLT and reinforce the perspectives offered by SLA.

Theories of experiential learning will be the focus of the chapter as these are particularly relevant to TBLT. The chapter begins by outlining key principles of TBLT as reference points for discussing experiential learning. Some key theories are then outlined and TBLT principles and practices are weighed against them to determine the extent to which the essential aspects of experiential learning theory have been addressed in the TBLT literature to provide an educational rationale for TBLT and point to possible directions for future work.

The first three principles form the foundation of TBLT in relation to other approaches to second language (L2) instruction:

1. *Learning by doing:* In TBLT, language learning takes place *through* task performance rather than *for* task performance. Language learning is seen primarily as an *incidental* process that takes place in line with learners' communicative needs.
2. *Individual development:* Learning takes place in line with learners' internal syllabuses. Tasks provide the space for learners to integrate task content and their own language resources. In TBLT, learners use their own language to successfully accomplish tasks in their own ways.

155

3. *Relevance:* Tasks present learners with real communicative demands. The abilities that are developed in connection with tasks are thus directly relevant to learners' communicative needs and their conceptions of what being proficient in a language involves.

In TBLT, the learner is thus the agent in the learning process, and teachers or course designers serve to facilitate this process through planning and implementation of learning opportunities. This process of facilitation typically involves additional principles by which learners' performance of tasks is optimized:

4. *Interaction:* Although not all target tasks involve interaction, TBLT provides ample opportunities for learners to negotiate meaning and develop shared understanding based on their own L2 resources. Interaction is a driving force in language acquisition (Long, 2015), and learners must be able to negotiate solutions to the range of tasks that they face *effectively* and *appropriately* (Ellis, 2003).
5. *Input-based tasks (listening, reading):* In addition to opportunities to perform interactive tasks, learners at different ages and proficiency levels can benefit from performing receptive tasks in which they are not *required* to produce language (Ellis, 2001, 2018a: Long, 2015; Shintani, 2016).
6. *Output-based tasks (speaking, writing):* Likewise, in addition to opportunities to perform interactive tasks, learners must have opportunities to produce extended discourse (Yule, 1997), test hypotheses and notice the aspects of language that connected discourse requires (Swain, 1995).
7. *Focus of form:* There is not a one-to-one relationship between task performance and language learning. Learners' attention must be drawn to forms that are difficult to acquire incidentally during the performance of communicative tasks (e.g. Long, 1991b, 2015; Ellis, Basturkmen and Loewen, 2002).
8. *Supporting performance:* Learners need opportunities to optimize their own task performance by being provided with time to plan and reflect on their performances as well as repeated opportunities to complete tasks and improve their performances (e.g. Skehan et al., 2012).
9. *Individual differences:* Learners have different aptitude, motivation and anxiety profiles. Optimizing the performance of learners with different learner profiles on tasks requires adjustments to task-based instruction (TBI) (Chapter 5; Robinson, 2011).

These nine principles illustrate the focus on the learner and the learning process in TBLT. These principles are consonant with twentieth-century educational philosophy and will be the focus of the present chapter. The chapter will begin with Dewey's (1913, 1938) theory of interest and effort in education and the ways in which TBLT is consistent with this theory. However, the roots of this theory stretch back to the eighteenth century (see Samuda and Bygate, 2008; Long, 2015, for reviews). Subsequent developments in educational theory related to Dewey's work will then be outlined and applied to contemporary TBLT practices. Recent empirical work will then be summarized that points to was of expanding TBLT practice in line with the educational theories discussed.

Learning by Doing

Experiential learning involves learners acting on and refining what they know in order to achieve specific outcomes and objectives (TBLT Principle 1). In particular, the aim of instruction is to develop the learner's ability to independently observe and evaluate immediate conditions and organize their own means to achieve their purposes within a given context (Dewey, 1938, p. 28) (TBLT Principle 2). In designing instructional materials, it is thus essential that educators tap into the possibilities inherent in ordinary experience (p. 89) and make learning relevant to learners (TBLT Principle 3). This section will provide an overview of Dewey's theory of developing experience. In this theory, affect and cognition are integrated and inseparable. As Swain (2013) points out, this is also the case in Vygotsky's sociocultural theory of mind (1978, 1987, 2000; Chapter 4). Subsequent work has tended to address one dimension or the other, however, and the cognitive dimension of learning has been the dominant concern in TBLT.

Dewey (1938) argues that for meaningful growth to occur, the learner must be the agent in the learning process. This requires *intelligent effort* on the part of the learner (p. 69). Intelligent effort, according to Dewey, involves learners initiating activity, taking control of it, and understanding the consequences of different behavioural alternatives in achieving different ends. Dewey argues that to generate intelligent effort, learners must feel personally involved in the purposes which direct their actions (1938, p. 67) and have a sense of responsibility for the outcome of learning activities (pp. 53–61). According to Dewey, a genuine purpose always begins with an impulse or a desire on the part of the learner, and the intensity of this drive will ultimately determine the strength of the effort that the learner puts forth in transforming this impulse or desire into a plan of action and a method for achieving its fulfilment. Impulse and desire give impetus to action, but intelligent effort directs it towards an end (p. 69).

Dewey (1913) elaborates the role of interest and effort in the learning process. In doing so, he distinguishes interest from feeling. Dewey defines *feelings* as mental states that do not lead to further action on the part of the learner, and he argues that it is a mistake to orient instruction towards learners' feelings. For example, activities might amuse learners for a while (e.g. hearing anecdotes or jokes, watching movies, listening to popular songs), and learners may enjoy the diversions that these activities provide, but this type of feeling of enjoyment quickly dissipates and learners immediately require new stimuli from the teacher to maintain their attention. According to Dewey, instructional activities aimed only at pleasing or amusing learners have no real educational value. In contrast, Dewey argues that the essential characteristic of educational activities is that they generate interest on the part of learners. Dewey uses *interest* in a technical rather than colloquial sense. According to Dewey, it has two essential characteristics. First, interest, in contrast to feeling, relates to an object external to the learner and generates *action* on the part of the learner aimed at achieving that object. In other words, we are interested *in something*, and this object of interest channels our attention and our subsequent behaviours. Second, interest, in Dewey's sense, is always personal. Any object of interest, by definition, must be perceived by the learner to be connected with his or her sense of self or well-being in some way. In other words, we have some *personal investment* in anything that we are genuinely interested in. For Dewey, interest is the driving force behind intelligent effort on the part of the learner, and effective instruction *must* tap into learners' current interests and build on learners' current knowledge and abilities if meaningful development is to result.

According to Dewey, interest, which is embodied and personal, generates *intelligent effort* in the form of *unified activity* (i.e. activity in which means and ends are suffused and transform one another). In a unified activity, learners allocate attention unreservedly and are absorbed in the activity which drives them. There is no distinction between means and end. Rather than having to push themselves to continue, they have difficulty pulling themselves away. Thus, in Dewey's theory, interest is primary and intelligent effort in the form of unified activity on the part of the learner follows naturally. Two key questions remain. The first is how interest results in the development of learners' abilities, and the second is how interest might be generated in the types of learning tasks used in TBLT.

Regarding how interest relates to ongoing development, Dewey (1913) argues that interests become more complex and involve more factors as they take on a longer time span (e.g. an interest in causal debates in high school can lead to interest in dialectic methods in Plato and eventually to the study of the Ancient Greek language at university). For Dewey, the development of interest involves two processes: (1) a direct interest generates a range of indirect interests, and (2) these indirect interests eventually supplant or at least marginalize the original interest. In learning an L2, for example, a romantic attachment during an undergraduate study abroad programme (direct personal interest) might lead to the need to communicate in a foreign language (an indirect interest). This language ability might then lead to a subsequent internship in a company abroad after graduation, and the internship might in turn lead to a specialized degree in international business and formal study of the language, which has become an interest in itself. These qualifications might then lead to personal interest in the specialized target tasks required to secure a permanent position and promotion in a company abroad. This example illustrates Dewey's (1913) argument that learners' experience develops from an initial state of direct embodied interest which is driven by the learner's current impulses and desires. It is also associated with the learner's sense of self and well-being. The specialized interests associated with the learner's ultimate target language needs would not have existed without the learner acting on an initial personal drive.

This brings us to the question of how such embodied and personal interest might be engendered in the design of pedagogic tasks for TBLT. Dewey addresses this issue at the abstract level of the conditions that must be engendered in materials design. Concrete ways in which these principles might be operationalized in both the design and implementation of tasks in TBLT will be addressed in the section 'Personal Investment and TBLT'. Dewey (1913) argues that the subject matter of instructional activities must provide learners with a means of self-identification and generate self-initiated action. Other people play an important role in most learners' sense of self. Humans generally have a natural desire for intimate contact in the form of sympathy, approval and shared understanding when they interact with one another. Learners' social needs are also deeply suffused in the objects of their interests and often play a key role in the genesis of these interests. Dewey argues that learners are naturally interested in topics and content that create sympathy, approval and shared understanding with others. Social and emotional needs motivate learners' interest. And when the learner's social or emotional sense of self is invested in classroom work, the likelihood increases of their engaging in *unified activity* and putting forth *intelligent effort* in completing classroom activities.

The difficulty for the course designer is in tapping into the background experience of individuals and determining how this experience might be incorporated to drive the learning of new subject matter (Dewey, 1938, p. 75). Instructional materials must create conditions that incorporate previous experience and current interests and build on these experiences and interests to lead to new experiences (p. 80). However, current definitions of tasks in TBLT typically focus on the cognitive demands of performance and learners' allocation of attention during performance (TBLT Principles 4–9). Little work has been done to systematically address the issue of learners' interests in the sense the term is used in Dewey's theory of experience. Some researchers argue that if instruction is relevant to learners' L2 needs that interest will take care of itself (e.g. Long, 2015, p. 65). Others argue that the issue can be dealt with by selecting tasks and topics that are generally interesting to the population of learners in question (Prabhu, 1987; Yule, 1997; Ellis, 2003). Only recently has attention been devoted to ways of designing and implementing tasks to engage the learner socially and emotionally and generate personal investment in L2 task performance. Recent work on task engagement (e.g. Lambert, 2004, 2017; Aubrey, 2017a, 2017b; Butler, 2017b; Lambert, Philp and Nakamura, 2017; Stroud, 2017) begins to provide a systematic basis for addressing Dewey's notion of interest in TBLT. This work will be discussed later in this chapter, together with concrete ideas for how tasks might be designed and implemented to develop a personal investment in learning and engage learners socially and emotionally in the learning process.

The Affective Dimension of Learning by Doing

Maehr's theory of personal investment provides a basis for modelling the role that learners play in performing tasks in the TBLT classroom. Maehr's theory suggests that five classes of variables determine the meaning that classroom activities have for learners. Learners bring a range of motivational traits to the classroom that result from their previous experiences and the sociocultural context in which the programme is situated. While these traits may be amended over timescales of weeks, months or years, teachers are typically more concerned with how learners' motivational state can vary within the time period of a given lesson as a result of the instruction that they provide. In terms of the subconstructs of L2 motivation (see Kormos, Kiddle and Csizer, 2011 for a data-based discussion), relatively fixed motivational *traits* might include ideal L2 self, international orientation, intrinsic/instrumental goals for learning, peer pressure, parental

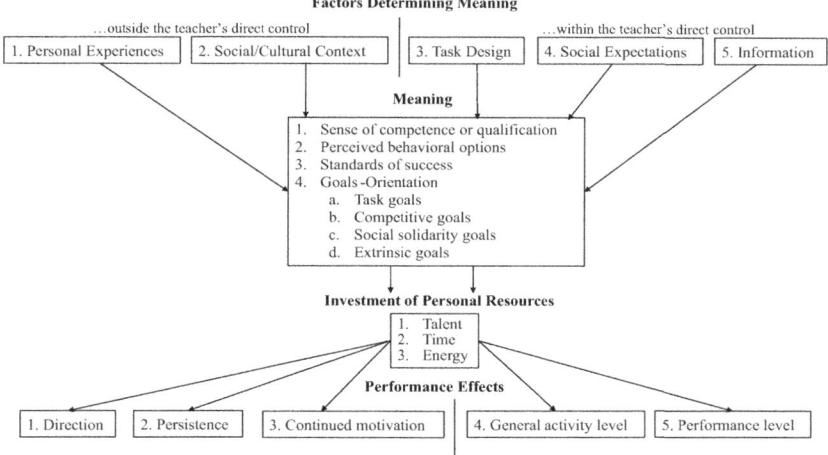

Figure 6.1 Maehr's theory of personal investment
Source: From Lambert (1998)

encouragement, technology, anxiety. Motivational *state* variables will depend on the immediate context but, on the other hand, might include learners' motivational intensity, their satiation control, their resourcefulness and their sense of self-efficacy.

The first two classes of variables at the top of Figure 6.1 might thus function as resources that can be drawn on in planning instruction rather than independent factors that can be manipulated in instructional design. The other three classes of variables at the top of Figure 6.1, however, are within the teacher's immediate control in planning and implementing instruction. The design of the tasks used in instruction, the social expectations established in the classroom and the information provided to learners can be modified, with direct effects on learners' performance during specific lessons.

All five classes of variables at the top of Figure 6.1 contribute to the *meaning* that instructional activities have for learners. Maehr defines *meaning* as a technical term, comprised of learners' (1) sense of competence, (2) perceived behavioural options, (3) standards of success, and (4) goal orientation (i.e. whether learners are trying to improve their ability to perform the activity, compete with one another, develop social solidarity or achieve some extrinsic goal such as a test score or a promotion).

The meaning that an activity has for learners will, in turn, determine learners' willingness to invest their personal resources into the performance of it. If an activity is meaningful for learners, they will be more willing to become involved in its performance in terms of voluntarily devoting their personal talents, time and energy into completing it. Thus, the learner will be more likely to complete the activity *well* rather than *well enough*.

Finally, personal investment in instructional activities on the part of the learner will have concrete performance effects. According to Maehr, the first three types in the bottom of Figure 6.1 are the direct result of learners' level of personal investment, and they are thus the best indications of it. These are: (1) learners' *direction* or their decision to work on the activity rather than to devote their attention to something else (e.g. their mobile phone or what their partner did over the weekend), (2) learners' *persistence* or their willingness to continue working on the activity for a longer period of time without the need for continual encouragement and support from the teacher (cf. Crookes and Schmidt, 1991), and (3) learners' *continued motivation* or the extent to which they are willing to revisit the activity in subsequent lessons.

Personal Investment and TBLT

In Lambert's (1998, 2004, 2017) adaptation of Maehr's theory of personal investment for TBLT, tasks are designed to incorporate learners' interests and sense of self and to use this experience to drive L2 use and build new experiences in the classroom. Lambert's work focuses on the respective benefits of tasks based on learner-generated content (LGC) and those based on teacher-generated content (TGC) in TBLT (see Lambert, 2017; Lambert and Zhang, 2019). In LGC tasks, the immediate classroom context creates the physical, social or emotional need that drives the language that learners use. Instead of exclusively relying on fixed content supplied by instructors and materials writers based on what teachers think learners will be interested in, tasks can also be designed to allow learners to generate *context-specific* content that is based on real experience. Specifically, Lambert argues that for learners to have a personal investment in L2 task performance, they must choose and discuss content that: (1) they think is genuinely interesting, (2) they genuinely want to share with the specific interlocutors they are working with on the task, and (3) they genuinely think these interlocutors will be interested in hearing. As argued later in this chapter, these three criteria might be argued to define the conditions for any authentic language use whether it takes place inside or outside of the classroom.

By designing tasks to tap into the real-life thoughts, experiences, activities and talents that interest learners and occupy their attention on a daily basis, all learners (even those who are not good at languages) have the opportunity to make a personal investment in classroom interaction. An example for lower-intermediate learners might be asking them to recommend local restaurants or other venues that they like, want to share, and think their partners might actually visit (Lambert, Gong and Zhang, in press). Another example for higher-intermediate learners might be choosing an anecdote about something that happened to them that they think is funny or interesting, want to share with the specific person they are working with, and think that this person will enjoy hearing (Lambert et al., 2017). Finally, an example for advanced-level learners might involve discussing unfortunate situations they have experienced and trying to arrive at an agreement on who is responsible (Lambert and Minn, 2007; Lambert and Zhang, 2019). Consistent effects for these LGC tasks on L2 use have been documented across task types and target languages. Before discussing these effects, however, the construct of personal investment must be disambiguated from related constructs in the TBLT literature.

Partially overlapping proposals for task selection and implementation include the relevance of tasks for learners in terms of the current or future needs (Long, 2015), the provision of background knowledge in conjunction with task performance (Robinson, 2011), learners' familiarity with task content (Prabhu, 1987; Ellis, 2003) and learners' control over task content (Foster and Skehan, 1996). Personal investment in the sense described implies a degree of each of the variables. However, it is a distinct construct in that none of these variables, individually or in combination, necessitate personal investment. For example, personal investment in the form of LGC might be argued to imply a degree of *relevance* to learners as their language use is connected with their own experience. However, something may be relevant to learners' current or future external needs for the language, but meet no urgent need (physical, social or emotional) within the immediate context. An example might be the need to translate user manuals for new machinery or summarize L2 economic news articles in the first language (L1). These were determined by a needs analysis in Japan to be tasks that Japanese English majors at a public university are likely to have to complete if they enter trading companies after graduation (Lambert, 2010). However, tasks connected with these needs generated very little interest or effort on the part of learners. It is possible, of course, that learners' experience would grow to include these indirect interests eventually but learner external needs as determined by

Lambert's needs analysis may have been too distant from learners' current interests and social and emotional needs to generate personal investment in task performance.

Personal investment through LGC will also imply a degree of *background knowledge* related to task content (Robinson, 2011). Again, however, background knowledge does not imply personal investment. For example, it is possible for a learner to have grown up with a father who was very interested in golf or in fishing. This might provide her with a degree of background knowledge about these activities and what is involved. This knowledge may in turn facilitate her development of a conceptual framework for completing tasks associated with these activities in the classroom. As useful as this background knowledge might be in facilitating her language use on tasks in other ways, however, it does not imply that the learner would have any more interest in completing a task connected with the topic of fishing or golf than she would in completing a task that she knew nothing at all about. In fact, she may be more interested in the new topic.

Finally, *familiarity* with and *control* over task content represent similar cases. In a typical map task which requires learners to describe routes and draw them based on the descriptions (see Prabhu, 1987; Yule, 1997; Long, 2015 for examples), a materials writer might ask students to describe the real routes that they take to and from school every day rather than narrate a random route on a generic map (e.g. Foster and Skehan, 1996). The task will certainly be more *familiar* to learners, and it may also allow them more freedom to structure task content and encode language in line with their current L2 resources. However, this familiarity and control is unlikely to impact learners' interest or personal investment in the performance of the task in the sense outlined. Familiarity in itself does not create any interest or urgency in the outcome of the task. Learners are unlikely to have any more interest in telling someone about their route to school than they would in discussing a random route on a generic map – nor is their interlocutor any more interested in hearing about it. As Paradis (2004) points out, in such pedagogic tasks learners are more motivated by the fact that it is their turn to speak rather than by any physical, social or emotional need for their partner to successfully understand the route that they are describing. In contrast, if learners are asked to think of a restaurant or club in the city that they frequent and really like, want to introduce to the specific interlocutor(s) they were working with for a task and think that these interlocutor(s) may actually visit, they may be more likely to have a physical, social and emotional need to ensure the semantic, pragmatic and interpersonal effectiveness of the conversation.

Personal Investment and L2 Performance

Initial empirical research on the effect of personal investment on L2 use during task performance has produced promising results. Lambert's early work on the topic (1997, 2002, 2004) suggested that content produced by learners in earlier tasks in a given sequence may function as learner-generated input to subsequent tasks and thus promote learners' personal investment in the learning process. Lambert and Minn (2007) subsequently investigated how a range of task types in different discourse genres (instruction, narrative and opinion), each designed to contrast learner-generated and teacher-generated task content, affected the number of utterances that served to expand on the semantic content of the tasks as well as the range of lexical items the learners employed. This study was replicated with L2 speakers of Chinese (Lambert and Zhang, 2019) using a broader range of performance variables, including engagement in L2 use, speech processing and clause combination strategies. It was found LGC tasks resulted in more engagement, more fluent speech processing and the use of devices which create pragmatic meaning (see Tables 6.1 to 6.3), but that TGC tasks resulted in more clause combination and focus on the language code. Finally, Lambert et al. (2017) compared thirty-two learners' performances on narrative tasks in which the solution to a culturally relevant and familiar problem was explained based on

Table 6.1 Instruction task discourse based on LGC

Original Chinese	English translation
啊。你不用粉底吗？	Ah. Don't you use foundation?
对对对。	Correct, correct.
哇!	Wow!
如果放粉底，我觉得心里有点儿别扭。不太习惯。	If I put foundation, I feel a bit awkward. Not used to do that.
啊，皮肤不能呼吸的感觉？	Ah, the feeling that the skin can't breathe?
***	***
大概用多长时间？	How long will it take?
大概用二十分钟就够了。	About twenty minutes is enough.
哇，很快。	Wow, very quick.
嗯，很快。我不知道怎么化妆。（笑）	Well, pretty fast. I don't know how to make up. (laughter)
没关系。很美。（笑）	It doesn't matter. You are very beautiful. (laughter)
不如你呀。（笑）	Not as good as you. (laughter)

Table 6.2 Narrative task discourse based on LGC

Original Chinese	English translation
欸，口水掉在那个馅儿里边？ 对对对对对。然后我妈妈说，哇，你的口水在里面！然后我妈妈说，啊，一点点口水没问题。（笑）	Eh, your saliva fell into the stuffing? Yes, yes, yes, yes, right. My mother said, 'Wow, your saliva is inside!' Then my mother also said, 'Ah, a little bit of saliva, no problem.' (Laughs)
嗯，然后拌完水饺，就煮嘛。煮完，先煮的给姥爷。姥爷，我帮忙，这个水饺好不好吃？姥爷说，比一般的更好吃.（笑）（笑）有那个口水的效果。 可能。	Well, having finished mixing the dumpling stuffing, we boiled dumplings. My grandpa was invited to eat first. I asked him, 'Grandpa, I helped with making dumplings, do they taste good?' He answered, 'They are more delicious than the usual ones.' (Laughs) (Laughs) That's the effect of the dribble. Possible.

Table 6.3 Opinion task discourse based on LGC

Original Chinese	English translation
留学的时候很孤单嘛, 不是吗？	It's very lonely when one studies abroad, isn't it?
留学就可以…	Do you mean when one studies abroad, they then can . . .
然后，有了帅哥就…	And there's this handsome guy, then. . .
可以吗？	Is that ok?
不是，我没有说可以，可是，我觉得没办法。	No, I didn't say that it's okay to have an affair, but I feel it is simply one of those things.

picture strips supplied by the researcher with those in which they were asked to select a problem that: (1) they had actually experienced and solved in the past, (2) they felt was genuinely funny or interesting and wanted to share, and (3) they thought their partner would be genuinely interested in hearing. Results showed that learners tended to speak more, elaborate more, clarify more and support one another more through back-channelling behaviour when discussing tasks that created a personal investment in the learning process through LGC.

The examples in Tables 6.1, 6.2 and 6.3 serve to illustrate the type of personally invested discourse that occurs as a result of LGC across three discourse genres (instruction, narration, opinion). The samples are taken from Lambert and Zhang (2019). They were produced by L1 Japanese students speaking Chinese as an L2. The two speakers are twenty-one-year-old undergraduate Japanese females majoring in Chinese at a large public university in Japan.

In the first sample (Table 6.1), the learners are completing an instruction task based on LGC. The speaker has just finished explaining a method that she uses for putting on her cosmetics that saves her time. The listener expresses her interest.

In terms of the amount of language and interaction produced, the conversations on LGC tasks were roughly comparable to TGC tasks (see Lambert and Zhang, 2019, for details). As the excerpt in Table 6.1 illustrates, however, there was a personal dimension to the learners' conversations on the LGC tasks that was not present on the TGC tasks. The speaker elaborates on her own feelings, and the listener shares her own experiences to demonstrate her understanding before further elaborating in line with her own interests. Furthermore, the closing sequence demonstrates the pragmatic device of self-deprecation in response to praise, and the learners then proceed to personally complement one another. Their emotional investment is reinforced through laughter. Use of such devices to create pragmatic meaning was absent on comparable TGC instruction tasks (Lambert and Zhang, 2019).

In the second sample (Table 6.2), the learners are completing a narrative task based on LGC. The speaker has just finished a story about an event that took place while she was preparing dinner with her mother, and the listener expresses her surprise.

The excerpt in Table 6.2 demonstrates how the rapport between learners was deepened on this LGC tasks. The elaborative details of the conversation related more closely to the learners personally and emotionally. The listener encourages the speaker with laughter and humour, and the speaker plays along by elaborating the details of her story. The interaction was quick and animated, and the atmosphere was humorous and light-hearted. This contributed to a rapport between the learners that is frequently absent on pedagogic tasks in the classroom.

In the final sample (Table 6.3), the learners are completing an opinion task based on LGC. The speaker has explained a complicated affair that took place while her friend was studying abroad, and the students are trying to decide who was responsible. The excerpt begins with a comment by the listener.

What is apparent in the three excerpts in Tables 6.1 – 6.3 is that pragmatic language use takes on a role in learners' task-based interaction. The learners' role in the content makes strategic language use necessary. In the excerpt in Table 6.3, learners use pragmatic devices such as tag questioning to elicit agreement, uncompleted sentences to deliver veiled challenge, mitigated questioning, unarticulated confrontation and softened tone. Such devices are what Sabet and Zhang (2015) refer to as vague language, which functions to create pragmatic meaning such as tentativeness, self-protection, collaboration and cooperation. There is simply no need for the use of such strategic devices in many of the pedagogic tasks that are based on content supplied by the teacher or materials designer. While such tasks may aid learners in developing interactive competence or gaining control of unfamiliar language associated with specific task content, tasks based on LGC may help to engage the learner personally and ensure the need for pragmatic language use. As TBLT relies primarily on incidental learning (TBLT Principle 1), learners cannot be expected to acquire pragmatic devices such as those in Tables 6.1 to 6.3 if the tasks they complete do not involve the level of personal investment that necessitates their use.

Strengths of LGC and TGC Tasks within the L2 Curriculum

Although this chapter has pointed out several advantages of incorporating tasks based on LGC in TBI, there are many aspects of L2 instruction that may be better suited to TGC tasks. The contrasts in Table 6.4 illustrate the need for a balance of both LGC and TGC in TBI.

Recent research on the relative effects of LGC and TGC (e.g. Lambert, 2017; Lambert and Zhang, 2019) indicates that LGC tasks often tend to result in fluent use of known language, with most negotiation of meaning being limited to negotiation of content. Furthermore, as

Table 6.4 Strengths of LGC and TGC tasks within the L2 curriculum

Learner-generated content	Teacher-generated content
Fluency	Complexity
Control of known language	Experimentation with new language
Negotiation of content	Negotiation of form
Pragmatic competence	Interactive competence

illustrated in this chapter, LGC tasks might engender the type of pragmatically authentic interaction that is often lacking in pedagogic tasks supplied by teachers and materials writers.

In contrast, TGC tasks may result in learners experimenting with more syntactically complex discourse and the negotiation of form (Lambert and Zhang, 2019). TGC tasks might thus be best suited for promoting noticing and the ongoing development of learners' linguistic competence during meaning-focused communication.

Personal Investment and Task Implementation

This chapter has so far focused on task design. However, it may also be possible to engage the learner personally in achieving task outcomes through task implementation. One possibility is in grouping learners to perform tasks. Aubrey (2017a, 2017b), for example, found that learners in a homogenous EFL context who worked with intercultural interlocutors reported being more absorbed in the performance of oral tasks in the classroom and that this intercultural contact also resulted in improved turn-taking during task performance. Phung (2017) reports similar findings in a heterogenous English as a Second Language (ESL) context for learners' preferences for tasks, arguing that grouping learners with those different to themselves creates a greater need to communicate and that this positively affects learners' preference for tasks as well as increasing the negotiation of form and content that takes place during task performance. In short, language learners come into the classroom with a range of individual differences (L1, background knowledge, proficiency level, gender, etc.) and grouping learners to create gaps in these differences during the performance of tasks may be one means of generating interest in task performance.

Another means of engendering personal interest during the implementation of tasks might be the use of goal-setting devices over repeated task performances (e.g. Reese and Wells, 2007; Butler, 2017b; Stroud, 2017). Reese and Wells (2007) and Stroud (2017), for example, report positive effects over semester-long studies in English as a Foreign Language (EFL) conversation classes for implementing a goal-tracking system based on conversation cards weighted for different point values for varying behaviours during task performance (e.g. giving reasons to support opinion, disagreeing with a partner's opinions, clarifying unknown meanings, confirming understanding, interrupting, correcting misunderstandings, etc.). In both studies, these goal-tracking systems were found to have positive effects on learners' L2 use as well as their affective response to instruction as measured by questionnaires. Similarly, Butler (2017b) points out the popularity of digital instructional games employing avatars as motivational devices to keep students playing and reinforce positive learning behaviours. These devices allow learners to earn credits for positive behaviours which they can use to maintain and develop their avatar's appearance in the game. Implementing tasks with goal-tracking systems of this kind may offer a means of engendering interest in task performance. In most approaches to goal-tracking, the assumption, based on self-determination theory, is that the use of such extrinsic motivators will ultimately lead to intrinsic motivation on the part of learners when a certain level of proficiency is reached (e.g. Reeve and Lee, 2014; Oga-Baldwin and Nakata, 2017). In short, some learners may benefit from being provided with a task-extrinsic means of control over their own progress in the form of game elements they can identify with at a personal level.

Personal Investment and SLA

The crucial issue, of course, is how personal investment, or interest in Dewey's sense, might be related to SLA. Neither Dewey's experiential learning theory nor Maehr's theory of personal investment specifically address language. Work in neurolinguistics (e.g. Lamendella, 1977; Paradis 1994, 2004; Schumann, 2001), however, provides a basis for conceptualizing the relationship between personal investment and language learning on tasks. The limbic system is a group of interconnected structures dedicated to linking visceral states and emotion to cognition and behaviour (Mesulam, 2000). Recent models of the limbic system (e.g. Catani, Dell'Acqua and de Schotten, 2013; Lovblad, Schaller and Vargas, 2013) identify components that work in unison to assess and encode new memories. Lovblad et al. (2013) argue that the hippocampus deals with the factual content of memory, whereas the amygdala assigns emotional content to memories and acts to enhance memory formation by increasing the importance of events. Personal investment in task-based language use could thus result in better registration and encoding of both form and meaning during incidental language learning (Paradis, 1994, 2004). Memory for the language used during task performance may be one way in which personal investment impacts L2 learning. Empirical work by Keenan, MacWhinney and Mayhew (1977) and MacWhinney, Keenan and Reinke (1982) has demonstrated effects on memory for both form and meaning when L1 conversations involve personal as opposed to factual content. Furthermore, recent empirical work with beginning-level L2 learners by Lambert, Gong and Zhang (in press) has found that both immediate and delayed lexical recall is better for LGC than TGC lexical items.

A second possibility for measuring the impact of personal investment in TBLT is through indicators of engagement in language use during task performance. Engagement has been a mercurial construct in L2 research and has tended to piggyback on trends in research on information processing and cognitive-interactionist theories of SLA. Since the late 1990s, aspects of L2 performance that have been investigated in connection with the notion of motivation and engagement have ranged from the number of words and turns used (Dörnyei and Kormos, 2000) to the amount of intake and pushed output (Batstone, 2002), learners' use of corrective feedback (CF) (Hyland, 2003), language-related episodes (Storch, 2008; Baralt, Gurzynski-Weiss and Kim, 2016), language awareness (Svalberg, 2009), and most recently a combined set of measures from interactionist research (Lambert et al. 2017) matched to a model of performance engagement from general education (Fredricks, Blumenfeld and Paris, 2004; Philp and Duchesne, 2016). In all cases, engagement has been measured in relative terms of learners doing more of what other theories of SLA have argued to be relevant for learning. The construct of engagement itself and how it relates to SLA is currently undertheorized.

In addition to its impact on memory and L2 performance, however, personal investment may also affect learners' sense of absorption or 'flow' during task performance (Csikszentmihalyi, 1975, 1990; Egbert, 2003; Aubrey, 2017a, 2017b). Flow might be an important indicator of learners' emotional engagement on tasks (Aubrey, 2017a, 2017b). Aubrey (2017a) argues, based on Egbert (2003), that one factor contributing to learners' experience of flow during task performance is that the content of the tasks is perceived as important, urgent or meaningful. A second factor is learners' control when they perceive themselves as enacting a choice over task topic, content or procedures. Aubrey (2017b), in a follow-up analysis of learners' post-task reflections, makes the case that such flow experiences can lead to a sense of accomplishment and self-confidence, which can facilitate the attainment of flow states in subsequent tasks. If this is the case, questionnaires eliciting learners' self-reported levels of flow during L2 task performance (see Egbert, 2003; Aubrey, 2017a, for examples) or post-task diaries documenting learners' retrospective thought processes and perceptions (Aubrey, 2017b) may provide an important and feasible means of gaging the extent to which materials designed to engender interest on the part of learners have worked in the classroom.

Implications for TBLT Principles

Although TBLT is generally consistent with Dewey's theory of experiential learning (TBLT Principles 1–3), the focus has been primarily on the cognitive dimension of learning (TBLT Principles 4–9). Current approaches to TBLT conceptualize tasks in two primary ways. The first is in terms of learners' real-world needs and the relevance that this has for them (Long, 2015; Robinson, 2011). The second is in terms of learners' cognitive and interactive needs for incidental SLA in instructed settings (e.g. Prabhu, 1987; Yule, 1997; Ellis, 2003). In both approaches the role of learners' personal interest in completing tasks has been a secondary consideration which has been assumed to be a by-product of relevance to future needs (Long, 2015) or has been left to teachers and materials writers to decide based on what they feel will appeal to learners (Prabhu, 1987; Yule, 1997; Ellis, 2003).

In Dewey's theory of experience as well as Vygotsky's theory of mind, however, the affective dimension of learning is central to subsequent cognition. As we have seen in this chapter, Dewey argues that interest is always embodied and personal, and that it provides the driving force behind both unified activity and intelligent effort in achieving new objectives. Learning is thus a personal process in which learners act on their current impulses and experiences to achieve objects of interest that are connected with their sense of self and well-being. These objectives might be shared personal understanding in social interactions in the classroom or achieving a much-needed job or promotion to support one's family. One way or the other, learners who achieve their best are typically personally invested in their learning and take an agentive role in what they do. The role for learners is too often missing in the types of interactive pedagogic tasks used in TBLT research and instruction. We might thus add a tenth TBLT principle to the list at the beginning of this chapter.

10. **Personal investment:** To optimize learning opportunities on tasks, learners must take an agentive role in the learning process. TBLT must incorporate learners personally so that task interactions and outcomes reflect their sense of self and well-being.

Until recently, the affective dimension of task-based learning has received little attention in the TBLT literature. By incorporating ample opportunities for learners to tailor task content based on their personal drives and experiences to the specific classroom context in which they are working, TBLT researchers and practitioners might generate more opportunities for intelligent effort, unified activity and pragmatically authentic communication in classrooms.

Conclusion

This chapter has presented an educational perspective on many TBLT practices based on Dewey's (1913, 1938) theory of experience and subsequent work on the affective dimensions of learning by Maehr (1984). It has been argued that while the cognitive dimension of L2 performance has received considerable theoretical and empirical attention in TBLT, the affective dimension is only beginning to be theorized and researched. This chapter suggested directions for addressing this gap in TBLT theory and practice by summarizing some initial empirical evidence on the different approaches to engendering personal investment and interest through task design and the implementation of tasks in the classroom. The chapter has also suggested some directions for evaluating the effects of these approaches on memory, language use and learners' experiences during task performance.

Part III
Pedagogical Perspectives

The chapters in Part II had a primary focus on the theory and research that informs task-based language teaching (TBLT) but they also considered pedagogical issues. The primary focus of this part is on the pedagogy of TBLT but we will continue to draw on research to support the proposals we advance. The three chapters in Part III address the following questions:

- What principles inform the selection and sequencing of tasks in a task-based course?
- What does a task-based lesson consist of?
- What methodological principles underlie proposals for implementing a task in the classroom?
- What kind of assessment is compatible with TBLT?

Chapter 7 addresses what tasks to include in a task-based course and how the tasks selected can be sequenced to assist learning. The chapter examines four different proposals for designing a task-based course. In Prabhu's Communicational Language Teaching Project (CLTP), the syllabus serves as an *operational* construct. That is, it has low internal structure and leaves implementation issues to be decided by teachers based on their experience of what works in their instructional context. Prabhu aimed to select tasks on familiar topics that would motivate students to engage mentally in using language to achieve meaningful outcomes. The tasks were sequenced intuitively by drawing broadly on a set of general principles such as cognitive demand and type of gap involved (i.e. information, reasoning, opinion). In contrast, Long's syllabus functions as an *illuminative* construct, aiming to bring what is learned in line with what is taught. That is, tasks in his syllabus have a training function. Target tasks are identified first by a needs analysis and then restructured into pedagogic tasks. They are sequenced based on their frequency and criticality as revealed by the needs analysis and also in terms of the cognitive demands they impose. Robinson also views the syllabus as serving an illuminative purpose. His is the most ambitious proposal as he proposes a syllabus that takes into account the cognitive complexity of tasks, their propensity for promoting the kinds of interaction that facilitate acquisition, and the cognitive abilities and affective dispositions of individual learners. Central to sequencing tasks, however, is their cognitive complexity. Finally, Ellis, like Prabhu, treats the syllabus as an *operational* construct. He identifies a range of factors that influence task complexity (e.g. the linguistic level of the input and whether the task outcome is closed or open) but suggests that sequencing tasks is largely a matter of intuition that can be guided only roughly by such factors. In Ellis' proposal – unlike the other proposal in Chapter 7 – there is room for a more traditional, structural module to fit alongside a task-based module in a complete course.

Chapter 8 considers the other side of language pedagogy – the methodology for implementing tasks. It identifies a range of options relating to each of the three phases of a task-based lesson – the pre-task phase, the main task phase and the post-task phase. The viability and effectiveness of the different options is considered in relation to both research findings and the recommendations found in popular teacher guides. Pre-task options have three purposes: (1) to motivate students to perform the task, (2) to prepare them to perform it, and (3) to encourage the use of strategies that will help them. Various options are considered with special attention given to pre-task planning and the various ways in which this can be carried out (e.g. in terms of its focus and the time allocated). The key option in the main task phase is within-task focus on form. Various ways of accomplishing this are considered – in particular corrective feedback (CF). Another main task option that research has shown impacts on task performance concerns whether learners perform a task with or without time pressure. Of the post-task options, asking learners to repeat a task has attracted the most attention of researchers. Various types of repetition (exact, content and procedural) are considered along with the relative strengths of each. The chapter does not seek to be prescriptive but it does point to particular options that research has shown to be effective.

Chapter 9 discusses how tasks can be used for purposes of assessment. The chapter begins by reviewing some general issues in testing to create a foundation for considering task-based assessment – the different functions of tests (proficiency, achievement, diagnostic), summative and formative evaluation; norm versus criterion referencing; washback. It then outlines the theory of testing that underlies task-based assessment, arguing that it must take account of both competences (e.g. grammatical, sociolinguistic and strategic) and the ability to use language. The interactive approach to testing is then contrasted with the real-life approach. The challenge facing task-based assessment is how tasks can provide evidence of learners' ability to use an L2 that is generalizable (i.e. not limited to the particular task used in a test). Drawing on research discussed in Chapter 4, a proposal is advanced for designing assessment tasks that can provide evidence of learners' overall proficiency by showing their ability to use language that is complex, accurate and fluent. The chapter concludes by looking at the development of task-based tests in three case studies.

7 Task-Based Syllabus Design

Introduction

The perceived importance of allowing learners opportunities to employ their linguistic repertoire under relatively natural conditions has generated discussion on the use of tasks in L2 instructional design since the 1980s, and the role that tasks might play within the language syllabus has been an issue of considerable debate (e.g. Brown and Yule, 1983; Brown et al., 1984; Candlin, 1987; Prabhu, 1987; Nunan, 1989; Yule, 1997; Ellis, 2003; Willis and Willis, 2007; Robinson, 2010, 2011; Skehan, 2014a; Long, 2015). In task-based syllabuses, tasks function as the primary unit in selecting and sequencing course content. There is considerable theoretical support for using tasks in this way in syllabus design (Long, 1985, 2015; Skehan, 1998, 2014; Robinson, 2001, 2011; Ellis, 2003, 2018a), and initial attempts have been made to develop courses in line with these theoretical rationales (e.g. Kelly and Kelly, 1996; Lambert and Hailes, 2002; Benevides and Valvona, 2008).

Tasks have also been used to *support* syllabuses organized around other units of analysis (e.g. grammatical structures, lexis, topics, situations). These task-supported syllabuses have gained support in English as a Foreign Language (EFL) contexts in different parts of the world (see Shehadeh, 2005; R. Sheen, 2006; Littlewood, 2014), and they are also supported by well-established learning theories (DeKeyser, 2007; Ellis, 2018a). Published sets of teaching material have also appeared which are in line with these theories (e.g. Kelly and Kelly, 1996; Cutrone and Beh, 2014; Harris and Leeming, 2016). Some researchers argue that the theories of learning associated with task-based and task-supported syllabuses are incompatible (e.g. Long, 2015). Others argue that when certain conditions are met they can be complementary in facilitating instructed L2 learning (Ellis, 2018a). The present chapter will compare key proposals for designing task-*based* syllabuses as well as some ideas on how task-based syllabuses might be introduced in programmes where a more traditional structural syllabus is in use.

Like any approach to syllabus design, proposals for task-based syllabuses must address procedures for task selection (how the content to be included in the course is to be determined) and task sequencing (how course content is to be ordered). In addition, however, approaches to syllabus design differ in the aims of the syllabus and consequently in the scope of the syllabus within the broader curriculum. The present chapter will discuss four proposals for designing syllabuses based on tasks. Each of these approaches will be compared in terms of: (1) the aims and scope of the syllabus within the L2 curriculum, (2) the procedures by which tasks are selected, and (3) the principles on which tasks are sequenced. In the final sections of the chapter, examples of how these approaches have been put into practice in designing actual L2 syllabuses used in EFL instruction in Japan will be considered, and the pros and cons of each approach will be summarized.

Prabhu's Approach to Syllabus Design

The Communicative Language Teaching Project (CLTP, also known as the Bangalore Project) was devoted to developing a L2 curriculum for use in general English classes in public secondary schools in India between 1979 and 1982. The syllabus used in the project was organized according to topic, and a range of tasks, loosely sequenced based on their procedural demands, were suggested to help teachers cover each of these topics with their learners. The distinctions that Prabhu (1987) makes regarding the role of this syllabus in instructional design are helpful in comparing subsequent developments.

One key distinction that Prabhu (1987) makes is between syllabuses which are intended to function as *operational* constructs in the curriculum and those that are intended to function as *illuminative* constructs. When a syllabus is designed to function as an operational construct in the L2 curriculum, the aim is to provide course content as a resource for teachers to construct their lesson plans and reach curricular goals with different learners in the varying classroom contexts in which they teach. This type of syllabus has low internal structure and leaves methodological and implementational issues to be determined by teachers based on their experience of what works at the local level and the problems that different learners face in the classroom. In short, the syllabus specifies only *what* will be taught, not *how* it will be taught. The content of syllabus is fixed, but how the teacher uses this content is flexible.

By contrast, when a syllabus is designed to function as an illuminative construct in the L2 curriculum, the aim is accountability for both what will be taught and for what will be learned as a result. The focus at the planning stage is on ensuring accurate prediction so steps are taken to bring what is taught and what is learned into careful alignment. In achieving this end, the line between syllabus and methodology naturally blurs, and the syllabus takes on a much broader role within the curriculum. Illuminative syllabuses are frequently used in subjects which are based on lists of content items that must be taught together with discrete-point questions that assess learners' mastery of this content. Illuminative syllabuses are also used in workplace training. Employees are briefly trained in how to perform key tasks (e.g. cleaning bathrooms at an airport, preparing a hotel room before check-in, detailing an automobile at the dealer before it is picked up, preparing a jet for take-off, etc.). Trainees' performances on tasks are then evaluated according to a checklist of the points on which they have been trained to ensure that they can do the tasks properly (e.g. mirrors have been cleaned, soap dispenser refilled, floor mopped, bins emptied, air freshener used, etc.). In both content instruction and workplace training, what is learned can be brought closely in line with what is taught. Syllabus content is divided into discrete points that all learners can be expected to master with little or no variation. Methodology is reduced to explanation and feedback.

Scope

Prabhu's syllabus was designed to function as an *operational construct*. It specified what would be taught at a low level of internal structure and allowed teachers to make intuitive decisions and adjustments to ensure adequate mastery of the syllabus content. The motivation for this was in line with the aim of the project's curriculum. The curriculum aimed to develop a general capacity in learners that would allow them to acquire the skills necessary for mastering any number of tasks that they face in the future. Prabhu refers to this capacity as *grammatical competence* and he used communicative tasks as tools to develop this competence rather than to train learners to perform these tasks as ends in themselves. He points out that developing competence in a language is a variable process and that a syllabus cannot be expected to anticipate all sources of challenge for different learners in different classrooms.

Selection

In Prabhu's approach, syllabus content was organized in terms of topic areas (e.g. monthly calendars, maps, school timetables) rather than in terms of tasks. Prabhu's primary concern in selecting topics was generating the *interest* and *effort* necessary to engage learners mentally in the process of using language to achieve meaningful outcomes. To achieve this end, content was selected for the project with a view to allowing learners to draw on their background knowledge and experiences. As we have seen in Chapter 6, there is a strong educational rationale for selecting tasks that draw on established areas of knowledge. Lambert, Philp and Nakamura (2017), for example, found that tasks which draw on content which learners found interesting, wanted to share and thought that their partner would enjoy hearing about resulted in increased engagement in language use in the classroom. There is also good theoretical and empirical evidence to suggest that it might result in improved memory for both content and language (see Lambert, 2017; Lambert, Gong and Zhang, in press; Chapter 6 of the present volume).

Prabhu defines the pedagogic tasks used in the CLTP as *pieces of logical thinking*. According to Prabhu, successful tasks had five characteristics: (1) a clear outcome, (2) clear criteria for success, (3) a balance of predictability and unpredictability, (4) content which allowed learners to draw on their background knowledge, and (5) content that generated interest and sustained engagement. Pedagogic tasks meeting these five criteria were selected to support each topic area specified for the syllabus (e.g. listening to stories of the 'whodunit' kind and completing them with appropriate solutions, see Prabhu, 1987, pp. 138–43, for more examples). However, it is worth noting that the tasks used in the CLTP also seem to have met the criteria of 'tasks' established by Ellis (see Chapter 1) in that they typically required a focus on meaning, involved a gap that necessitated language processing, required learners to draw on their own resources in completing them and resulted in a communicative outcome beyond practising language for its own sake.

Sequencing

The tasks selected for each topic in the syllabus were then sequenced. The primary criterion for this sequencing seems to have been the mental procedures that learners might have to engage in arriving at the task outcome. Prabhu distinguishes three levels of procedural demand that filling the gaps required to arrive at task outcomes might entail (see Chapter 1):

1. *Information gap:* Transfer of given information related to a topic.
2. *Reasoning gap:* Derivation of new information from given information through processes of inference, deduction, calculation, collation, application or identification of relationships/patterns.
3. *Opinion gap:* Identification and articulation of personal preferences, feelings or attitudes in response to a given situation.

Under the topic of 'maps' (Prabhu, 1987, p. 139), for example, we find a sequence of six versions of a map task sequenced to increase in difficulty according to these three levels of procedural demand. Learners initially (1) *identify* and (2) *describe* locations on a map. They then (3) *draw* maps based on instructions and (4) *draw* routes on maps based on instructions. Up to this point, only information transfer (the lowest level of procedural demand) is involved in the sequence. However, the next task requires learners to reason based on available information by (5) *deciding* forms of transport when given information on bus routes, fares, etc. (i.e. deriving new information from existing information). Finally, the last task requires learners to (6) make a decision about the best place for new facilities such as a hospital or a school. The last task in the sequence thus requires the identification and articulation of a personal preference in response to the situation which, according to Prabhu, represents the highest level of procedural demand.

On careful examination, however, other factors used in sequencing the tasks in the project can be identified (see Table 7.1). Procedural demand is thus one factor among others. This illustrates Ellis' (2003, 2018a) point that tasks are invariably *conglomerations of features* that work together to impact the demands placed on learners (see Chapter 3).

Prabhu's approach to task sequencing was thus an expedient one, but it seems to have met with some success in the context in which it was used.

Table 7.1 Prabhu's criteria for task sequencing

1	Information provided	Amount, type, variety, circumstance
2	Reasoning needed	Number of deductive, inferential or calculative steps
3	Precision needed	Level of interpretation and expression required
4	Experience assumed	Experience of task purpose and constraints
5	Abstractness involved	Reference to concepts vs. objects and actions
6	Language mode required	Receptive vs. productive; oral/aural vs. written
7	Cognitive demands	Information transfer, reasoning, opinion

As noted, the purpose of the syllabus in the CLTP was simply to provide teachers with a set of landmarks and suggestions for working on a topic in the classroom. Teachers were free to adjust or eliminate specific tasks based on each group's needs and problems. In terms of the level of specification of an operational syllabus of this type, Prabhu (1987, pp. 87–8) argues that the syllabus needs to include four types of information to provide teachers with the resources that they need: (1) the topics to be covered (monthly calendars, maps, school timetables, itineraries, etc.), (2) information connected with each topic (schedule contents, prices, distances, etc.), (3) the procedures to be used in addressing each topic (inference, calculation, collation, application, etc.), and (4) the outcomes to be reached (the shortest time, the lowest cost, the most symmetrical pattern, etc.).

Thus, Prabhu believes a language syllabus should function as an *operational construct* in the L2 curriculum and specify course content at a low level of internal structure. His fear is that an over-specified syllabus will reduce what learners and teachers can bring to the learning process and that the outcome will be unified levels of learning associated with *task training* rather than individual development and the general problem-solving capacity associated with *language education*. He argues that *training* involves mastery of a series of fixed stages to criterion-level performance on specific real-world tasks, and *education* involves mastery of a general capacity that allows learners to engage in adaptable behaviour and ongoing learning on any future tasks. Prabhu (1987, p. 91) claims that the aim of a language syllabus is to enable the learner to employ language for meaning exchange and, in the process, to achieve conformity to linguistic norms. However, his focus throughout is the subconscious acquisition of language through rational thinking (reasoning, inferencing etc.).

Prabhu's work on the Bangalore Project has made a seminal contribution to the field, but subsequent theories of task-based instructional design are in agreement that something more is needed at the syllabus level and during implementation if learners are to acquire the ability to complete tasks *and* achieve conformity with linguistic norms in doing so.

Long's Task-Based Syllabus

Long (1985, 2015) argues that the syllabus should be conceptualized, organized and assessed in terms of *tasks*. In contrast to Prabhu's approach to syllabus design, where the focus was on using tasks as tools to develop a general language capacity, the focus in Long's approach is on the ability to perform specific tasks. This change of focus affords several practical advantages for the syllabus designer. Syllabuses aimed at language competence of any kind must face the fact that language development is a holistic, organic and variable process that is difficult to assess in terms of fixed stages which are the same for all learners. Syllabuses aimed at the ability to complete specific real-world tasks, on the other hand, can potentially avoid this issue by subordinating language to what it is used to accomplish, namely tasks. In fact, this is how abilities are typically evaluated outside of the language classroom. As we have seen earlier in the chapter, in workplace training there is a high degree of alignment between what is taught and what is learned, and instructional content can be divided into discrete points that all learners can be expected to master with little or no variation.

To take an example, consider the situation of non-native speakers of English who work on the floor of furniture stores or car dealerships in English-speaking countries. One of their most important duties will naturally be achieving sales. Their manager knows that customers come in ready to buy or not. If they are ready to buy, the job of the showroom staff is to facilitate rather than inhibit that process. The manager will know through experience, at least tacitly, what this involves. It might involve greeting the customers at the right time, shaking hands, maintaining a smile, incorporating children in the decision-making process (What do you think about this car? Which one do *you* like?), comparing products in a given range, discussing prices and options, completing the appropriate paperwork to close transactions etc. Initial and on-the-job training may involve spending some time going through these things with trainees, asking them to observe experienced sales staff for a period, bringing certain things to their attention that went well or badly, and then observing them as they do these things themselves to ensure that they are done adequately, intervening whenever necessary to bring performance up to standard. All employees would be expected to do the things that are taught, and a checklist, explicit or tacit, might be used to ensure that they are performing well. The employees' linguistic competence is subordinated completely to the tasks that need to be performed. The training process and evaluation process themselves are not aimed at *grammatical competence* as in Prabhu's project. The focus is on successful task performance. Language is seen as a by-product or artefact of successful task performance. Task performance in Long's sense is thus *trainable* and *measurable* in terms of *objective criteria* that apply to *all learners*.

Scope

By subordinating language to task performance as it is in the real world, Long's syllabus can function as an *illuminative* construct within the curriculum. It can bring what is learned in line with what is taught and thus become accountable for what is *learned* as a result of instruction. Long defines *tasks* broadly as the events that learners participate in 'in everyday life, at work, at play, and in between' (Long, 2015, p. 108). He does not attempt to define tasks at the syllabus level in terms of conditions that connect them to language acquisition. In fact, at this level, he does not attempt to connect them to the use of language at all. In Long's approach, the pedagogic tasks that learners work on in the classroom are direct reflections of real-world tasks. In addition to tasks in which language plays a central role such as 'buying a pair of shoes' or 'making a hotel reservation', the examples of tasks Long (2015) provides include those in which language plays only a distal role if it is necessary at all (e.g. 'painting a fence', 'dressing a child' or 'weighing a patient').

Selection

In Long's approach, the tasks which constitute the content of the syllabus are identified based on a needs analysis (Long, 2005, 2015). Long argues that this provides a rational and empirical means of content selection in contrast to approaches such as Prabhu's, which rely on teacher or course designer's intuitions about what is interesting and challenging for their learners. Second, it is essential for accountability in the case of learners who have educational and career goals involving the target culture or who have to survive socially in target language communities (Long, 2015, pp. 63–83).

The process by which tasks are selected for the syllabus involves three stages of analysis (Long, 2015, pp. 223–7). The first is identifying the things that learners will need to do in everyday life (e.g. making or changing a plane, train, hotel, restaurant or theatre reservation). The outcome of this analysis is a list of *target tasks* that learners need to be able to complete. This list, however, provides only the 'raw input' for a task-based syllabus. Following this, the second stage of analysis involves classifying these target tasks into *task types* or more abstract superordinate categories based on their common features (e.g. making reservations, changing reservations) in order to meet the needs of heterogeneous groups of learners efficiently. When several *target tasks* overlap, such as in the example of different types of reservations, it would be uneconomical to treat them all separately in the syllabus so this intermediate step of identifying task *types*, according to Long, provides a more efficient basis for initially organizing course content. Long also points out that target tasks that are unique to specific subgroups of learners might be eliminated at this stage and only task types which all learners need might be selected for inclusion in the syllabus. Finally, when the list of task types to be included in the syllabus has been determined, the final stage of analysis in Long's approach to task selection is to create *pedagogic tasks* connected with each task type. These pedagogic tasks serve as the actual content of the syllabus (e.g. filling out or changing a reservation form while listening to a telephone call; role-playing customers and clerks who are making/changing reservations, etc.). The ultimate goal in selecting pedagogic tasks for a syllabus, according to Long, is to provide adequate coverage of each task type by ensuring that learners develop the skills necessary to complete the target tasks they represent.

As an example of how Long's approach to selecting tasks for a syllabus was put into practice, Lambert (2010) conducted an analysis of the English language use of graduates over a twenty-five-year period from an English programme at a Japanese university. The analysis generated a broad range of tasks which overlapped in varying degrees. In order to incorporate a representative number of the target tasks specified by informants in key areas of job placement, task types representing a broad range of specific tasks were initially established (e.g. locating information on the Internet, locating information in newspapers, translating users' manuals, translating e-mail messages, editing teaching materials, editing contracts, etc.). Only after this initial classification was it possible to create a reasonable number of yet more abstract task types in the sense that Long suggests (e.g. locating information, translating from English to Japanese, editing English documents, etc.). The process was a dynamic rather than a linear one, which required considerable intuition and experience with the cultural milieu and the educational context in which the syllabus would be implemented.

Sequencing

Before developing sequences of pedagogic tasks connected with each task type, Long (2015) recommends initially arranging the various task types that will be included in the syllabus in relationship to one another based on 'the relative frequency and or criticality of the task as determined by the needs analysis' (p. 233). In other words, the task types which learners can be expected to encounter often or that are the most essential for their success in reaching their goals will be addressed earlier in the syllabus, whereas those that they will need to complete less frequently or which are not as critical to their success will be addressed later. Selecting tasks based on a needs analysis thus has the added advantage of providing a principled basis for the initial arrangement of task types to be included in the syllabus content.

Following this initial sequencing of task types, pedagogic tasks representing simplified versions of each task type are sequenced in relationship to one another, in line with learners developing capacity to complete them. The goal is that the demands of the versions of these pedagogic tasks will increase until they match the demands of the target tasks represented by the task type. The last task in each module should thus be a full 'proxy' or 'virtual' version of a target task that learners need to complete outside of the classroom, and this task will be used as an 'exit task' to assess learners' abilities to deal successfully with this target task on the basis of which the task type and associated pedagogic tasks were created.

In terms of the specific factors used to grade the demands of versions of a given task, Long advocates using factors related to the intrinsic complexity of the targeted task. According to Long, task intrinsic complexity relates to the inherent, unchanging qualities that make tasks more or less challenging. The examples that he provides are those identified in early proposals for L2 task design by Brown and Yule (1983) and Brown et al. (1984). These factors include: (1) the number of components, elements and steps in a task, (2) the distinctiveness of task's components, elements and steps, and (3) the dislocation in time and space of the task content in relation to the speaker. Long also acknowledges the importance of Robinson's (2001, 2010) SSARC (simplify, stabilize, automatize, restructure, complexify) model of task sequencing which will be discussed in the section 'Robinson's Task-Based Syllabus'.

To take a concrete example, in comparison to the task sequence related to 'maps', which was summarized in the section 'Prabhu's Approach to Syllabus Design', Long provides a sequence of eight pedagogic tasks to prepare learners to 'obtain and follow street directions': (1) learners listen to recordings of real examples of a native speaker giving directions to orient them to the demands of the target task; (2) they follow short fragments of oral directions on a map; (3) they follow longer directions to more distant locations on the map followed by questions asking them to confirm their location (street name, nearby buildings, etc.); (4) they work in pairs to read out fragments/questions and follow/answer them; (5) they listen to directions and follow routes marked on an authentic map as they listen; (6) they listen to directions from a starting point on the map, trace the route as they listen and answer questions about where they are at the end; (7) they complete the same task more rapidly with no breaks; (8) they complete a simulation of the target task 'obtain and follow street directions' which acts a form of assessment for the module. Thus, Long's syllabus is more illuminative in scope than Prabhu's syllabus. Long's approach provides a more detailed level of description which includes not only the content to be taught, but a considerable amount of information about how it is to be taught (4, 7) and what is to be learned as a result (1, 8). In other words, the traditional distinction between syllabus and methodology begins to blur.

Thus, as we have seen, Prabhu (1987) believed that the cognitive demands of tasks could drive the development of L2 learning in terms of grammatical competence and allow flexible behaviour and the capacity for ongoing learning on the part of learners. As this competence, and the processes by which it develops at the individual level, are variable, Prabhu opted to leave the specifics of how these learning processes would be engendered for teachers and learners to negotiate in the classroom based on their intuition and experience. In contrast, Long's approach (1985, 2015) avoids the problem of variability in L2 acquisition at the syllabus level altogether by focusing on task learning and subordinating language to what it is used to accomplish. In this way, Long is able to propose a syllabus which aims to account for unified, criterion-based learning outcomes for *all* learners based on the things that they need to accomplish in their lives and careers. Long's task-based syllabus functions as an illuminative construct with respect to task learning. This change in focus from language learning to task learning has had a seminal effect on the field of instructed second language acquisition (ISLA) in terms of both theory and practice. The problem, of course, is with the accountability of the syllabus as a language syllabus as well as a task syllabus. The goals of stakeholders (learners, parents, teachers and educational administrators) are often not only to accomplish tasks but to develop the linguistic resources to accomplish them in comparable ways to proficient speakers of the target language. While language learning and task learning overlap at times, there is not a one-to-one relationship between them. If a syllabus is to be accountable as a language syllabus, evidence of how tasks relate to the specific processes of L2 learning is required. Long's syllabus does not deal with this directly. It is left to be dealt with through focus on form as a set of procedures to address language problems as they arise in situ (see Chapter 2).

Robinson's Task-Based Syllabus

Scope

Robinson (2001, 2010, 2011) provides a theoretical foundation for connecting task performance to specific processes of L2 performance and acquisition. He outlines what Prahbu would term an *illuminative* task-based language syllabus par excellence. To account for the specific language learning processes that students will engage in in the classroom, Robinson (2010, 2011) proposes a syllabus that takes into account factors relating to the situational and cognitive demands of tasks as well as factors that affect the difficulty that learners will experience with tasks based on their individual differences. See Chapter 3 for a detailed account of the Cognition Hypothesis (CH) that underlies Robinson's ideas about a task-based syllabus. The proposed syllabus involves a relatively high level of specification and takes on a very broad scope within the language curriculum.

Selection

Robinson adopts Long's (1985, 2015) definition of tasks as the things that learners have to do outside of the classroom for the purpose of initially identifying and determining the communicative conditions of the tasks that learners will complete in the classroom. This requires the type of behavioural needs analysis that Long advocates. However, Robinson (2011) also argues that it is necessary to understand the cognitive, ability and affective demands that tasks place on learners if predictable gains in L2 performance and learning in the classroom are to be ensured. The selection of tasks in Robinson's approach thus involves analyses related to three aspects of task demand: (1) an initial *behavioural analysis* of tasks in situ to identify target tasks and determine their essential communicative conditions, (2) an information-theoretic analysis of the cognitive demands that tasks place on all learners to determine how they should be graded and sequenced into syllabuses to promote balanced L2 learning, and (3) an *ability analysis* to determine the difficulties that learners of different aptitudes and motivational profiles will experience in completing them (Robinson, 2011, pp. 5–8) so that learners can be matched with tasks suiting their individual needs.

The first stage of task analysis involves a behavioural needs analysis of the type discussed in the section 'Long's Task-Based Syllabus', in the subsection 'Selection' to identify the real-world tasks learners need to complete as a basis for selecting tasks for the syllabus. Robinson claims that six types of information about target tasks should be collected at this stage: (1) the list of target tasks, (2) the interactive demands of these tasks and the roles that they imply for learners, (3) the subtasks that make up these tasks, (4) the steps needed to complete the tasks and their subtasks, (5) discourse samples of proficient speakers completing the tasks, and (6) criterion measures of success in completing these tasks. This information will be used to set up the essential structure of the syllabus and establish the situational and interactive demands that govern language use in the classroom. This involves the goal orientation of tasks (open/closed, convergent/ divergent), the division of task-essential information between participants (shared, one-way, two-way), the number of learners involved in a task, the contributions required (productive, receptive), and whether the outcome of the task is subject to negotiation of meaning or not. The information acquired during this first stage of task selection can also be used to inform the grouping of the learners in terms of proficiency levels, gender, familiarity, content knowledge, status and cultural background. According to Robinson, all of these aspects of pedagogic tasks fall into the category of *task conditions*. They are part of the essential structure of the target tasks that motivated their inclusion in the syllabus, and they are fixed based on an initial behaviour analysis. They are *not* subsequently manipulated in sequencing tasks within the syllabus.

The second stage in selecting tasks for the syllabus is classifying them based on the information-processing stages involved between input, output and interaction. According to Robinson, this will consist of analyses related to component task achievement and the sequencing of sub-task learning (2011, p. 7). Robinson does not discuss exactly what these forms of analysis entail or the specific procedures by which they might be conducted, but he notes that Skehan's (1998, 2009a) theory of how the cognitive demands of tasks can be classified and manipulated during instruction has been the most influential example of this type of analysis in the field of second language acquisition (SLA). Presumably, Robinson's approach to sequencing tasks demands in terms of whether they direct or disperse learners' cognitive resources during task performance (to be discussed in the section 'Robinson's Task-Based Syllabus', in the subsection 'Sequencing') is another. Briefly, Skehan argues that tasks allowing exemplar-based processing, by drawing on learners' current language resources, promote the development of fluency and accuracy, and that tasks requiring rule-based processing push learners to experiment with new and partially mastered language and will result in increased complexity (see Chapter 3). For instructional purposes, Skehan argues that tasks which force learners to alternate between both types of processing be balanced across the syllabus so that learners develop the ability for dual-mode processing. In this way, fluency does not dominate at the expense of ongoing development nor does ongoing development dominate at the expensive of fluency. In the first case, learners would chat fluently using broken language. In the second case, they would know a lot of language that they cannot use in real time. Robinson's (2011) argument is that an information-theoretic analysis of this type will provide a basis for determining how the cognitive demands of tasks can be controlled for all learners through the manipulation of factors in the design of tasks.

The first two stages of task selection in Robinson's approach thus make a clear distinction between the situational conditions of real-world tasks, that were the focus of Long's approach, and the range of cognitive demands and psycholinguistic processes that in rudimentary form was the focus of Prabhu's approach. This distinction is very important as it potentially provides Robinson with the conceptual means of bridging the gap between broad definitions of tasks as the things that learners need to accomplish outside of the classroom and narrower definitions of tasks as tools for promoting cognitive processes related to L2 use and acquisition in the classroom. To achieve this end predictably, however, Robinson's approach necessitates a third dimension of task analysis which involves identifying factors affecting how learners of different aptitude and affect profiles will respond to them.

Robinson acknowledges that individual differences in learners affect how they perform tasks and that specific task characteristics will make some tasks better suited to individual learners than others (2011, pp. 23–6). For Robinson, the third stage in the selection of tasks is thus the analysis of the abilities (aptitudes) and affective dispositions (motivation) that tasks favour so that tasks can be adjusted to accommodate the individual differences of learners. Robinson identifies four types of aptitude that can be argued to affect learners' performance and learning on tasks: (1) working memory capacity (tasks without visual support during performance could favour learners with higher working memory capacity); (2) executive control (tasks that require dual-tasking could favour learners who can switch quickly from one task to another); (3) causal reasoning ability (tasks requiring complex arguments to be structured could favour learners with high causal reasoning ability); (4) sensitivity to the mental states of others (tasks that require learners to speculate on why different people behaved the way that they did could demand a high level of sensitivity to the mental states of others). Likewise, Robinson argues that factors related to output anxiety, self-efficacy, self-regulation, openness to experience or tolerance of ambiguity could also affect learners differentially. For example, performance on tasks with an open solution as opposed to a single correct answer may cause problems for students with a low tolerance for ambiguity and result in unpredicted variation in the language used. However, in terms of the implications of ability and affect analyses for task selection, Robinson claims that to optimize and unify learning gains on tasks, learners of differing dispositions will need to be matched with tasks which suit their affect and ability profiles and reduce variability due to individual differences in aptitude and affect. He does not discuss how tasks catering to individual differences might be incorporated in the design of task-based syllabuses, however. We will return to this point in the section 'Ellis' Task-Based Syllabus'.

Sequencing

Robinson's approach to sequencing tasks is based only on the cognitive factors in their design. Factors relating to the interactive and situation demands of tasks remain fixed throughout the syllabus, as explained. Ability and affect demands of tasks are likewise not used in sequencing tasks in the syllabus but to match tasks to learners of different individual difference profiles. Robinson's approach to sequencing involves two sets of cognitive demands, which could be argued to relate directly to the complementary cognitive processes of *analysis* and *control* (Bialystok, 1994). Briefly, Bialystok argues that analysis is related to the destabilization, restructuring and development of the language system, whereas control is related to the stabilization of the language system in terms of fluent access to current resources. She argues that these two processes account for the development of symbolic systems and complex skill acquisition over the human lifespan. In Robinson's model, task design factors that *direct* learners' cognitive resources (e.g. attention, working memory) to specific features of task content and the language needed to express it could be argued to relate to processes of analysis, whereas task factors which *disperse* learners' cognitive resources over several aspects of the larger performance context could be argued to relate to processes of control. The examples he provides of *resource-directing* factors are: (1) the number of elements in the task, (2) the temporal and spatial displacement of these elements, (3) the need to make the reasoning (spatial, causal, intentional) explicit, and (4) the need to make perspectives on elements explicit. All of these tend to be explicitly grammaticalized in English and they direct learners to specific task content and require them to grammaticalize that content. Examples that he mentions of *resource-dispersing* task factors, on the other hand, are: (1) the number of steps in tasks, (2) the relationships between these steps, (3) the inherent structure of the task, (4) the need to multitask, (5) time to plan, and (6) familiarity with the task (Robinson, 2011, p. 7). In contrast to Skehan's (1998, 2009a) model of cognition and L2 performance summarized in 'Robinson's Task-Based Syllabus', in the subsection 'Selection', Robinson argues, based on work by Neumann (1987) and Sanders (1998) that increasing the resource-directing demands of tasks will promote greater effort towards production and more vigilant monitoring of output, impacting language production in terms of both complexity and accuracy as well as increasing uptake from input.

Robinson (2010) proposes a three-stage procedure for manipulating these two types of cognitive task design factors in sequencing tasks within a syllabus. He refers to this as the SSARC model of L2 task sequencing. This model was briefly introduced in Chapter 3. The first stage involves *simplifying* the new task in terms of *both* the resource-directing and resource-dispersing factors in its design. This provides initial support for performing the new tasks. It also allows learners to access their current L2 resources and *stabilize* these resources in relationship to the new task. The second stage is increasing resource-dispersing task demands (keeping resource-directing demands constant) until these demands match those of the target task on which the new task is based. This stage allows learners to *automatize* the L2 resources brought to bear in the first stage. The third stage then involves increasing resource-directing task demands. These factors bring the new task closer in line with the target task that learners need to complete, destabilizing the linguistic strategies they have brought to bear on the new task in the previous two stages and requiring learners to analyse and *restructure* these L2 resources in line with the demands of the full version of the target task, evidently *complexifying* the language that they use in the process. If the task is particularly challenging, this cycle is repeated until learners can complete full versions of the new task that are equal to the target real-world task it represents.

An example of how Robinson's SSARC model of L2 task sequencing was put into practice in developing a task-based syllabus for a EFL programme in Japan will be discussed later in this chapter. This example will illustrate the high level of specification involved in an illuminative task-based syllabus that aims to predict language learning processes for all learners. Robinson's approach to task-based syllabus design was the first with the potential to bridge the gap between the approaches of Long, who focuses on training and assessing task ability rather than language ability, and Prabhu, who focuses on language ability but leaves the issue of how tasks relate to learning processes to be negotiated by teachers in the classroom.

Ellis' Task-Based Syllabus

In contrast to Long and Robinson, Ellis' position on the task-based syllabus might be seen as a return to the approach used by Prabhu. Like Prabhu, his position is that a syllabus cannot anticipate all sources of variation that will occur for different learners and across different classrooms. Ellis argues that pedagogic tasks are conglomerations of the features that interact with one another and with a full range of individual and contextual variables to produce the learning processes that take place in the classroom. A research agenda aimed at predicting performance and learning based on tasks would have to identify the effects of myriad variables in all of the possible combinations in which they occur in tasks when used with different learners and in different contexts. Robinson (2011), for example, identifies thirty-six variables related to task–learner interactions. It is not difficult to imagine a research agenda of this complexity expanding exponentially with each new variable and receding beyond the event horizon of ISLA. In addition, however, Ellis' position, again like Prabhu's, is that an illuminative syllabus would be undesirable, even if it were possible, as it limits what teachers and learners bring to the learning process in terms of the intuitive decisions and adjustments that they make in optimizing learners' mastery of syllabus content. A third issue Ellis mentions is feasibility. He points out that it is not clear what an illuminative syllabus connecting tasks to language learning might look like. For example, it is not clear how tasks might be matched to learner profiles in practice. Even if researchers were able to demonstrate a finite number of learner types, it would be unrealistic in most language programmes to develop and implement separate syllabuses for each of them in order to control for the effects of individual differences on performance and predict the specific learning processes that learners will engage in while performing tasks.

Scope

Ellis (2018a; see also Chapter 10) thus returns to Prabhu's position on the role of the syllabus in the language curriculum, advocating a syllabus which functions as an operational construct. Ellis makes a clear distinction between task-as-workplan and task-as-process (see Chapters 1 and 4). The former is the domain of syllabus design while the latter is the domain of methodology. Ellis thus limits the role of the syllabus to a workplan for teachers to help their learners achieve competence in the language rather than training learners to perform a specific set of tasks. Unlike Prabhu, however, who is interested in grammatical competence, Ellis sees the purpose of task-based instruction (TBI) as developing interactive and pragmatic competence so that learners can negotiate understanding effectively and appropriately on the range of tasks that they may face in the future. For this goal to be reached in the classroom, it is necessary for teachers to adjust the task online as it is being performed to take account not only of individual difference but of fluctuations in classroom dynamics in order to ensure learning. Specifically, Ellis (2003) distinguishes between 'performance options' and 'process options'. The former refers to options that can be planned in advance, whereas the latter can only figure in situ as the task is performed. Examples of the latter variables might be: (1) whether, when and how long specific learners need to plan, (2) whether and how they can best benefit from repeating tasks, (3) whether they can better benefit from imposing a time limit on task performance or whether they should be allowed to do it at their own pace, (4) whether and to what extent they can benefit from performing receptive versions of pedagogic tasks and what the focus of these tasks should be, (5) how receptive versions of tasks can best be integrated with productive versions of tasks for a given group of learners, (6) whether the social roles and conditions of tasks should be adapted to learners' affective dispositions, and (7) when and how to provide effective feedback for learners of different aptitudes and motivations within a given class. In short, rather than attempting to ensure specific learning processes (automatization, restructuring, etc.) in advance, Ellis' position is that teachers can best ensure these processes by matching tasks to learners' individual differences as the tasks are performed in the classroom.

Unlike Long and Robinson, Ellis (2009a) defines 'task' not in real-world terms, but as a language learning tool. He argues that for tasks to develop interactive and pragmatic L2 competence, they must: (1) focus learners on meaning rather than form, (2) have a communicative gap that necessitates communication, (3) require learners to draw on their own resources in completing them, and (4) result in a communicative outcome beyond the use language for its own sake (see Chapter 1). Ellis' definition of task thus focuses on the conditions necessary for authentic processing of language and the development of a general capacity to use language that is not be limited to specific tasks, but which he argues will transfer to any number of tasks that learners may complete in the future. The integrity of tasks, according to this four-part definition, ensures that teachers' workplans involve tasks. If any of these four criteria are missing, the resulting activity may correspond to what Ellis refers to as a *situational grammar exercise* rather than a task (Ellis, 2009a).

Selection

Ellis (2018a; see also Chapter 10) argues that different approaches to selecting specific tasks will be required for different learners. In the case of learners with specific occupational needs involving the target language (e.g. nurses, flight attendants, hotel staff, receptionists, sales staff, etc.), tasks should be selected based on a needs analysis as suggested by Long (2015). However, in the case of children or general-purpose language learners, tasks might be selected based on criteria similar to Prabhu's: (1) the intrinsic interest that tasks for learners, and (2) learners' previous experience or familiarity with them. A typical example of general-purpose learners might be English majors in Japanese universities. These learners frequently have very little contact with English after graduating and entering the Japanese workplace. However, they are very motivated to develop social and interactive competence in English for personal development and are keen to use it in any situation that affords them the opportunity. Ellis argues that, provided tasks have the four criteria to ensure their integrity as learning tools, any of the approaches to task selection discussed in this chapter may be appropriate depending on the goals and interests of the learners in the programme for which the syllabus is being designed. In other words, Ellis recognizes the case for selecting tasks that cater to the target needs of learners where this is possible, but that otherwise different criteria to select tasks for a general-purpose language course are needed.

Sequencing

Whether tasks are selected based on real-world tasks or whether generic tasks are selected which engage learners' interest and backgrounds, once the list of pedagogic tasks to be included in the syllabus has been determined, Ellis (2003) suggests grading and sequencing tasks in terms of factors relating to four aspects of their structure: (1) the input they provide, (2) the interactive conditions they entail, (3) the reasoning they require, and (4) their resulting outcomes. Based on

Table 7.2 Ellis' criteria for task sequencing

	Easy		Difficult
Input factors			
1	Non-verbal input	Written input	Aural input
2	High-frequency lexis		Low-frequency lexis
3	Shorter, simple sentences		Longer, complex sentences
4	Static information	Dynamic information	Abstract information
5	Few elements/ relationships		Many elements/ relationships
6	Structured		Unstructured
7	Here and now		There and then
8	Familiar		Unfamiliar
Interactive factors			
9	Two-way		One-way
10	Single task		Dual task
11	Dialogue		Monologue
Reasoning factors			
12	Information gap	Reasoning gap	Opinion gap
13	Few steps		Many steps
Outcome factors			
14	Pictures	Written	Oral
15	Closed		Open
16	Descriptions	Instructions/narratives	Arguments

Source: Ellis (2003)

a review of the literature, Ellis suggests sixteen potential factors which might be used as a basis for sequencing decisions in these four areas (see Table 7.2).

It should be remembered, however, that Ellis does not suggest that these criteria be prescribed in a fixed format in developing programmes, as Robinson does, but rather that they function as a set of resources and guidelines. According to Ellis, teachers will develop a task-as-workplan and then carefully monitor the resultant behaviours in the classroom (i.e. the task-as-process) and make adjustments to ensure that task sequences work to provide the opportunities necessary for learners to reach task outcomes and develop competence. The resources that they use to do this will vary in different contexts and with learners of different aptitudes and affective dispositions. Ellis' task-based syllabus, like the syllabus proposed by Prabhu (1987), thus provides content for teachers to promote L2 learning and leaves the critical issue of supporting learners of differing motivations and aptitudes to be dealt with by teachers, based on their experience with their learners and the behaviours that occur as tasks are performed in the classroom.

Ellis (2018a; see also Chapter 10) also provides a rationale for a modular syllabus which incorporates modules based on a task-based syllabus along with modules based on a traditional structural syllabus organized in terms of targeted grammatical and lexical forms. He argues for an approach in which a task-based syllabus is used at the lower level of proficiency until learners gain fluency in the language. The structural syllabus then begins to play a progressively greater role at the intermediate and advanced levels. However, he also points out two other alternatives for pairing structural and task-based syllabuses, which he favours less. In the first, a structural syllabus is used at the early stages of proficiency (as is typical of current practices in many programmes), followed by a task-based syllabus at the later stages. In the second, both types of syllabus are used in parallel at all levels of proficiency. If the third approach is adopted, however, Ellis points out that it is essential that the two syllabuses be kept separate (e.g. taught on different days). If the task-based syllabus is used to practise what is taught in the structural syllabus, the integrity of the task-based syllabus is compromised and the result is a task-supported syllabus rather than a modular syllabus. In this way, learners have the opportunity to access the full range of their own L2 resources to complete tasks. Ellis argues that his modular curriculum represents a feasible way to begin using TBLT in many international contexts. Thus, although Ellis' approach to task-based syllabus design does not attempt to predict performance or provide accountability for the learning that will take place in the classroom, it has the advantage of being more practical and feasible in many contexts internationally in which teachers and programme designers might otherwise struggle with a task-based approach or not have the freedom to use one at all.

Applications

Before concluding, it will be helpful to consider how some of the approaches that have been outlined in this chapter have been put into practice. Two actual task-based syllabuses that have been used with EFL learners in Japanese universities will be considered. The first example (Lambert and Robinson, 2014) will illustrate a task-based syllabus which is based on an analysis of the future needs of Japanese English majors at public university in Japan. The syllabus is intended to function as an *illuminative* construct within the L2 curriculum in that it is highly structured and aims to account for the specific learning processes (automaticity, restructuring etc.) that take place at different stages for all learners. In contrast, the second example (Kelly and Kelly, 1996) will illustrate a task-based syllabus in which tasks were selected based on the materials designer's experience and intuition of tasks that are intrinsically interesting to Japanese EFL learners and that are likely to develop their general interactive competence in using English. Unlike Lambert and Robinson (2014), this syllabus functions as an *operational* construct within the L2 curriculum in that it has a relatively low degree of structure. In addition to the main task sequence, it provides optional exercises for teachers to draw on in supporting different learners in different contexts.

Example 1:

The SSARC model of L2 task sequencing

This example is a task-based syllabus used with English majors at a Japanese university (Lambert and Robinson, 2014). A task-based needs analysis revealed that summarizing English-language materials was one of five critical task types for English majors at the university (Lambert, 2010). In the module, task sequences were developed to train learners in summarizing English-language short stories. The picture strips used in the first four lessons of the syllabus were taken from Trondheim (2007) and adapted for the pedagogic tasks used in each sequence. This children's book consists of thirty highly comparable sixty-frame pictures stories involving a protagonist (Mr I) and his series of frustrated attempts to steal a piece of a pie cooling in a window.

The example consists of a module of six lessons. The first two were based on simplified versions of the stories in which frames relating to mental states were removed so that the narrative consisted only of a series of physical actions and motion paths. The first lesson was intended to activate learners' current L2 resources in connection with the task and draw their attention to resources that they had already learned for conjoining clauses and expressing different types of motion in English. It was thus connected with the simplify-and-stabilize phase of Robinson's (2010) SSARC model. The second lesson was intended to automatize the resources that learners brought to bear in Lesson 1 and was connected with the *automatize* phase of the SSARC model. The focus was on extensive, time-pressured use of relevant language forms in different contexts.

The third and fourth lessons were based on longer picture strips (sixty frames), which included frames representing both actions and the mental states of the characters involved in the narrative. The third lesson was intended to force learners to restructure and complexify (the final phase of the SSARC model) the resources that learners brought to bear in Lesson 1 and automatized in Lesson 2 in line with the demands of adding mental states to their narratives and the verbal subordination processes that facilitate such narratives. The fourth lesson was then intended to provide more extensive practice of the resources that learners had brought to bear in Lesson 3 and develop flexibility in applying them in new and diverse contexts, returning to the *automatize* phase of the SSARC model.

Finally, the fifth and sixth lessons were based on authentic English-language short stories. In the fifth lesson, learners summarized Japanese short stories in English translation, and in the sixth lesson, they summarized original English short stories. The purpose of the fifth lesson was again to provide them with exposure to language used with each story and notice the gaps between their own production and the production of their native-speaking peers. It was thus connected with further *restructuring* and *complexifying* their language for summarizing stories. Learners were expected to pick out the important events in the story, say what they thought the characters were thinking and feeling to behave the ways that they did, and try to provide some conclusion of their own regarding what the stories mean. In the sixth lesson, the purpose was again to *automatize* the resources brought to bear in Lesson 5 and develop fluency and flexibility in applying what each learner had acquired in different contexts.

The task sequences in each lesson illustrate how the syllabus relates directly to the learning processes that are intended to occur:

Lesson 1: *Activate* and *stabilize* current L2 resources for narrating *physical actions*

Task 1: Each learner in a group of four has a different twenty-four-frame picture strip story limited to overt actions. They summarize their stories as best as they can so that the others can sequence scrambled sets of pictures. They are given time to prepare and make notes next to each frame.

Task 2: Learners complete cloze activities based on transcriptions of their native-speaking peers completing the narratives from Task 1. The focus is on coordinating conjunctions used to combine clauses. They first guess the missing conjunctions, then listen to check their answers.

Task 3: Learners repeat Task 1 eight frames at a time. Next to each frame, options for verbs of motion are provided (e.g. came back, walked over, snuck over, etc.) for learners to choose from as they tell the story. They perform the task three times in pairs, changing partners each time.

Task 4: Learners listen to two different native speakers narrate a new story. They use cloze transcripts to guess missing conjunctions and verb particles for verbs of motion then listen and check their answers.

Task 5: Learners repeat Task 1 after ten minutes of planning time.

Revision: Learners read the transcripts of native speaking peers telling the four stories they told in class, identify useful language and expressions, and write a narrative of a new story incorporating this language.

Lesson 2: *Automatize* current L2 resources for narrating *physical actions*

Task 1: Learners retell the stories from Lesson 1 (Tasks 1 and 5) three times each to different partners each time under time pressure. Listeners make notes to tell each story back to the original speaker, who confirms or corrects key facts.

Task 2: Learners repeat the procedures for Task 1 with the new stories that they completed for homework under progressively increasing time pressures.

Task 3: Learners read cloze versions of transcripts of the stories in Task 2 with bold type used to focus their attention on subordinating conjunctions for combining clauses.

Task 4: The procedures in Tasks 1 and 2 are repeated in telling and retelling new stories. Learners are given ten minutes to plan.

Revision: Learners read transcripts of the stories told in class, identify useful language and expressions, and write two letters to a friend summarizing two of these stories. They include what they believed each character was thinking and why they behaved in the way they did to activate their current L2 resources for the subsequent lesson.

Lesson 3: *Restructure* and *complexify* L2 resources for narrating *physical actions* and *mental states*

Task 1: Learners summarize the stories they had prepared for homework, telling them three times each to different partners each time.

Task 2: Learners listen to a narration of a full (sixty-frame) story consisting of frames connected with actions and mental states. They listen statement by statement, writing the number of the statement connected to each frame. Multi-clause statements sometimes correspond to multiple frames.

Task 3: Learners guess the missing verbs in twenty statements made that attribute mental states to characters (Mr I *noticed that* ..., He was *surprised that* ..., etc.), and listen to check their answers.

Task 4: Learners complete a dictation task of five statements made and label the function of each statement (provide background, establish goal, state outcome, draw a conclusion etc.).

Revision: Learners study transcripts of statements from Task 2 in relation to the frames of the story they described. The examples involve subordinated constructions relating to mental states and expressing motivations for the story. They prepare a narration of the full sixty-frame version of the stories that they had summarized in Lesson 1 (Task 1) with mental state frames included.

Lesson 4: *Automatize* new L2 resources for narrating *physical actions* and *mental states*

Task 1: Learners tell the stories they had prepared for homework in pairs and make notes on ways to improve them based on language their partner used in telling her story.

Task 2: Learners listen to narrations of the full sixty-frame versions of the stories they prepared for homework and note how these narratives differ from their own.

Task 3: Learners read twenty statements expressing cause-and-effect relationships used with gapped connector words (i.e. in order that, so, as a result), guess the missing words and listen to check.

Task 4: Learners summarize new sixty-frame stories (actions, intentions, motivations). They have five minutes to prepare.

Revision: Learners review transcripts and write 1,000-word summaries of a new sixty-frame story. They also read one of four short stories by Haruki Murakami and prepare to summarize it in the next class.

Lesson 5: *Restructure* and *complexify* L2 resources for summarizing *authentic short stories*

Task 1: Learners take turns summarizing their Murakami stories in groups of four.

Task 2: Learners listen to a recording of a proficient speaker summarizing of one of the Murakami stories and identify which of the forty-eight words were used to explain the mental states (e.g. remembers, wonders, hopes, anticipates).

Task 3: Learners listen to a summary of a second story. They identify events from the story which were mentioned or left out.

Task 4: Learners listen to a summary of a third story. They identify statements that are true and false.

Task 5: Learners listen to a summary of a fourth story. They identify the conclusion made.

Task 6: Learners repeat Task 1 after ten minutes of planning time.

Revision: Learners review transcripts of the Murakami summaries from class with key elements highlighted. They also read one of four short stories by Ernest Hemingway and prepare to summarize it in the next class. They pick out the important events in the story, say what they think the characters are thinking and feeling to motivate their actions, and provide a conclusion on the story's meaning.

Lesson 6: *Automatize* L2 resources for summarizing *authentic short stories*

Task 1: Learners form groups of four and work in pairs to summarize their Hemingway stories three times each to different partners each time without time pressure. They thus tell their story three times and hear three other stories once each. Each time they make notes and retell the story that they heard back to their partner, who checks and corrects any problems.

Task 2: Learners change to a new group of four. They repeat Task 1 under increasing time pressure.

Example 2:

A modular approach to the task-based syllabus

The second example of a task-based syllabus is from a published textbook for use in courses aimed at developing oral English skills in Japanese universities (Kelly and Kelly, 1991). The book provides an interesting example of how task-based and task-supported structural syllabuses might be used in parallel for learners of differing motivations and aptitudes based on enjoyable and cognitively engaging content. The task sequences in the book are organized around solving mysteries through detective work (e.g. catch a killer, disarm a bomb, identify counterfeits, perform rescues, catch a thief etc.). The tasks were not selected based on an analysis of the situations that learners might face in the future, but based on the materials designer's experience of what is intrinsically interesting to the targeted student population and the opportunities that they provide for learners to develop the interactive skills that they need in order to complete the range of tasks that they will face in the future. As none of the tasks could be argued to be more frequent or critical for learners, the arrangement of task types within the syllabus seems to have been a matter of convenience or intuition.

The example is taken from Unit 2 of the book and involves a sequence of tasks which involves finding and disarming a bomb. Learners work together in pairs to share information in order to complete a three-task sequence: (1) find the apartment in which the bomb is hidden, (2) find the piece of furniture in which the bomb is hidden, and (3) follow instructions for disarming the bomb. In the first task, learners each see the outside of six apartments. One learner has the view of these apartments in the morning, and the other has the view in the afternoon. They are told that two changes were made outside of the apartment containing the bomb between morning and afternoon. They work together based on their own L2 resources to describe each of the entrances and find the one with two differences. In the second task, they move to the interior of the apartment to identify the piece of furniture in which the bomb is hidden. One has a picture representing a perspective on the interior of the apartment, and the other has a floorplan from a rotated perspective. They must describe and compare the ten objects in the room in relationship to one another in order establish a shared perspective and identify what the shape on the floorplan containing the bomb corresponds to in the room. Finally, in the third task, they disarm the bomb. Both of the learners have pictures of the same bomb consisting of several different colour wires, a timer, a battery and some explosives. However, one learner has a precise eight-step sequence for disarming it labelled on this diagram (cutting, disconnecting, turning off, etc.), and the other does not. The speaker must explain these steps to the listener, who must ask any questions in order to execute each step accurately by marking the diagram.

As learners complete each task sequence in the book, they have a checklist to write their answers. When they are finished with the sequence, the teacher evaluates this checklist and allocates points for correct answers. The teacher often has some flexibility in the level of precision required in learners' answers so that higher-proficiency learners can be pushed to be more precise than lower-proficiency learners. Students then enter their points for each task sequence into the back of the book to track their progress across the course. In the end, they are awarded a level of achievement based on the quality of their detective work rather than their English. The entire book is set up as a detective school in which they must solve multiple mysteries, and the focus throughout is thus on achieving these task outcomes rather than on the language used.

In addition to the task sequences and the goal-tracking system, an additional sequence of task-supported language exercises is provided for each task sequence in a separate part of the book. Based on the motivation, aptitude and ability of their learners, teachers can choose to leave this material out entirely or draw on it in part or in whole before, during or after the task sequences, based on the needs of each group. The resources consist of vocabulary items which might ease learners' cognitive load while completing the tasks, input-based tasks and slot-and-frame structures which draw attention to key functions for negotiating meaning (asking for more information, confirming, clarifying, asking to repeat, expressing uncertainty, etc.) when completing each task sequence. Finally, two comparatively simple versions of the tasks in the main task sequence are provided for learners to practice using these resources. The first is typically a simplified version of one of the tasks in the main task sequence (identify T-shirts by describing shapes in relationship to one another), and the second is typically an open task allowing learners to discuss content of their own (design a T-shirt and describe it so that you partner can draw it).

Clearly, the purpose of the course provided in Kelly and Kelly (1991) is not to train learners to complete the specific tasks involved in locating and disarming bombs in the future, but to provide engaging pedagogic tasks which develop their interactive competence in using English to negotiate understanding on a range of tasks in the future. Likewise, the syllabus is not intended to determine the learning processes that will take place for all learners, but to support the teacher in ways in which learners at different levels of proficiency, motivation and aptitude profiles might be aided in successfully completing the task sequences in the syllabus, thereby improving their interactive competence in English.

Conclusion

It should be clear from the discussions in this chapter, that each of the approaches to task-based L2 syllabus design that have been covered are with the essential principles of TBLT outlined in Chapter 1, and that they all have advantages and disadvantages which will make them more or less appropriate to the needs of teachers and learners in different instructional contexts. In concluding, it will be helpful to compare the strengths and limitations of each.

In the approach advocated by Long (1985, 2015), the focus is on learners' ability to perform specific real-world tasks that they are likely to encounter outside of the classroom. As in other forms of workplace training, syllabus content is selected and organized in terms of the frequency and criticality of these target tasks that learners need to complete, and learners are trained with initially simple, progressively more demanding, versions of each task so that they can master what performance of the full task requires. At the syllabus level, L2 development is seen as a by-product of task learning. Learners acquire the language necessary to complete tasks incidentally as a function of learning to complete tasks effectively and efficiently. Focusing on task learning rather than language in this way avoids the problems of variability in SLA and provides criterion-based learning outcomes for all learners that directly reflect what they need to accomplish outside of the classroom.

However, L2 learners and policy makers are often interested in developing more than the ability to accomplish specific tasks. Many stakeholders in language education are interested in developing the general competences that proficient speakers bring to bear on tasks. Robinson's (2010) approach to task-based syllabus design provides a solution to accounting for broader L2 development as a product of performing tasks. By attempting to specify the cognitive and affective demands of tasks in addition to identifying the tasks themselves, Robinson's approach aims to predict the language learning processes that will take place on tasks. While an admirable goal for research, this approach might not be feasible for L2 practitioners in contexts with mandated tests and curricular content.

In this regard, Ellis (2018a, Chapter 10) argues that a modular approach to task-based language teaching will not only allow practitioners to experiment with tasks within the context of current language curricula, but that this combination of approaches might complement one another and lead to learning outcomes that neither approach can achieve easily on its own. Like Prabhu (1987), however, Ellis advocates an operational syllabus over an illuminative syllabus, even if an illuminative syllabus were possible in a given context. He argues that seeing to the details of L2 development on tasks is best done by teachers in situ with specific groups of learners. Ellis argues that the syllabus should not function to dictate the procedures used in the classroom, but that it should provide teachers with resources and freedom to address the needs of learners differing in motivation and aptitudes as well as fluctuations in classroom dynamics.

8 Methodology of Task-Based Language Teaching

Introduction

The methodology of task-based teaching refers to the various options for task implementation that may affect the affective and linguistic aspects of task performance and the learning that results. This chapter seeks to explore options and ideas that are empirically informed and/or theoretically justified, to stimulate thoughts for further research, and to expand pedagogical choice building on available research and current practices. The chapter will foreground the importance of making evidence-based decisions, reflecting 'the centrality for research' in a task-based approach in comparison with 'communicative language teaching' that is comprised of some loose concepts devoid of theoretical and empirical support (Skehan et al., 2012). Three types of evidence are drawn upon in this chapter, including: (1) empirical evidence, which consists of the methodological options reported in the research and the findings regarding the effects these have on the process and product aspects of task-based learning; (2) practical evidence, which takes the form of pedagogical recommendations proposed by teacher guides; and (3) theoretical claims on the benefits and limitations of task-related procedures.

The three types of information roughly correspond with Long's (2015) evaluation criteria for the validity of the methodological principles he proposed for the implementation of task-based language teaching (TBLT). Long claimed that the principles are based on at least one of the three major criteria: theoretical motivation, empirical support and logical argumentation. The three criteria were illustrated through the example of corrective feedback (CF), the utility of which is supported by multiple theories (theoretical motivation), a large amount of research (empirical support) and arguments (logical arguments, not claims of independent, well-established theories) such as that of Lydia White (1987), who worried about the impossibility of unlearning errors related to first language influence merely through positive evidence. Long states that due to various constraints, there has been a lack of research in certain areas, but language teaching cannot be 'put off for a few years while the research is carried out' (p. 301). Therefore, alternative criteria such as theoretical motivation and logical argumentation are in order.

In his discussion of the methodology of task-based teaching, Long (2015) made a distinction between methodological principles and pedagogical procedures. Methodological principles are language teaching universals, informing teachers of what should be done; pedagogical procedures are specific steps teachers follow in implementing the principles, specifying how it should be done. Long (2015) only elaborated some methodological principles ('elaborate input', 'provide negative feedback', etc.) without discussing pedagogical procedures, on the grounds that there are an infinite range of options to instantiate the principles and the job of how to implement a principle should be left to the local teacher. In this chapter, we do not make a distinction between principles and procedures (although our discussion will centre more on the latter); rather, we take a bottom-up approach providing a detailed description of the various options available for teachers at each stage of a TBLT lesson. We will consider these options in terms of the three stages of a task cycle: pre-task, main task and post-task (Ellis, 2003).

Dividing the task cycle into the three stages provides a convenient framework to discuss the procedural aspects of a task-based lesson (Willis, 1996; Ellis, 2003; see also Chapter 1). The pre-task stage serves to prepare learners for the main task and the post-task stage is where learners engage in follow-up activities after the task is completed. Ellis (2003) pointed out that among the three stages, only the main task stage is required. However, as we will see, pre-task and post-task activities are critical to achieving the goals of task-based teaching, and there has been abundant research on the influence of the various options, especially pre-task options, on task performance and learning gains. It is necessary to clarify that although the three stages are discussed in the context of a single task-based lesson, they can occur in different lessons. For example, in preparation for a debate on gun control, the teacher may brainstorm the topic with students in the previous lesson to arouse their interest. Similarly, after completing the main task, students may be asked to reflect on their task performance in the next lesson. Furthermore, one component that applies to all three stages of a task cycle is participatory structure, which refers to the pattern of interaction a task involves. In the following sections, we will elaborate the various options for the three stages, followed by a brief discussion of participatory structure.

Pre-Task Options

Various activities can be conducted in the pre-task stage (see Table 8.1 for a summary), some of which have been examined through empirical research. To know what activities should be included in the pre-task stage, it is important to understand the goals of pre-task activities. First, pre-task activities serve to motivate learners, arousing their interest and building up their expectations. To motivate learners, teachers may inform students of the relevance of the task to their personal life, the real world and/or their study goals (see Dembovskaya (2009), discussed in Chapter 5, for example pre-task motivating strategies). Giving students a reason to perform the task is especially important in foreign language settings or for learners who have no prior experience with tasks and who may have negative perceptions about a task-based approach. Willis and Willis (2007) noted that for comprehension (reading and listening) tasks, having students make predictions about the content of the aural or written text, such as by using the title or subtitles and accompanying visuals, is an especially effective motivating strategy. Although task motivation has significant theoretical and pedagogical value for a task-based approach, there has been very little research on this aspect of TBLT (see Chapter 5).

The second goal of pre-task activities is to prepare learners for the upcoming main task. Learners' preparedness for a task means that (1) they are clear about the task procedure and expected outcome, and (2) they are equipped with the adequate resources required for task completion including the relevant linguistic and schematic knowledge – background information about the topic. It should be clarified that here linguistic knowledge refers to lexical or vocabulary knowledge, not knowledge about grammar or morphosyntax. Whereas vocabulary is essential for task completion, grammar is often not important although it may facilitate the accuracy of communication. The controversy over whether to teach grammar in the pre-task stage will be addressed in the next section. Furthermore, it is important to clarify that the purpose of providing learners with the necessary vocabulary is to scaffold rather than stipulate the language needed for task performance.

The third goal of pre-task activities is to provide learning opportunities which may have an effect on learning outcomes or task performance. For example, responding to a survey or quiz about the topic of the subsequent task may encourage learners to think and talk about

Table 8.1 Summary of pre-task methodological options

Options	Description	Recommendations
Pre-task planning	Learners are given time to plan the content and language of subsequent task performance	• 1 – 3 minutes of planning seem ideal, but teachers should customize the length of planning according to learner and task characteristics • During planning, teachers may consider allowing students to make notes, work with language materials, and plan in their L1, L2 or both. • No planning is an option
Pre-task focus on form	Pre-task grammar instruction: learners are taught a grammar rule before task performance	• Make sparing use of pre-task grammar instruction because it may affect learners' fluency and the complexity of their speech production.
	Pre-task modelling: learners are provided with a model performance	• Be careful about what to model because the model has a significant impact on learners' task performance.
Other options	Topic preparation: provide content knowledge about the topic	• Too much background knowledge reduces negotiation
	Teacher scaffolding: perform a similar task together with learners	• Help learners with task procedure
	Vocabulary preparation	• Teach vocabulary to prepare learners for task performance but do not require them to use prescribed words

grammar and to look up new words. Allowing learners to plan may free up their attention, leaving more cognitive space for focusing on linguistic forms during task performance. Modelling how to negotiate meaning and form in the pre-task stage may increase the incidence of language-related episodes (LREs) in learner–learner interaction (see Chapter 4), which may lead to learning gains.

Pre-Task Planning

Pre-task planning, sometimes called strategic planning, is a pedagogical option that allows learners time to plan the content and language of their task performance before the main task. Pre-task planning is probably the most researched pre-task option in task-based research, and the intensity of the interest is both theoretically and empirically motivated. Theoretically, task planning has been extensively investigated to verify Skehan's Limited Attention Capacity Hypothesis (LACH) (see Chapter 3), which states that pre-task planning may ease the pressure on learners' limited cognitive resources during task performance and mitigate the trade-off between the various aspects of speech production such as complexity and accuracy. The findings of planning research have often been cited to support Skehan's theory and counter Robinson's Cognition Hypothesis (CH), which states that there is no trade-off between complexity and accuracy because they draw on different resources, and that what affects learners' task performance is the processing demands of the task, rather than learners' limited attentional capacity. Pedagogically, some teachers consider it important to allow students some time to plan to make them more prepared and to make performing a task in a second language (L2) a more pleasant experience. Others, however, hold that pre-task planning may deprive students of the opportunity to practise how to use L2 knowledge in spontaneous communication. Planning is also of relevance to language testing. Wigglesworth and Elder (2010) argued that planning contributes to the fairness of an oral test by reducing learners' stress and anxiety to enable them to achieve their best possible performance. In the following, we summarize planning research with a view to demonstrating how the findings can inform pedagogical decisions.

The Effects of Pre-Task Planning. The effects of pre-task planning can be investigated in two ways: in terms of its influence on learners' task performance and on the learning gains that result from performing the task. Task performance concerns what happens while learners are performing a task, namely the process features of task-based instruction (TBI). Learning gains, which are measured through pre-tests and post-tests, pertain to the product aspect of TBI. To date, the majority of studies have investigated task performance, and only one study (Romanova, 2010) has examined the impact of planning on learning gains. The study will be discussed in the section on main task options because it also examined two during-task options: within-task planning and online feedback.

Ellis (2009b) synthesized the research on the effects of pre-task planning on task performance in terms of the complexity, accuracy and fluency (CAF) of learners' speech production. He reports that the research has shown consistent effects for planning on fluency and complexity but its effects on accuracy have been variable and unstable. Ortega (1999) also noted mixed findings regarding the influence of pre-task planning on accuracy: 'When the accuracy findings for all planning studies are taken together, it is also difficult to see any consistent patterns' (p. 134). Crookes (1989) was one of the first studies examining the effects of pre-task planning. In this study, forty adult L1 Japanese English as a Second Language (ESL) learners were divided into two groups and performed two monologic tasks. The planning group was allowed ten minutes to plan and the other group performed the tasks without planning. The study found significant effects for complexity in terms of lexical variety and syntactic complexity measured by words per utterance, subordination and S-nodes per utterance, but no difference was found for general accuracy measured through the number of error-free T-units.

Why does pre-task planning have stronger effects on fluency and complexity than accuracy? The primary reason seems to be that learners spend most of the planning time organizing the content, rather than language, of their task performance, which eases the burden on the conceptualizer and leads to more fluent and complex language. Sangarun (2005) reported that regardless of whether learners' attention was directed towards content or language, their planning primarily focused on meaning. During task performance, learners must match the planned content with the relevant linguistic items, leading to more complex language. The elevated complexity is probably obtained at the expense of accuracy, confirming Skehan's LACH.

Duration of Planning. In most studies investigating pre-task planning (e.g. Ortega, 1999; Fu and Li, 2017), learners are allowed ten minutes to plan – a practice based on Mehnert's (1998) study, which is probably the first to examine the impact of length of planning on learners' performance. In this study, thirty-one L1 English and L2 German learners were divided into four groups and performed two oral tasks. The four groups were allowed to plan for zero, one, five and ten minutes respectively. When the data for both tasks were combined, the results showed that, for fluency, all planning groups outperformed the no-planning group, and the effects were incremental, that is, longer planning time led to higher levels of fluency. For accuracy, planning had a significant effect compared with no planning, but the effects were non-linear in that the one-minute planning group showed higher accuracy than the five-minute and ten-minute groups. For complexity, the ten-minute planners outperformed all other groups but were only significantly better than the five-minute planners; the non-planners showed higher scores than the one-minute and five-minute planners. Overall, the results showed that the length of planning time had the largest effect on fluency, less on accuracy and least on complexity, and that the effects were non-linear. However, the sample size of the study is small, with seven to eight participants in each group. Therefore, the generalizability of the findings is limited.

Li, Chen and Sun's (2015) study was conducted in a testing condition – learners were informed that their test performance counted towards their final grades for the course. The planning lengths they investigated were zero, one and five minutes, and thirty seconds. For fluency, the effects were incremental but plateaued after three minutes, and thirty seconds did not make a difference. For accuracy, the one-minute, three-minute and five-minute groups outperformed the zero-minute and one-minute groups but after one minute, there was not much difference. For syntactic complexity, the thirty-second, two-minute and five-minute groups outperformed other groups. Finally, for lexical complexity, the one-minute group did best. Overall the results showed that planning below one minute did not seem to work and that the effects were non-linear and tended to plateau after one or three minutes.

In another study that was claimed by the researchers (Wigglesworth and Elder, 2010) to be conducted under a testing condition, three planning lengths were examined: zero, one and two minutes. The researchers failed to find any benefits for planning in terms of either objective CAF measures or subjective ratings. Their explanations for the null effects for planning were: (1) learners couldn't remember what they planned, and even if they did, planning might have affected only the first few utterances, not the whole task performance; (2) the task performance was monologic and unpressured, which allowed learners to plan online and so made pre-task planning superfluous. Although this study was conducted using tasks similar to those in an International English Language Testing System (IELTS) test, it is not a 'pure' testing study because the learners' task performance did not affect their course grades or career development.

Whereas the tasks in these studies were monologic and the participants were adult learners, Philp, Oliver and Mackey (2006) examined interactive tasks where the learners were children. The study showed that no planning and two-minute planning led to more CF than five minutes, no planning resulted in longer utterances and five-minute planning enhanced grammatical complexity. The researchers argued that planning made learners familiar with the content and removed the need for negotiation, hence less feedback and shorter utterances. They also exemplified how too much planning caused trouble for classroom management with children, who can become restless more easily than adults.

The research reviewed above suggests that allowing students to plan for one to three minutes (maximum five minutes) seem ideal and practical, and this recommendation is based on the following grounds. First, one to three minutes of planning seem effective in facilitating CAF performance, and after three minutes, task performance seems to plateau on some measures. Second, although in many studies ten minutes is the default time, longer planning time does not always lead to better performance. In fact, the effects of planning duration are often non-linear, with shorter planning times showing larger effects. Third, in real classroom settings where teachers are often under time pressure, it is not always feasible to allocate ten minutes for pre-task planning. Fourth, for tasks involving interaction, planning increases learners' familiarity with the content and reduces the need for negotiation – a feature that is a main source of learning, according to the interactionists (Pica, 1987; Long, 1996; Gass, 1997; see Chapter 2). Fifth, in child language classes, too much planning causes management difficulty. We would like to point out that that we do not wish to make it a hard rule for teachers to follow. Teachers are task executers, and they are able to make the best decisions regarding the length of planning based on the nature, difficulty and goals of the task and other idiosyncratic constraints imposed by the local instructional setting. We also need to acknowledge that the results of the planning studies were very mixed, which makes it difficult to arrive at definite conclusions.

Finally, in the research on the influence of the amount of time for planning as well as the research on planning in general, the duration of planning is invariably imposed by researchers, and learners are never given the freedom to decide how much time they need for planning. Also, in existing research, duration of planning is operationalized as a categorical variable. If learners are allowed to plan as long as they wish or need to, the duration of planning can be analysed as a continuous variable, and a correlation analysis can be conducted to ascertain whether longer planning time is associated with better task performance.

Other Options. There are a number of other aspects of pre-task planning of relevance to pedagogy and research. The first concerns notetaking during planning. In most studies (e.g. Park, 2010; Li and Fu, 2017), learners are allowed to make notes without writing complete sentences to ensure that (1) they did plan, and (2) they will not provide a scripted performance. However, doubts about the value of scripted performance have not been empirically tested, and it would be interesting to investigate the effects of different types of scripted planning, such as discrete phrases, complete sentences and complete scripts, on task performance. Second, in most planning studies or studies investigating the impact of the procedural and conceptual aspects of tasks on CAF, the tasks are purely output-based, and learners have no linguistic input prior to task performance. They were either asked to watch a silent video clip (Skehan et al., 2012) or view a picture with no accompanying L2 input (e.g. Ortega, 1999). While this practice may increase the internal study of the research, it deprives learners of the opportunity to learn from input, which is 'the *sine qua non* of acquisition' (Gass and Mackey, 2015, p. 181). Third, the language of planning is of particular pedagogical interest. In Park's (2010) study, learners were allowed to plan either in their L1 or L2, whereas in Mehnert (1998), only the L2 was allowed. In Ortega (1999), learners listened to a taped version of the narrative in their L1 before starting to plan to 'avoid too much individual variation in the story lines ... and to reduce the cognitive load of the narrative task' (p. 122). Park's and Ortega's studies show how learners' L1 can be judiciously used in the planning stage, given that such use has been criticized as a concern for implementing a task-based approach (Carless, 2004). Fourth, the research on planning, as well as the underlying theory (Skehan, 2014a; see also Chapter 3 of this volume), has primarily focused on CAF, not the acquisition of new linguistic knowledge. Therefore, the benefit of planning seems to be restricted to the retrieval, proceduralization and automatization of previous knowledge, which is critical to ultimate L2 attainment. However, the scope of the research should be expanded to include various options of form-focused instruction (FFI) (Ellis, 2016). We will discuss an example of such research in the section on within-task options later in this chapter.

To conclude this section, a final comment is in order: no planning is an option. While planning has been advocated and shown to be a useful pedagogical technique that leads to improved performance, an alternative position is warranted, that is, no planning also has a place in task-based methodology. Ortega (1999) reported that in her study twelve out of the thirty-two learners disliked the idea of planning because: (1) the tasks were simple enough, which made planning superfluous, (2) task performance is a matter of L2 proficiency and providing extra time does not necessarily help, (3) their planning notes were taken away before task performance (although this is a problem with the research design, not with planning per se), and (4) they thought that planning introduced more anxiety because then they would be expected to be more linguistically correct. Furthermore, as Robinson (2011) argued, it is important to increase task complexity along resource-dispersing variables (relating to the procedural aspects of tasks) such as by not allowing time to plan in order to encourage spontaneous communication.

Pre-Task Focus on Form

Skehan and Foster (2001) argued that the meaning-oriented nature of communicative tasks may distract learners from attending to the linguistic code and that some form-focusing strategies are needed to attract learners' attention to linguistic forms during task performance. In a similar vein, Kim (2013) pointed out that the purpose of including form-focusing techniques in the pre-task stage is 'to raise learners' awareness of these forms during planning time as well as during task performance' (p. 10). It is important to distinguish two broad types of form-focusing strategies: explicit and implicit. Explicit strategies overtly draw learners' attention to linguistic forms, such as through grammar explanation or input enhancement (e.g. by highlighting instances of a particular structure in the input). Implicit strategies induce learners' attention to forms indirectly by pre-task planning, which increases the chances for attention to form, or by providing a model performance demonstrating how to negotiate forms during group interaction (Kim, 2013). It must be pointed out that the explicit–implicit distinction is best seen as a continuum, not a dichotomy. In the following, we discuss two pre-task form-focusing options that have been researched: pre-task grammar instruction and pre-task modelling.

Pre-Task Grammar Instruction. Whether to provide explicit grammar explanation in the pre-task stage is of theoretical and pedagogical significance. In Long's (2015, 2016) model of TBLT, pre-task grammar instruction is not an option on the grounds that learners may not be developmentally ready for the preselected structure. Long argued that focus on grammar must happen reactively when learners experience difficulty with linguistic forms required for meaning-making. Skill acquisition theory (DeKeyser, 2013) holds that learners must have declarative knowledge, which can be learned through pre-task grammar instruction, proceduralized in subsequent skill-specific task performance and then automatized through repeated practice. Ellis (2003, 2017a) calls this approach task-supported language instruction, which he distinguishes from the purely task-based approach advocated by Long.

From a pedagogical perspective, those opposing pre-task grammar instruction (e.g. Willis, 1996) worry that explicit grammar instruction predisposes learners to focus on the target structure, with the result that they may treat a task as language practice rather than a site for information exchange. This practice, it is argued, will subvert the meaning-primary principle of task-based teaching. Proponents of pre-task grammar instruction contend that learners need grammar knowledge to perform a communicative task and that teachers prefer to teach grammar before asking students to perform a task (Littlewood, 2007; Shehadeh, 2012). Teachers' preference for pre-task grammar instruction has been examined in research. For example, van de Guchte et al. (2017) interviewed five experienced 'task-based language teachers' (p. 2) in a Dutch secondary school about the necessity of such instruction. They all indicated that they taught grammar explicitly before asking learners to perform an oral or written task. Their argument was that most other Dutch teachers taught grammar in their classes and so that they wanted to ensure that their students knew the same grammar rules as other students. However, to date, there is a lack of research on students' perceptions about TBLT.

What has research demonstrated about the influence of pre-task grammar instruction on task performance and learning effects? To date, Ellis, Li and Zhu (2018) is the only study that has investigated this question. In their study, ninety 8th-grade Chinese English as a Foreign Language (EFL) learners were divided into three groups. One group received a ten-minute grammar lesson on how to use the English passive voice before performing two similar dictogloss tasks. During each task, the teacher presented a story on PowerPoint, then the students worked in pairs to practise retelling the story, and finally they took turns to report the story to the rest of the class. A second group performed the two tasks without receiving pre-task grammar explanation. The researchers measured students' task performance during the reporting stage through CAF. The results suggest that pre-task grammar instruction had a harmful influence on learners' task performance in terms of the CAF of their speech production. Probably the grammar instruction caused them to focus their attention on the target structure at the sacrifice of overall performance. Also, although the grammar instruction led to more frequent use of the target structure, it failed to make the learners more accurate in producing it. The results of this study suggest that it might be better to avoid pre-task grammar instruction. However, this does not mean grammar should not be addressed at some point in a task-based lesson. Both Ellis (2009a) and Long (2016) acknowledge the importance of focus on form in TBLT. The question is when and how the focus on form should happen.

Pre-Task Modelling. An alternative to grammar instruction in the pre-task stage is modelling. This involves techniques that serve to: (1) clarify task procedures, (2) demonstrate expected group dynamics (e.g. how to negotiate with other group members), (3) provide linguistic and pragmatic support, and (4) afford learning opportunities by focusing on a particular linguistic structure. Modelling has many variants, and it is important to attend to the details of the modelled performance because they can influence how learners perform the task.

Kim (2013) reported a study where Korean middle school EFL learners participated in a pull-out programme designed to enhance their oral proficiency. The learners were divided into two groups. One group viewed a task modelling video before performing the task and the other did not. Both groups attended three 45-minute treatment sessions, and during each session they performed a focused task targeting English question formation. The modelling group watched a two-minute video clip showing how to deal with linguistic problems relating to question formation, such as by providing feedback to each other. For example,

A: How many types of pets?
B: No, you should use an auxiliary verb first (in students' L1 – Korean)
A: How many types of pets do they have?

The modelling performance was provided by the researcher and the learners' own English teacher. The scripts were written by the researcher. The instructional effects were measured by examining LREs, defined as utterances where learners 'talk about the language they are producing, question their language use, or correct themselves or others' (Swain and Lapkin, 1998, p. 326) during planning and task performance, and also by means of pre- and post-tests. L2 development was operationalized as the number of learners who produced questions at a higher developmental stage in the immediate and delayed post-tests. The results showed that students in the modelling group produced significantly more LREs than the control group and the number of students who advanced to higher stages of question formation was significantly greater than the control group.

Kim's (2013) study is insightful for a number of reasons. First, it shows how to draw learners' attention to linguistic forms through modelling. Used properly, modelling can serve as an effective alternative to grammar instruction, which, as we noted, may affect learners' task performance. However, the study did not examine CAF, so it is not clear whether modelling, like grammar instruction, has a negative impact on learners' task performance. Second, in Kim's study, in the video two teachers modelled the task that was to be carried out by the students but this in effect removed the 'gap' in the task. It might have been better if the teachers had modelled a similar task rather than the same task. Third, in the modelling video, the teachers used the students' L1 to comment on each other's language use, which led to the students making extensive use of their L1 in the LREs during the pair work. This study shows that modelling has a powerful influence on how students perform a task.

Another study that provides valuable information on modelling is van de Guchte et al. (2017). This study examined the influence of language-focused and meaning-focused modelling on the use of the target structure as well as on overall complexity, as represented by the learners' use of coordination and subordination. Forty-eight 9th-grade L2 German learners at a Dutch school were divided into two groups, both watching two videos of two girls describing a school cafeteria to persuade potential students to enrol in the school. The target structure was locative prepositions. While watching, the language-focused group was asked to write twelve sentences that the actresses used to describe the locations of the objects in the cafeteria, while the meaning-oriented group was asked to answer eight questions about how the presenters in the video persuaded prospective students to enrol in the advertised school. After watching the videos, the students were allowed to plan for ten minutes, writing down ten keywords, which were later taken away. Then the students were asked to describe a school cafeteria shown in a picture, which served as the post-test. A similar task was completed before the treatment as the pre-test and three weeks later as the delayed post-test. The results revealed an overall trade-off between the use of the target structure and overall task performance. The language-focused group attempted more frequent and accurate use of the target structure but the meaning-focused group showed greater linguistic complexity. The study did not measure overall accuracy or fluency so it is not clear what influence the two different types of modelling had on those two aspects of overall task performance.

The way the modelling was provided in this study has implications for pedagogy. First, in contrast to the modelling in Kim (2013), which was conducted by two teachers, in this study the modelling was provided by two actresses whose ages were similar to the students'.

The researchers stated that peer (instead of teacher) modelling videos were used 'to increase the chance of identification, confidence, and motivation' (p. 7). The authors also pointed out that students in the current cohort could be used to model performances for students in future semesters. Second, this study shows the importance of carefully designing and conducting the model performance. Modelling may influence learners' use of language, whether they orientate to meaning or form when they perform the task, and the affective aspects of task performance such as their confidence and motivation.

Other Pre-Task Activities

Other activities that might be included in the pre-task stage include developing learners' schematic knowledge of the task topic, providing scaffolding and teaching vocabulary (Ellis, 2003). The purpose of developing schematic knowledge is to increase learners' familiarity with the content domain of the task. This aspect of task familiarity – namely, topic familiarity – is distinguishable from familiarity with the procedure of a task. Topic familiarity frees up learners' attentional resources allowing them to allocate more resources to the formal aspects of a task. In addition to the potential benefits in enhancing task performance, task familiarity may have a positive impact on motivation. In research on reading, topic familiarity has been found to facilitate vocabulary learning (e.g. Pulido, 2007) but it has not received much attention in research on oral production tasks. Skehan (2009a) noted that a task with familiar content (as in personal narratives) led to greater fluency and accuracy but less complexity than a task with unfamiliar content (as in a narrative and an argumentative task), suggesting a positive effect for tasks with less familiar content. Therefore, while teachers need to ensure that learners have sufficient background information, there is also a case for tasks with less familiar content.

Teacher scaffolding refers to the level of assistance teachers provide to enable a task to be completed successfully. Scaffolding is a concept of the sociocultural theory (Lantolf, Thorne and Poehner, 2015; also see Chapter 4). The type and amount of assistance is not predetermined but needs to be determined in flight as the task unfolds. One such example can be found in the Bangalore Project (Prabhu, 1987) where the teacher performed a pre-task with the students by means of question/answer before asking students to perform the main task independently. This is not the same as modelling as the teacher does not provide a model performance. Rather the teacher aims to provide 'other-regulation' to enable the development of 'self-regulation', namely the ability of the learner to perform a task without assistance.

According to Willis and Willis (2007), learners should receive assistance with the vocabulary required for task completion in the pre-task stage. However, as Ellis (2003) warned, pre-teaching vocabulary my result in learners treating the task as a practice activity for the pre-selected words. Willis and Willis float the idea of 'linguistic mining' as an alternative to direct teaching. For example, the teacher could give students a questionnaire on the topic of the task prior to task performance and leave it to the students to take the initiative to understand the meanings of key lexical items by consulting their peers or a dictionary. Students can also draw up a list of words that they deem important for performing the task individually and then compare lists, resulting in a list of items that are of central importance for performing the task. But teachers should avoid requiring students to use specified words when performing the task to prevent it becoming a vocabulary exercise.

Options for the Main Task

In this section, we examine different types of within-task focus on form (see Table 8.2), particularly CF, which has been the focus of a large amount of research since the late 1990s (see Chapter 2). We conclude this section by exploring other considerations that may affect the way learners perform a task and the resulting learning outcomes.

Within-Task Focus on Form

Within-task focus on form refers to attention to linguistic problems while the task is ongoing. As explained in Chapter 2, it can be preemptive or reactive (Ellis, Basturkmen and Loewen, 2002). In preemptive focus on form, the teacher draws the learner's attention to form in anticipation of a linguistic problem or the learner makes a language-related enquiry to the teacher or a peer. In reactive focus on form, attempts to address linguistic forms are made in response to errors learners produce in their task performance. Reactive focus on form has been referred to as CF and is viewed by Long (2015) as the primary way of doing focus on form. Within reactive focus on form, Ellis et al. (2002) made a further distinction between conversational and didactic focus on form, with the former referring to situations where linguistic errors are dealt with to resolve communication breakdowns and the latter to situations where errors do not cause communication breakdowns and where language is treated as an object. A related distinction is that between planned and incidental focus on form. In planned focus on form, the teacher makes an a priori decision

Table 8.2 Summary of within-task methodological options

Options	Description	Recommendations
Within-task focus on form	CF: provide feedback on errors arising during task performance	• Use mixed feedback • Start with a prompt and provide a recast in the absence of self-correction
	Integrated focus on form	• Interrupt a task to address linguistic forms
Other options	Within-task planning: no time constraint is imposed on task performance	• Use within-task planning with beginners
	Access to support	• Provide access to linguistic input such as word cues • Do not provide access to non-linguistic input such as pictures
	A surprise element	• Introduce a new element to increase amount of production and motivation
	Interim goals	• Add interim goals to increase task structure and task accountability

to target a linguistic structure consistently; in incidental focus on form, the teacher addresses linguistic forms in a contingent manner and it is not planned ahead of time.

Another distinction, which has been the focus of the research by Spada et al. (2014), is between integrated and isolated focus on form. According to them, integrated focus on form is 'provided within communicative/content-based activities', whereas isolated focus on form is 'provided separately from communicative/content-based activities' (p. 457) and thus corresponds to the provision of explicit instruction in the pre-task stage of a lesson. Thus the difference between integrated and isolated focus on form is that the former is embedded in communication and the latter occurs in separate blocks of grammar instruction. Integrated focus on form, they further explained, includes both CF and rule explanations during brief time-outs while learners are performing a task. Thus, it would seem that such form-focusing techniques include both online feedback which does not interrupt the communication flow as well as rule explanations that temporarily put the ongoing communicative event on hold.

Within-task focus on form constitutes integrated focus on form in Spada et al.'s terms.

Among the various options of within-task focus on form, CF has received the most attention in research, because of its importance in second language acquisition (SLA) and language pedagogy (Ellis and Shintani, 2014). CF refers to responses to learners' production errors or comprehension problems that occurred during a task. Lyster and Ranta's (1997) seminal study identified six types of CF: recasts, repetition, elicitation, clarification request, metalinguistic clue and explicit correction. For example, for the error in the utterance 'There are many big livers in Africa', where 'rivers' is mispronounced as 'livers', the teacher can respond by:

1) Using a recast – reformulating the wrong sentence: 'There are many big rivers in Africa.'
2) Repeating the error: 'Liver?'
3) Eliciting the correct form from the learner: 'There are many big ...'
4) Making a clarification request: 'Sorry?'
5) Providing a metalinguistic comment: 'There is something wrong with your pronunciation of "liver".'
6) Alerting the learner to the presence of an error and supplying the correct form: 'No, not "liver", "river".'

These six CF types can be further divided into explicit and implicit depending on whether learners' attention is drawn to errors. Recasts, for example, have been examined as an implicit CF type, and metalinguistic clues as explicit feedback (e.g. Ellis, Loewen and Erlam, 2006). However, what determines the level of explicitness of CF is not just the type but the context in which the CF occurs. The CF types can also be classified as output-prompting (clarification, elicitation, repetition and metalinguistic clue) versus input-providing (recasts and explicit correction) depending on whether they encourage learner repairs (Lyster, 2004). These different types of CF are discussed in greater detail in Chapter 2.

In terms of the participatory structure of CF in a classroom setting, CF falls into two broad categories: peer CF and teacher CF. Peer CF can be incidental, in which case learners respond to each other's errors in an ad hoc way during group work (Adams, Nuevo and Egi, 2011), or planned, in which case errors are responded to consistently in a controlled manner. Sato and Lyster's study (2012) exemplified how planned CF was provided. In their study, learners worked in groups of three: a storyteller who told a narrative incorporating a variety of errors, an error detector who had to provide CF (recasts or prompts) on the errors, and an observer who recorded whether the errors were corrected and reported the observations at the end.

With regard to teacher CF, the literature indicates three ways the teacher may respond to students' errors: during teacher–student interaction, during teacher–class interaction or during student–student interaction. Teacher–student interaction can be further divided into one-way and two-way interactions. In one-way teacher–student interaction (Sheen, 2010; Yang and Lyster, 2010; Li, Ellis and Zhu, 2016), the teacher provides CF during the reporting stage of a communicative task after students have completed group work. Two-way interaction typically happens in a question/answer format where the teacher interacts with a single student and provides CF on his/her errors (Yang and Lyster, 2010; Goo, 2012). Teacher–class interaction occurs in situations where the teacher performs the task together with the whole class. For example, in one of the treatment activities in Lee and Lyster (2016), the teacher made a series of commands, all students reacted, and the teacher provided CF when students made mistakes in understanding his commands. Finally, CF can also be provided while students work in groups as in van de Guchte et al. (2015), where the teacher circulated the class, interrupted students and provided CF while they were performing communicative tasks.

Next, we would like to highlight two points that teachers should heed based on CF research. First and foremost, teachers should not hesitate to provide CF, given clear evidence of its facilitative effects on L2 development (Ellis, 2010; Li, 2010; Lyster and Saito, 2010; Nassaji, 2016). Task-based teachers should recognize that CF is an ideal alternative to pre-task grammar instruction, which, as we have seen, can affect learners' overall task performance and makes learners treat the task as a grammar exercise. Also, CF addresses linguistic forms during communication and thus may facilitate the development of communicative competence (Spada et al., 2014). It motivates the learner to attend to the input while he/she is struggling to find the correct form to convey meaning (Long, 2015). Thus, linguistic knowledge acquired via CF is proceduralized through immediate application in subsequent performance during the ongoing task (Li et al., 2016). One caveat is that teachers may worry about the harmful effects that CF has on students' motivation. However, Li's (2017) meta-analysis of studies of teachers' and students' attitudes towards CF indicates that students are overwhelmingly positive about CF (with an 89% endorsement rate for the importance of CF), although teachers are much more hesitant (with a mere 39% agreement rate). Furthermore, Zhang and Rahimi (2015) found that students' preference for CF was not related to their anxiety level. Therefore, the detrimental impact that CF can have on the affective aspects of learning is perhaps less acute than teacher guides like to suggest (see Ellis and Shintani, 2014).

Second, regarding which type of CF should be provided, we recommend using a variety of types instead of a single type. The research has shown an overall advantage for explicit feedback over implicit feedback although the difference may disappear over time (Li, 2010). Prompts have been found to be more effective than recasts in classroom settings (Lyster and Saito, 2010). The comparative effects of prompts vs. recasts also led to a debate between Lyster and Ranta (2013) and Mackey and Goo (2013). Prompts push the learner to reflect on his/her own language use, involve deeper cognitive processing, and help learners become better at consolidating and automatizing previously learned linguistic knowledge. Recasts are generally non-intrusive, provide both positive and negative evidence, and may be especially useful for learning new linguistic structures. However, the relative effects of different types of CF are context-dependent. Recasts, for example, can work very well in classroom contexts where students are oriented to attend to form. Instead of choosing one type over the others, perhaps the best way is to provide mixed CF, for example starting with a prompt to elicit self-correction followed by a recast if the learner fails to self-correct (Li et al., 2016). A second option is to start with recasts to establish an initial knowledge base and then follow up with prompts to consolidate the new knowledge. Similarly, the teacher may start with a few instances of explicit feedback to direct students' attention to the linguistic target but then switch to implicit feedback which is less disruptive (Yilmaz, 2013a). Teachers need to experiment with CF to find out what works best for them in their own instructional context.

Other Within-Task Options

Another within-task option is whether to allow learners to carry out planning while they are performing a task. In a within-task planning condition, learners are not given a time limit and so can perform a task without time pressure. However, this feature has been operationalized differently in the research. In Ahmadian and Tavakoli (2011) and Li and Fu (2017), learners watched a video and were then given an unlimited amount of time to complete the narratives. They were encouraged to plan the content and language while performing the tasks. In Wang's study (reported in Skehan et al., 2012), however, learners watched a slowed-down version of a video and told the narrative simultaneously. The methodological differences between these studies may explain their different findings. While Ahmadian and Tavakoli (2011) and Li and Fu (2017) found an advantage for within-task planning in enhancing accuracy and complexity at the expense of fluency compared with both no planning and strategic planning, Wang failed to find any difference between within-task planning and no planning.

Both of these studies examined CAF, not learning. Romanova (2010), however, conducted a study examining the effects of within-task planning on learning gains in comparison with pre-task planning and no planning. L2 Russian (L1 English) learners performed a picture description task where they told a narrative based on pictures displayed on a computer screen. The within-task planners performed the task at their own pace but had no time to plan before starting the narrative. The pre-task planners were allowed five minutes to see the pictures beforehand but they performed the task under time pressure, while the non-planners were not allowed to plan either before or during task performance. All groups received recasts on their third-person singular errors while performing the task. Both online and pre-task planning were found to be more effective than no planning when recasts were provided, but online planning was more effective than pre-task planning in contributing to the effects of recasts and resulted in more noticing and more modified output. This was because in the pre-task planning condition 'the unavailability of online planning time during interaction may inhibit acquisitional processes due to the limitations of WM [working memory], just like in the NP [no-planning] condition' (p. 865). To sum up, it would seem that within-task planning may assist with the formal aspects of task performance and also have a positive effect on learning. This might be especially true for beginner learners who may need more time to plan and monitor their speech performance.

A second possibility concerns the degree of support while performing the task. This can take the form of planned notes, input materials (images, videos, texts, etc.) or reference tools such as dictionaries. In research on the effects of pre-task planning, typically learners are not allowed to refer to their planned notes or any reference tools during task performance, which Ortega (1999) considered undesirable from a pedagogical perspective. A related idea is allowing learners to borrow from the input materials of the task as it is performed, which Ellis (2003) suggests should be encouraged. In Robinson (2007c), learners were required to complete three oral tasks that differed in complexity. Learners had access to a list of key phrases while performing the tasks. Robinson found that when performing the more complex tasks, the learners referred to the word list more frequently. He considered access to notes as a useful way of helping learners perform more complex tasks, echoing

Ellis' the idea about borrowing from input information. However, asking learners to refer to task prompts such as photos (Révész, 2009) or videos (Skehan et al., 2012) increases learners' processing load and can affect task performance. Therefore, it would seem that while access to linguistic input may afford learning opportunities, access to non-linguistic input such as picture cues may have a negative effect. To avoid increasing learners' processing load, perhaps learners should be given the freedom to decide whether they want to refer to available input or supporting materials.

Other within-task options mentioned in TBLT guides (Ellis, 2003; Willis and Willis, 2007) include using a clear task format (tables, diagrams, etc.), introducing a surprise element or new information half way through the task, and setting clear interim goals (that is, making the outcome of each stage of a task clear and specific). Although these options have not been subjected to empirical research, they are pedagogically valuable in that they help learners to engage with a task, lead to more output and so on.

Post-Task Options

Post-task activities are follow-up activities that build on the main task (Table 8.3). The purpose is to provide learning opportunities by: (1) asking learners to repeat a task, (2) addressing linguistic forms that had been shown to be problematic for the learners in the main task, and (3) engaging learners in reflective activities. The first option encompasses different forms of task repetition, which has received much attention in the research. The second option concerns the various techniques teachers may draw on to address linguistic forms explicitly. The third category involves activities encouraging learners to reflect retrospectively and introspectively on their task performance. In the following, we elaborate on each of these three broad categories of post-task activities.

Task Repetition

A task can be repeated in different ways and, depending on whether the repetition involves the content of the task, the task procedure or both, three types of task repetition can be identified: exact repetition, procedural repetition and content repetition. In exact repetition both the content and procedure are repeated. This type of repetition has been referred to as 'task repetition' in the literature (e.g. Kim and Tracy-Ventura, 2013) but in order to distinguish task repetition as a

Table 8.3 *Summary of post-task methodological options*

Options	Description	Recommendations
Task repetition	Learners are asked to repeat a task. Three types of repetition are possible: exact repetition, procedural repetition and content repetition.	• Procedural repetition is ideal • May mix procedural and content repetition • Feedback may be provided between repeated tasks
Explicit focus on forms	Post-task feedback	• May ask learners to perform another task after providing feedback on their task performance
	Providing a model	• Learners may listen to the audio recording of a task • Learners may read a script of a model performance
	Other options	• Learners may engage in consciousness-raising (CR) activities where they extrapolate rules based on given materials • Learners may perform input processing activities that force learners to attend to linguistic forms to process meaning • Learners may be asked to 'grammatize' a gapped text where some linguistic features (e.g. plural) are missing
Reflection	Reflective accounts	• Ask learners to reflect on various aspects of their task performance
	Transcription	• Ask learners to transcribe their task performance • Integrate transcription and other post-task options such as teacher feedback

concept and task repetition as a technique, we refer to the latter as exact repetition. As an example of exact repetition, Ahmadian and Tavakoli (2011) asked learners to perform a narrative after watching a fifteen-minute silent video and then repeated the task one week later. Another example is Gass et al. (1999), where the exact repetition group (called content repetition by the authors) watched the same Mr Bean video episode three times and performed a narrative after each viewing.

In procedural repetition, learners follow the same steps each time they perform the task but the content is different for each performance. For example, in Gass et al. (1999), the procedural repetition group (which the authors called 'different content group') watched four different Mr Bean episodes about different topics. In Patanasorn (2010), in the procedural repetition condition, pairs of learners completed three decision-making tasks where they followed similar steps but the topics for each task were different. For example, in one task, learners exchanged information about two suspects for a crime and discussed who was the perpetrator; in another, they decided who was the greatest footballer based on information about two candidates. In Kim and Tracy-Ventura (2013), Korean EFL learners performed three information exchange tasks following similar procedures but each was on a different topic: hosting an American friend, describing school events/activities and discussing mayoral candidates.

In content repetition, the repetition involves the same content but the procedure is different. In Patanasorn (2010), the content repetition group performed three different tasks involving the same information. In the first task, called story completion, they worked together to complete a narrative about a prime ministerial candidate. In the second task, which is called information exchange, they worked with a new partner to tell their narratives. Finally they performed a decision-making task with another new partner, arguing why their own candidates should be elected. In this study, content repetition happened through recycling the same information in a different format with a different partner/interlocutor. Another procedural variation involves setting different time limits for each repetition, as in Thai and Boers (2015), where learners performed the same narrative task three times, within three, two and one minutes respectively, each time with a different listener. Still another option is to repeat the task in a different modality. For example, after performing an oral debate task, learners could be asked to summarize the main points of the debate in writing. Similarly, after a listening task, learners could be asked to read a passage on the same content/topic.

Several other methodological aspects of task repetition are worth mentioning. One is the number of repetitions. In some studies (e.g. Ahmadian and Tavakoli, 2011; Skehan et al., 2012), a task is repeated only once and the second performance is treated as the outcome of task repetition. In Kim and Tracy-Ventura's (2013) study, in the identical repetition condition, the learners performed the same task three times. A second methodological variable is the interval of repetition. In addition to immediate repetition (e.g. Thai and Boers, 2016), other intervals reported in the literature include one day (Kim and Tracy-Ventura, 2013), two to three days (Gass et al., 1999), one week (Ahmadian and Tavakoli, 2011) and fortnightly (Bygate, 2001). A third aspect concerns whether task repetition happens by learners performing the task individually (Ahmadian and Tavakoli, 2011) or in pairs/groups (Kim and Tracy-Ventura, 2013).

An essential question is whether task repetition has any benefits for L2 learning. First, with regard to identical repetition, the studies involving monologic tasks show that it enhanced CAF on the same task (Gass et al., 1999; Bygate, 2001; Ahmadian and Tavakoli, 2011; Skehan et al., 2012). However, the effects tend not to transfer to new tasks (Gass et al., 1999; Bygate, 2001). The studies involving group interaction produced mixed results. Patanasorn (2010) found that identical repetition did not have any effect while Kim and Tracy-Ventura (2013) reported that identical repetition led to improved accuracy in learners' use of the English past tense but that this group's speech was less complex and fluent on the post-tests compared with the pre-tests. Second, procedural repetition led to an improvement in ratings of a performance of a new task (Gass et al., 1999), improved accuracy in the English past tense (Patanasorn, 2010; Kim and Tracy-Ventura, 2013) and improved linguistic complexity (Kim and Tracy-Ventura, 2013). Third, content repetition led to improved global fluency but reduced accuracy in the past tense (Patanasorn, 2010).

Based on the available evidence and bearing in mind that more research is needed on the comparative effectiveness of the three types of repetition, we suggest that exact repetition, which requires learners to repeat the same task multiple times, is not the ideal option in task-based teaching. Exact repetition not only results in unstable effects on task performance or learning outcomes but it may also be perceived negatively by learners (Plough and Gass, 1993; Kim and Tracy-Ventura, 2013). Kim and Tracy-Ventura (2013) also reported that exact repetition led to fewer LREs than procedural repetition. The researchers suspected that this might have been because learners were already familiar with the content, which removed the need for them to negotiate for meaning. In contrast, procedural repetition, where learners follow similar steps but work with different information, has proven to be more useful and motivating. It has the potential to provide new learning opportunities in the case of input-based tasks when learners are exposed to more varied linguistic structures and vocabulary. One possibility is to mix content and procedural repetition by retaining part of the content and the whole or part of the procedure. Finally, one option that is largely missing from the research literature on task repetition is providing some kind of intervention between the first and second performance of a task – for example, providing feedback on the first performance.

Explicit Focus on Forms

Earlier in the chapter we argued that pre-task grammar instruction can affect learners' overall task performance by causing them to focus on the linguistic target, with the result that the taskness of the task is subverted. One way to address the limitation of pre-task grammar instruction is to delay it to the post-task stage, as Willis and Wills (2007) and Skehan (1998) have consistently advocated. Long (2016) also argued that an explicit focus on forms is a useful option in the post-task stage of a lesson because it is reactive (i.e. it addresses attested problems with form). Post-task focus on form caters to learning by providing opportunities for learners to practise producing structures they found difficult when they performed the task. Teachers can use the input materials to exemplify the usage of the linguistic target and design various form-focused activities based on the materials. Also, addressing linguistic forms after learners have struggled to use the appropriate forms to convey meaning enables them to see the need to learn and is therefore more motivating than pre-task grammar instruction. However, to date there has been little research on the effects of post-task focus on form. In the following, we discuss the options and benefits of post-task feedback and then address some other types of form-focused techniques.

Post-Task Feedback. One way to provide CF is to hold a plenary feedback session addressing the typical errors that the teacher observed the students making while they were performing the task. Li et al. (2016) conducted a study on the relative effects of immediate and delayed feedback. In the immediate feedback condition, learners received feedback on English passive voice errors while they were telling a story to the class, whereas in the delayed feedback condition they received feedback on their errors after the task had been completed. When providing post-task feedback, the teacher quoted an error she had noted and asked the learner to self-correct: 'Josh, you said "three people killed". Can you say it again?' If the learner failed to self-correct, the teacher then provided a recast: 'Three people were killed.' The researchers found that delayed feedback was effective but not as effective as immediate/within-task feedback in facilitating the learning of the target structure. They suspected that this was because, unlike the learners who received immediate correction during task performance, those who received delayed feedback did not have an opportunity to apply the learned knowledge during the performance of the task. The implication is that the effects of delayed feedback might be boosted if learners were asked to perform another task after the feedback session. However, this option needs to be empirically examined.

Providing a model. Lynch (2009) proposed extending the scope of feedback to include sample performances of the same tasks by more competent speakers or native speakers so that learners can self-correct by noticing the gap between their own performance and the correct models. This can happen by asking learners to listen to the audio recording of the task and/or read the script of the performance. Lynch surveyed sixty international postgraduate students at a British university and asked them to comment on the post-task options that they thought would help them notice their errors in their role plays. The respondents preferred to receive sample performances (recordings or transcripts) after, rather than before, the role plays. Encouraging self-correction by providing a model after performance has several benefits. First, it encourages a comparison of the correct model with the learners' own utterances, provides opportunities for self-repair and fosters learner autonomy. Second, the focus is only on learners noticing their errors rather than mastering structure productively, which they may not be developmentally ready for. Third, it can prevent learners feeling embarrassed as a result of being corrected by the teacher in front of other students. However, post-task modelling also has limitations. For example, some errors may be ignored because they are too complicated and/or because learners just focus on meaning. Also error correction happens in a haphazard rather than systematic way and is unfocused.

Aside from CF, the teacher can also provide positive feedback. For example, the teacher may note down useful words or advanced structures learners used during the task (Willis and Willis, 2007) and build on that during the post-task stage by eliciting more examples.

Other Form-Focused Strategies. We do not intend to provide a full account of the strategies for explicit FFI (for a detailed account of various aspects of explicit instruction, see Ellis and Shintani, 2014). Rather, we will highlight several input-based techniques. One such strategy is called consciousness raising (CR), which Ellis (1997) defined as 'a pedagogic activity where the learners are provided with L2 data in some form and required to perform some operation on it, the purpose of which is to arrive at an explicit understanding of some linguistic properties of the target language' (p. 160). Essentially CR is an inductive approach that caters to the learning of explicit linguistic knowledge. In a typical CR activity, learners are provided with input materials, either aural or written, from which they extrapolate linguistic regularities relating to grammatical features that they failed to use or used incorrectly when they performed the task. Ellis (2003) argued that CR activities meet the criteria for tasks because they provide opportunities for authentic communication as learners work together to work out the rule for a grammatical feature. In other words, CR tasks make grammar a topic to be talked about. In this sense, CR tasks do not need to be limited to the post-task stage of a lesson. They can figure as main tasks but they have a clearer role in the post-task stage of a lesson.

Another strategy is called processing instruction, which is based on VanPatten's (2015) input-processing theory. A primary principle of the theory is that learners tend to prioritize meaning over form when processing linguistic input and therefore teachers need to design activities that require learners to conduct form-meaning mapping. Asking learners to fill in past forms in a text, for example, does not require form-meaning mapping because learners can simply add '-ed' to verbs without having to understand the connection between the past forms and the meaning they encode. An alternative is to ask learners to listen to a text with a mix of tenses such as the present, the future and the past and identify just those events that happened in the past. Similarly, an activity that provides clues that enable learners to decode the meaning without processing the form obviates the need for form-meaning mapping. For example, imagine an activity aimed at helping the learner understand the English causative constructions (i.e. 'have somebody do something', 'have something done', etc.) where a learner is given the sentence, 'Jill had her husband washthe dishes.' The sentence is accompanied with a photo showing a man cleaning dishes. In this scenario, the learner could use the photo as a clue to answer the question without having to process the target structure. The alternative is to remove the photo so that the learner has no clues to rely on to understand the meaning of the linguistic structure.

The third strategy, consistently advocated by Willis and Willis (2007), is called 'grammatizing', where learners are required to restore the linguistic items or features that have been left out in a text. This is an ideal strategy for integrating focus on form into the input materials of a task. For example, the teacher could show a sentence: 'He sometimes asked me to wash his car or cut the grass, but I was never forced to do it.' Then some words are erased: 'He__ asked me__ wash his car or cut __ grass, but I was never __ to do__.' The number of words deleted can be varied, making the activity more demanding – for example, 'He__ __ me __ wash his __ or ___ ___ grass, but I ___ never ___ to do ___.'

Reflection

Learners can be asked to reflect on various aspects of the completed task including the task itself and/or their own or their peers' performance. We divide reflection activities into two types: reflective accounts and transcription. Learners' reflective accounts refer to self-reports about what they think they learned during the task, their evaluation of their task performance, their perceptions of the design features of the task including its objective, nature and difficulty, their attitudes towards the task and their opinions about how to improve it. This involves asking learners to complete a simple questionnaire.

Transcription involves learners providing a transcript of their own or a peer's performance. Transcription can be used in various ways and in conjunction with other post-task strategies such as post-task modelling, CF, etc. For example, the learner could transcribe his/her own performance, edit or reformulate the transcript, and/or compare the transcript with the script of a sample performance. These activities can be undertaken independently or in collaboration with peers and can be integrated with teacher feedback. However, to date there has been little research on the effects of different types of transcription on learning outcomes.

Participatory Structure

Discussions of task-based teaching are often based on the assumption that a task must be performed in pairs or small groups, but this is a mistaken notion – there are different types of participatory structure. Participatory structure refers to the way interaction occurs in a task, which can be divided into four types: individual, student–student, teacher–class and student–class (see Table 8.4) (Ellis, 2003). In an

Table 8.4 Participatory structure of task-based interaction

Participatory structure	Prototypical form of interaction	Pattern of interaction
Individual	Intrapersonal	Individual student
Social	Interpersonal	Student–student
		Student–class
		Teacher–class

individual participatory structure, students work on a task or part of a task independently. Student–student interaction occurs when students engage in group or pair work. Student–class interaction occurs when one student or a group perform a task with the rest of class. Teacher–class interaction occurs when the teacher interacts with the whole class. The following jigsaw task can be performed in different ways involving any of the four different structures.

In this task, students are given five jumbled pictures depicting a story. The task can be performed individually by asking students to sequence the pictures independently before telling the story in oral or written form. The task can also be performed in group work, where each member is given one picture and describes what happens in his/her picture; they then work together to arrange the pictures in the right order. The task can also be performed via the student–class structure, where one student is asked to describe the pictures in the right order to the rest of the class, who arrange the pictures based on that student's narrative. Similarly, the task can be performed between the teacher and the whole class, in which case the teacher tells the narrative and the whole class sequence the pictures accordingly.

Conclusion

In this chapter, we have discussed various methodological options available to teachers in the three phases of a task-based lesson. For the pre-task stage, we reviewed the literature on pre-task planning, pointing out that while this is a necessary and useful step, longer planning time does not necessarily result in better task performance. Based on the findings of the research and taking into consideration the constraints imposed by local instructional settings, we recommended three minutes as an optimal duration, which can be shortened or extended depending on teachers' own judgement. We also recommended exploring the possibility of allowing learners the freedom to decide on how much time they need to prepare for the main task. With regard to pre-task grammar instruction, drawing on empirical evidence and theoretical and pedagogical perspectives, we argued against such practice. Teachers may experiment with alternative form-focused strategies such as pre-task modelling. Another valuable pre-task strategy is to work with students and scaffold their performance of a task before asking them to perform it (or a similar task) independently.

For main task options, we considered ways in which teachers and learners can focus on form as a task is being performed. We argued that CF has proven to be an effective instructional device. However, instead of a single feedback type, we proposed teachers use a variety of corrective strategies, for example a prompt followed by a recast or alternating between explicit and implicit feedback.

For the post-task stage, we started by identifying three types of task repetition: exact repetition, procedural repetition and content repetition. We went on to show, based on research, that exact repetition is not an ideal strategy and that procedural repetition has proven to be more useful and effective. We then explored different post-task options such as modelling and various types of explicit FFI. Finally, we explained different ways in which learners can be encouraged to reflect on their performance of a task, including the use of transcriptions of the students' performance of the task.

Regarding participatory structure, we clarified that a task can be performed in different ways involving different types of interaction and that it is a misconception to consider group work the only way. An example task-based lesson is provided in an appendix that exemplifies participatory structures and other options of the three stages of a task cycle.

Appendix: An Example Task Lesson

Task Description

This is a dictogloss task adapted from Li, Ellis and Zhu (2016, 2017). It is a focused task aiming to facilitate middle school EFL learners' comprehension of the English passive voice and elicits their production of the structure. The task requires learners to listen to a narrative presented by the teacher, work in pairs to practise retelling the story and take turns to report the story to the rest of the class after the pair work. The lesson contains two tasks that are based on different content but follow similar steps. This is called procedural repetition.

Li et al. (2016, 2017) examined the effects of different form-focused options in different phases of the task cycle, and we include the alternative options in the lesson plan described as follows.

Task Materials

The task materials include two narrative texts embedded with thirty cases of passive use. They were tailored to the level of the learners in terms of length and difficulty.

Task 1 Narrative: A Car Accident

There was a bad car accident yesterday. Three people were killed. Also one child was injured. Her leg and arm were broken. Her face was seriously cut. She was driven to the local hospital. Her injuries were treated there. The relatives of the girl were told about the accident.

A witness said, 'The car was hit by a big truck. It was badly damaged.' The truck was travelling on the wrong side of the road. The driver of the truck tried to run away. But he was stopped, and he was arrested. He was taken to the police station for questioning. Some bottles of beer were found in his car. He was charged with drunk driving. He was locked in a police cell.

Task 2 Narrative: An Earthquake

Kiki was raised in a small house in the countryside. One day he was playing when suddenly there was a big earthquake. He was knocked down by the falling bricks. Then the walls fell down. He was trapped in the house. It was very dark. Kiki was badly hurt and could not move. Later Kiki's mom came back home. She saw the house was destroyed. She thought her boy was buried in the house. She shouted out to him. He could not hear her because he was covered with bricks.

Some dogs were brought to search for him. Kiki was found. The bricks were removed. Kiki was pulled out of the wreckage of the house. He was carried to the local hospital. He was put in an emergency room for treatment. He was given special food to help him recover. He was allowed to leave the hospital after one month.

Lesson Plan

Stages	Procedure	Participatory structure
Pre-task	The teacher asks a few brainstorming questions about drunk driving to arouse students' interest and provide background knowledge.	Teacher–class
	The teacher introduces the instructions for the task.	Teacher–class
	The teacher teaches vocabulary to facilitate task performance, but students are not required to use the words in their subsequent task performance.	Teacher–class
	Optional: pre-task grammar instruction. The teacher explains the use and formation of the English passive followed by controlled practice where students judge the grammaticality of the ten passive sentences.	Teacher–class
	The teacher presents the narrative three times. She/he reads it aloud, presents it on PowerPoint, and reads it aloud again.	Teacher–class
Main task	Students work in pairs to practise retelling the story by referring to given clues. They are required to add an ending to the story.	Student–student
	They are asked to take turns to report the narrative to the rest of the class, with one student telling half of the narrative before passing the speaker's role to the other. Other students listen and compare their endings to the speakers'. They vote for the best ending at the end of the task.	Student–class
	Optional: the teacher provides CF on the learners' errors in their use of the passive voice. The feedback package consists of a prompt to encourage self-correction, followed by a recast in the absence of self-correction.	Teacher–class
Post-task	Option 1: the teacher provides feedback on the students' errors in passive use.	Teacher–class

(continued)

(cont.)

Stages	Procedure	Participatory structure
	Option 2: the teacher provides grammar explanation about the passive voice if this is not done in the pre-task stage.	Teacher–class
	Option 3: the students receive the script of the narrative and reflect on their own performance.	Individual
	Option 4: students are asked to perform another task following similar steps based on the second narrative text.	The above patterns are repeated

9 Task-Based Testing and Assessment

This chapter starts with a general introduction to the basics in testing since these underpin a specifically task-based approach to assessment. It then gives a brief survey of significant general theorizing in the field, leading to an outline model of language testing and language test performance. This is followed by the main section of the chapter, describing the components of this model, focusing on the role of 'ability for use', the influence of the task and the factors that are relevant to performance rating, all linked to the relevance of task research. Several challenges for task-based testing are then addressed, while the concluding section provides a survey and critique of four practical attempts to test in a task-oriented way.

An Introduction to Testing

Essentially, testing consists of the elicitation of data so that decisions can be made which are reliable, valid, fair and useful. Each of these words is central to language testing. Elicitation of data could mean completing a multiple-choice test or writing an essay or undertaking a speaking task. Decisions may be about how much learning has taken place (as with achievement tests), or whether someone has the appropriate language to do a certain job (a form of proficiency test), or even whether someone comes in the top 10 per cent of a group (and can be offered a place on another course). Tests also need to be reliable, in that they should lead to information (and decisions) which are consistent and not clouded by the chance factors in the data that have been elicited, or the scoring or rating that is done by different individuals. Tests also need to be valid, in that they measure what they are supposed to measure (and not what it is more convenient to measure). And they need to be useful, and make worthwhile contributions. This is less tangible than measuring for reliability (for which all sorts of heavy-duty statistical techniques are available), but just as important. It might mean that a test score is not obtained just for the sake of it, to be put in a filing cabinet (or computer file) and forgotten. It might also mean that the test itself needs to have a positive influence, or washback, on the world around it, and influence teaching or preparation beneficially. Ideally, doing well on a test should connect fairly clearly with how effectively one uses language in the real world – a potential source of strength for task-based approaches. Language testers, over the years, have developed a range of procedures to structure the way all these claims can be examined, regarding data elicitation, reliability, validity, fairness, utility and washback. Indeed, one could characterize language testing as an inherently self-reflective area (even if, on occasions, one may consider that particular examples of testing could be subjected to more searching scrutiny). All these issues are just as relevant when assessment is task-based as when conventional testing procedures are used.

Some other basic distinctions are relevant. The first of these is between summative and formative testing. Summative evaluation generally comes at the end of a course, and is likely to be in numeric form, a judgement of how well someone has done on a test. The information from summative evaluation may well go to outsiders, e.g. school principals, education authorities. It is not likely to have a direct impact on the detail of instruction. Formative evaluation is likely to be collected during a course, and its central purpose is to feed into ongoing instruction. The information that it gathers is likely to have diagnostic features, but it may not be individual-focused, instead more concerned with finding out how a course as a whole can be made better while it is still running. A second distinction concerns score interpretation. One approach, norm-referencing, relates a particular score to the scores of other people, e.g. when a score is shown to be higher than 60 per cent of other test takers. A contrasting approach, criterion-referencing, relates the score directly to the real world, and whether a score is consistent with someone being about to do something specific, e.g. function as a hotel receptionist. Norm-referenced approaches can also be used to make connections with the real world, but these connections are necessarily indirect, and additional research is required to link real-world performance to a norm-referenced base. For example, it could be established that someone two standard deviations above the norm on a particular language test is probably able to handle the language demands of a university course. Criterion-referenced approaches, in contrast, reduce the amount of inferencing involved, because criterion-referenced language tests are likely to contain procedures which have more natural relationships with the real world. As we will see, a task-based approach to testing leans more towards a criterion-referenced approach for interpreting the meaning of scores.

Underlying Language Testing Theory

Any approach to task-based testing needs good theoretical foundations. Essentially, this basic theory has to deal with a number of issues and tensions:

- the role of any underlying competences;
- they way such underlying competences are mobilized into actual performance;
- the tension between generality (likely to be based on underlying competences and abilities) and specificity (a need to be able to analyse and sample particular examples of language use).

The major approaches in the literature to theorizing communicative abilities all wrestle with these issues (Carroll, 1961). Arguably the first major attempt at this challenge was Canale and Swain (1980), followed by Canale (1983). Canale and Swain (1980) proposed three underlying competences: grammatical, sociolinguistic and strategic. These were later supplemented (Canale, 1983) with the addition of discourse competence. Clearly these competences are meant to be underlying in nature and to represent knowledge bases which can be drawn on in actual communication. In other words, in addition to the more conventional grammatical competence, there is the assumption that there is a knowledge base relevant to sociolinguistic and discourse issues, and that any rounded approach to measuring underlying competences will need to sample each of these. Most interesting of all is strategic competence. Canale and Swain (1980) proposed this as a capacity for improvisation when other competences are lacking, e.g. a vocabulary item or a discourse marker to help conversational flow. Strategic competence would then be drawn on to overcome a resulting communication problem. Sadly, empirical investigations have not been particularly supportive of this version of communicative competence. Harley et al. (1990), in quite a large-scale study, did not find much confirmatory evidence for the four-component structure or for the functioning of strategic competence.

The Canale–Swain approach was overtaken by the more ambitious formulation of Bachman (1990; Bachman and Palmer, 1996, 2010). This approach also has an underlying competence structure, but with important differences to Canale and Swain (1980). Overall communicative competence is divided into organizational and pragmatic competences. The former is then further divided into linguistic competence and textual competence, while the latter is subdivided into sociolinguistic competence and discourse competence. Interestingly, Bachman (1990) does provide some evidence supporting this structure and the arrangement and interrelationships of the different sub-competences, although this empirical support cannot be regarded as extensive. In general, though, we have a more convincing view of the structure of communicative competence. More interesting still in Bachman's account is the role of strategic competence. According to Canale and Swain (1980) this only had a compensatory role. For Bachman it is central, and effectively the mediator between underlying competences and actual communicative language use. It is not primarily compensatory, but at the heart of all *normal* communication. It is concerned with things such as goal-setting, assessing a situation, planning, drawing upon background knowledge and so on. So here we have a feature, labelled a competence, which permeates actual language use. The other competences may have important foundational roles and act as resources for the communication that takes place.

Bachman (1990) also made a distinction between what he termed interactive-ability and real-life approaches to testing. The implicit emphasis in the discussion so far has been on the interactive-ability approach. To return to one of the foundational issues in language testing, there is a tension between the limited amount of data that is obtained in testing situations on the one hand, and the desire to generalize as widely as possible on the other. An interactive-ability approach attempts generalization by effectively sampling from underlying competences in a way which permits maximum generalization potential, but with testing formats which meet interactional authenticity criteria. In other words, although the emphasis here is on competences, the testing contexts which are used need to trigger natural use of language on the part of the test takers.

This perspective, then, contrasts with a real-life approach which emphasizes the uses for language that a candidate will encounter. Testing, in this view, needs to develop methods to systematically research patterns of future language use, since these will be the basis for test items, or tasks, that will be used in testing. Bachman (1990) and Bachman and Palmer (1996, 2010) attempt to provide such a systematic framework to structure the ways needs analyses are conducted for testing purposes. Indeed, many other needs analysis approaches to testing have taken a similar approach, as in vocational or occupational or English for academic purposes (EAP) testing. This is easier when a restricted set of circumscribed language situations and

Figure 9.1 An outline model for task-based testing

uses are concerned, but more difficult when the range of situations and language demands is broader, even if such cases are more circumscribed than 'general language use'.

These different proposals for language testing models (Canale and Swain, 1980; Bachman, 1990) have foregrounded the need for assessment to be based on communicative uses of language. Skehan (1996, 2001) attempted to make connection between such approaches and task research by outlining a related model which places task centrally within testing. A revised version is shown as Figure 9.1.

The task is central in this model and is the basis for the performance which is generated. To the left of the task are two general areas, relating to the test taker, which are mobilized and provide the foundation for this task performance. These are underlying competences and an ability to mobilize and access these competences, under communication conditions. To the right of the task are the judgements that are made about the performance. First, in this regard, we have the raters, but also the rating scales that they use. The outcome of this stage is the score which is assigned to the performance.

Little further will be said here regarding underlying competences. A formulation such as Bachman's is assumed, comprising the different components mentioned. It is assumed that test takers have such underlying competences, to varying degrees, that these have an important impact on performance, and that the score that is assigned will in turn be influenced by them. It is assumed that task research has relatively little to say about such competences, at least at present. But next we come to ability for use. This implicates a language user's capacity to mobilize underlying competences in naturalistic communication, in real time and in actual contexts. It is assumed, for example, that two people with similar underlying competences might differ in actual performance because they vary in how effective they are in accessing and mobilizing these competences in an appropriate manner. When testing aims at predicting to real-world language use, competences are not enough: we also have to consider capacity to use these competences. Task research, it is argued, may have a great deal to say here. Even more clearly, the task itself, the next part of the model, is likely to have an impact on performance. Tasks are not neutral devices – they may themselves have an impact on performance, and so the performance which is rated may partly depend on the task which was chosen and the conditions under which it was done. Once again, task research may have a lot to contribute to transforming the model in Figure 9.1 from a schematic account to a more empirically grounded proposal. Next we turn to raters and rating, significant foci for research within language testing, as researchers have explored whether different raters might use different standards in rating performance, or if different emphases with rating scales might introduce a lack of systematicity into the assigned scores. The relevance of such research unquestionable. But task researchers have put considerable effort into how task performance might be measured, what its dimensions are and how different levels of performance might be distinguished. This research, too, may have relevance to testing, since it could, potentially, provide empirical grounding for the rating scales which are used and the judgements which are made.

Testing typically ends with a score, and it is assumed that the score will reflect what we want it to reflect. What Figure 9.1 brings out clearly is that the score which is assigned, in a task-based approach to testing, may reflect underlying competences, and/or ability for use, and/or the actual task which was undertaken and the conditions and context that were used, and/or the particular raters and rating scales. This is a formidable and confusing set of influences, and shows that the practice of testing is fraught with difficulty. The point in itemizing these different influences is to reveal that the model shown in Figure 9.1 is rudimentary, and that a major contribution of task research to testing is to bring some clarity to the contributions of these different influences, as well as the potential each of them has for introducing a lack of standardization in testing. The sorts of things that task researchers have explored, in other words, can begin to fill in details regarding the different components in the model.

Task Research and Task-Based Testing

The central three components from Figure 9.1, ability for use, task, and raters and rating, have been presented as potential clouding influences on the score which may be assigned in a test. If there is such a potential, it is useful to explore if task research can clarify how such clouding might function, and so this section will explore what contribution such research can make to understanding testing. It will examine tasks, including task conditions, ability for use, raters and, more precisely, rating.

TASKS AND TASK CONDITIONS

Broadly there are two approaches in this section: generalizations which emerge from narrative enquiry and findings from meta-analyses. Regarding the first, if we consider that task research started to gain momentum from the late 1980s, then we now have a range of task studies that could form a basis for any claims that are made through traditional narrative accounts. Such research has frequently used a complexity, accuracy, lexis and fluency (CALF) framework, which eases connections between studies, and it has also tended to explore task types and characteristics, on the one hand, and task conditions, on the other, as we have seen in other chapters in this volume. The research, as we have seen, has had theoretical linkages, often connected with the respective accounts provided by the Limited Attentional Capacity (LAC) approach and the Cognition Hypothesis (CH) (see Chapter 3).

We have seen, for example, task characteristics and influences on performance such as:

- structured tasks raise accuracy and fluency, and sometimes complexity;
- tasks requiring information transformation or integration raise complexity;
- tasks based on familiar information raise fluency and accuracy;
- time perspective influences performance;
- tasks with more elements raise accuracy slightly;
- tasks with support raise fluency.

We have also seen research which clarifies the influence of task conditions, such as:

- strategic planning raises complexity and fluency, and sometimes accuracy;
- online planning (i.e. less time-pressured performance) raises accuracy;
- post-task conditions raise accuracy, and sometimes complexity;
- repetition raises complexity, accuracy and fluency (CAF), but does not have a strong effect on lexis.

One would like to say that these generalizations are robust and strong, but it has to be admitted that what is proposed here represents no more than tendencies (as is discussed in the third part of the Issues in

Table 9.1 Overview of meta-analytic results

Task feature	Complexity	Accuracy	Lexis	Fluency
Resource-directing	0.13	0.13	0.28	−0.09
Resource-dispersing	−0.77	−0.73	−0.27	−0.34

Task-Based Testing section, regarding a difference in consistency between tasks themselves and task conditions). But even so, the relevance for testing is clear. If test tasks vary in any of the listed characteristics or conditions and this variation is not handled in a principled way, then the interpretation of particular tests may be compromised, since the basis for comparing performance on one set of tests with another set of tests, or with real-world language use, can be questioned. For example, if two tests, intended for use at the intermediate level (say), contrast one test using an unstructured task, with unfamiliar information, without support and without planning with another test using a structured task based on familiar information, visual support and ten minutes of planning time, comparison between the two tests is going to be difficult, if not impossible.

This argument is supported if one considers the results of meta-analyses. Table 9.1 is a reduced version of Table 3.3, based on Malicka and Sasayama (2017), and shows results from the most extensive meta-analysis that we have available in the field.

The meta-analytic results mostly confirm the generalizations which have emerged from the narrative analyses. This study was more driven by the CH, hence the prominent distinction between resource-directing and resource-dispersing variables. These more macro categories suggest that resource-dispersing variables have much larger and more consistent effects on CALF measures than do the resource-directing variables. At a more detailed level (and see Table 3.3 for details), planning, repetition, task structure and task support show consistency with the narrative enquiry generalizations, with only familiarity revealing a different pattern.

This pattern of results is also consistent with a claim made in Skehan (2016), as already noted in Chapter 3. This is that task conditions tend to produce more consistent and larger influences on CALF measures. Task characteristics, he argues, do not generate comparable levels or such dependable results. He suggests that this is understandable through the easier connections between task conditions and the stages within the Levelt model, as indicated through quantitative and qualitative research with, for example, planning. Most of the resource-dispersing variables in Table 9.1 are, essentially, task condition variables, whereas most of the resource-directing variables are task characteristics. So essentially the meta-analytic results are consistent with Skehan's claim.

We come back to the point made earlier in this section – if task characteristics and task conditions are built in to test tasks in an uncontrolled and unsystematic way, there is a danger that the score someone receives will not be any sort of transparent measure of underlying competences or ability for use, but rather that the task and task conditions which have been used have intruded into the measurement. The potential for unfairness is clear.

There is, though, an important caveat. This analysis tacitly assumes that task research findings are directly generalizable to testing contexts, in other words, that these results – for example, on structured tasks or on planning – operate in the same way when the context is testing. There are reasons, unfortunately, why reservations are needed. Iwashita, McNamara and Elder (2001) used insights from task research, with variables such as planning, perspective, immediacy and adequacy, but in a testing context. They report that the sorts of effects found in task research were not evident. Khabbazbashi (2017) compared the Test of English as a Foreign Language Internet-Based Test (TOEFL iBT) and real-life (academic-context) performances and reports that the iBT performance was slightly more complex but less accurate than more naturalistic performances, although informal language was more evident in the real-life performances. Khabbazbashi (2017) also reports small but inconsequential topic effects. Brooks and Swain (2014), also researching the TOEFL iBT format, confirm the greater complexity finding for the test-condition iBT, with slightly lower accuracy and less informal language. So these studies suggest that task effects do not translate easily, consistently or strongly to a testing context.

Even so, one has to say that there are not many studies applying task characteristic variables in the testing domain. Planning, though, has been more extensively researched in relation to a testing context. We saw that Iwashita et al. (2001) reported little planning effect with TOEFL-origin tests. This was confirmed by Wigglesworth and Elder (2010), who used International English Language Testing System (IELTS)-like speaking tests. Brief planning periods (zero, one, two minutes) produced no effects on ratings or on CALF measures, with the possible exception of a small effect on complexity. Interestingly, planning time was positively regarded by participants. Nitta and Nakatsuhara (2014) also investigated planning, with First Certificate tasks from the Cambridge system. Ratings showed a small but significant effect for fluency measures and also for ratings. Nitta and Nakatsuhara (2014) report that planning was associated with parallel or asymmetric interaction styles (Galaczi, 2008), and non-planning with a more effective collaborative style. The planning period was three minutes, but all participants looked at visual items pre-task, thus providing a form of planning across all conditions. The two planning studies to show positive effects in a testing context are Tavakoli and Skehan (2005) and Xi (2005), who both showed significantly elevated performance under planning conditions.

The results of these planning studies are clearly mixed, and it is certainly possible that variations in research design might be a factor underlying inconsistencies in results, such as different lengths of time for planning, since the testing-oriented studies tend to use shorter pre-task planning periods. O'Grady (in press) goes some way to overcoming these problems. He contrasted an exposition task with a narrative, picture-based task, under planned and unplanned conditions, with several planning intervals, ranging from thirty seconds to ten minutes. He reports a planning effect for the five- and ten-minute conditions, with this being more effective for the narrative (the possibly more complex task) than the exposition task. But this effect, though detectable, is not large, and is reported as 0.36 of a logit, in the context of a five logit levels being distinguishable in the dataset.

Summarizing this range of studies, it seems reasonable to conclude that task and task condition effects are relevant for testing, but it cannot be concluded that they suggest consistent or large influences. The database is not extensive, and it is clear that we can learn more about the particular operationalizations of task characteristics and task conditions in the future, and that this may lead to more impact on performance, whether this is in terms of ratings or CALF measures. But in the main, the influence is not huge, and it seems the sorts of effect sizes from planning research are not matched in testing contexts.

One can interpret this in different ways. The most obvious is to say that a testing context is a great leveller. Test takers, who are abundantly aware that their performance is being scrutinized, may mobilize attention to maximum advantage and perhaps try to emphasize more challenging language, and especially, try to avoid error. Any research-based effect for something like planning might then be attenuated. In this case, testers might reasonably conclude that they have 'license' not to be overly concerned about differences between tasks or differences between conditions, and accordingly claim that test scores are fair reflections of more underlying abilities. But an alternative interpretation is to question the interactional authenticity of many testing formats. It could be argued that if effects which are well established in the task literature do not reproduce in a testing context, then this questions the naturalness of the data which is elicited and the potential this data has for generalization to real-world contexts. Of course, it might be argued that task performance is not totally natural, but if it is the case that such performance is more natural than what happens in many testing contexts, then the test-elicited data may be a less dependable base for use outside a testing context.

We turn next to a relatively recent development in task research – the use of tasks for the assessment of pragmatic ability (Roever, 2011). Roever and Kasper (2018) argue that existing testing procedures have a strong psycholinguistic emphasis. They suggest that pragmatic abilities, i.e. the use of language in context to achieve pragmatic goals, often in longer encounters and interactions, is not sufficiently reflected in current procedures, and that the use of tasks, as an assessment vehicle, may enable this imbalance to be redressed. Roever and Kasper (2018) point to this aspect of communication ability as one urgently needing research and development.

Pragmatic abilities, though, are wide-ranging, and incorporating them within task-based testing certainly contains its challenges. We range from a relatively circumscribed focus on speech acts, to wider aspects of an interactional competence, such as the capacity to handle sequential organization in more extensive encounters or texts, turn-taking, implicature, a capacity to access appropriate routine formulae, and the ability to ensure there is cohesion and coherence. Beyond this, there is the capacity to handle breakdown and repair, and even to use non-verbal means of communication. And even beyond that, scope to engage in co-construction of discourse and to be effective in using language contingent on the contributions of an interlocutor. The scope for task research is considerable here, and the corresponding challenge for testing equally large.

As with all testing, there is a 'scope for generalization' issue here. The different aspects of pragmatic ability concern scale (how large the language use task is, and hence, how much the language user has to sustain performance); organization (and how important it is to clarify linkages between one's own contributions as well as those of an interlocutor); context (with the wide range of different contexts where language might be used, with the myriad differences they may embody); and freedom (in degree of scope for an interaction (say) to be co-constructed and take unforeseen paths). Any attempt to measure pragmatic ability, and to be able to generalize to real-world performances, will need to sample amongst these possibilities in a systematic and principled way.

The last aspect mentioned here, freedom, itself introduces additional complexity. Tasks vary in how predictable the language they elicit actually is. But if one wants to assess pragmatic ability it is likely that a task will not simply provide opportunities for speakers to demonstrate turn-taking ability or capacity to anticipate problems and repair, but in addition they may co-construct the discourse that emerges so that a task, quite naturally, evolves in unpredictable unforeseen ways. The task will then have worked as a task, but it introduces the difficulty that different candidates, doing the same task, push the task in different directions. In testing, this may be problematic, since comparing test-task performances may mean not comparing like with like. The standardization that is a desirable quality in testing may not be attainable. As Timpe-Laughlin (2018) indicates, this creates difficulty not simply for rating (do raters try to make allowances for this, and if so, how?), but also for tasks used in parallel forms of tests, or for choice of interlocutor and for interlocutor influences on a candidate's performance. There may also be issues of fairness since some candidates may be more equipped through previous experiences to have familiarity with a variety of contexts (and context is central to pragmatic ability), with this possibly being connected with issues of wealth and travelling. So while the assessment of pragmatic abilities is very important, it is also difficult, even compared to the challenges faced by testers elsewhere.

Despite this gloom, interesting work has been done. Concerning speech acts, Ekiert et al. (2018) devised a series of (computer-delivered) tasks, comparing making a complaint, giving advice and delivering a refusal. They found that the complaint > advice > refusal sequence indicated greater difficulty for their participants, but this sequence only applied at a lower-proficiency level. Higher-proficiency participants performed on the tasks at equivalent levels. The suggestion is that refusal may be slightly more difficult to handle than the other speech acts. Youn (2018) also researched speech acts (recommendation, requests, refusals), all in an academic context. Youn (2018) also used conversation analysis techniques to confirm that the interactions that the tasks provoked had natural characteristics, an interesting way of validating the functioning of the tasks concerned. Role plays were used, structured to produce different speech acts such as refusing, requesting, agreeing. It was found that the role play, which required participants to write a 'request letter', was the most difficult. Youn (2018) used item response analysis to establish this, while FACETS results suggested that, broadly, tasks and scales were neutral as regards the results obtained.

These two studies (Ekiert et al., 2018; Youn, 2018) are quite structured and targeted. Two other studies are much wider ranging, and bring out the challenges that using tasks to assess pragmatic ability entail. Norton (2013) was interested in the potential of tasks to elicit co-construction, and particularly with large-scale testing formats where there is a need for standardization. Using the Cambridge Main Suite format (see the section 'The Cambridge Main Suite of Tests') with a scripted interviewer performance, he was able to show that there is some, though not extensive, deviation from the script, so some degree of co-construction is possible in this context. He suggests though, that less educated testees may be less effective in exploiting these co-construction possibilities. As with Youn's (2018) study, Lam (2018) was also interested in wider interactional competence, and focused on the potential for, and detection of, contingency in performance. In a Hong Kong context, with English-medium secondary school students, Lam (2018) argues that two group interaction tasks provoked many opportunities for interactional abilities to be used (and provides a discussion of the different components of such abilities as in formulating (paraphrasing), accounting (repackaging) or extending a previous speaker's utterance). He also suggests, through conversation analysis (CA), that contingency moves were evident in the performances. He argues that the existence of such moves demonstrates the richness and naturalness of the interactions, but simultaneously, the difficulty of using such tasks for testing, since the importance of such contingency shows how interactions can be co-constructed, and so difficult to compare in any standardized way.

Conclusions

We see from this section, then, that tasks and task conditions influence performance. The bulleted points indicate what narrative accounts have suggested, and, coupled with the largely complementary findings from meta-analyses, give some empirical foundation for this claim. Test constructors clearly need to take such results seriously, and we will see examples of this in the section 'Practical Approaches'. But we have also seen the challenge in applying task research findings to testing contexts. We have seen that this transfer often does not occur in a straightforward manner, or effects seem to be smaller when testing is involved compared to the broader area of task research. There are important research design issues here, and possible non-application in testing studies of the exact operationalizations used in task research. But the challenge is real, and there is scope for additional research that is obviously important. As a final point, we can also now see more clearly that attempts to use tasks to assess pragmatic abilities have considerable promise. This line of research is relatively new, and the range of findings is not extensive and does not, as yet, present too coherent a picture. There is, though, considerable potential, and encouraging progress has been made. For all that, there is the point that this may be the area where the limits of testing are most exposed. The fundamental tension between standardization and comparability on the one hand, and freedom to co-construct discourse and allow natural and unpredictable development on the other, may be difficult to reconcile.

Ability for Use

Tasks themselves, though, are not the whole story. While actual performance on a task depends on task characteristics and task conditions and also draws on underlying competences, all of this is mediated through the concept of *ability for use*. Bluntly put, this means that underlying competences may be considerable, but if they are not mobilized into actual performance, communication is impaired. In contrast, if limited underlying competences are marshalled effectively, the performance that results may go beyond what might be expected on competences alone. It is useful, therefore, to explore what ability for use might consist of. Two preliminary points are helpful. First, we are dealing with something pretty close to Bachman's strategic competence, with its stages of assessment, goal-setting and planning. This too was focused on how actual communication is achieved against the background of underlying competences and how these competences are mobilized for performance. But Bachman's account is not specifically task oriented, nor does it embrace the factors that can now be located within ability for use. Allied to this, a second point is that the Levelt framework, covered in Chapter 3, is highly relevant for the functioning of ability for use and clarifies how the functioning of each of the Leveltian stages, as well as the relationship between them, is very important.

Two influences within ability for use concern the Conceptualizer stage. The first concerns the way the Conceptualizer handles issues such as assessing a situation, selecting what to say, taking a stance and then organizing propositions into the pre-verbal message (cf. Bachman's account, as covered in the section 'Underlying Theory'). Decisions about all these things influence the likely propositional content of what is going to said and also the pragmatic considerations which will influence these propositions. Context will be an important driver here for how the underlying ideas are selected and organized. Linked to this is the general knowledge base that can be drawn on to underpin these processes, knowledge of the world and of interactions within it, and also of sociolinguistic expectations and pragmatic conventions. None of this directly implicates the underlying language-oriented competences, but provides the foundation for the ideas that will be expressed and, indeed, is what leads to the pre-verbal message. It is assumed that people vary in how effectively they are able to marshal Conceptualizer processes of this sort.

Then we have two influences more linked to the Formulator stage and to the psycholinguistic processes that underpin actual language production. First, the second language mental lexicon (SLML), discussed more extensively in Chapter 3, is, in itself, an underlying competence, but ability for use is relevant when we consider aspects of the lexicon which make it more effective in communication. Here we have issues like the speed of operation of the SLML as well as access skills, the richness of what is held in lemmas, the connections of lemmas to one another and the completeness of what is retrieved. All of these are going to vary between individuals, and are distinct from more conventional views of what a competence consists of. In addition, within the SLML, there is the range of formulaic language which can be drawn on. As we saw in Chapter 3, formulaic language eases processing demands and if the language user can draw upon ready-made language chunks, the need to allocate attentional resources to computation is reduced. The second Formulator influence here is working memory, which concerns the resources and attention that are available as a message is built. Those with larger working memories, other things being equal, will have more ability to organize ideas and then access linguistic resources, with this being particularly important under any communicative pressure. As indicated in Chapter 3, it is interesting that working memory is an important individual difference factor in online planning studies, but not in strategic planning. It has to be concerned, that is, with the effectiveness with which underlying competences are assessed and brought to bear in actual communication.

The two remaining components of ability for use implicate both Conceptualization and Formulation stages. A compensation ability connects with the Canale and Swain (1980) framework, and also with Hulstijn's (2015) account of second language (L2) performance. It is the ability to handle problems when they occur during communication, either because underlying competences are lacking or because there has been some sort of misstep which needs to be retrieved. To include this ability here suggests that this is a consistent capacity to deal with the unforeseen. Linked with this resourcefulness is the capacity to monitor more effectively, and to act upon that monitoring. If things are going well, it is possible that monitoring, as a process, may be close to inactive, but if someone is operating at close to or outside their comfort zone, effective monitoring may pre-empt what might become more serious problems later. Finally we have metacognition, which is slightly more Conceptualizer oriented but nonetheless relevant for Formulator operations also. It concerns the L2 user's insights into their underlying competences and other aspects of ability for use, and the way these need to be used flexibly in a given communication situation. Metacognition is pervasive in its use, as on occasions the L2 user makes adaptations to be realistic about what they can achieve, even changing the focus of Conceptualization because of insights regarding limitations in ability and in the SLML (Skehan, 2018). Pang and Skehan (2014) bring this out clearly from their qualitative study of planning where it is clear that some learners modified what they did during the planning period to make it more likely that they would produce language commensurate with their abilities and not allow over-ambition to lead them into difficulty. L2 speakers clearly vary in their skill with metacognition (as they vary with other aspects of ability for use) and this then has an important influence on communicative effectiveness.

If this analysis of ability for use as a mediator for underlying competences in actual performance is accepted, the impact on effective assessment is considerable. Of course, there are techniques to measure underlying competences, possibly reliably and validly, and such measurements have considerable use and meaning. But if ability for use has this important mediating role, such competence-oriented measurements have to be balanced by approaches to testing which allow it to come into play. Not to do so is to miss testing a very important part of communicative ability, and so generalizations as to how people can use language in real situations are compromised. Tasks then become an important vehicle to allow ability for use to manifest itself, since they can potentially require the language user to cope with time pressure, with a need to relate language to ongoing discourse and context, and to use language appropriately.

Raters and Rating

There is an additional aspect of Figure 9.1 that requires more comment, and which brings out another potential contribution of task research. This is measurement, and the way task-related performance is rated. The convention in assessing spoken and written performance is to use global and analytic rating scales. Global scales tend to be an amalgamation of the analytic, and so won't be discussed separately here. Analytic scales typically cover grammar, vocabulary, accuracy, pronunciation, range, fluency, organization, coherence, task fulfilment and so on. The history of language testing makes frequent reference to the construction of rating scales and the basis for providing descriptions of performance at different levels which are valid and reliable, as well as comprehensible to raters and consumers of language test results. A considerable amount of expertise has been developed in such scale construction, reflected in systems like the Common European Framework of Reference for Languages (CEFR) (Council of Europe, 2001, 2008) or the Foreign Service Institute system and so on. But there have also been periodic calls to base scale construction on a more secure empirical footing, both with respect to the dimensions of performance and also the details in the scale descriptions (Fulcher, 1996).

In parallel, task research has given considerable importance to the measurement of CALF. There is a considerable degree of correspondence here (although this is far from absolute), and so complexity (with tasks) has a resemblance to grammar and range (in language testing), accuracy is simply accuracy, lexis relates to vocabulary and fluency maps onto fluency (and what is often termed 'delivery'). This raises the possibility that there are a number of areas where findings from task research can make useful contributions to the content of rating scales that are used in assessment and to their empirical base.

Skehan (2018) explores what task research has revealed in this regard. For example, he shows that the two measures of complexity most used in task research, subordination and words-per-clause do not correlate particularly highly and appear to measure different things. This confirms Inoue's (2013) finding of the same effect, actually obtained in a testing context. The former reports a median correlation across a number of studies (and different conditions within each) of –0.03, and the latter, across a smaller number of tasks, of also close to zero. This has the interesting implication that rating scale measures of complexity in a testing context really need to address these two areas separately, and include descriptors relevant to each. In contrast, the task research findings concerning measures of accuracy suggests that they broadly do the same thing, whether one looks at errors-per-clause, or measures based on error gravity, or one examines measures of length of clause that can be used accurately. So with accuracy the results suggest that developing analytic rating scales is relatively straightforward and likely to be consistent with measurement approaches in task research.

With fluency things are less clear. The task research suggests that speed, breakdown and repair form separate sub-dimensions of fluency. This division might then be the basis for different aspects of fluency rating scales, since it appears that the three areas have some independence from one another. In addition, there seems something of a tension, within fluency, between discourse and clause-linked influences (Skehan, 2018). The former are concerned with dysfluencies which manifest themselves at analysis of speech (AS) or clause boundaries, whereas the latter connect more with within-clause problems, indexed by such things as mid-clause silent and filled pauses and repair. Tavakoli (2018) also presents interesting proposals suggesting that different fluency measures are effective in distinguishing between CEFR levels, with speed distinguishing between levels from A2 to B2/C1; silent and filled pausing distinguishing between A2 and the higher levels; and mid-clause pauses between A2/B1 and B2/C1. Once again, the implications for the detail of rating scales which are used to measure performance are intriguing. Finally, with lexis, task researchers broadly use measures of lexical diversity (i.e. corrected type-token ratios) and lexical sophistication (typically the 'penetration' of a performance by less frequent words). The former measures a speaker's (or writer's) capacity to avoid recycling the same words, while the latter seems to reflect a capacity to draw upon a wider underlying lexicon. Interestingly, measures of each area do not particularly correlate (Skehan, 2009b), and so these two aspects of lexical performance (and so vocabulary ratings of test-task performance) need to be kept distinct. Once again, task research has the potential to illuminate what needs to be included in analytic rating scales.

Findings such as these have considerable potential to influence what is covered in the rating scales that are used in language testing. They may provide more valid and empirically based input to the wording of scales and also, thereby, possibly bring rating scales and discourse analytic measures into a greater degree of congruence. One example of this could be O'Grady's (in press) work in developing what he terms EBB (empirically derived, binary choice-oriented (to simplify decision-making) and boundary-oriented) scales, regarding the different levels in rating scales. Detailed performance analysis in task research could be an important impact in such an approach. In any case, returning to Figure 9.1, it is clear that rating, and information for raters, are other areas where task research has an important potential contribution to make to language testing.

Conclusions

The model outlined in Figure 9.1 was schematic and preliminary. The discussion since then has covered a great number of studies, and shown that the model is now grounded in a good deal of research.

There is, of course, much still to do, but already we have a framework which enables us to relate task research to testing, and not simply to testing speaking. We know much more about task effects and task condition effects. Measurement procedures from the task domain have been shown to be clearly relevant to the process of rating test performance. Ability for use, perhaps less grounded in research studies than the other components of the model, nonetheless has clear relevance for our understanding of effective testing. Above all, ability for use provides a way of thinking about the relationship between interactive-ability and real-life approaches. By focusing on the details of processing, in addition to simply looking at task characteristics, we may have a basis for generalizing more effectively from particular, and necessarily limited, test tasks, provided that processing demands can be linked to wider patterns of language use. It may be that, following a task-based approach, the interactive-ability and real-life approaches to testing are not as different as they may at first sight seem.

Issues in Task-Based Language Testing

The previous section, 'Task Research and Task-Based Testing', has tried to argue for a task-based approach to testing, to link such testing with task research, and to sketch out a model which organizes the way tasks can be related to the assessment situation. It has considerable promise. But there are a number of issues which need discussion – issues which indicate there is also progress yet to be made. We will discuss four of these: the contrast between real-life and interactive-ability approaches, given the role tasks can play in assessment; the conundrum of task difficulty; the central issue of whether task performance is predictable; and finally the enduring challenge of achievement testing.

Real-Life vs. Interactive-Ability Approaches

A thread running through this entire chapter so far is the contrast between real-life and interactive-ability approaches to language testing (Bachman, 1990). The former takes as a starting point real-life tasks, and so the purpose of assessment (not to mention instruction) is to identify relevant real-life tasks and then to model assessment tasks upon them, as advocated by Long (2016) and Norris (2016), and Bachman and Palmer's (1996) Target Language Use (TLU) approach. The emphasis here is on the real-life relationship between pedagogic and assessment tasks, and some approaches (Brindley, 2013; Wigglesworth and Frost, 2017) see this as what task-based testing is.

This approach, assuming the accuracy of the real-life uses which are identified, has the enormous advantage of a very good basis for prediction to such situations, as well as the potential to devise scoring procedures which reflect what is important in real-life tasks. Sampling, in this view, is focused and is more likely to achieve comprehensive coverage of a limited domain. Later in the chapter we will explore one application of this approach.

Obviously the central strength of this approach – that there is a clear relationship between test-tasks and real-world language uses – presupposes that the range of real-world language uses is sufficiently identifiable and restricted. In one sense, this strength is also a weakness – the prediction to such real-life tasks may be good, but the consequence is that prediction to other real-life tasks may be compromised precisely by the precision of the match that is the basis for such effective prediction. The range of prediction may therefore necessarily be narrow. Interestingly, another critique that is made of the approach (Bachman, 2002) is that real-life contexts which are targeted are rarely as uniform as the approach would require. Bachman (2002), for instance, gives the example, from Norris et al. (1998) of two tasks which may be both superficially concerned with the same theme, but which differ markedly in other respects. This follows Skehan (1984) who critiqued English for Specific Purposes (ESP) testing on a similar basis – different domains contain vastly contrasting sub-specialities, for example, psychiatry and dermatology are both within medicine but very different in language use.

The alternative, the interactive-ability approach, also has its strengths and weaknesses. Sampling, traditionally, has been on the basis of underlying competences, perhaps linked to some target-language use system, although this, necessarily, will be nothing like as precise as the alternative real-life approach. This sampling will attempt representative coverage, but of a much larger domain, and in many cases the domain involved, as with general proficiency tests, can only be very considerable indeed. But if the sampling is maximally effective, then the generalization to real-world performances can be wide-ranging, even if less exact about particular real-life events. Even so, the problem is that the relationship between the sampling and the ultimate real-language use situations is not clear.

In his formulation of this distinction, Bachman (1990) makes it clear that the tasks which are used in testing need to generate interactional authenticity, in other words, a use of language which resembles real-life language use and which engages abilities in a similar way to what happens in such contexts. In addition, he proposes that strategic competence, as he formulates it, is important in making a bridge between underlying competences and actual communication. What we have seen in this chapter is that tasks and the reconceptualized ability for use could be an important basis for sampling and the generalization that is then enabled. By trying to draw upon a variety of tasks and task conditions, the data base which will emerge will be a more robust basis for connecting with a range of language use situations. What will be discovered is underlying processing capacities, and these are likely to provide a better basis for predicting how well people will do in future unspecified situations. This needs to be coupled with sampling of ability for use, for probing how effectively test takers can handle issues such as effectiveness of Conceptualization, speed and effectiveness of SLML access, capacity to use working memory, metacognitive processes, compensation and so on. The specific tasks that are used may not be general in nature, but the underlying competences that they trigger could be a better basis for generalizing than simply targeting underlying competences. In this way, a task-based approach to testing, it could be argued, is a better justification for using an interactive-ability approach, and also, possibly for avoiding the limitations of a real-life approach.

Of course, there is a lot of work that needs to be done here. The findings on task characteristics are suggestive more than definitive as a base for predicting actual performance, despite the generalizations mentioned. Conditions, perhaps, are more promising, but even here there is the issue of replicating task condition research findings in a testing context. Further, while ability for use as a construct is interesting and has great potential, tying down its different components and establishing the detail of their influences is a challenge for the future. But these factors do have considerable potential relevance for testing, and it is to be hoped that in the future they will motivate a great deal of testing research.

The Difficulty of Test Tasks

One aspect of Figure 9.1 requires further discussion. The task box in the figure is highly likely to be influenced by both Conceptualizer and Formulator issues. These are important for the general influences that they have on performance. They are also relevant to the concept of difficulty in language testing. Conventional testing, armed as it is with some complex statistical procedures, is able to arrange test items on a cline of empirically established difficulty, where that difficulty is based on information regarding the proportion of test takers who pass an item, and the extent to which individual items conform to a 'model' of difficulty (McNamara, 1996). With task-based approaches to testing, we are well beyond individual items which can straightforwardly be passed or failed. The performances that are elicited are multidimensional and complex, and do not lend themselves to simple passing and failing decisions. Pollitt (1991) notes that in assessment there is something of a division between approaches which count things (as with the items in conventional tests) and approaches which rate performance. It is the latter approach which is relevant to testing, as the multidimensional nature of performance is likely to be rated for things such as range (close to complexity in task-based performance), accuracy, vocabulary, pronunciation, and outcome or task fulfilment, as we have just seen. This richness of performance, coupled with the fact that with tasks one cannot have large numbers of 'items', means that measuring performance is much more complex, and in turn, that making decisions about difficulty is also much more complex, since tasks may push different aspects of performance in varying directions, and so the multidimensional nature of what is said or written makes it difficult to develop a one-dimensional scale of difficulty.

Skehan (2018) proposes in this regard that it is useful to separate notions of task difficulty in testing into those which are Conceptualizer-linked and those which are Formulator-linked. In the former case what would be manipulated are the ideas that make some tasks more conceptually difficult than others, such as information which is more extensive or more abstract, or operations which are more complex. Then with Formulator influences one would be looking to vary performance features which have an impact on access to the SLML, and the speed and ease with which language can then be built and syntactic frames assembled. Skehan (2018) proposes that the influences on making tasks more difficult or complex in these two cases are different, and that if one is developing a series of tasks as the sampling basis for assessment, it is helpful to keep them apart, both conceptually and with actual test-task development. In this way one can perhaps obtain a more rounded view of performance and a better basis for generalization. Table 9.2 exemplifies how this might work.

The essential point here is that sampling combinations of easy and difficult tasks and conditions for each of the stages of speech production can be more effective in giving a comprehensive account of a candidate's communicative competence. The details in the different cells in this figure are sketchy and incomplete, essentially only exemplifying, but as task research accumulates, we will have a better idea as to how to build in different degrees of difficulty in a testing situation and how to probe different aspects of ability. The figure offers a framework that could be very useful in testing.

Table 9.2 Level of difficulty linked to Conceptualizer and Formulator influences

	Conceptualizer easy	Conceptualizer difficult
Formulator easy	• Unpressured communication • Familiar, structured information, only requiring retrieval	• Unpressured, small-scale communication • Extending, planning, reasoning, transformation
Formulator difficult	• Pressured communication, heavy input, monologic, non-negotiable • Familiar, structured information; emphasis on retrieval	• Pressured communication; heavy input; monologic; non-negotiable • Extending, planning, reasoning and transformation

The Predictability of Tasks and Task Conditions

In Chapter 3, and also earlier in this chapter, the predictability of tasks and task conditions have been discussed. Indeed, two approaches which try to account for regularities in task and task condition effects have emerged. The LAC approach proposes that these are numerous, and that actual performance is the conjoint result of the combinations of influence which may operate in any one task, such as when a structured task (and such tasks lead typically to greater accuracy) with planning opportunities (generally associated with higher complexity and fluency) produce raised performance in the three CAF areas. The CH, through its resource-directing, resource-dispersing distinction, makes predictions about the effects of the various examples of each of these categories. Each of the approaches has generated a considerable amount of research and the database we have available is extensive, as meta-analyses, such as that of Malicka and Sasayama (2017), make clear.

Task research, then, through theory and through empirical work, has provided clear indications that there are important generalizations one can draw on. But Skehan (2016) expresses words of caution. Reviewing the available research, he suggests that the consistency in effects of task characteristics (in general, and not just associated with the two more theoretical approaches just mentioned) is disappointing. There are many interesting avenues to explore (task structure, task complexity, information type and organization and so on) but the evidence is not strong that they produce effects, let alone substantial effects. He suggests that task conditions are associated with more consistent findings, with this applying to pre-task planning, online planning (i.e. lack of time pressure during actual performance) and repetition.

It is clearly the case that language testing needs to take account of this theorizing and research in L2 task performance. But we have also seen that when language testing studies have tried to incorporate variables from task research, there has been far from a simple replication of what happens. We have seen that comparing TOEFL iBT performance to real-life performance sees the latter associated with slightly higher complexity but lower accuracy (Brooks and Swain, 2014; Khabbazbashi, 2017). Studies of planning, in general, do show an effect on performance, in a testing context, but the effect tends to be small, and likely more important with CALF measures than with performance ratings (Wigglesworth and Elder, 2010; Nitta and Nakatsuhara, 2014; O'Grady, in press). It is also reported that the effect is not so great as to lead to different rating levels being assigned (from FACETS analyses). There are important research design issues with these results, in that we have not seen a systematic examination of the relevance of variables identified in task research for a testing context, e.g. task complexity or time pressure. Nor have variables which have been used, principally planning, been operationalized in the same way in testing as in task research (with perhaps the exception of O'Grady). So the jury is still out. But one does have to say that so far task research can only be suggestive as regards a testing context. There is considerable promise but it has yet to be realized.

This discussion relates to two important challenges to task-based testing raised by Bachman (2002). First, he suggested that progress in task-based testing requires that tasks which function in the same way generally be identified, so that they are dependable influences upon performance. As we have seen, the findings on this issue since Bachman's critique was published have not been replete with suggestions which meet his criterion. Some are, possibly, such as the usual suspects of planning, time pressure during performance and some task characteristics such as structure. But generally, his point is still relevant. His second critique, and this was perhaps in response to the Hawai'ian EAP project, was to suggest that the prospects for a task-based approach to testing, or at least real-life testing, are limited because a key issue is that tasks (and presumably task conditions) interact with individuals such that one cannot assume that a given task, condition or task condition bundle will work in the same way with different people. There will be differences in background knowledge, training, experience, preferences, which will mean that a particular task, even if it were of a particular 'difficulty', would not be responded to in the same way by different individuals. Short of identifying task characteristics which operate in a 'candidate-independent' way, the hope of regarding a task as a dependable unit of testing is limited.

This is an interesting criticism. There are two reasons, though, why it may not have so much force given the view of task-based testing that is promoted here. First, there is the issue that a lot of task research has been done since the critique was originally made. We are now in a position, as noted, to propose some reasonably powerful generalizations, even if task researchers would like to be able to report more! Second, and returning to Figure 9.1, the clearer prominence and understanding we have regarding ability for use is another force that clarifies some of the variance in test scores which might otherwise be regarded as error. Performance does not depend solely on tasks and task conditions. If we can understand more about how the different aspects of ability for use function, we can design more effective assessment procedures and have a clearer basis for generalizing to real-life performance. After all, to take one example, if working memory interacts with processing conditions and time pressure, we have first of all identified what might otherwise be regarded as an unforeseen interaction, and second of all, we are focusing on something which would be relevant to performance in the real world. If working memory, for example, confers an advantage in some real-life language use, then we have to be attuned to that effect.

But we are left with what might be the greatest challenge of all to the predictability of tasks (and test tasks) – the importance of co-construction. As we saw in the discussion of pragmatic abilities, effective communication requires much more than knowledge of an underlying system. There is also a need to understand how L2 speakers handle pragmatic demands and how they function effectively in terms of interactional abilities. This, naturally, requires test formats to incorporate interaction, and this leads to a considerable problem in that once a candidate in a testing situation is confronted by the need to interact, there is the possibility that the interlocutor will exert an influence on the candidate's performance. But even more challenging, if the interaction is allowed to develop naturally, in whatever direction seems appropriate to the interactants, then a lack of standardization is introduced. In other words, co-construction does present very serious challenges (Timpe-Laughlin, 2018) for any capacity to compare performances of different candidates (since they may not have been doing the same thing even though the starting point was the same) or parallel forms of tests (since this follows from the previous difficulty – if a given starting point can lead to different development, two (or more) different starting points can only make matters worse). In the second part of this chapter, in the section 'Practical Approaches to Task-Based Testing', we will see how attempts to overcome this difficulty have been made. For now, it has to be recognized as a serious concern – if tasks are to meet criteria for naturalness and unpredictability, their use in testing is not at all straightforward.

Achievement Testing

Long (2015) suggests that the most urgent area for progress in task-based testing is that of achievement testing, and indeed there are a number of ways of justifying this. The first is that this is the area which has shown least development since the late 1980s or so. Proficiency testing, whether interactive ability or real life, has seen some important developments, but testing linked to teaching has languished in comparison. There is great scope for improvement, in other words. But even more important is the consequence of lack of development in this area. Washback, as we have seen, is an important test quality. If task-based teaching is not matched by task-based assessment, and even worse, if assessment focuses on more formal aspects of language, the achievements of a task-based approach will be compromised, as learners (and parents and educational systems) will inevitably prioritize what is tested. So the need for educational systems to match task-based instruction (TBI) with task-based assessment is vital.

There are, of course, many reasons for this lack of progress. Test construction and validation are expensive and time-consuming and so it is no coincidence that the greatest activity is associated with proficiency tests, especially where these are well funded, as with major international testing organizations. Teachers are far less resourced in this regard, and also typically lack the same level of technical and computing expertise that is routinely used in effective test validation processes. Qualities such as reliability, validity, fairness, usefulness are just as important with achievement tests as with proficiency tests, but are more difficult to attain given the resourcing typically available. There is also, perhaps, the issue of a lack of theory for the development of achievement tests, something which reflects a disconnect between L2 acquisition research, on the one hand, and classroom and textbook-based instruction, on the other. Achievement testing needs to be based on what has been taught, but many approaches to teaching, and this may well include some versions of TBI, may not be based on a clear view of development and acquisitional progress, which does not help in designing tests which are meant to reflect progress.

In one respect, though, achievement testing ought to be simpler. The 'target' of such testing is what has been taught, and so the challenge in designing tests should be to devise effective ways of sampling so that tests cover the different aspects of teaching in a systematic way. The emphasis in such cases is to establish content validity. More traditional approaches to teaching lend themselves to this fairly well, in that the items of a syllabus can be sampled, and performances on test items can then be totalled, even with the prospect of giving diagnostic information about aspects of the syllabus which have been covered. Things are more difficult with task-based approaches. Test tasks are likely to require performances to be generated, which are time-consuming (enabling fewer 'items') and require more complex rating procedures. In addition, the units in task-based teaching are less likely to lend themselves to generating representative items. So the tester has a number of additional problems to face, not least as (as Chapter 7 demonstrated) notions of syllabus in the task-based area are less definitive or precise. In fact, compared to the textbook dependence of much conventional teaching, task-based achievement tests may require classroom observation to discover what has actually been taught, or even individual-tailored tests, given the freedom and non-prescriptive approach in task-based achievement tests.

The difficulties are clear, but how might they be overcome? Obviously a first and very important approach is for teachers to develop achievement tests on the basis of the task-based classes they have taught. This is feasible, and even minimal investigation of the functioning of such tests will be valuable to establish some degree of reliability and effective measurement. But this will be demanding on people with a very limited amount of time. More realistic, given the likelihood of coursebooks being used, is for publishers to make greater efforts to develop task-based tests for coursebooks which make claims about the use of tasks as part of their methodology. Large coursebook series now routinely do contain testing material, but this is often fairly conventional in nature. Publishers need to take more responsibility for matching the approach to testing with a claimed approach to instruction. They have considerable resources, and such coursebook series have very large budgets. Producing a range of testing materials which teachers can draw upon, as needed, should become the norm.

An alternative approach, if teaching is carried out under the aegis of a state educational authority, is for collaboration with institutions of higher education or with testing bodies. In this way professional expertise can come from the institution concerned but there can be collaboration with teachers involved in the process of test development itself. Consequently, hard-pressed teachers can work within a wider framework, but be supported in their efforts. This promotes the possibility that tests will be locally relevant and reflect the reality of TBI, but that the tests themselves can meet professional standards. Indeed, more widely collaborative action can lead to the production of resource banks for testing which, cumulatively, can grow and provide a basis for selection of tasks of known qualities.

One final initiative might be of note. Harrison (1982) describes a system where sets of different coursebooks were analysed for the tasks that they used and then these were taxonomized through content and functions/notions. Test tasks were then developed targeting different content areas and, within this area, a range of mini-tasks were devised. These were assembled into a 'challenge sheet', with claimed differences in difficulty. This was done in collaboration with actual teachers. But what was innovative in this work is that the challenge sheets were then given to the students themselves, who were given responsibility for saying when they were ready to take on the detailed items within each challenge sheet. The interlocutor was another student, who was responsible for the 'validation' that the mini-task had been done adequately. Each challenge sheet contained ten or so mini-tasks, and the student in question could only approach the teacher when all ten tasks had been validated by other students. In this way, considerable assessment was carried out, but the teacher's workload was considerably eased. The system required significant centralized development work, but it then led to considerable washback as students were given much more responsibility than is usual for language process within the task-based system.

The final section of the chapter will include a couple of examples of achievement-testing projects.

Practical Approaches to Task-Based Testing

This section will present four case studies in task-based testing. These bring out the relevance of the preceding discussion, and at the same time indicate how practical problems can be solved to make a task-based approach a reality. They comprise a project to develop a testing procedure in a university EAP system (a real-life approach); a set of publicly available commercial tests (an interactive-ability approach); some tests to accompany a coursebook series; and a series of testing ventures within an educational system (with these last two examples both functioning as achievement tests).

The Hawai'i Performance Assessment Project

Many of the principles and difficulties of a task-based approach to testing are illustrated by a testing project which originated at the University of Hawai'i, and which is documented in two book publications. Norris et al. (1998) describe the development of the bank of test items and provide a rationale for the approach. Brown et al. (2002) provide an account of considerable practical work with this item bank and their work contains rich statistical data. The purpose of the project was to develop a wide range of prototypical tasks which would 'represent real-world tasks that might face university students studying a second or foreign language' (Norris et al., 1998, p. 71). In other words, this is clearly a real-life approach. On the basis of an extensive needs analysis, a very large number of such tasks was generated. The tasks fell into seven general categories:

- health and recreation/entertainment (eighteen tasks);
- travel (sixteen tasks);
- food and dining (thirteen tasks);
- at work (seventeen tasks);
- at the university (nineteen tasks);
- domesticity (fifteen tasks);
- environment/politics (six tasks).

The test tasks which were developed, more than one hundred in total, covered this range of themes. They each of them met criteria for 'taskiness' (e.g. giving medical advice; enquiring about financial support (in a university context); advertising for a housemate; planning a presentation), and were mostly associated with relevant support materials. The authors developed a difficulty rating scheme for each task, based on three areas, with two subcategories of each (loosely based on Skehan, 1996):

- Code complexity:
  - range;
  - number of input sources.
- Cognitive complexity:
  - organization of input;
  - availability of input.
- Communicative demands:
  - mode;
  - response level.

Each subcategory had two values (− and +), yielding six ratings in total, generating a score range of 1 (the easiest level of task, based on six minuses) to 6 (the most difficult, with six plusses). Each general and specific category were provided with copious descriptive material, and high reliability was achieved in the ratings, which were calculated by category difficulty and overall test task difficulty.

At first sight the project is more obviously consistent with Bachman's real-life approach, in that the different tasks outlined in the Hawai'i project relate to studying at a university, and so have clear real-world relevance within that sphere. In that respect, effective sampling of behaviour can be claimed quite straightforwardly through surveys of language use in such contexts, systematically sampled, as they were. But Norris et al. (1998) were introducing a scheme to assess difficulty which has resemblances to what I have proposed here. It also has connections with Bachman's interactive-ability approach to testing, since these categories concern more general processing. The approach, that is, melds a real-life task choice approach with an interactive-ability notion of difficulty.

The research team also developed two types of rating scale. The first was task specific and, using five steps ranging from clearly inadequate to adept, provided clear descriptions of the different levels of skill needed to complete a task. Impressively, a different task-specific set of descriptors, at the five levels, was developed for each separate task. In addition, a task independent scale was developed, also with five steps. Generic descriptors were provided for code command, cognitive operations and communicative adaptation. Self-ratings were also collected as part of the research project.

The project was largely successful in what it set out to achieve. Extensive analyses of the dataset showed that performance ratings, both task specific and task independent, were highly reliable, so that judgements of performance on the different tasks were consistent and dependable. The project demonstrated, in other words, that although the tasks and the performances might be considered complex, the judgements made about those performances amply met conventional statistical standards. In addition, there was important validity evidence. Different reference groups took the different tests, and these reference groups had fairly clear differentiation in general ability levels. The data patterned strongly in accordance with differences between the various groups.

The one area where the research could be regarded as disappointing (and this is an important disappointment) concerns the relationship between estimated task difficulty and actual performances on tasks of different proposed difficulty. The authors indicate that they had hoped that a clear relationship in this area would have been the basis for claims of generality. The capacity to relate tasks to difficulty in a principled and empirical way would enable more powerful claims to be made about generality and how test tasks could be chosen to make more precise statements, and then perhaps go beyond the particular test tasks chosen. So the weak-to-moderate relationship that is reported is a disappointment. The correlation between predicted difficulty and actual performance that is reported is −0.43 (negative being appropriate here), and so this suggests there is room to improve the predictability of difficulty with tasks. This is consistent with discussions elsewhere in this book suggesting that linking task characteristics to predictable language use, including task difficulty, is often extremely problematic. It also connects with the discussions relating to Table 9.2, where a somewhat different account of task difficulty is proposed.

But this point should not diminish the achievements of the Hawai'ian research group. They have produced a wide range of tasks which address a particular assessment problem in a systematic way. They have demonstrated very impressive validity and reliability evidence. They have also contributed in a major way to the development of rating scales, and added to our understanding of the relationship between adapted and general rating scales. The research was extensive and practical, and has demonstrated how much effort is required to meet conventional testing standards within a task-based framework. It was essentially a collaborative research project, and this is the only way, frankly, outside a testing organization, where such thoroughness could be possible. What has been achieved is a resource which can be drawn on by others. The project is a milestone in our field. It also, interestingly, fits in very well with the task definition from Chapters 1 and 13: meaning primacy; a goal which needs to be addressed; learners relying on their own language resources; and a clearly defined outcome.

The Cambridge Main Suite of Tests

The Cambridge Main Suite is an important set of public examinations, used all over the world. In fact it can be regarded as a set of separate tests, each appropriate for a particular proficiency level; however, in more recent years the relationship between the different tests has been articulated more clearly and, in addition, the connection of these tests to the CEFR has been clarified. The tests (and each is associated with a CEFR level) comprise the Key English Test (KET) (CEFR A2, Waystage), the Preliminary English Test (PET) (B1, Threshold), the First Certificate in English (FCE) (B2, Vantage) and the Certificate in Advanced English (CAE) (Effective Operational Proficiency: C1). (There is also the Certificate of Proficiency in English, CPE (Mastery: C2), which will not be considered here, since it effectively functions at close to native-speaker level.) The stakes are high with these tests.

They are available worldwide, and have to attain very high standards of test construction, scoring and reporting. In addition, they need to be available in multiple forms (and regular new forms) to ensure security. They are, broadly, interactive-ability tests that try to assess more general ability in English. Since they function from CEFR A2 Waystage up to C1, Operational Proficiency (and beyond, with C2, Mastery), they have to deal with a very considerable range in ability. Relatively recently they have undergone a major process of construct validation and are related to Weir's (2005) socio-cognitive model, particularly in relation to cognitive and contextual validity factors. The former largely derives from the application of the Levelt (1989, 1999) model, and the latter is concerned with setting factors (task and administration) and demands (linguistic and interlocutor). Extensive analyses are provided of how research relates to the different aspects of the socio-cognitive model (e.g. Galaczi and ffrench, 2010), and how these different factors are exemplified in the different tests within the main suite (Weir, Vidakovic and Galaczi, 2014).

What is relevant here is whether the tests at the different levels, and the subsections which comprise them, represent a task-based approach to testing. To explore this question, we will focus here on the speaking test component of the different tests (Galaczi and ffrench, 2010), and the illustrations will be in terms of the publicly available material, drawn from the Cambridge English website (Weir et al., 2014).

Broadly, it cannot be said that the details of what is done in the different tests comes directly from the task literature, but at the same time, a great deal of task research is drawn on when the sub-tests are discussed, and familiar variables from the task literature are in evidence. Galaczi and ffrench (2010, p. 170) suggest that complexification within the main suite set of tests involves the following features:

- a move from controlled to semi-controlled to open-ended response formats;
- a move from greater to lesser support (visual and otherwise);
- a move from familiar topics, with stronger examiner influence, to more open-ended topics and more general topics;
- an increasing amount of time for each task type (note: not a difference in time pressure here, but more a need for more extended language use);
- a move from factual to evaluative discourse;
- a move from persuasion and description to exposition and argumentation;
- a move from personal and concrete information to non-personal and abstract information.

Each of these bullet points is based on variables which, one way or another, have featured in task research and been the basis for performance effects. So there is some degree of congruence between the preoccupations and theorizing of task researchers and what is done to develop greater complexity within the main suite tests. There are, of course, other factors in task research not so prominently represented. The distinction made earlier in this chapter between Conceptualizer and Formulator influences on difficulty and complexity is not so clear. Other variables, such as planning, are not represented (although they are mentioned in relation to cognitive validity in the Cambridge tests). Broadly, though, there are clear connections between the design features evident with the tests and the approach taken within task research.

A brief description of testing material for the speaking tests, taken from the Cambridge English website, will make some of these issues clearer. The KET, identified at A2 level, has two parts and is conducted with an interlocutor and a pair of candidates. In the first part, the interlocutor asks candidates fairly easy questions such as 'Do you think English will be useful for you in the future? What did you do yesterday evening/last weekend?' In the second part each candidate is given information, such as about a museum or a bookshop, and the other candidate in each case is required to ask questions about that information. Brief prompt material is provided. The PET (CEFR B1) has three sections. The first section is broadly similar to the KET. In the second part there is more complex input material, entirely visual, and this is the basis for the two candidates to talk to each other, drawing on the visual suggestions, to formulate advice, for example, on somebody's visit to a city for the weekend. So the task is supported, contextualized and has a clear outcome. But it also requires conversation management. The third part also has a visual prompt, for example, requiring people to respond to pictures about things that people are doing at home. The intention is to push candidates to taking a longer turn. Each candidate completes the picture description task, and then they have to talk to one another about what they themselves do at home.

The FCE is regarded as B2 level, and has four parts. The first is similar to the previous levels, in that the interlocutor asks questions, although the focus for these questions is more wide-ranging, even though the personal nature remains. The second also has similarities to the KET, but in this case a degree of comparison is involved, as well as the need to respond to more general and judgement-provoking questions from the interlocutor. The third part requires interaction based on input, which requires some processing (such as how to attract tourists to a town), and then some reasoning and justification in connection with this. Part Four in this example, also interactive, develops the tourism theme but moves to holidays more generally and issues connected with them, requiring the capacity to express opinions and justify them. Finally, the CAE is regarded as C1 level, and like the FCE has four parts. Part One, similar to FCE, is interlocutor-driven and could be considered 'extended personal'. Part Two is similar to FCE Part Two, but perhaps with a little bit more justification in the responses made to pictures. There is also greater prominence for talking about the feelings and motives of those in the pictures. Part Three uses a visual prompt (in the form of a splash diagram) and requires conversation between the candidates about decisions, e.g. choosing a university. The focus is not on the decision itself but on the process of decision-making, the factors which are important and how decisions can be justified. Part Four develops this theme, going beyond the concrete and specific decisions covered in the third part, and is concerned with decision-making in life generally. It is more abstract, requiring the student to link this to their own personal experiences and to offer more difficult justifications.

It is clear in all the subsections of the tests that language is being elicited so that it can be evaluated. The examiner is clearly in charge and orchestrates events either closely (Part One) or with some degree of freedom for the candidates (Parts Two to Four). The candidates are given every opportunity to display a range of language, likely to the limit of what they can do, with this being partly in response to direct questions from the examiner or in interaction with another candidate. As the bulleted points indicate, there is also organized development in what candidates are given the opportunity to do across the levels of the main suite. It is evident that we are dealing with an interactive-ability approach to testing, and that the formats provide many occasions where ability for use needs to be brought into play. But this analysis does not, in itself, establish 'taskiness'. At the very least, there is a strong communicative dimension to all the encounters in the speaking test. Perhaps the most prominent and obvious connection with tasks comes at the lower levels (KET and PET) where there are clearer outcomes for the tasks which are given (cf. the museum and bookshop tasks, the visit to a city). At higher levels there are structured encounters, interaction, longer turns and the opportunity to use a range of language abilities, but not the same focus on task achievement as at lower levels. This is obviously good in provoking wider sampling and opportunity to stretch language, and so may be inevitable in testing at higher levels. Perhaps the one other thing of note is that when the examiner is involved, there is restriction in the spontaneity of what is said. Interlocutor contributions are scripted, and so there can be little doubt that unequal discourse is involved and lack of scope for the candidate to shape what is said. But this may well be inevitable if challenges to fairness and equal opportunities are to be met. All in all, this range of tests does indicate that, where the testing of speaking is concerned, there is considerable prominence for the use of tasks in a very widely used public examination. To return to a point made earlier, the washback that is likely from these tests is vital: one could not prepare for these tests by learning lists of grammar or vocabulary items.

Developing Task-Based Tests to Accompany a Coursebook

Major coursebook series have been one of the most significant developments in the teaching of English as a Foreign Language (EFL), and since the late 1970s such coursebook series have changed in interesting ways. They are now far more comprehensive, and typically contain a considerable quantity of integrated supplementary material, much of it delivered through multimedia. In addition, the 'input' to the classroom teacher for each lesson or sequence of lessons is far more extensive now, with the result that the teacher has, arguably, less of a developmental, or mediating or adapting role. Such coursebook series tend to claim communicative approaches almost routinely, but importantly often contain a lot of more traditional material.

It is intriguing that, despite the massive financial commitments made by publishers towards such series, one area has remained surprisingly unchanged – that of assessment. Where coursebook series provide testing materials, even when major claims are made towards communicativeness, the testing materials are remarkably traditional. In view of that, we will go back some years in the case study in this section, and examine the testing materials from the COBUILD course (Willis and Willis, 1988), a series consisting of three volumes (at three proficiency levels), which claims to be task-based (with important lexical connections also). The series is distinguished by having a separate testing book (Fried-Booth, 1989), and so this provides an interesting opportunity to explore to what extent the testing materials respond to the nature of the materials themselves.

The testing book for the three-volume series contains ten tests, three for the first volume, three for the second and four for the third. The tests have a standardized format, and contain sections on vocabulary and pronunciation, grammar, reading, writing and listening. In addition, at the third level the reading tests sometimes contain material on dictionary skills. No statistical information is provided on any of the tests concerned.

The vocabulary, pronunciation and grammar sections of each test are fairly traditional in nature, with multiple choice, fill in the blanks and matching formats. The only additional thing to say here is that the COBUILD course has vocabulary features (linked to a Birmingham University corpus of spoken and written English), with the course materials written to incorporate designated (and important) sets of words that arose from this corpus. The tests then focus on this material, and so there can be claims of content validity. The reading and listening components of each test can be described as communicative, rather than task-based. With reading, interesting and challenging material is presented. This often has a magazine-article quality, and then meaning-oriented questions are asked about such material. The focus is very much on meaning, although on occasions there are sections which ask for synonyms to be found from within the reading passages. So while the material is real-world based, and the questions asked are genuinely meaningful, these are not real-world tasks. The same can be said about the listening tests. These are based on recordings, where the test item may range from choosing amongst multiple-choice illustrations, to filling in blanks in a form, to making choices from several statements. The listening material is given at a reasonable but not excessive pace, and the decisions that have to made are totally meaning-focused, but once again, it is difficult to claim a real-world relationship. The most task-based section of the various tests is consistently the one on writing. Here the test contains similar sorts of tasks to those which figure in the Hawai'ian project, with context, input materials and a specific need to communicate something which has a real-world connection. Even so, some of the time there are transformation exercises and more communicative activities which are more generic in nature. But compared to the other sections, criteria of 'taskiness' are more clearly met.

On balance, then, the COBUILD tests are more communicative than completely task-based. Even so, it should be said that, compared to other major coursebook series, they are more concerned with tasks and communication than most. Most such series claim to be communicative, and even task-based, but the mismatch between professed aims and any associated testing material is much greater. If, then, we are concerned with washback, the COBUILD tests just reviewed do complement, to a considerable degree, the aims of the broader series and the units which compose it. Returning to the general task definition (meaning primacy, gap to be addressed, learners use their own resources, clear outcome), the tests in question go some way to achieving this, and they demonstrate that task-oriented coursebook series can achieve useful testing. But the match here is not as great as it was with the Hawai'ian tests. The Cobuild tests are less convincing with all of the individual criteria at some point or another. So we have an interesting contrast between two sets of 'task-based' tests. On the other hand, they do sample from the coursebook materials reasonably effectively, and this may well be more important.

Task-Based Testing within an Educational System

The case studies we have examined so far concern what might be considered to be elective contexts – in each case learners choose to study a language. The fourth case is slightly different in that it concerns a mandated education system, in Belgium. Colpin and Gysen (2006) describe a whole series of task-based tests developed within this context, for learners of various ages and for different contexts. They also discuss many of the associated issues in developing task-based tests.

The range of tests that were developed included (for more examples, see Colpin and Gysen, 2006):

1. Six-year-old immigrant children who have finished kindergarten and are entering primary education. The test is intended to indicate to their new teachers their new classes' Dutch language proficiency.
2. A test for twelve- to sixteen-year-old children assessing their Dutch language proficiency at the end of their first year in reception in Belgium. The test was designed to establish functional language proficiency in Dutch.
3. An adult education setting, aiming at discovering whether a basic level of Dutch L2 proficiency has been attained. It is used to decide if non-native Dutch speakers have reached a level to enable them to enter vocational training.

Many interesting and vital points emerge from the development of these (and related) tests. The first of these is the importance of collaborative effort. The driving force for the development of these tests was the Centre for Language and Education (CLE) in Brussels. This is a government-funded centre, which then receives commissions for the development of tests to achieve particular goals. The CLE has considerable expertise in TBI and in task-based assessment. It was also resourced sufficiently to produce such tests, which then became available within the Belgian education system for widespread use. So the tests had impact, but they required an organizational structure and adequate financing for their production. It was not teachers in particular educational contexts who were able to produce the tests. A second point which flows from this first one is that the test development teams could bring considerable sophistication to bear in what they did. The CLE team were very aware, for example, of the threats to reliability in performance testing, and made strong efforts to counter sources of error in the test results that they obtained (such as taking great care that instructions were clear and were understood, and incorporating multiple tasks, to the extent that time pressures allowed, to gain a more rounded estimate of performance). They were also aware of validity-linked developments in the field, and so drew upon the task-based literature in the way they tried to deal with task difficulty, for example.

The test development team was also concerned with curriculum issues. One consequence of this was a strong awareness of washback. A related feature of their work was that research was conducted to gather feedback from teachers on their reactions to a move towards more task-based assessment. This research revealed clear reservations on the part of teachers regarding what could be achieved if assessment involved tasks. What this meant was that if washback was to be positive, it was important to work with teachers so that they were convinced that not using traditional testing techniques did not mean effective assessment was not taking place. In other words, merely introducing a more task-based approach to assessment is not enough. For washback to be positive, so that approaches to teaching itself become more task-based, working with teachers becomes essential.

An Evaluation of the Case Studies

The four case studies cover a range of language testing contexts. They are united in the way that they demonstrate the feasibility of task-based testing, with prospective university students, with general learners looking for certification, with students following a major coursebook series and with learners within a state educational system. In each case test developers solved a range of problems, and produced sets of tests which are task-based and which address the different educational contexts. This alone is important, because it shows what can be done.

But there are differences between the four case studies which go beyond the obvious, the things such as differences in age, in first language (L1)/L2 combination and in the uses of language that are important in each case. One concerns the number of people involved in test development. The Hawai'ian, Cambridge and Belgian tests were the products of considerable collaborative work. In the first of these cases, a set of researchers worked together; in the second, massive numbers of specialists (system developers, task developers, production departments, international administration systems, statistical experts) all worked together to develop and stockpile many test tasks; in the third, a centre was at the heart of test development, and it is clear that teams of staff worked on the tests in question. The COBUILD tests were a smaller scale affair, with one lead developer, plus the two authors of the actual coursebook series. In addition, the Hawai'ian, Cambridge and Belgian tests are associated with statistical investigation while the COBUILD tests do not seem to be. Even so, given the content orientation of these actual tests, the argument for validity is less statistical and more concerned with content itself. But the different test initiatives do give some indication of the resources required (principally time) to develop and validate task-based tests.

Connected with this, the Hawai'ian, Cambridge and Belgian teams were more ambitious in what they attempted. In the first case a testing system was developed which interestingly combines interactive-ability and real-life elements. In the Cambridge tests, separate tests were combined to function within a wider proficiency range, and were essentially interactive-ability in nature. In the third, a series of essentially distinct tests were produced, with a strong achievement connection but also with summative qualities. It is not surprising, therefore, that larger numbers of test developers were involved.

All the approaches to testing, though, share some qualities. It is clear that while all of them have a summative emphasis, each lends itself to the generation of formative information which can feed back into instruction. The tests generate numbers and these numbers can enable important summative decisions to be made, but the information contained through the test formats can provide clear indications of areas of weakness, both for individuals and for courses of instruction. Related to this, even though all of them generate numeric scores, they also have a criterion-referenced element, in that completing the tests is likely to provide direct information as to how language can be used in the real world and with tasks which connect with real-world events. These qualities, formative evaluation and criterion-referencing, are significant strengths for the tests concerned.

Conclusion

This chapter has covered a considerable amount of work in task-based assessment. We have seen that task-based research is highly relevant to the area of testing, providing a framework and principled basis for what would otherwise be a loosely focused communicative approach to assessment. Of course, a great deal more research is needed, but it is already clear that task research is relevant to the design of assessment procedures and to the interpretation of results. There is also the important claim that a task-oriented view of assessment may go some way to reconciling the interactive-ability and real-life approaches by showing how tasks can be based on researched characteristics and conditions, and by analysing the processing demands required for task completion. This may provide a better basis for making test-linked generalizations.

We have also seen some impressive practical developments in task-based assessment, and these have shown what can be done. But these successful practical initiatives also bring out the need for adequate resourcing if task-based tests are to be constructed and validated. Testing is not cheap, and so major developments are most likely to be associated with situations where resources are available. It is to be hoped that consortia, such as that described in task-based testing in Belgium, can go some way to mitigating the importance of finance and resourcing. This would start to address the point made earlier in this chapter – that the single most important area for development is progress in the construction of task-based achievement tests (Long, 2015).

Part IV
Investigating Task-Based Programmes

By and large, the research we have addressed so far has been theoretically motivated, carried out by researchers and concerned with the performance of individual teaching or assessment tasks. Clearly, though, there is a need to investigate complete task-based programmes from the perspective of teaching, the stakeholders involved in them and the learning that results. This section seeks to do this by addressing the following key questions:

1. How effective is task-based language teaching (TBLT) in comparison to more traditional approaches?
2. How can TBLT programmes be evaluated?
3. What do evaluations of TBLT programmes tell us about their viability and effectiveness?
4. What practical problems arise in introducing a TBLT programme and how can these be addressed?

Chapter 10 seeks an answer to the first of these questions by reviewing comparative method studies. These are studies that have investigated the relative effectiveness of TBLT vis-à-vis some other, more traditional approach such as presentation–practice–production (PPP). Such studies are notoriously difficult to design and often suffer from design flaws. Overall, to date the studies do point to the superiority of TBLT in a variety of instructional contexts – e.g. state schools in India and English-for-specific-purpose courses in the United States – but there is a clear need for more studies. The chapter concludes with some guidelines for the design of future studies.

Chapter 11 seeks answers to Questions 2, 3 and 4 by evaluating (rather than 'researching') TBLT programmes. The studies that have undertaken this are not comparative in nature and do not aim to contribute to the theories that underpin TBLT. Rather they are practice-oriented, addressing whether TBLT 'works' and what might be done to make it work more effectively. The chapter begins with a discussion of TBLT as an innovation and illustrates how the general factors that are known to affect the success of educational innovations can be used to predict and explain the success or failure of particular TBLT programmes. The chapter then reviews a number of actual evaluations – both macro-evaluations where complete TBLT programmes were studied and micro- evaluations where teachers (not researchers) carried out evaluations of specific tasks in their own classrooms. Drawing on these evaluations, the chapter ends with a discussion of the major problems that teachers face in implementing TBLT and also suggests some solutions.

10 Comparative Method Studies

Introduction

Long (2015) distinguished two kinds of programme evaluations. *Descriptive studies* aim to investigate whether a particular programme is achieving its goals and whether it should be abandoned or, more likely, modified in the light of the evaluation. Such studies consider programs *in situ* and focus on the nature of the instructional processes that result from the implementation of the programme and on students', teachers' and stakeholders' evaluations of it. In contrast, *experimental studies* are comparative in nature and examine the learning outcomes of the different approaches by means of tests. Ideally, they have a pre-test/post-test design and randomly formed groups. However, as Long acknowledged, true experimental designs are often not possible in institutional settings as it is usually only possible to use intact classes. In this book we have elected to examine these two types of programme evaluations in separate chapters. In this chapter we focus on studies that have compared task-based language teaching (TBLT) with some other teaching approaches and have briefly included a post-test. In Chapter 11 we will consider descriptive programme evaluations.

Comparative Method Studies

Comparative method studies seek to determine which of two or more language teaching approaches is most effective. Such approaches are notoriously difficult to implement and many suffer from a number of design problems. Ellis and Shintani (2014) listed the design features of a sound method comparison study (see also Long (2015)):

1. Pre-tests are needed to establish that there are no differences in the groups taught by the different methods at the outset.
2. The study should include a control group that just completes the testing regime in order to establish that learning takes place in the

experimental groups. Without a control group is not possible to determine whether any gains from pre- to post-testing are simply the result of a test practice effect or of general exposure to the target language.
3. The study should establish through observation that the process features which are evident when the approaches under study are implemented correspond to the external descriptions of these approaches. If there is no difference in the instructional processes, then the study lacks internal validity.
4. The instruction should be carried out by the same teacher to guard against the possibility that any learning differences which are found are the result of variations in the teachers' background and general teaching abilities. It is also necessary to ensure that the learners in the different groups are equivalent in background.
5. The study needs to ensure that the tests used to measure learning outcomes are not biased in favour of one of the methods being compared. It is, however, very difficult to ensure content-fair testing (Beretta, 1990).
6. Ideally, too, the study should investigate the effect of the different methods on individual learners as well as on groups in order to see whether individual learner factors mediate the effectiveness of each method.

Few of the studies we will consider satisfy all these criteria. In the concluding section we will evaluate the studies in terms of them.

We also acknowledge that the construct of 'method' or 'approach' is problematic in several ways. Kumaravadivelu (2001), for example, has critiqued 'method' on the grounds that it requires teachers to simply implement a set of externally described prescriptions about how to teach and thus disempowers them. He argued that teachers need to be free to write their own 'script' rather than perform a script given to them. Larsen-Freeman (2000) also argued that methods cannot be understood as prescriptions for classroom behaviours and imposed on teachers as a strict set of procedures to follow. The method/approach construct is problematic in another way. No method is monolithic and so narrowly prescribed that there are no options for how it can be implemented. This is especially true of the two approaches we will be examining in this chapter – presentation–practice–production (PPP) and TBLT. Each stage of a PPP lesson can be implemented in a variety of ways. For example, the presentation of the target grammatical structure can be inductive or deductive. The availability of options is equally true for TBLT, as was made clear in Chapter 1. For example, there are different views about whether learners' attention should or should not be directed to form while they are performing a task (see for example, Willis and Willis (2007) and Long (2015)) or whether the tasks selected should mirror the target tasks that learners need to perform in real life (see Chapters 1 and 7).

These problems have led some commentators to propose that method comparisons should be discontinued. However, advocates of both PPP and TBLT have argued the need for such studies. Advocates of PPP such as R. Sheen (2006) insist that it is dangerous to propose new approaches such as TBLT purely on theoretical grounds without 'long-term trialling in normal classrooms' (p. 273) and without evidence that they result in superior learning to well-established approaches such as PPP. While Sheen is wrong to claim there has been no long-term trialling of TBLT (see, for example, Van den Branden, 2006), Long (2015, 2016), one of the main advocates of TBLT, has also accepted the need for comparative studies.

Long (2015) argued that experimental studies should first be carried out under laboratory conditions where it is possible to control potentially confounding variables and then extended to classrooms to check if the findings of the laboratory studies have ecological validity. However, we considered laboratory-based studies in Part II of the book, so we have elected to focus only on classroom-based studies in this chapter. Ultimately we believe that only studies carried out in classrooms will enable a true comparison of approaches that were designed for the classroom. We acknowledge, however, that the findings of such studies, even when well designed, are limited because of the difficulty of controlling the cluster of variables that are inevitably present in the holistic setting of a classroom.

Method Comparison Studies

Studies comparing TBLT and another approach are of two basic types. In some studies, which we will call 'general programme comparisons', TBLT is compared to some pre-existing programme. In these studies, the TBLT programme constitutes an innovation – that is, TBLT has been introduced into a teaching context where a more traditional approach has been the norm. A good example of such a study is Beretta and Davies' (1985) comparison of Prabhu's (1987) Communicational Language Teaching Project (CLTP) and the well-established Structural-Oral Situational Method. In such studies, it is common for multiple classes to be allocated to each approach, all taught by different teachers and with no random assignment of students to classes or even of classes to type of instruction. Often there was no pre-testing of the students; comparisons were made solely on the basis of post-tests.

In other studies, however, the comparison between TBLT and another approach was built into the design of the study. That is, separate groups were formed and the types of instruction to be compared were devised based on explicitly formulated theoretical and methodological principles (e.g. 'focus on forms' versus 'focus on form') and implemented in accordance with them. These studies investigated the effects of the instruction on the acquisition of specific linguistic features (vocabulary or grammar) by means of both pre- and post-tests. We refer to such studies as 'focused comparative studies'. A good example is Shintani's (2016) comparative study of TBLT and PPP, which we will discuss later. We will first consider programme comparisons and then focused comparison studies.

General Programme Comparisons

A characteristic of the four programme comparisons we will consider here is that they all involved instructional programmes that were not specifically designed for purposes of research – that is, the courses that were compared were all institutionally scheduled. The contexts and learners of these courses were very different – beginner-level learners in high schools in India (Beretta and Davies, 1985), relatively advanced learners of Spanish in a university programme for business and economics in Belgium (de Ridder, Vangeheucten and Gomez, 2007), limited proficiency students in a Spanish course for border control agents in the United States (González-Lloret and Nielson, 2015) and a computer-delivered programme for intermediate-level high school students learning Turkish as a foreign language (Arslanyilmaz, 2013). The obvious differences in these programme comparisons preclude reaching clear conclusions but they can be seen as affording insights into the relative effectiveness of TBLT in very different instructional settings.

Beretta and Davies (1985) compared Prabhu's (1987) CLTP (i.e. TBLT) with the Structural-Oral Situational Method, a version of PPP (a teacher-centred, form-oriented instructional method). The study took place in India with beginner-level secondary school students. The TBLT programme involved a series of communicative tasks with no direct teaching of specific linguistic items. The PPP courses consisted of the presentation and practice of sentence patterns through drills and situational grammar activities with the underlying aim of developing automaticity in their use. Beretta and Davies measured learning through a battery of tests that included a test favouring the TBLT experimental group (i.e. a task-based test), one favouring the PPP comparison group (i.e. a structural test) and three neutral tests (i.e. contextualized grammar, dictation and listening/reading comprehension tests). These tests were only administered at the end of the school year (i.e. there was no pre-test). The results showed that the task-based group performed better than the comparison group on the task-based test whereas the comparison group performed better on the structural test. However, on the three neutral tests, the task-based group showed a clear advantage over the structural group. Beretta and Davies argued that the task-based learners demonstrated superior acquisition as even though these learners had not been explicitly taught specific grammatical structures they were able to deploy the grammar they had learned more readily.

Ridder et al. (2007) compared two Spanish programmes for third- and fourth-year university business and economics students, who were assigned randomly to two groups. Both groups participated in course components consisting of form-focused instruction (FFI) involving presentation followed by practice with communicative activities (apparently a version of PPP). The comparison group then worked individually on compiling an individual dossier about twelve Spanish companies followed by an oral test where they gave a brief presentation about these companies. The experimental group worked in pairs in a series of task-based workshops directed at preparing an advertisement for a brand-new project. Ridder et al. argued that whereas the comparison's assignment required them to use their acquired knowledge in a similar context to the rest of the programme, the experimental group needed to make creative use of their acquired knowledge in a new context. Measurements of the learners' oral performance were taken at the end of the programme using ratings of pronunciation, fluency, intonation, sociolinguistic competence, lexical competence and grammatical competence. The experimental group outperformed the comparison group on grammar, vocabulary and social adequacy but there was no difference on fluency and the comparison group performed better on pronunciation and intonation. A problem with this programme comparison – acknowledged by the authors – is that the final oral activity used to measure learning outcomes was not equivalent; the learners in the comparison group carried out the oral presentation individually with an examiner whereas the data for learners in the experimental group were derived from conversations they had with their partners.

González-Lloret and Nielson (2015) evaluated a newly introduced task-based Spanish for Specific Purposes programme designed for students preparing to become border patrol agents in the United States. The project involved three empirical studies. The first included twenty students from the TBLT programme, who were compared with nineteen students who had participated in the previously taught grammar-based programme. The participants in both courses completed an oral picture-guided narration task after they had finished the course, which lasted for approximately 150 hours over seven weeks. Their narratives were audio recorded and analysed in terms of fluency, lexical complexity, syntactic complexity and grammatical accuracy. The results showed that those students who had received the task-based instruction (TBI) displayed significantly greater fluency and syntactic complexity. However, there were no significant differences between the two groups in lexical complexity and grammatical accuracy. González-Lloret and Nielson argued that the TBLT course was superior in developing those abilities that were the main aims of the TBLT approach (i.e. oral fluency and complexity) and just as effective in developing grammatical accuracy, which was the principal aim of the traditional, grammar-based approach. The second study was not comparative but we will consider it briefly here. A whole cohort (n = 256) of TBLT programme participants took a computer-scored oral proficiency test as pre-test and post-test. The test afforded scores for overall proficiency, sentence mastery, vocabulary, fluency and pronunciation. The results showed that participants improved significantly in all categories and that the benefits of the instruction were evident at all levels of proficiency. These two studies show that the TBI resulted in all-round development of second language (L2) proficiency and was more effective than the conventional structure-based approach.

Arslanyilmaz (2013) investigated the comparative effects of computer-delivered TBI and FFI by analysing the learners' production during the computer-mediated lessons. The researcher assigned thirty-eight high school students in two intact classes to the TBI or the FFI group and held seven 40-minute computer-mediated sessions over seven days. The students in the TBI group engaged in two-way information-gap tasks where pairs of learners interacted in a chat room to complete the task. These learners were encouraged to refer to a video-recorded model of a conversation between two native speakers for guidance. The FFI group listened to the same audio samples of native speakers as the TBI group but then completed controlled activities (e.g. fill-in-the-gap activities) with the teacher. Arslanyilmaz (2013) audio recorded and transcribed the lessons. The FFI class was 'dominated by the teacher's talk' (p. 310) with limited opportunity for students to speak. An analysis of the learners' production in terms of accuracy, fluency and lexical complexity showed that the learners in the TBI group were more fluent. There were no statistically significant differences between the two groups in lexical complexity or accuracy but

Arslanyilmaz argued that the TBI group scored higher in both aspects and that the differences did not reach statistical significance only because of the small sample size.

These studies have a number of methodological limitations. As Beretta and Davies' (1985) study was a *post hoc* evaluation, the participants were from different age groups, and the length of instruction varied depending on the four schools involved in the study. Also, as there was no pre-test, we do not know whether differences existed between the groups before they started their instructional programmes. De Ridder et al.'s (2007) study seems a very *ad hoc* evaluation; not only was there no pre-test but the learning outcomes were measured using non-equivalent methods. González-Lloret and Nielson (2015) carefully planned their studies, including a pre-post assessment of the learners' general oral proficiency as well as group comparisons between the TBLT and grammar-based courses. However, as González-Lloret and Nielson acknowledged, the study was limited in a number of ways, particularly the lack of a pre-test in the first study and of a comparison group in the second. Arslanyilmaz's (2013) study only examined the learners' speech production within the lessons and, as such, did not address whether the TBLT instruction resulted in better L2 acquisition. All in all, then, although they do provide evidence of the effectiveness of TBLT, no clear conclusions about the relative effectiveness of TBLT and a more traditional approach are possible. In this respect, the focused comparative studies we consider next are more insightful.

Focused Comparative Studies

Focused comparative studies are more theoretically oriented. These studies compared two instructional approaches (TBLT and PPP) in order to investigate two clearly defined constructs – focus-on-form (FonF), where the primary focus is on meaning but with attention to form when communicative or linguistic problems arise, and FonFs, where the instruction explicitly addresses predetermined linguistic forms. We will examine four such studies: one is longitudinal (Sheen, 2005) and three are relatively short term (de la Fuente 2006; Shintani, 2013, 2015). As discussed here, Sheen's study was unsatisfactory in a number of ways, making clear conclusions impossible. However, the three short-term studies afford clearer evidence in support of the FonF approach.

Sheen (2005) compared the effects of a one semester-long (seven-month) 'strong communicative language teaching (SCLT)' course with a FonFs course involving PPP on the learning of two grammatical structures (i.e. WH interrogatives and adverb placement). The learners were grade 6 elementary French-speaking students in Canada aged eleven and twelve. The PPP instruction consisted of explicit descriptions of the target structures, controlled practice exercises and opportunities for free production. Different teachers taught the TBLT and PPP classes. Sheen administered three tests – an aural written comprehension test, an oral interview (scored for correct use of the target structures) and a grammaticality judgement test (GJT). However, he presented results for only the latter two. In the oral production test, which was conducted as a pre-test, post-test and delayed post-test, the PPP group demonstrated some improvement in the two target structures whereas the TBLT group failed to show any improvement. In the GJT, which the researcher administered at the end of the study, only the PPP group improved their scores. Sheen concluded that the PPP instruction was more effective than the TBLT instruction. The major problem with Sheen's (2005) study was that while he provided detailed descriptions of the PPP instruction, he offered no account of the procedures for the TBLT instruction except to say that the students participated in 'enjoyable tasks and game activities' (p. 288) with 'FonF opportunities' (p. 289). However, there is no information about how often the students in the TBLT class experienced focus on form directed at the target structures and, in fact, Sheen noted that the lessons offered few opportunities for corrective feedback on the use of either target structure. In other words, it would seem that in fact there was no or very little focus on form in the TBLT lessons. There are also a number of design issues that are problematic. Sheen's testing clearly favoured the PPP group and none of the tests examined the learners' ability to produce the target structures in spontaneous communicative speech – arguably the best way of measuring the effect of instruction. Also the two groups received instruction from different teachers, with Sheen, an advocate of PPP (see Sheen, 1994), teaching the PPP class.

We will now examine three short-term studies that investigated TBLT: two of these examined vocabulary acquisition (de la Fuente, 2006; Shintani, 2013) and one examined incidental grammar acquisition (Shintani, 2015). These studies controlled instructional factors more strictly and also provided more detailed descriptions of the research procedures and the instruction. For these reasons they afford more convincing results than Sheen's study.

De la Fuente (2006) included process descriptions of the interactions that took place in the FonF and FonFs instruction as well as measuring learning outcomes. Thirty university students in an elementary Spanish class were divided into three groups: the PPP group (FonFs), the

TB-NEF group (task-based without explicit instruction) and the TB-EF group (task-based with explicit instruction). The explicit instruction was provided after the learners had completed the task, and this focused on the morphological, phonological and spelling problems the learners had manifested when performing the task. The TB-NEF group simply repeated the same task. The lessons targeted fifteen Spanish words, with which all the participants were unfamiliar. The PPP learners received fifty minutes of instruction consisting of the three phases of PPP – explanation of the new words (presentation), controlled oral and written production exercises (practice) and a role play performed in pairs (free production). The students in the two TBLT conditions worked on a restaurant task in pairs, where students needed to negotiate the meaning of the target words in order to complete the task. The TB-NEF group repeated the same task twice in the lesson, whereas the TB-EF group received the same controlled exercises as the PPP group instead of repeating the same task. The researcher measured acquisition using a discrete-item oral production test.

The different types of instruction resulted in no statistically significant differences in the immediate post-test. However, in the delayed post-test, the two TBLT groups outperformed the PPP group. Examining the interactions that occurred in each group, de la Fuente (2006) found that the TBLT instruction provided more opportunities for learners to negotiate for meaning, produce the target words and retrieve the target words online than did the PPP lessons. By examining the process features of the instruction, de la Fuente was able to offer an explanation of why the TBLT groups learned the target words better than the PPP group. However, it could be argued that it was the opportunity to produce the target words that can account for the TBLT groups outperforming the PPP group. Without examining the learners' actual exposure to the target words or the opportunities to produce them during the instruction, it is not clear that the interactional processes de la Fuente identified were responsible for the advantage found for the TBLT groups. The study also had some methodological limitations. As de la Fuente admitted, the learning outcomes were only measured by means of a discrete-item oral production test and there was no control group. However, this study is illustrative of the kind of process-product approach that is needed to investigate the comparative effects of instruction.

Shintani's (2013) study also included a process analysis. She analysed both the nature of the interactions that took place during instruction, the extent to which the learners were exposed to the target items in the input and whether they produced them in their output.

The learners were forty-five Japanese children, all aged six, with no prior experience of any L2 learning. Shintani divided the learners into three groups: FonFs (i.e. PPP), FonF (i.e. TBLT) and control. The two experimental groups received nine 30-minute lessons over five weeks. The PPP group completed five activities in one lesson, which followed the three phases of PPP. The learners first saw the thirty-six target words on flashcards with Japanese translations. The students then engaged in 'fun activities' requiring the students to produce the words repeatedly. The TBLT learners completed three input-based tasks that required them to listen to the teacher's commands and demonstrate that they had understood them by selecting the appropriate flashcards. However, the teacher used flashcards only for nouns; adjectives only appeared in the teacher's spontaneous utterances when she sought to help the students to understand her commands and select the appropriate cards – for example, by referring to the size or colour of an object. The thirty-six target words included twenty-four nouns and twelve adjectives. The researcher measured both receptive and productive knowledge of the target items in a pre-test, a post-test conducted one week later and a delayed post-test conducted four weeks later. The production tests included a discrete-point test and a task-based test.

Both the PPP and TBLT groups outperformed the control group in the acquisition of nouns. The TBLT group outperformed both the PPP and the control groups in the acquisition of adjectives. The process analysis demonstrated that although the PPP group produced the target words during the lessons more frequently than the TBLT group, the quality of their production differed dramatically. In the PPP group initiation–response–feedback (IRF) exchanges predominated, so that the learners' production of the target items was almost always teacher-initiated. In contrast, the TBLT group engaged frequently in student-initiated negotiation where they were exposed to and in some cases voluntarily produced both the nouns and the adjectives.

Shintani (2015) drew on Laufer and Hulstijn's (2001) claims about the importance of cognitive load for vocabulary learning to explain her results. She used the process data to evaluate the 'need', 'search' and 'evaluation' of the use of the target words in the two groups, and she concluded that the interactions that comprised the instruction imposed a greater cognitive load for the adjectives in the TBLT lessons than in the PPP lessons. Both the PPP and the TBLT instruction involved 'need' (i.e. an externally imposed or self-imposed task requirement to attend to a word). But whereas the TBLT group engaged in 'search' (i.e. the attempt to find the meaning of an unknown L2 word or to find the L2 word form expressing a concept), the PPP group did not do so because the teacher explained the meaning of the target words at the beginning of each lesson. 'Evaluation' (i.e. the comparison of a target word with other words and assessing whether a word fits its context) was required in the PPP but only in a limited way when the learners responded to the teacher's feedback. The TBLT learners needed to engage more deeply in 'evaluation' because they were required to infer the meaning of an adjective when the teacher elaborated her commands after the learners had failed to comprehend her initial command, and also because the students used adjectives to seek clarification when negotiating understanding a command. Shintani (2015) argued that this constituted 'strong evaluation' as it required generative rather than just selective choice. Table 10.1 summarizes the differences in the TBLT and PPP in terms of 'need', 'search' and 'evaluation'. Shintani concluded that it was the difference in the cognitive load imposed by the two types of instruction that led to the TBLT group outscoring the PPP group for adjectives.

As part of the same study, Shintani (2015) also investigated the incidental acquisition of two grammatical features – plural-*s* and copula *be* –neither of which was explicitly taught in either the TBLT or the PPP lessons. As with the vocabulary study there were nine repeated lessons in the FonF (i.e. TBLT) group and in the FonFs (i.e. PPP) group. The learners in both groups were exposed to multiple exemplars of the two structures in the teacher's utterances but were not required to produce the forms. Acquisition of plural-*s* was measured by means of a task-based production test and discrete-point comprehension and production tests. The acquisition of copula *be* was measured by discrete-point and task-based production tests. The results demonstrated that the TBLT group acquired plural-*s* but not copula *be*. The learners in the PPP group acquired neither structure. Analysing the classroom interactions, Shintani (2015) showed that there was a functional need for the learners to attend to plural-*s* in the TBLT classroom but not in the PPP classroom. Copula *be* is a redundant feature and thus there was no functional need to attend to it in either classroom. Shintani argued that the focus on form that occurred quite naturally in the TBLT instruction enabled the learners to distinguish the meanings of plural and singular nouns. In the PPP instruction, however, the feedback only focused on whether the learners had produced the correct noun form, which did not enable the learners to make a form-meaning mapping for plural *-s*.

The focused comparative studies we have considered are a mixed bunch and certainly do not provide conclusive evidence of the superiority of TBLT. Sheen's (2015) study reported results that suggested PPP was more effective than TBLT in enabling learners to acquire

Table 10.1 'Need', 'search' and 'evaluation' in PPP and TBLT

	PPP		TBLT			
		Nouns and adjectives		Nouns		Adjectives
Need	+	Production was necessary to complete the activities.	+	Comprehension of the nouns was necessary to complete the tasks.	+	Comprehension of the adjectives was useful to complete the tasks.
					+	The use of the adjectives was motivated by the tasks.
Search	–	The pictorial image of the words (word meaning) was provided.	+	Engaging in or observing negotiation of meaning.	+	Inferring the meaning of the adjectives.
Evaluation	+	Positive and negative feedback on production was provided.	+	Choosing the correct noun card.	+	Feedback on the noun choices was provided.
			+	Feedback on the noun choices was provided.	++	Finding the appropriate adjectives for negotiation.

Note: –: an absence of an involvement factor; +: moderate presence of an involvement factor; ++: strong presence of an involvement factor.
Source: Shintani (2015, p. 58).

specific grammatical features but, as we have pointed out, the design problems with this were so great as to preclude any conclusion. The other studies by de la Fuente (2006) and Shintani (2015) were better designed and point to a clear advantage of TBLT, especially where longer-term learning is concerned. These studies also involved comparisons of the process features of the types of instruction being compared and were able to show that active engagement by learners in the TBLT lessons promotes acquisition. Clearly, though, more studies that investigate learners with different levels of proficiency and different target features, and that, crucially, are longitudinal, are needed.

Conclusion

Tables 10.2 and 10.3 summarize the comparative studies we have examined and also indicate to what extent they took account of the key design factors that were outlined earlier in this chapter. The programme comparisons are clearly very limited – as indeed the researchers who conducted them admitted. They satisfy few of the good design criteria for such studies. Only González-Lloret and Nielson (2015) investigated the instructional processes in the second of their studies but did not investigate learning outcomes. Thus we cannot be sure that there were in fact clear differences in the types of instruction being compared or that these differences were responsible for the learning outcomes. In these general programme comparisons there were no pre-tests or control groups and teacher and learners factors were not controlled for. Only group results were reported. Only Beretta and Davies (1985) attempted to avoid testing bias. However, these studies do at least point to the potential advantage of TBLT over more traditional forms of instruction in authentic classroom contexts.

The focused comparison studies varied in the extent to which they satisfied the criteria for well-designed comparative studies. Sheen's (2006) study included a pre-test and also controlled for learner factors. But it did not examine process features (except in anecdotal comments), it did not control for the teacher factor, it only examined group differences between the TBLT and PPP learning outcomes, there was no control group and the tests were arguably biased in favour of the PPP group. De la Fuente's (2006) study included discussion of the instructional processes but there was no pre-test, it did not control for learner factors, only group comparisons were reported and only one type of test was administered – a discrete-point test – which was biased in favour of the PPP group, although, in fact, this group performed less

Table 10.2 General programme comparisons between TBLT and PPP

Study	Beretta and Davies (1985)	Ridder et al. (2007)	González-Lloret and Nielson (2015): Study 1	González-Lloret and Nielson (2015): Study 2	Arslanyilmaz (2013)
No. of participants	390 (4 schools)	68	256	39	28
Treatment duration	1–3 years	1 full academic year	8 weeks	8 weeks	7 days (7 sessions)
Target features	General proficiency	General proficiency	General proficiency	Oral CAF	Oral CAF
Measurements	Task-based test: ■ structural test ■ contextualized grammar ■ dictation ■ listening/reading comprehension	Ratings of oral production: ■ pronunciation ■ fluency ■ intonation ■ sociolinguistic adequacy ■ vocabulary ■ grammar	Oral proficiency test: ■ overall proficiency ■ sentence mastery ■ vocabulary ■ fluency ■ pronunciation	■ fluency, lexical complexity, syntactic complexity and accuracy on an oral production	■ CAF in oral production during the tasks
Results	Mixed but overall TBLT > PPP	Mixed but overall TBLT > PPP	TBLT > PPP	TBLT > PPP	TBLT > PPP

Instructional processes examined	No	No	No	Yes	No
Pre-test	No	No	No	No	No
Teacher factor controlled	No	Not clear	No	No	Not clear
Learner factors controlled	No	Yes – randomly formed groups	No	No	No
Testing bias avoided	**Yes**	**Yes**	**Yes**	**Yes (measured accuracy)**	**No (only free production)**
Inclusion of a control group	No	No	No	No	No
Effect on individual learners as well as on groups examined	No	No	No	No	No
Teacher factor controlled	No	Not clear	Yes		No

Table 10.3 Focused comparison studies

Study features	Sheen (2005)	De la Fuente (2006)	Shintani (2013)
No. of participants	48	30	45
Treatment duration	6 months (4 hours per week)	1 day (50 minutes)	5 weeks (9 lessons)
Target features	Interrogative form, adverb placement	15 words	36 words
Measurements	■ oral interview GJT	■ discrete-item oral production test classroom interaction	■ discrete-point oral production test ■ task-based oral production test ■ classroom interaction amount of input and output during the lessons
Results	PPP > TBLT	TBLT > PPP	TBLT > PPP
Instructional processes examined	No	Yes	Yes
Pre-test	Yes	Yes	Yes
Teacher factor controlled	No	Not clear	Yes
Learner factors controlled	Yes	Yes	Yes
Testing bias	No (only discrete point)	No (only discrete point)	Yes
Inclusion of a control group	No	No	Yes
Effect on individual learners as well as groups examined	No	No	Yes

well than the TBLT groups on it. Both of Shintani's (2013, 2015) studies satisfied all the criteria.

De la Fuentes' (2006) and Shintani's (2013, 2015) studies point to the superiority of TBLT for both vocabulary and incidental grammar learning. However, caveats need to be acknowledged. First, these studies operationalized TBLT in very different ways. De la Fuente, for example, investigated oral tasks that required learners to produce language spontaneously and negotiate for meaning to complete them. Shintani's studies, in contrast, employed input-based tasks where student production was optional whereas her comparison (PPP) group completed output-based tasks. Thus two aspects were confounded – TBLT versus PPP and input-based versus production-based instruction. However, arguably this is inevitable given that TBLT can only be implemented for complete beginners by means of input-based tasks.

As was pointed out in the Authors' Preface and in Chapter 1, TBLT does not constitute a monolithic approach. Different versions exist, as is clearly evident in how TBLT was operationalized in the studies we have examined. Thus care must be taken in not overgeneralizing from the results of studies that investigated a particular version of TBLT. PPP is also not monolithic and can be implemented in different ways. Thus, all that these studies show is that the particular version of TBLT they investigated led to superior outcomes than the particular version of PPP with which it was compared. This reflects the inherent problem with comparative method studies that we mentioned in the 'Introduction' to this chapter. It is difficult to generalize the findings of such studies to make claims about the superiority of one type of instruction given that 'method' is an external construct which will become manifest in variable ways when it is implemented.

There is a final issue that needs to be considered. The well-designed studies showed that TBLT was advantageous where the acquisition of *specific* linguistic forms was concerned. That is, they constituted examples of what Ellis (2012) called 'local' comparative studies. With the exception of González-Lloret and Nielson's (2015) study, they did not investigate other aspects of L2 development – complexity, accuracy and fluency (CAF), for example. Clearly, though, if it is to be argued that TBLT is superior to traditional forms of teaching such as PPP, it is necessary to provide evidence that it is not just superior in enabling learners to acquire specific linguistic features but also superior in helping the development of their overall proficiency. This means that researchers need to investigate the incidental acquisition that inevitably occurs in the exposure to the 'input', 'output' and 'interaction' that any type of instruction provides. One of the essential claims of TBLT is that such incidental acquisition is enhanced when learners perform tasks. Shintani's (2015) study did compare the incidental acquisition that occurred in the TBLT and PPP lessons but it focused narrowly on two grammatical features. What is needed are longitudinal studies that can inform about the relative effectiveness of different approaches on general proficiency – in effect, carefully designed programme evaluations. But as we have seen these are likely to be plagued by design problems, in particular the difficulty of controlling for all the variables that impact on classroom instruction. Thus it may be that while comparative studies (especially longitudinal ones) are needed to address the doubts of traditionalists such as Swan (2005a) about TBLT, even then clear answers about the relative effectiveness of the different approaches will be difficult to achieve.

The assumption of a comparative method study is that it can provide a generalized picture of which of two methods is the more effective. We have seen that the studies that have compared TBLT with PPP manifest a number of methodological problems. Perhaps the biggest challenge lies in the very nature of comparative method studies as they tend to (and perhaps must) prioritize ecological validity over predictive validity. Implementing different approaches inevitably involves a variety of factors that can potentially affect learning. Controlling all these factors is not realistic, considering that the ultimate goal of comparative method studies is to provide practical advice to teachers. We can ask, therefore, whether there is a case for conducting comparative method studies. We believe there is. In order to accept a new teaching approach, teachers need to know whether it is likely to be more effective than their current approach.

How, then, can we ensure that comparative method studies are well designed and also informative for teachers? Ellis (2012) suggested that researchers should design 'local' comparative method studies involving relatively short periods of instruction and focused on specific linguistic features rather than 'global' studies involving long periods of instruction and assessing general language proficiency or achievement. We have seen that those researchers who conduct longitudinal studies have struggled to control for the various factors that can influence outcomes. Although many of the short-term studies had the same methodological problems as the longitudinal ones, a few have provided some clear findings. These studies were premised on the assumption that externally defined constructs (for example, FonF and FonFs) result in different processes when they are implemented by teachers in a particular pedagogical context. When a comparative method study includes an examination of how the methods were implemented and how the learners responded to them, the results are arguably more convincing and more informative. The analysis of the process features in de la Fuente (2006) and Shintani (2013, 2015) demonstrated that when learners have the opportunities for FonF while engaging with tasks it has advantages over PPP.

Arguably then, it is the comparison of process features that is most revealing. As Kumaravadivelu (2001) pointed out, for 'language pedagogy to be relevant, it must be sensitive to a particular group of teachers teaching a particular group of learners pursuing a particular set of goals within a particular institutional context embedded in a particular sociocultural milieu' (p. 538). Seedhouse (2005a) emphasized the difference between the task as 'workplan' and the task as 'process' (i.e. what is actually happens in a particular teaching context). Larsen-Freeman (2000) suggested that methods should not be understood as prescriptions for classroom behaviours and imposed on teachers as a strict set of procedures to follow. We need to develop an understanding of how different manifestations of TBLT result in different classroom processes and how these processes affect the learning that takes place.

We will conclude this chapter by reviewing the guidelines for conducting comparative studies and the extent to which the studies summarized in Tables 10.2 and 10.3 conformed to them.

- Studies should examine the process features of instruction (what happens in the classroom) along with the product of the instruction (what the students learned). Shintani (2015) and de la Fuente (2006) attempted to do this.
- Studies need to control for factors other than instructional variables – such as the teacher and learners. Controlling for teacher factors can be achieved by ensuring the same teachers instruct both groups of learners, as in Shintani's (2005) study. The learner factors can be controlled for by conducting pre-treatment tests as in de la Fuente (2006) and Shintani (2005), to establish the equivalence of the two groups being compared.
- Studies should guard against test bias. Four of the studies only used discrete-point tests, which are likely to favour explicit types of instruction. Arslanyilmaz's (2013) assessed learners' production in free production activities, which showed that TBLT instruction was superior. Three studies used multiple tests to guard against bias. According to Beretta and Davies (1985), TBLT instruction possessed advantages not only in the test that was biased in its favour but also in tests designed to be 'neutral'. González-Lloret and Nielson (2015) included fluency and complexity measurements that they consider favour TBLT and accuracy measurements in the grammar-based programme. Shintani (2005) demonstrated that the two

groups showed similar gains in both types of tests for nouns but that the TBLT outperformed the PPP in all tests for adjectives.
- Studies should include a control group. Most of the studies looked at in this chapter did not include a control group; as such, it is only possible to interpret the results in terms of comparative effects, not in terms of either method's effectiveness. The only exceptions were Shintani's studies.
- Studies should examine incidental acquisition (i.e. they should not just measure the learning of the linguistic items targeted by the instruction but also the acquisition of non-targeted features that arise naturally as the different approaches are implemented). Only Shintani (2005) did this.

Overall, the comparative method studies do indicate that TBLT is more effective than traditional approaches. However, given the problems with comparative method studies, greater insight as to the strengths and limitations of TBLT and PPP might be achieved through descriptive programme evaluations. Such evaluations focus on complete courses. They examine the instructional processes that arise when a particular approach is implemented more narrowly and they often elicit the subjective evaluations of the participants. Descriptive programme evaluations may also help our understanding of how different versions of TBLT result in different classroom processes. In Chapter 11 we review descriptive evaluations of TBLT.

11 Evaluating Task-Based Language Teaching

Introduction

For many teachers task-based language teaching (TBLT) constitutes an innovation. This is especially the case in instructional contexts where the established approach to teaching involves a structural syllabus, explicit instruction and controlled practice exercises (i.e. what Long (1991a) called 'focus-on-forms'). Introducing task-based teaching into such contexts is likely to pose a number of problems for both teachers and students. It is for this reason that there is a need to move beyond the kinds of controlled experimental comparative studies we considered in Chapter 10 to examine how teachers and students respond to TBLT in specific instructional contexts. This calls for evaluation studies rather than research.

Evaluation has fundamentally different goals from formal research, which is directed at either testing or building theoretical positions. In the case of tasks, the research has typically been experimental, often laboratory-based, and studies have covered a relatively short period of time (not even a complete lesson in most cases), although, as we saw in Chapter 10, there have been some longer comparative studies (e.g. Shintani, 2016). Skehan (2003) commented that 'applications of research findings do not really make sufficient connection with most classroom decision-making' (p. 9). Arguably, evaluation studies are better equipped to speak to the issues that teachers and learners face as they constitute 'a more encompassing and more contextually relevant approach' (Norris, 2015, p. 28) where there is 'systematic attention to the constellation of factors that make up a learning environment' (p. 35). Evaluations are not concerned with theoretical issues (although they may still inform about them). Rather they are directed at accountability (i.e. showing how TBLT works under what circumstances and with what effects) and also at development (i.e. identifying how aspects of the approach can be improved for subsequent use in the same instructional context).

Norris (2009b) provides a brief historical sketch of educational evaluation. Early evaluations of language programmes in the 1960s and 1970s were summative in nature, aimed at demonstrating the effectiveness of a method (often in comparison with another method) by administering language proficiency tests at the end of the period of instruction. By the 1980s, driven in part by funding agencies such as the British Council, the focus switched to investigating the accountability of specific training programmes and began to look beyond outcomes and products by gathering evidence about the processes involved in implementing a programme using a variety of data collection instruments. In the 1990s a more pragmatic approach to evaluation emerged that took account of the uses to be made of an evaluation study (see, for example, Alderson and Beretta, 1992). Norris notes that this pragmatic orientation continues to the present day. The evaluations of TBLT we will consider in this chapter are essentially pragmatic in nature; that is, they addressed how particular tasks or programmes were carried out in particular instructional contexts, with what achievements and with what problems.

First, though, we will consider what insights can be gained by viewing TBLT as an innovation. Then we will describe different types of evaluation. This will provide a basis for reporting the findings of empirical evaluations of both complete TBLT programmes and of individual tasks. The chapter concludes with a discussion of the problems of implementing TBLT that these evaluations have identified, along with suggestions for how they might be addressed.

TBLT as Innovation

One approach to evaluating TBLT is predicting whether it is likely to prove a success when it is introduced into a particular instructional context. This involves asking what factors are likely to impact on the successful introduction of TBLT. Table 11.1 lists the general factors that evaluations of innovations have found can influence their uptake. Such a list is helpful in two ways. First, it can be used to explain why an innovation was successfully implemented. Second, it helps innovators to develop a good understanding about an innovation they are planning, which, as Van den Branden (2009) noted, 'constitutes the crucial first step in a process that may ultimately lead to the implementation of an innovation' (p. 662).

Let us consider two different teaching contexts and apply the characteristics shown in Table 11.1 to try to explain why one innovation did in fact prove successful while a second projected innovation is less likely to succeed.

Table 11.1 Factors determining the success of innovations

Attribute	Definition
Initial dissatisfaction	The level of dissatisfaction that teachers experience with some aspect of their existing teaching.
Feasibility	The extent to which the innovation is seen as implementable given the conditions in which teachers work.
Acceptability	The extent to which the innovation is seen as compatible with teachers' existing teaching style and ideology.
Relevance	The extent to which the innovation is viewed as matching the students' needs.
Complexity	The extent to which the innovation is easy to grasp.
Explicitness	The extent to which the rationale for the innovation is clear and convincing.
Trialability	The extent to which the innovation can be easily tried out in stages.
Observability	The extent to which the results of the innovation are visible to others.
Originality	The extent to which the teachers are expected to demonstrate a high level of originality in order to implement the innovation (e.g. by preparing special materials).
Ownership	The extent to which teachers come to feel they 'possess' the innovation.

Source: From Ellis (1997, p. 29).

TBLT in Flanders

In this case we examine an actual project. The Educational Priority Policy issued by the Flemish government in Belgium aimed at enhancing the quality of Dutch language education at primary, secondary and adult levels, with a view, in particular, to enable pupils at risk and adult immigrants to benefit from the educational and occupational opportunities open to them. The predominant approach at the beginning of the project was teacher-centred and audiolingual. Responsibility for introducing TBLT was assigned to the Centre for Language and Education at the Katholieke Universiteit of Leuven, which undertook the design of programmes and the training of teachers. Members of the centre were available to work with large schools teams, educational counsellors, policy makers and educationalists to support the step-by-step introduction of TBLT (Van den Branden, 2006).

There are a number of factors listed in Table 11.1 that can explain the success of this innovation. There was a general dissatisfaction with the audiolingual approach, teachers were helped to see that TBLT matched their students' needs, the rationale for the innovation was made clear to teachers, it was introduced step by step and teaching materials were provided, reducing the level of originality required by the teachers. Publications relating to the project have shown that the introduction of TBLT in this context was largely successful (see Van den Branden, Van Gorp and Verheist, 2007).

Elementary Schools in Japan

In this case we describe a context where TBLT has not yet been introduced but might well be. English was introduced in elementary schools in Japan in 2002 and became compulsory for 5th and 6th grades in 2006, but only as a 'foreign language activity'. In 2020 it will become a 'school subject' with designated textbooks and formal assessment (Aoki, 2016). A communicative approach has been mandated. It is expected that elementary schoolteachers will take responsibility for teaching English although it is likely that many will lack oral proficiency. In all probability, too, the teachers will have had no experience of learning English through TBLT.

An inspection of Table 11.1 suggests that these teachers will struggle to implement TBLT. While it may be the case they were dissatisfied with the traditional approach they experienced in their own language education (a positive factor), there are many probable negative factors. For example, implementing TBLT in the conditions that the teachers work in will be difficult, TBLT may not be seen as relevant if the methods of assessment are the traditional ones common in Japan and teachers will need to demonstrate a high degree of originality unless teaching materials are made available to them. Thus, although TBLT is the ideal approach for introducing English at the elementary level in Japan (Ellis, 2017b), it is questionable whether it will be successful unless substantial support is provided. Carless' (2004) evaluation of the introduction of TBLT into Hong Kong elementary schools (discussed later) found many problems even though, in many respects, Hong Kong constitutes a more favourable context for its introduction than does Japan.

These two contexts have some similarities but also some conspicuous differences. In both cases, dissatisfaction with existing approaches provides the platform for innovation and in both innovation was officially mandated. The main difference lies in the level of support teachers receive. In Japan it remains to be seen what kinds of support will be provided – but we are not optimistic – whereas in Flanders external support and a communication network were established from the start, enabling the teachers to develop a sense of ownership with regard to the innovation.

Viewing TBLT as an innovation and applying the criteria for successful uptake of an innovation is instructive because it allows for the effective planning of a TBLT programme. However, as Van den Branden (2009) pointed out, 'the power of innovations should be measured by whether learners are making more progress than before an innovation was implemented' (p. 669). This calls for the evaluation of programmes. In the rest of this chapter we will consider reports of actual evaluations of TBLT. We begin with a consideration of what evaluation involves and the different types of evaluation.

Types of Evaluation

Some of the studies we considered in Chapter 10 can be thought of as evaluation studies. For example, Long (2015) and Norris (2015) consider Beretta and Davies (1985) an evaluation study. However, this evaluation did not account for the holistic, pragmatic and programmatic nature of TBLT that is the goal of evaluation studies. In this book we have elected to remain more faithful to the aims of evaluation studies by distinguishing those studies that are purely product-focused – such as Beretta and Davies' study – which we considered in Chapter 10 and evaluation studies that address how TBLT is implemented in this chapter.

Evaluators have in general been concerned with the evaluation of whole programmes – see, for example, Norris (2009b) and Alderson and Scott (1992). R. Ellis (2011), however, pointed out that such evaluations are not necessarily in accord with teachers' ideas of what evaluation involves. He suggested that teachers are less likely to focus on whole courses or programmes and more likely to be interested in whether specific activities 'work' in the context of a particular lesson. A distinction can be made, therefore, between macro- and micro-evaluations. Figure 11.1 shows the different types of evaluation based on this distinction. The broken line indicates that macro- and micro-evaluations are potentially connected.

A macro-evaluation can be carried out: (1) to establish to what extent a programme/project is effective and efficient in meeting its goals, or (2) to identify in what ways it might be improved. This is what Weir and Roberts (1994) refer to respectively as an 'accountability evaluation' and a 'development evaluation'. Applied to TBLT, a macro-evaluation looks at a complete TBLT course. Most evaluations of language teaching have involved macro-evaluation. In early evaluations (e.g. Alderson and Beretta, 1992; Weir and Roberts, 1994; Kiele and Rea-Dickens, 2005, and the special issue of *Language Teaching* (vol. 13.1 on 'Understanding and improving language education through

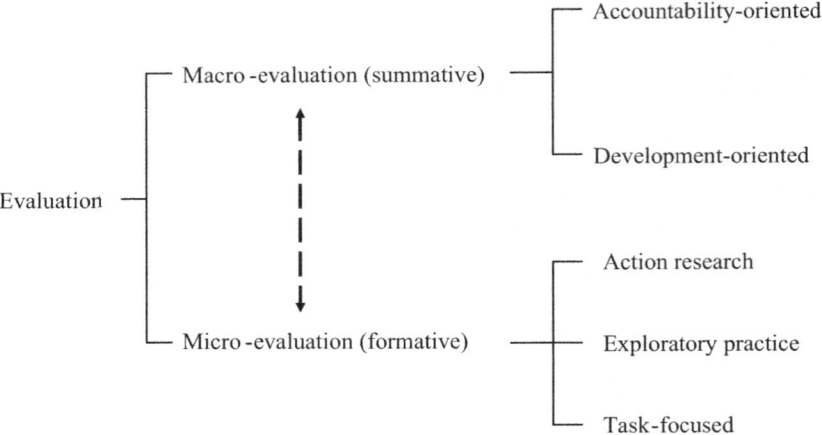

Figure 11.1 Types of evaluation

program evaluation') reports of macro-evaluations dominated but few concerned TBLT. In Alderson and Beretta (1992), for example, there was only Beretta's own study of Prabhu's TBLT project. Subsequently, reflecting the increased interest in TBLT since the 1990s, there have been a number of macro-evaluations of TBLT programmes (see, for example, Carless, 2004; Van den Branden et al., 2007; East, 2012; Hu, 2013; Nielson, 2014).

A micro-evaluation has a narrow focus on some specific aspect of the curriculum. Probably the most well-known type is action research (Burns, 2010) but we will also consider exploratory practice (EP) (Allwright, 2003, 2005) and an approach that takes as its starting point a specific task (Ellis, 2015a). Micro- evaluations have investigated such issues as the motivational value of using tasks (Loumpourdi, 2005), how to incorporate tasks into lessons based on traditional textbook materials (Muller, 2005), the extent to which it is possible to predict the language that will be needed to perform specific tasks (Cox, 2005), the effect of students' reporting the outcome of a task publicly on the quality of their language output (Johnston, 2005) and the effect of training students to use meaning-negotiation skills on task performance (Lee, 2005).[1] While such evaluations often draw on the theories that inform task-based research, they reflect the specific questions that teachers are interested in and are action-oriented.

The distinction between macro- and micro-evaluations correlates in part with another distinction – that between summative and formative evaluation. In a summative evaluation, a programme is assessed on its completion to decide whether it should be discontinued or continued and in the case of the latter what modifications are needed. In a formative evaluation, a programme is assessed during its development, with a view to providing information that can be used to modify it as it continues. Winke (2014) identified the key aspects of formative evaluation: students' progress is monitored regularly based on work they complete in class, it aims to provide continuous feedback to both the teacher and students, and it encourages reflection. A summative evaluation is typically macro in type while a formative evaluation is micro. A summative evaluation is generally conducted by an outsider while a formative evaluation is more likely to be undertaken by a single teacher or perhaps collaboratively with other teachers. A formative evaluation will necessarily involve the evaluation of individual lessons and, perhaps also, individual tasks. A summative evaluation can involve the collection of evidence not just at the end of a programme but throughout its implementation. Thus, a series of micro-evaluations carried out for formative purposes can contribute to the final summative evaluation.

Irrespective of the type of evaluation, effective evaluations need to collect a variety of evidence – documentary, qualitative and quantitative. R. Ellis (2011) suggests that an evaluation can be student-based, response-based or learning-based (or any combination of these). A student-based evaluation collects information about how the students responded to the teaching (i.e. how engaged they were) using self-report methods such as rating slips, questionnaires, interviews, focus groups and written commentaries. Similarly, a teacher-based evaluation obtains information about teachers' perceptions about TBLT. A response-based evaluation addresses whether the students responded to the task-based activities as intended by the designer of the materials or the teacher(s) using them and whether the students were successful in achieving the intended outcomes of the tasks. It involves observing or recording task-based lessons and also collecting documentary records of task outcomes. A learning-based evaluation looks for evidence that some learning has taken place in terms of new linguistic knowledge and greater control over existing linguistic resources or discourse skills. It may require the administration of tests but evidence of learning can also be obtained through the detailed analysis of lesson transcripts.

Macro-Evaluations of TBLT

Table 11.2 provides a summary of a selection of macro-evaluations of TBLT. These evaluations cover TBLT programmes in a variety of

Table 11.2 A selection of evaluations of TBLT programmes

Study	Context	Purpose	Evaluation type	Findings
Beretta (1989, 1990) Language – English	Secondary schools in southern India (Prabhu's Communicational Language Teaching Project (CLTP).	To establish to what extent TBLT was being implemented in accordance with the CLTP's principles.	Response-based: recordings and observations of selected lessons.	Very mixed – most of the teachers not directly involved in the project failed to implement TBLT effectively due to lack of oral proficiency in English.
Carless (2004) Language – English	Primary school classrooms in Hong Kong.	To see how teachers were attempting to implement TBLT in their classrooms and what their attitudes were towards TBLT.	Response-based: data collected by means of classroom observation of lessons and semi-structured interviews with teachers.	Overall, the tasks represented language practice activities rather than genuine communication and the teachers manifested a poor understanding of what a task was. Teachers expressed concern about use of first language (L1) and discipline (noise) issues.

Watson-Todd (2006) Language – English	University students in Thailand – TBLT course developed by teachers.	To evaluate the continuation of the TBLT course, including changes made to it as it evolved from one year to the next.	Response-based by inspecting documentation from the course; teacher-based through interviews and records of end-of-year meetings to discuss the course.	Various changes made to the course over time; fewer tasks, greater emphasis placed on explicit instruction and increased emphasis given to examinations rather than continuous assessment. These reflected 'a move away from a "pure" version of task-based learning towards a more mixed methodology' (p. 9).
McDonough and Chaikitmongkol (2007) Language – English	Innovative task-based course for students at Chiang Mai University, Thailand, developed by teachers involved in the programme.	To investigate what teachers' and students' attitudes to the new TBLT course were and what concern teachers had about its introduction.	Response-based and teacher/student-based: a variety of data collection instruments including task and course evaluations, observations by teacher participants and researcher, and interviews with teachers.	Learner independence increased; teachers became more positive about lack of grammar over time; students recognized the real-world relevance of the course. Changes subsequently made to course to address the need to help students' adjust, to provide support through supplementary materials and to reduce the number of activities in each lesson.

(*continued*)

Table 11.2 (cont.)

Study	Context	Purpose	Evaluation type	Findings
Hu (2013) Language – English	Introduction of TBLT in Chinese elementary and high schools.	To investigate teachers' beliefs and practices in using TBLT in their classrooms.	Response- and teacher-based: classroom observations; interviews with teachers; documentary evidence (e.g. instructional materials).	Three levels of implementation of TBLT identified: (1) denial (teachers continued to function as examiners), (2) passive acceptance (teaching based on textbook), (3) active application (teachers expressed positive views about TBLT but by and large implemented only a weak form of TBLT).
Nielson (2014) Language – Chinese	Online task-based course for high school students in USA based on needs analysis.	To investigate whether the performance-based assessments (PBAs) built into the course worked, whether the students' Chinese proficiency improved and how the tasks could be improved.	Student-based and learning-based: results of the PBA tasks; Likert scale survey completed five times during the course.	Overall participation declined except for conversation partner sessions; the PBAs were effective in assessing students' level of ability in performing particular tasks; task completion not an adequate measure of task performance.

González-Lloret and Nielson (2015) Language – Spanish	Eight-week programme for US Border Patrol Agency based on needs analysis.	To investigate whether the students' Spanish proficiency improved as a result of the task-based programme and to gauge students' opinions about the course.	Learning-based and student-based: pre- and post-tests of students' oral proficiency; Likert scale surveys administered to both students in programme and those who had left and were in employment as border patrol guards.	Overall Spanish oral proficiency improved in both the more advanced and novice students; students held positive views about the course and believed it had helped them to in their jobs.

languages (English, Chinese and Spanish) and instructional contexts (elementary and secondary public schools, universities, specific-purpose contexts, online and face-to-face in classrooms). There is a focus on TBLT as an innovation, as in all the studies TBLT is a recent introduction. For this reason, perhaps, most of the studies are concerned with the extent to which TBLT was effectively implemented in the different contexts and teachers' attitudes to its introduction. As a result, most of the evaluations were response and/or student/teacher-based in their methodology. However, two of the most recent evaluations (Nielson, 2014; González-Lloret and Nielson, 2015) were also learning-based. The comparative aspect of González-Lloret and Nielson's evaluation was considered in Chapter 10; here we also consider information about the student-based component of this evaluation. Data collection methods in the evaluation studies listed in Table 11.2 were diverse, including classroom observation, questionnaires and interviews, and tests. We will first examine three of these evaluations in detail before attempting a summary of their findings.

English in Indian Secondary Schools

To the best of our knowledge, the first macro-evaluation of a task-based programme was Beretta's (1989; 1990) evaluation of Prabhu's (1987) CLTP. Beretta's evaluation was a follow-up to Beretta and Davies' (1985) comparative study of the learning outcomes of the CLTP and the traditional Structural-Oral Situational Approach which we considered in Chapter 10. Beretta (1989) focused on teachers' error correction practices. He reported that 'the treatment of linguistic error was largely consonant with the project's statements about the kinds of attention that are appropriate to a focus on meaning and that this could be distinguished from the ways of treating linguistic error that are attributable to a focus on form' (p. 283). However, he went on to suggest that this might have been because the input tasks used in this project meant that there was limited learner production, reducing the likelihood of learners making errors and thus the need for teacher correction. Beretta (1990) examined the historical narratives from fifteen teachers and rated them according to three levels of implementation of the task-based approach: (1) orientation (i.e. the teacher demonstrated a lack of understanding of task-based instruction and failed to implement it), (2) routine (i.e. the teacher understood the rationale of the project and was able to implement it effectively), and (3) renewal (i.e. the teacher had adopted a critical perspective and could demonstrate awareness of its strengths and weaknesses). Beretta found that 40 per cent of the teachers were at Level 1, 47 per cent at

Level 2 and 13 per cent at Level 3. However, when he distinguished between regular and non-regular teachers involved in the project, he found that three out of four regular teachers (yet none of the non-regular teachers) were at Level 1. Beretta concluded that task-based instruction of the kind practised in the project is not easily assimilated by regular classroom teachers in southern India. He pointed to these teachers' lack of English proficiency as one reason for their failure to adopt task-based teaching. Beretta's qualitative evaluations of the classroom processes evident in the CLTP suggested that it did not consistently result in the kinds of teaching described in Prabhu (1987).[2]

English in Primary Schools in Hong Kong

Carless' (2004) evaluation took the form of case studies of three primary schoolteachers, who were described as 'young, capable and open-minded'. The context was Hong Kong, where a new 'target-oriented curriculum' had been recently introduced into primary-level schools, requiring a shift away from traditional, teacher-fronted instruction to task-based instruction involving group work. Data were collected through classroom observations (seventeen per teacher) and interviews. Carless presented his evaluation in terms of three classroom episodes (one for each teacher), which he used to illustrate his general findings. In Episode A selected students came out to the front of the class, were blindfolded and then tried to guess what fruit they were holding. In Episode B students worked in groups to answer questions about some photographs they were given. In Episode C the class was divided into groups of six and then tried to draw a picture based on the group leader's description of what he could see when he looked out of the classroom window. Carless reported that while two of the teachers had a fairly clear idea of what a task was, one teacher was vague, offering this definition: 'mainly has objectives and it can link pupil ability and understanding, conceptualizing, that kind of communication' (p. 648). The teachers varied in their views of the mother tongue, one believing that the lesson should be conducted entirely in English but the other two seeing some value in allowing students to use the L1 (e.g. to work out how to do a task). The teachers experienced tension between their desire to carry out the tasks and their wish to maintain a quiet and orderly classroom, with the result that 'concerns over noise and discipline inhibited implementing task-based language teaching' (p. 656). Finally, Carless noted that too much time was spent on non-linguistic activities such as drawing. Carless concluded by suggesting that a task-supported approach might be more effective in Hong Kong primary schools on the grounds that 'if English language structures are not pretaught, then beginning learners will probably not have sufficient English to use during tasks' (p. 658).

Spanish Special-Purpose Programme

González-Lloret and Nielson (2015) reported a comprehensive evaluation of an eight-week Spanish specific-purpose programme designed for the US Border Patrol Academy. TBLT was introduced as an alternative to the existing grammar-based course. Along the lines advocated by Long (1985, 2015), the course was based on a needs analysis of the target tasks that border agents are required to perform as part of their job. González-Lloret and Nielson (2015) conducted three separate evaluative studies. The first, which involved a comparison of the grammar-based and TBLT courses, was considered in Chapter 10. The second was a learning-based evaluation focusing on whether the TBLT course was successful in developing the students' oral proficiency in Spanish. The students completed a short oral proficiency test prior to the start of the programme and on its completion. Overall proficiency scores improved by 7.47 points. There was also a statistically significant improvement in vocabulary, fluency and pronunciation. The results of the test further indicated that both the most advanced students and novice students improved their level of proficiency. The third study was student-based. Both in-service and pre-service agents completed an electronic survey designed to investigate their perceptions of the strengths and weaknesses of the programme. The students reported they had enjoyed the course, they found it relevant to their jobs and they expressed a desire to keep on learning Spanish. However, many still felt they were not yet ready to talk to native speakers. Their comments on specific aspects of the course indicated their approval of specific task types such as role-playing but also their disapproval of a video game designed to provide an out-of-class learning experience. Commenting on this evaluation, Norris (2015) noted that it illustrates 'the diverse purposes to which an evaluation can and should be put' (p. 50). He emphasized that such evaluations of TBLT programmes are important in 'enabling a better understanding of how they work'.

Practitioner Research: A Place for Micro-Evaluations of TBLT

Macro-evaluations of whole programmes require careful planning and are time-consuming to carry out. For these reasons they are typically not carried out by teachers but by external evaluators. In contrast, the micro-evaluations of tasks that we will consider in this section were small scale and carried out by teachers in their own classrooms. They are examples of practitioner research. We consider three types of practitioner research that have been used to investigate TBLT – action research, exploratory practice (EP) and the micro-evaluations of tasks.

Action Research

Action research (Burns, 2010) is probably the best-known type of practitioner research. It involves a research cycle where teachers work on investigating small-scale aspects of their own practice in their own classrooms. The cycle involves a planning stage, an action phase where the plan is implemented, an observation phase where data is collected to investigate whether the plan has worked, and a reflection phase which can lead to further critically informed action (Carr and Kemmis, 1986). Action research is often problem oriented, with the teacher systematically researching solutions to a teaching problem that he/she has identified.

A good example of an action-research study investigating TBLT is Calvert and Sheen (2015). This study reports a teacher's attempt to design and use a task about housekeeping with low-literacy adult refugees. The effectiveness of the task was evaluated by inspecting the task outcome (a handout where the students had to enter information about housekeeping duties). This indicated that most of the students failed to complete the task successfully. Also, the students' responses to a post-task questionnaire revealed they had a negative attitude to the task. In the reflection phase of the study, the teacher identified a number of factors responsible for the failure – in particular, the learners' lack of familiarity with the format of the task and the linguistic demands the task placed on them. This led to several modifications being made to the task, reducing the amount of information the learners had to handle and simplifying the language. In addition, a new pre-task activity was introduced where the teacher first performed the task with the whole class, scaffolding the actions required of the learners and the language involved. When the students performed the modified task they were able to achieve the outcome successfully and this time evaluated it more positively. This study is informative because it reveals the kinds of problems that novice teachers have in designing and teaching tasks and also the value of action research in helping a teacher to solve initial problems. Another advantage of conducting the action evaluation is that it led the teacher (Calvert) to revise her initially unfavourable view of TBLT.

Weaver (2012) reported on an action-research study he carried out in a Japanese university. The focus here was on a formative assessment cycle, which Weaver incorporated into the implementation of his task. This cycle involved a needs analysis, task description (using the framework in Ellis, 2003), the development of assessment criteria based on both performance processes and the task product, the actual assessment of the students' performance of the task, and the provision of feedback directed at both the students and the teacher himself. Weaver (2012) claimed that the formative assessment of the kind he conducted 'can help teachers establish a framework for systematically implementing TBLT in their classrooms' (p. 307).[3]

However, doubts have been expressed about whether action research is the best way of conducting practitioner research. Formulating clear research questions is not something that teachers always find easy (Nunan, 1990). Also, the requirement that it is cyclical places a burden on teachers. It is difficult to see many teachers carrying out the study reported by Calvert and Sheen (2015), for example. Like formal research, action research is also technicist (i.e. it requires technical skills required to design the research and to collect and analyse the data). Rainey (2000) noted that, despite teacher educators' advocacy of action research as a way of creating a bridge between theory and practice, it has not been widely adopted.

Exploratory Practice

An alternative approach is EP, which Allwright (2003, 2005) promoted on the grounds that it is less likely to result in teacher/researcher burn-out. EP is not directed at solving problems but at developing an understanding of some aspect of 'the quality of life' in a specific classroom by integrating enquiry into actual classroom practice. In EP, students as well as teachers are practitioner-researchers. EP focuses on investigating 'puzzles' rather than 'problems'. These include puzzles that learners acknowledge about themselves (e.g. 'Why I don't speak English after nine years of study') as well as about teachers (e.g. 'Why do teachers have no time to answer students' questions') . Allwright (2005) listed the general principles that inform EP – e.g. 'involve everybody' and 'work for mutual development' – and offered some practical suggestions – e.g. 'integrate the work for understanding into the working life of the classroom' (Allwright, 2003, p. 130). A detailed account of how to conduct EP can be found in Allwright and Hanks (2009) along with narrative accounts of EP in practice.

Slimani-Rolls' (2005) study may not qualify as fully-fledged EP but it illustrates a number of the principles that inform it – in particular, incorporating data collection as part of the instructional activities of the lesson and emphasizing the contribution that learners can make to both their own and their teachers' understanding. Slimani-Rolls was interested in researching how task design factors affect the negotiation of meaning and the conversational adjustments that arise during it, which, as we saw in Chapter 2, has been the focus of a number of research studies. She investigated three tasks – a one-way information-gap task, a two-way information-gap task and a decision-making task. A quantitative analysis confirmed the results of other studies, namely that the two-way task resulted in the most conversational adjustments. But Slimani-Rolls also noted that the individual students differed widely both within the same task and across the three task types. She included the students in her investigation by asking them to explain their motives and attitudes to engaging in the negotiation of meaning and found that their behaviour was highly idiosyncratic and unpredictable, reflecting a host of affective, social and cognitive variables. The students very clearly had their own ideas about how to handle the tasks. Slimani-Rolls concluded by emphasizing that task-based research can benefit from treating a task performance as a puzzle which can be best understood through teacher and students engaging collaboratively in practitioner enquiry.

Allwright (2005) conceived of EP as involving long-term action on the part of the teacher and students. One of his key principles is 'Make the work a continuous enterprise.' (Allwright, 2003, p. 130). It is therefore perhaps not best suited to the in-depth micro-evaluation of tasks. I turn now to an alternative form of micro-evaluation – one that takes as its starting point a specific task and one that has potential to shed light on how tasks open up spaces for teacher development.

Micro-Evaluations of Tasks

A micro-evaluation of a task addresses a simple question 'Does a task work?' Ellis (2015a) outlined three general ways of addressing this question corresponding to the three general types of evaluation mentioned earlier in this chapter – student-based, response-based and learning-based. A student-based evaluation is the easiest to carry out as it does not involve any interruption to the normal conduct of the task. A response-based evaluation can also be relatively undemanding if it only involves collecting documentary evidence of the task outcome (e.g. the map showing the route students have drawn when following instructions). However, it becomes more demanding if the aim is to examine how students actually performed the task. This requires specially designed checklists or alternatively recording and transcribing the interactions that result from performing the task. The most demanding type of micro-evaluation is learning-based as it is difficult to find of way of measuring whether a single task results in discernible learning.

R. Ellis (2011) outlined a procedure for conducting a micro-evaluation of a task. The starting point is a clear description of the task. This helps the evaluator to see what needs to be evaluated and thus guides the planning of the evaluation. The objectives of the evaluation need to be stated. These will address whether the task is successful in achieving the goals a teacher has set for the task and also, perhaps, whether unexpected benefits occur (Eckerth, 2008). Data collection can take place before the lesson starts (e.g. by administering a short test) but is more likely to occur during the lesson as the task is performed (e.g. by observing or recording the learners' performance of the task) or after (e.g. by means of a short questionnaire to tap into students' perceptions of the task). Documentary evidence of the task completion also needs to be collected. Data analysis can involve both qualitative and quantitative methods but teachers may find it easier and more informative to analyse the data qualitatively (e.g. by inspecting a recording of the task performance to identify episodes that capture important aspects). However, simple descriptive statistics help to give a general picture. The analyses of the data guide the conclusions, where the teacher comments on whether the task worked and what changes are needed to improve it.

Hoogwerf's evaluation of a consciousness-raising (CR) task (reported in Ellis, 2008) serves as an example of a micro-evaluation. Hoogwerf's students were second-year Japanese college students enrolled in an eight-month study-abroad college programme. Hoogwerf designed a grammar CR task focusing on subject-verb agreement. The task consisted of: (1) a statement of the subject-verb agreement rule, (2) sentences serving as examples of the rule, and (3) sentences taken from the students' own writings to be completed by the students using choices provided. The students were asked to read the explanation of the rule and the examples provided and underline the subjects of the sentences and then supply the correct verb form from the choices provided. She identified two main objectives for the task: (1) to raise the students' awareness of subject-verb agreement, and (2) to enhance the students' motivation to attend to what she considered a fossilized error. Hoogwerf undertook both an objectives model evaluation and a developmental evaluation; that is, she wanted to see whether her task had 'worked' and how she might improve it. She undertook a student-based evaluation by examining the comments that the students made about the task in their journals, a response-based evaluation by observing the students while they performed the task and by collecting in their written answers, and a learning-based evaluation by examining the students' free writing before and after the task to see if there was any evidence of increased accuracy in subject-verb agreement.

The students' journals indicated they were positive about the task. The students commented on the fact they liked composing their own sentences and many of them asked for more CR tasks. The response-based part of the evaluation revealed that the students worked quickly and eagerly on the task in a manner notably different from their normal classroom behaviour. Also, the students' answers were nearly all correct. However, with the exception of the top three writers in the class, there was no evidence of improved accuracy in the students' subsequent writing. Hoogwerf concluded that the task had worked in so far as it raised students' awareness of subject-verb agreement and increased their motivation to attend to fossilized errors in their writing but she acknowledged that it did not lead to improved accuracy in the students' free writing. Overall, Hoogwerf felt that her experience of evaluating the task was valuable and stated that she planned to use more CR tasks in the future.

Ellis (2015a) reported a number of other micro-evaluations of tasks. These were undertaken by teachers enrolled in a TBLT course as part of an MA programme. The teachers first designed their own tasks, planned how to evaluate them and then collected data for the evaluations while implementing the tasks in their classrooms. Ellis reports that the teachers chose the tasks to evaluate for very different reasons – their perceptions of their students' needs, to fulfil the aims of the course they were teaching, to test their understanding of research findings or simply through a desire to engage their learners more fully. They also approached how they developed their tasks differently. Johnson (2000) found that less experienced teachers used 'task frame' (e.g. the participatory organization or the skills to be practised) as a starting point for designing a task, whereas more experienced teachers opted mainly for 'task genre' (e.g. information gap) or 'task function' (e.g. describing a person). He also noted that the teachers varied in terms of whether they opted for a 'language-oriented' or 'task-oriented' approach. The teachers in Ellis (2015a) adopted a similar mixed approach to developing their tasks. However, whereas Johnson found that the teachers he investigated did not draw on research involving tasks, Ellis reported the some of his teachers did make use of the research-based knowledge they had acquired on their MA course.

Ellis noted that his teachers were very aware that every task has a context and that this can influence both how the task is performed and what is learned as a result. For example, the teachers recognized the importance of sequencing activities in order to ensure that a task works effectively. Thus, even though they were asked to evaluate only the main task, their evaluation reports revealed the importance they attached to pre-task and post-task activities. In other words, they saw their tasks as part of a complete lesson. In this respect their approach differed from that of many researchers who have focused narrowly on the performance of a single, specific task.

Another general finding of the micro-evaluations was that a task does not result in the same 'activity' when it is performed by different students – as claimed by sociocultural theory (see Chapter 4). One teacher noted that there were marked differences in the students' negotiation of meaning. One pair engaged much more extensively in the negotiation of meaning than another pair, worked harder to resolve the communication problems that arose and was more successful in doing so. There was also a difference in how these pairs negotiated. The pair that negotiated extensively did so by means of clarification requests whereas the other pair employed confirmation checks. Clearly, the same 'task' resulted in very different interactional processes for these two pairs of students. The students also varied in their perceptions of the purpose of the tasks they were asked to perform. In sociocultural terms, they had very different 'motives' for the 'actions' they carried out. For example, two of the students performing a dictogloss task thought it was a communicative activity whereas a third student in the same group saw it as a grammar practice activity. Micro-evaluations of tasks are valuable because they help teachers to understand the factors that are responsible for the differences that arise in how the same task is performed.

The response-based part of a micro-evaluation involves examining both the 'product' (i.e. whether the learners are successful in achieving the outcome of the task) and the 'process' (i.e. what transpires when the task is being performed). One of the conclusions that Ellis (2015a) came to after examining a number of micro-evaluations was that closed tasks are advantageous because they allow teachers a quick and easy method of determining whether a task has 'worked'. All the teachers' micro-evaluations investigated task processes using a variety of techniques drawn from the task-based literature (e.g. negotiation of meaning; language-related episodes). In particular, they were interested in the level of learners' 'engagement' with the task. One teacher, for example, developed an observation chart to record behaviours that were indicative of motivation, enjoyment and task fatigue The same teacher also used a 'reflection questionnaire' to record his own responses about the students' participation in the task once the lesson was over. This concern with 'engagement' lends support to current work on task engagement which we discussed in Chapter 6.

All the micro-evaluations in Ellis (2015a) included a student-based component – mainly by asking the students to complete a short questionnaire about their perceptions of the task. In this respect the evaluations differed again from research studies, where collecting such data is rare. Arguably finding out how learners orientate to a task is crucial because it will affect how they perform it. It is also worth pointing out that asking students to complete a short questionnaire can be seen as part and parcel of the pedagogy of task-based teaching (i.e. it constitutes a legitimate post-task activity).

Micro-evaluation of tasks is a convenient way to conduct practitioner research. It is arguably easier for teachers to take as their starting point a particular teaching activity they are interested in than a 'problem' or a 'puzzle'. The teachers who conducted the micro-evaluations in Ellis (2015a) reported they found them of value in developing their understanding of TBLT. However, they also noted that such evaluations were time-consuming and that they were unlikely to undertake them in their day-to-day teaching. Micro-evaluations of tasks clearly have value in teacher education programmes, however. One way of making them more practical for teachers might be to develop a set of guiding principles along the lines that Allwright (2003) has done for exploratory practice. Ellis (2015a) concluded with a list of such principles (e.g. Data should be collected in a way that is practical and that enhances the pedagogic value of the task and the evaluation should be seen as a mutual enterprise.

Final Comment

Samuda (2015) sees tasks as devices for creating pedagogical spaces. She commented 'a task has the capacity to open up a space for learning and teaching' (p. 282). The value of the practitioner research considered in this section is that it focuses on how tasks create pedagogical spaces – that is, how tasks are interpreted and reshaped as they are performed. Practitioner research inevitably addresses how context determines the choice of task and how the enactment of the task dynamically constructs the context as it is performed. We have suggested that micro-evaluations of tasks carried out by teachers in their own classrooms have special value in this respect. As Van den Branden et al. (2007) observed 'tasks on paper and tasks in real classrooms may differ from each other in an astonishing number of ways' (p. 3). Micro-evaluations of tasks are ideally suited to investigating this. They take 'task' – the fundamental element in TBLT – as the starting point and then investigate how a specific task mediates the teaching and the learning that take place.

Implementing TBLT: Problems and Some Solutions

The evaluation studies we have considered point to a number of problems that can arise in implementing TBLT – especially when it constitutes an innovation and teachers are struggling to make it fit into their instructional context. It is, however, unwise to overemphasize these problems. Long (2016), for example, dismisses the claim of Bruton (2002a) and Swan (2005a) that TBLT is not suited to foreign language contexts because of the limited number of hours of instruction each week in typical programmes. He commented 'inadequate instructional time and lack of L2 [second language] exposure outside the classroom are real problems for all kinds of LT (language teaching), not just TBLT, and not just in foreign language settings' (Long, 2016, p. 26). Long's point is well made. In identifying the problems with TBLT it is important not to assume that these only apply to TBLT. Nevertheless, the evaluation literature does point to a number of problems. These can be grouped according to whether they concern the teacher, the students or structural issues within the education system.

Problems Involving Teachers

One problem that figures in a number of evaluation studies is that teachers do not always have a clear grasp of what a 'task' is. We noted this in Carless' (2004) evaluation of TBLT in Hong Kong elementary schools. Hu (2013) also noted that the Chinese public schoolteachers of English he investigated had very different ideas of what a task was – some simply equated it with exercises in their textbook. Lin and Wu (2012) likewise found that none of the Taiwanese teachers they interviewed could give a clear definition of a task. This problem can be put down to inadequate training but even when this is available teachers still seem to struggle to fully grasp what a task is. Erlam (2016) reports on an in-service teacher education programme for teachers of foreign languages in New Zealand. As part of this programme she asked the teachers to design their own tasks, which she evaluated in terms of whether they satisfied the four criteria for a task proposed by Ellis (2003) – see Chapter 1. She found that the teachers' tasks more often than not failed to satisfy criterion (3) – namely, 'learners rely mainly on their own linguistic and non-linguistic resources'. In other words, the tasks the teachers developed often involved the explicit presentation of target language.

The difficulty teachers experience in defining what a task is reflects another more general problem. Teachers implementing TBLT frequently express concern about their students' grammatical development (Watson-Todd, 2006; McDonough and Chaikitmongkol, 2007; East, 2014; McDonough, 2015). But this problem is arguably more imagined than real as there is clear evidence that grammatical development does take place in TBLT (Beretta and Davies, 1985; Shintani, 2016). The real problem here is the difficulty that teachers have in recognizing that grammar can be acquired incidentally and that incidental acquisition can be more effective for the development of communicative abilities than the intentional language learning to which traditional language teaching caters. Unless teachers are ready to accept the utility of incidental acquisition they are likely to opt for a weak version of TBLT (i.e. task-supported language teaching), which incorporates explicit instruction in the pre-task phase of a lesson. In other words, the fundamental issue is the theory of language learning that teachers have internalized. Unless teachers buy into the theory of language learning that informs TBLT (i.e. a theory of incidental acquisition) they are unlikely to implement it effectively. Helping teachers to understand how languages are acquired 'naturally' should be a major goal of teacher education for TBLT.

The tendency teachers have to resort to a weak version of TBLT and to fall back on traditional modes of teaching is exacerbated when teachers lack proficiency in the target language or lack confidence in their proficiency (Butler, 2004; Jeon and Hahn, 2006). Again, though, lack of proficiency is a problem no matter what the teaching approach. The solution is again effective teacher training programmes. It is also worth noting, however, that one way teachers can improve their own ability in the L2 is by using it in task-based teaching!

Several commentators (Littlewood, 2007, 2014; Butler, 2011) have pointed to the conflicts that exist between TBLT and traditional culturally embedded teaching approaches. This is especially the case in Asian contexts where it is claimed that Confucian notions that emphasize knowledge as residing in books and the teacher as the primary source of knowledge are incompatible with an approach that emphasizes experiential learning. Samimy and Kobayashi (2004), for example, claimed there is a cultural mismatch between communicative language teaching and the Japanese culture of learning. However, as Butler (2011) pointed out, this problem has been overstated. She noted that the cultural backdrop of Asian language classrooms varies considerably; for example, the culture of primary classrooms in Japan is in fact well suited to the introduction of TBLT. Also, it should be noted that TBLT does not require the total abandonment of traditional roles. The post-task phase of a lesson, for example, affords opportunities for a more traditional approach to teaching. What is needed is training that helps teachers to modify the role they adopt in accordance with the varying purpose of instructional activities in a TBLT lesson.

Teachers have sometimes been found to experience problems in managing task-based lessons, especially when the students work in small groups. Carless (2004) found that primary schoolteachers in Hong Kong were concerned that TBLT resulted in noise and discipline problems. However, this can be a problem with group work in general, not just with TBLT. Also, TBLT does not necessitate group work. Where students are unused to performing tasks, it might be advisable to begin with input-based tasks with the whole class, where the teacher has greater control over what transpires.

A final problem concerns teachers' perception that planning TBLT lessons imposes too great a workload on them. East (2014), for example, found that this was one of the main 'negative characteristics' of TBLT that teachers in an in-service teacher education programme in New Zealand mentioned. The teachers pointed to the time required to design tasks and to monitor students' performance. This problem is very real given the lack of published task-based teaching materials. It can be addressed if teachers collaboratively develop a bank of task-based materials that individual teachers can draw on as needed – a proposal that Candlin (1987) made in his seminal article many years ago. This would, however, require some central organization of the kind found in the Belgium TBLT project (Van den Branden, 2006) or in the TBLT course that McDonough and Chaikmongkol (2007) evaluated.

Problems Involving Students

The evaluation studies indicate that students sometimes have problems adapting to TBLT (McDonough and Chaikmongkol, 2007; Butler, 2011). This can arise when students are used to teacher-centred instruction, where language is treated an object rather than as a tool, and as a consequence fail to see the point of performing tasks that cater to incidental rather than intentional language learning. This problem is not universal, however. Students in some contexts welcome TBLT. González-Lloret and Nielson (2015), for example, reported that the border patrol agents in the programme they evaluated welcomed a task-based approach as it equipped them with the Spanish they needed for their work. Bao and Kirkebaek (2013) also reported that Danish university students responded positively to a task-based Chinese course because they saw it as increasing their engagement, creating an interactive and interesting learning environment, and leading to effective learning. Students' perceptions of TBLT derive from their prior cultural experiences of classroom learning and are influenced by their motives for learning a language. In cases where negative views prevail, some learner training may be needed to develop students' awareness about the nature of language learning. In addition it may be helpful if teachers help students to see that they have learned some new language as the result of performing a task (e.g. by asking them to note down any new language at the end of a task or by means of an occasional oral or written quiz).

Another commonly voiced belief is that beginner-level learners cannot perform tasks because they have not developed the English proficiency needed to communicate. This problem, however, derives from the misconception that TBLT must necessarily involve 'speaking'. Clearly students cannot speak in English if they don't know any English. The solution is to introduce TBLT to beginner-level learners through input-based tasks where the teacher works to make the input comprehensible to the students. Shintani (2016) provides detailed advice about how input-based tasks can be successfully used with complete beginners.

A third perceived problem is that students resort to the use of the L1 when faced with communication problems that they cannot solve in English, resulting in the overuse of the L1 in the TBLT classroom (Carless, 2004). We saw in Chapter 4 that there are legitimate uses of the L1 in TBLT but, as Butler (2011) noted, it is not easy for teachers inexperienced in implementing TBLT to make judgements about when and how much L1 use to allow. This also needs to be a focus of teacher-education. Teachers can be introduced to some useful strategies for dealing with L1 overuse by students: (1) using input-based tasks where the students' responses are non-verbal, (2) performing speaking tasks in a whole class context rather than in small group work so the teacher can exert control over the use of the L1, (3) allowing pre-task planning time, which, as we saw in Chapter 3, can help students to formulate the language they need to perform a task, and (4) ensuring that the task poses a reasonable level of challenge to the students, arguably the most important strategy for guarding against L1 overuse.

Structural Problems

Structural problems are problems that arise as a result of the external requirements imposed on teachers that they are relatively powerless to change. There are two kinds – classroom-level constraints and societal-institutional-level constraints (Butler, 2011). A commonly mentioned classroom-level constraint is the large size of classes that make small group work difficult and allow little opportunity for individual students to use English (Li, 1998; Samimy and Kobayashi, 2004). This, however, is a problem with any teaching approach. Arguably, if TBLT is skilfully implemented it is more likely to ameliorate this problem than accentuate it. Again, input-based tasks have an important role here as they maximize students' exposure to the target language. Societal-institutional problems include the requirement placed on teachers to follow a structural syllabus and the prevalence of traditional examinations that emphasize grammatical accuracy over communicative proficiency and that assess by means of discrete-item tests. In some settings a structural syllabus is officially mandated even when TBLT is the recommended approach. Traditional tests seem to have a life of their own, stubbornly continuing to exist even when communicative language teaching has received official approval. TBLT can only be successfully introduced if: (1) the syllabus is task-based, and (2) students are assessed by means of performance-based tests involving the use of the same kinds of task as for teaching.

If teachers are constrained by a structural syllabus, TBLT is not possible. But it is still possible for them to employ tasks if they adopt a task-supported approach. We have seen in Chapter 1 that task-supported language teaching has its advocates and is supported by skill-learning theory. Samuda (2015) suggested that there is a need to investigate how tasks work out in both task-based and task-supported language teaching – a view we endorse. Key issues are whether prefacing the performance of focused tasks by explicit instruction directed at specific target structures actually results in the use of these structures when learners perform the tasks and also whether it affects the overall quality of the language used. Ellis, Li and Zhu (2018) reported an experimental study that showed explicit instruction did not result in greater accuracy in the use of the target structure and had a negative overall effect on the language produced. Micro-evaluations of tasks can shed further light on these issues.

Traditional methods of assessment involving indirect, system-referenced tests are arguably the greatest barrier to TBLT. The problem here is that teachers will teach to the tests. However, as Long (2016) pointed out there is evidence to show that TBLT enables learners to perform well in such tests. Also, even if teachers are faced with preparing their students for a high-stakes traditional test, they still have the option of incorporating performance-based assessment tasks into their courses. Two evaluation studies have shown the viability of this approach to assessment. Nielson (2014) included such tasks in her online task-based Chinese course and showed how they could support the task-based content of the course. Winke (2014) described a course where task-based assessments involving students self-assessing their own performance were incorporated into a Chinese language course. She was able to show a high level of correspondence between the students' and the instructor's rating of their performance on the tasks, pointing to the validity of learner self-assessment. Self-assessment also provides an answer to a question that teachers' often pose – namely, how to assess learners' speaking proficiency. It is often not practical for teachers to assess individual students' speech but students can be helped to self-assess in ways that will enhance reliability. Nevertheless, as Butler (2011) concluded, if TBLT is to thrive 'not only are changes in the exam system required, but also drastic changes toward learning and assessment in general in society are needed' (p. 46).

Conclusion

Throughout this chapter we have pointed to differences between researching and evaluating TBLT. Both are useful, of course, but arguably evaluation studies are especially valuable as they provide information about how TBLT works in actual classrooms. Evaluation studies shed light on whole courses (in the case of macro-evaluations) or on specific lessons or tasks (in the case of micro-evaluations). They show how teachers and students respond to TBLT, whether the task-based activities result in the kinds of behaviour intended and whether (and to what extent) learning takes place. The accumulated evidence points clearly to the effectiveness of TBLT in a wide range of instructional contexts. They show that teachers are capable of real change provided that they receive support. The factors influencing the success of innovations shown in Table 11.1 provides a useful checklist of the support needed to ensure that when TBLT is introduced it is successful.

The evaluations have also pointed out the problems that can arise. We identified a number of issues involving teachers and students along with some serious structural problems. While recognizing that many of these problems are not specific to TBLT, it is clear that serious consideration needs to be given to how they can be addressed. One is to acknowledge the contextual constraints and accept that a communicative approach is not appropriate or desirable in some settings (Bax, 2003). Another is to opt for a weak form of communicative language teaching. This is the solution favoured by Littlewood (2014) and Butler (2011). They argued that task-supported language teaching is more compatible with existing practices and more closely aligned with current methods of assessment in Asian contexts. Several of the evaluation studies summarized in Table 11.2 (e.g. Watson-Todd, 2006) reported that task-based courses mutated over time into task-supported courses. Teachers clearly do need to take account of contextual factors and make adjustments when needed but they also need to consider the evidence from comparative method studies (see Chapter 10), which indicated that presentation–practice–production (PPP) may be less effective than TBLT if the aim is to develop communicative abilities. Also, the macro-evaluation studies considered in this chapter (e.g. Van den Branden, 2006; McDonough and Chaikmongkol, 2007; González-Lloret and Nielson, 2015) provide convincing evidence that TBLT can be implemented successfully. Thus, while we acknowledge there can be a place for task-supported language teaching (TSLT), we believe that ideally it should not supplant TBLT. The answer is to address the problems of implementing TBLT, not to abandon it.

Evaluation studies do not just tell us what works and what doesn't. They also serve a teacher development function. This is especially true of micro-evaluations. They document actual TBLT lessons and how specific tasks work out in real teaching contexts. Unlike programme evaluations that are typically carried out by external evaluators, micro-evaluations are conducted by teachers in their own classrooms. They serve as one of the most effective ways of developing teachers' understanding of TBLT and how to implement it.

Part V
Moving Forward

In this final part of the book we address the following questions:

1. What criticisms of TBLT have been made and how can these be addressed?
2. What lines of research should researchers pursue to further understand the relationship between task and learning?
3. In what ways can theory and the praxis of TBLT be mutually informing?
4. In what ways can task-based research and task-based teaching profitably interface?

In line with the main aim of the book, we continue to explore the interface between research-based and pedagogical-oriented perspectives on TBLT.

Task-based teaching has been subjected to considerable criticism from teachers and teacher-educators who maintain allegiance to more traditional approaches to teaching. Chapter 12 considers these outsider-criticisms (i.e. criticisms that originate from opponents of TBLT) and the misunderstandings that underlie them, while also acknowledging a number of real issues they raise that need to be addressed if TBLT is to progress in the future. The chapter also looks at insider-critiques (i.e. issues raised by advocates of TBLT). One such issue concerns how to define and investigate complexity so as to arrive at a principled basis for sequencing tasks in a syllabus. We will see that there are different positions regarding such issues.

In Chapter 13 we take stock and suggest the future directions that we think TBLT should take. Theory and research about TBLT show no sign of losing vitality. We can expect researchers to both draw on and contribute to theories of L2 acquisition. We foresee that influences from neighbouring disciplines will grow. We also predict that TBLT will be increasingly mandated by educational authorities so there will be continued pressure for teachers at all levels (primary, secondary and tertiary) to adopt TBLT. Crucial to the successful uptake of TBLT will be the development of a testing regime that is compatible with it; so we envisage that task-based assessment will receive increased attention. The increasing importance of technology-mediated language instruction will also lead to the development of suitable task-based materials for online use and of research programmes directed at investigating these.

12 Responding to the Critics of Task-Based Language Teaching

Introduction

As might be expected in the case of a new approach that differs radically from mainstream approaches, TBLT has aroused considerable criticism. In part, this criticism has its origin in the suspicion in which research in general is held by some members of the language teaching profession. Swan (2005a), for example, talked of 'legislation by hypothesis', arguing that SLA researchers have foisted TBLT onto the profession, ignoring the realities of most classrooms. Hadley (2013) saw TBLT as the 'new orthodoxy' and as 'a new religion' and talked of 'the disconnect between scholarly proponents and classroom practitioners' (p. 194). This view that TBLT is just the product of armchair SLA researchers is mistaken, however. For a start, many of these researcher-advocates of TBLT (including the authors of this book) were once teachers themselves, and their advocacy of TBLT derives from their experience of the limitations of mainstream approaches juts as much as from research and theory. Also, TBLT has spokespersons from among teachers and teacher-educators (e.g. Estaire and Zanon, 1994; Willis, 1996; Cutrone and Beh, 2014), who do not see themselves as members of the SLA research community. It is unwise to dismiss research and to make a case against TBLT just because it is advocated by SLA researchers.[1]

TBLT critics sometimes fail to recognize that TBLT is an 'approach' rather than a well-defined 'method' (Richards and Rodgers, 1986). That is, it involves a quite varied set of theoretical principles, curricular designs, lesson plans and methodological strategies as we have tried to make clear in this book. There is a difference between task-based and task-supported language teaching (see Chapter 1) but even this distinction is not watertight, given that both can involve explicit instructional strategies. Critics, however, have ignored this variation and straitjacketed TBLT in order to set up their critiques. In so doing, they end up misrepresenting TBLT. By way of example, Table 12.1

Table 12.1 The characteristics of TBLT according to Swan (2005a)

Swan's list	Commentary
'Natural' or 'naturalistic' language use involving a primary focus on meaning rather than language.	This is a key principle. All versions of TBLT (and also some types of TSLT) see tasks as affording opportunities for 'natural' language use where the primary focus is on meaning.
Learner-centredness rather than teacher control.	This is a misrepresentation. Not all task-based lessons need involve group work. Tasks can be performed by the teacher working with the whole class. Group work can also be followed by teacher-led activities.
Naturalistic learning does not guarantee target-like accuracy, so some intervention is needed.	This is partially correct. Learners can acquire much language 'naturalistically' (i.e. while focused on meaning) but some forms are 'blocked' (Ellis, 2006) by the L1 or by their lack of saliency and for this reason intervention is needed.
Intervention can be best achieved by focusing on form while the overriding focus is on meaning.	'Focus-on-form' is an essential feature of TBLT. However, intervention involving focus-on-form need not be restricted to the online performance of tasks. Ellis (2016) outlined various ways of achieving a focus-on-form (see also Chapter 2).
Communicative tasks are the best vehicle for this approach.	Tasks are central to both TBLT and TSLT. All ways of focusing on form involve tasks. However, the pre- and post-task stages of a lesson need not be task-based (see Chapter 8).
Pre- and post-task activities can prime or boost noticing during communication.	This misrepresents because it is incomplete. Focus-on-form is directed at inducing 'noticing' *while* tasks are being performed. Pre- and post-take activities serve a number of different purposes including planning the language needed to perform a task in the pre-task stage and explicit learning in the post-task stage. 'Noticing' is just one of the psycholinguistic processes that TBLT aims to activate.

(continued)

Table 12.1 (cont.)

Swan's list	Commentary
Traditional approaches are ineffective and undesirable.	Some advocates of TBLT (e.g. Willis, Long and Skehan) do reject traditional approaches. Others (e.g. Ellis) propose a modular curriculum consisting of both a synthetic component (as in traditional approaches) and an analytic component (as in TBLT) – see Chapter 7.

summarizes the characteristics of TBLT that Swan (2005a) proposed as the basis for his critique along with a commentary on each characteristic he mentions. Swan correctly identified the two key tenets found in all versions of TBLT, namely the centrality of 'natural' language use where the primary focus is on meaning and the need for intervention involving focus-on-form. But he misrepresents TBLT in other respects (e.g. he fails to recognize the importance of teacher control) and under-represents it in others (e.g. by failing to recognize that focus-on-form is not just directed at 'noticing'). He seizes on the view espoused by some advocates of TBLT (e.g. Willis and Willis, 2007; Long, 2015) that traditional forms of instruction need to be abandoned in favour of TBLT and he ignores the proposals of other advocates (e.g. Ellis, 2003; Klapper, 2003) for a modular approach involving both TBLT and traditional approaches. Swan mistakenly assumes that there is a single set of principles that characterize TBLT and as a result many of his criticisms are unwarranted.

We find the same problem in Bruton's (2002a, 2002b) critiques of TBLT. He assumes that TBLT necessarily involves learners interacting in pairs or small groups and that the sole purpose of using tasks is to generate oral interaction. For Bruton, tasks 'exclude listening approaches' (2002a, p. 285) and there is no recognition that they can include reading and writing too. From this totally mistaken standpoint, Bruton went on to claim that TBLT is only tenable if the learners 'have some existing target language ability' (p. 285). Also, like Swan, he sees TBLT as marginalizing the intervention of the teacher. He fails to recognize that tasks can be performed in a whole-class participatory structure where the teacher plays the dual roles of a co-performer of the task and an instructor.

There are two groups of critics of TBLT. Outsider critics approach TBLT from an adversarial position. Included in this group are Sheen

(1994, 2003), Bruton (2002a, 2005), Widdowson (2003), Swan (2005a, 2005b) and Littlewood (2007, 2014). There are also insider critics – advocates of TBLT who are their own critics. They dispute key issues, such as the relative merits of real-world and pedagogic tasks and how focus-on-form can best be executed. They also acknowledge the problems that can impede the implementation of TBLT. We will first take a look at what the outsider critics have had to say and then consider the issues that concern the insider critics.

The Outsider Critics

In his defence of tasks and TBLT, Long (2016) distinguished 'non-issues' and 'issues'. The non-issues were those raised by the outsider critics, while the real issues were those that required serious consideration. Our view is a little different. Like Long, we see many of outsider critics' problems as non-issues, but we also see some of the problems they identified as real issues. We organize this section on the outsider critics accordingly.

Non-Issues

Problem 1: Tasks cannot serve as the units of a syllabus. Arguably the most serious problem identified by the outsider critics rests in the claim that task behaviours are not predictable and therefore cannot serve as syllabus specifiers. Bruton commented 'the lack of predictability of the language generated in many tasks make (*sic*) it likely that any form of planning for assimilation will be rather arbitrary' (Bruton, 2002a, p. 285). Seedhouse (2005b) argued in a similar vein by noting that the interaction that transpires when learners perform a task frequently does not match that intended by designers of the task. He claimed that for this reason it is impossible to plan a language course based on tasks-as-workplans.[2] There is in fact evidence to support such a position. In Chapter 4 we considered research based on sociocultural theory (e.g. Coughlan and Duff, 1994) that showed that the 'activity' that results from a 'task' varies according to the specific motives that different learners have for performing the task.

This problem is overstated, however. While the relationship between task-as-workplan and the activity it gives rise to is not a perfect one, a task can have predictive value, as shown in research that investigated how the design features of tasks can influence the complexity, accuracy and fluency of learners' production (see Chapter 3). In addition, focused tasks can be successful in eliciting the linguistic features they target (see Ellis, 2003). Thirdly, it is easy to design input-based tasks in a way that obligates learners to process pre-determined linguistic features contained in them. Fourthly, Bygate (2018) proposed that tasks can display 'pragmatic predictability' (i.e. the discourse phases that characterize the trajectory learners follow when they perform a particular type of task). Bygate investigated how learners performed a picture story task with each learner in the group holding one of the six pictures that made up the story. There was considerable consistency in how these learners moved through discourse phases involving description, comparison, interpreting, sequencing and finally narrating the story.

But predictability, especially of linguistic features, is a non-issue. Irrespective of whether it is or is not possible to predict the language use that occurs when learners perform a task, TBLT is premised on the assumption that it is not possible to predict what individual learners will *learn* from a task. In other words, the design of a task-based syllabus does not need to be informed by what Bruton called 'planning for assimilation'. Indeed, the fundamental rationale for TBLT is that such planning is not possible given that learners acquire language in a non-linear way, working on a number of different features concurrently, and moving only gradually towards mastery of them. The strength of the task-based syllabus is that it acknowledges the processes by which language is acquired naturally, removing the need to pre-determine what and when learners will acquire specific linguistic features. To dispute the validity of tasks as a basis for a syllabus it would be necessary to dispute the theory of acquisition upon which TBLT is based. This is exactly what Swan (2005a) tried to do by attacking the hypotheses which he claimed the theory is based on. In so doing, however, Swan ignored the large body of research that supports these hypotheses – as Long (2016) so admirably demonstrated in his defence of TBLT.

There is, however, a real issue behind the problem stated by Bruton and Seedhouse. If it is not possible (or desirable) to base the design of a task-based syllabus on linguistic grounds, the question arises as to what principles *should* inform the selection, grading and sequencing of tasks in a syllabus. This is an issue which will be considered in the later section dealing with insider critic issues.

Problem 2: TBLT does not help learners learn 'new language'. A common complaint of outsider critiques is that because TBLT emphasizes incidental language learning while performing tasks, it is inferior to traditional approaches that cater to intentional language learning through the presentation and practice of what Swan (2005a) terms 'new language'. Outsider critics, however, are not entirely dismissive of tasks as they see them as supplementary to linguistic approaches in helping to develop learners' oral fluency. As Swan (2005b) put it 'TBLT is not primarily a language teaching approach' as it is 'mainly concerned with improving learners' command of what they already know' (p. 254) – a view that reflects how tasks figured in communicative language teaching in the 1980s (see Chapter 1).

Whether learners can learn 'new language' incidentally through performing tasks is an important issue. If it is not possible – or if it only takes place inefficiently – then a case can be made for direct, teacher-led instruction of the kind favoured by the outsider critics. In fact, though, there is plenty of evidence that learners do acquire language incidentally as a result of performing tasks. Studies based on input-based tasks (e.g. Ellis, 2001; Shintani, 2016) show that when learners perform tasks, they acquire both new vocabulary and new grammatical structures (see Chapter 2). Other studies involving output-based tasks (e.g. Mackey, 1999; Spada and Lightbown, 1999) show that performing interactive tasks enables learners to progress along an acquisition sequence. Corrective feedback studies (e.g. Ellis, Loewen and Erlam, 2006; Yilmaz, 2013b) show that learners' grammatical accuracy improves when they perform tasks and receive feedback on their output. In fact, the SLA literature is replete with studies that demonstrate that incidental acquisition does take place when learners perform tasks and that this is true irrespective of whether acquisition is defined as involving new language, progression from one developmental stage to another or greater accuracy. Meta-analyses (e.g. Norris and Ortega, 2000; Goo et al., 2015) also provide clear evidence of the adequacy of incidental acquisition. As Long (2015) concluded 'incidental focus on form works' (p. 13).

Outsider critics might still argue, however, that incidental acquisition is less efficient than intentional learning and that, therefore, an approach involving the direct teaching of 'new' language is preferable to TBLT. The meta-analyses referred to in this section, however, show that focus-on-form is not statistically less effective than traditional focus-on-forms instruction. In Chapter 10, we examined a number of studies comparing TBLT with traditional approaches, such as PPP. We noted that these studies suffer from a number of methodological problems but that on balance they point to the superiority of TBLT over PPP, especially when acquisition is measured in ways that tap into learners' ability to use language in free oral communication.

Problem 3: There is no grammar in TBLT. This putative problem is really an extension of the previous one. Sheen (2003) claimed that in task-based language teaching there is 'no grammar syllabus' and went on argue that proponents of TBLT 'generally offer little more than a brief list of suggestions regarding the selection and presentation of new language' (p. 391). He was also critical of the fact that in TBLT any treatment of grammar only takes the form of quick, corrective feedback, allowing for minimal interruption of the task activity. Swan (2005a) insisted that TBLT 'outlaws' the grammar syllabus. Perhaps this view that that there is no grammar in TBLT originates in Willis' version of TBLT. Willis rejects focusing on form during the main task phase, arguing that to do so would interfere with fluency. However, other versions of TBLT see attention to linguistic form as a necessary feature of task performance.

In fact, in one way or another there is plenty of grammar in TBLT. In Ellis's (2003) version of TBLT, there is the possibility of designing focused tasks to address learners' specific grammatical problems. Swain and her co-researchers (e.g. Swain and Lapkin, 1995) have shown that when learners perform a focused task in pairs or small groups 'language-related episodes' occur frequently and that these are often successfully resolved and contribute to learning (see Chapter 4). Opportunities for focusing on grammatical form also occur in the pre-task and post-task stages of a lesson. Guided pre-task planning allows learners the opportunity to consider what grammar they will need before they start to perform the task. In the post-task stage, teachers can deal explicitly with observed grammatical difficulties (see Chapter 8).

Problem 4: Performing tasks encourages indexical and minimal use of the L2. Seedhouse (1999) criticized task-based language teaching on the grounds that the performance of tasks results in indexicalized and pidginized language because learners are over-reliant on context and thus do not need to stretch their linguistic resources. Bruton (2002a) also thought that asking learners to perform tasks leads to the development of a classroom pidgin. Widdowson (2003) noted that learners may be successful in achieving the communicative outcome of a task without any need to attend to their actual use of the L2.

Clearly a task can result in language consisting of single words and formulaic chunks – especially if learners are beginners. However, there is also plenty of evidence to show that tasks can give rise to much more complex and accurate use of the L2. Much depends on the nature of the task and the way it is implemented. Opinion-gap tasks can elicit more complex language use than information-gap tasks (Rulon and McCreary, 1986). Giving learners opportunities to plan before they perform the task also has a notable effect on the complexity – and in some cases accuracy – of the language used. Thus, the claim that tasks will inevitably result in impoverished learner output is unjustified. Much of the research on tasks has been directed at identifying the design features and implementation options that will attract learners' attention to form and motivate language that is more complex and/or more accurate (see Chapter 3). Furthermore, as Long (2015) pointed out, the kind of interaction typical in traditional language teaching – the ubiquitous initiate, response, feedback (IRF) exchange – is in fact much more likely to involve the 'narrow and restricted variety of communication' that Seedhouse (1999, p. 155) believed tasks resulted in.

Problem 5: TBLT is not suited to low-proficiency learners. Littlewood (2007) commented that speaking tasks are difficult for learners of low proficiency. However, this problem seems to derive from the commonly held belief that TBLT only involves speaking tasks. It is obvious that beginner-level learners cannot engage in the free speaking that oral tasks require. However, they can perform listening tasks. Ellis (2001) reviewed a number of studies involving what he called Listen-and-Do Tasks such as the Kitchen Task, where the learners listened to instructions about where to locate kitchen objects (represented in numbered pictures) in a kitchen (represented by a diagram of the kitchen). They demonstrated their understanding of the instructions by writing the numbers of the correct pictures in the correct position in the diagram of the kitchen. Ellis was able to show that performing this task resulted in learners learning the words for kitchen objects. Shintani (2016) showed that Listen-and-Do tasks can be used successfully with *complete* beginners and can contribute to the acquisition of grammatical features.

Learners do not begin the process of acquiring their L1 by speaking it. Rather they match what they hear in the input to the objects and actions around them and thereby acquire new words and grammatical forms. Input-based tasks cater to this process. The L2 resources that are built up through performing such tasks can then later be used in speaking tasks. It is important to note, however, that input-based tasks do not prohibit learners from speaking; they simply do not require it. Therefore, learners who wish to try speaking from the outset – and there are some – are free to do so.

TBLT is not just well suited to teaching learners of low proficiency but in many respects is better suited than more traditional methods that require speaking from the outset. The only way that traditional methods can elicit speaking from learners is by carefully controlling their output using models and slot-and-fill and substitution exercises. Input-based tasks provide learners when an opportunity to experience natural language use from the start and to build up procedural L2 knowledge which will then be available for speaking.

Problem 6: TBLT assigns the teacher a very limited role. Swan (2005a) complained that 'the thrust of TBLT is to cast the teacher in the role of manager and facilitator of communicative activity rather than as an important source of new language' (p. 391). He based this claim on the fact that TBLT is implemented through small group work, rather than in teacher-centred instruction. However, as noted above, the claim that TBLT requires the performance of tasks in groups is mistaken. It has probably arisen from the fact that much of the research has investigated speaking tasks performed in pairs or groups. In fact, as noted previously, group work is not an essential characteristic of TBLT. Prabhu (1987), for example, argued that effective task-based teaching needs to expose learners to good models of the L2 and that this requires the teacher to take charge of the task in a whole-class context. Input-based tasks require a teacher–class participatory structure. Even speaking tasks can be carried out with the teacher interacting with the whole class. In an information-gap task, such as Spot the Difference, the information can be split between the teacher and the students.

Nor is the teacher just a 'manager and facilitator of communicative activity'. The teacher serves as a major source of input in TBLT. In the case of input-based tasks, teachers need to function as 'navigators' (Shintani, 2016) by helping the students to understand the input through repetition and non-verbal clues. In the case of output-based tasks, the teacher has a major role to play in providing corrective feedback while students are performing a task. At times, the teacher may need to step outside the task to provide some brief explicit instruction in order to guide learners to make the link between a grammatical form and its meaning. In fact, in TBLT, the teacher needs to perform multiple roles. Long (2015), addressing the same non-issue, noted that 'the teacher's role in TBLT requires greater expertise, and is more important, more demanding and certainly more communicative than in PPP' (p. 24).

Some Real Issues

We turn now to some of the other problems mentioned by the outsider critics. These issues we consider 'real' in the sense that they raise important questions which need to be addressed.

Problem 1: 'Task' is an ill-defined construct. Widdowson (2003) claimed that 'the criteria that are proposed as defining features of tasks are ... so loosely formulated ... that they do not distinguish tasks from other more traditional classroom activities' (p. 126). Widdowson seized on the definition provided by Skehan (1998), who identified four key criteria for a task:

- meaning is primary
- there is a goal that needs to be worked towards

- the activity is outcome evaluated
- there is a real-world relationship

According to Widdowson the key terms such as 'meaning', 'goal', 'outcome' and 'real-world relationship' are ill-defined. Ellis (2009a) attempted to clarify; he pointed out that a task involves both semantic and pragmatic meaning (whereas an exercise involves only semantic meaning), that the 'goal' means a communicative goal, that the 'outcome' that is evaluated is again a communicative (not linguistic) one, and the 'real-world relationship' refers to language use that is interactionally rather than situationally authentic. In Chapter 1, we offered an extended definition of a task that we believe is tighter and better able to distinguish tasks from exercises. We included an additional criterion, namely 'learners rely mainly on their own linguistic and non-linguistic resources' to capture the fact that a task needs to involve learners in text creation not just text manipulation.

Nevertheless, problems still exist with the definition of a task. Van den Branden (2006) distinguished seventeen definitions of a task, which he divided into those that define a task in terms of language learning goals and those that define it as an educational activity. The proliferation of definitions is itself an indication of a definitional problem. In the applied linguistics literature, the term 'task' is often used to refer to just about any type of pedagogic or assessment activity. Questions can also be raised as to whether the tasks used in various research studies always qualify as tasks. For example, do text reproduction activities such as dictogloss require learners to use their own linguistic resources? Questions might also be asked about picture-composition tasks, which figure in many studies. Is telling a story when there is no communicative purpose for doing so a 'task'? Text-enhancement studies also raise questions. Are activities where all that the learners need to do is read a text with some words highlighted and then answer some comprehension questions really 'tasks'? Where is the gap in such activities? Where is the communicative outcome? Perhaps the distinction between a task and an exercise is less clear cut than has sometimes been claimed or assumed. Some activities – for example, cue-card dialogues (Revell, 1979) – seem to be task-like rather than fully fledged tasks. It is perhaps not so surprising that teachers are often very uncertain about what constitutes a 'task' (see Chapter 11).

It may not be possible to arrive at a watertight definition of a task and perhaps such a definition is not needed. Perhaps it is sufficient to simply call any activity a 'task' that requires the receptive or productive use of the L2 in a meaning-focused activity that involves text creation at some level. Nevertheless, synthesizing the results of task-based studies is going to be problematic given that the studies have been conducted with very different notions of what a task is.

Problem 2: Learners will resort to their L1 when performing tasks. A common criticism is that if learners are focused on achieving the task outcome, they will simply resort to the use of their shared L1 as the most efficient way of achieving this. Carless (2003), for example, reported that mother tongue use was one of the key issues raised by both teachers and teacher-educators when task-based language teaching was introduced into Hong Kong schools. Carless also noted that most of the teachers he interviewed took a pragmatic view on mother tongue use on the grounds that it was needed to maintain students' attention and involvement. He speculated that when teachers became concerned about the overuse of the mother tongue in group work tasks, they would simply resort to traditional, teacher-fronted teaching.

One response to this problem is to argue that it is not a problem at all and that the use of the L1 is entirely legitimate in TBLT. Sociocultural theorists have argued that the L1 can serve as a mediating tool for performing tasks in the L2 (see Chapter 4). Good practice in TBLT reflects current views about the value of the L1 for performing such functions as task management, task clarification, discussing vocabulary and meaning and even presenting grammar points (Cook, 2001). It acknowledges the naturalness of code-switching when there is a shared L1 (Macaro, 2001).

Nevertheless, overuse of the L1 in TBLT constitutes a real problem – especially in monolingual classrooms such as those in Hong Kong. However, it does not warrant the abandonment of TBLT. For a start, L1 overuse can arise in any approach to teaching. Also, there are various ways of mitigating it. The teachers and teacher-educators that Carless interviewed mentioned several – appointing language monitors to remind their classmates to use English, using a reward system for using the L2, performing tasks as a whole class or in pairs rather in than groups. The task-based research points to other ways. One is task repetition. Shintani (2011) found that when her beginner-level learners performed a task for the first time, they naturally drew on their L1, but that over time, as the task was repeated and the children grew familiar with both the procedures and the English needed to perform the task, they increasingly used English. In pre-task planning. learners can draw on their L1 to conceptualize what they want to say, which can ease the processing burden and give them time to formulate when they perform the task in the L2.

Problem 3: TBLT is not suited to 'acquisition-poor' environments. Swan (2005a) claimed that TBLT is not suited to 'acquisition-poor' environments, by which he meant foreign-language contexts where learners are dependent on the classroom for learning a language. He argued that in such contexts, learners need a more structured approach to ensure they learn the grammatical resources required for communicating. However, while grammar is certainly helpful for communicating, it is not essential. Research on early L2 acquisition both outside the classroom (e.g. Klein and Perdue, 1997) and inside (e.g. Ellis, 1984) has shown that L2 learners manage to communicate with no or very minimal grammar. They draw on a limited range of formulaic expressions and vocabulary in conjunction with context to express what they want to say. Grammar, in fact, comes later, driven by the need to express more complex ideas that require more advanced language. It would follow then, that if the aim is to foster communicative ability in learners from the start, an approach that focuses on lexis would be most effective – for example, the Lexical Approach (Lewis, 1993). Such an approach is entirely compatible with TBLT as tasks can serve as a vehicle for providing lexical input (see Ellis, 2001).

Nevertheless, as we have already noted, there is a concern – voiced by both the critics of TBLT and by many teachers – that there is no grammar in TBLT and reservations regarding TBLT seem to centre on this point. If grammar learning has a place in courses for beginner-level learners, however, it is not in the classroom but in self-study materials that can be made available for use outside the classroom (e.g. for homework). The learning that results from such materials is unlikely to feed directly into the learners' ability to communicate. Rather it results in explicit knowledge which according to some theories (e.g. Ellis, 1994) serves as a resource for monitoring output and for priming attention to grammatical forms that learners are exposed to in task-based input and thus indirectly – and only in due time – facilitating the implicit knowledge needed for communication. However, for beginner-level learners in acquisition-poor environments, their only access to communicative input is the classroom; for that, tasks – in particular input-based ones – are needed.

Insider Critics

As we noted earlier in this chapter, there is considerable diversity in TBLT. This diversity manifests itself in debate among TBLT advocates on a number of issues.

Issue 1: Task-Based Research Is Limited in a Number of Respects

One of Swan's major objections to TBLT was that the theoretical principles that underpin TBLT lacked supporting evidence from research. However, as Long (2015) pointed out, Swan's claim has little merit as there is in fact ample evidence to support each of the hypotheses (online, noticing and teachability) that Swan rejected. Nevertheless, there are some notable gaps in the research agenda that informs TBLT. Révész (2017) pointed to several. She noted that researchers have focused on the effect that task design and implementation variables have on task performance, but have generally neglected to investigate the relationship between task performance and developmental outcomes. She also pointed to the predominant focus on output-based tasks and the paucity of research that has investigated input-based tasks. A side effect of this is that misunderstandings arise about what TBLT entails, leading to false claims about its unsuitability for beginner-level learners. Révész also noted that young learners have received little attention and that 'relatively few task-based studies have been conducted in actual classroom settings, even though the aim of TBLT is to inform L2 pedagogy' (p. 9).

TBLT clearly needs to justify itself as a researched pedagogy and while some progress has been made in this direction (see Chapters 10 and 11), there are obvious gaps in need of attention. If TBLT is to claim it is relevant to all learners in all teaching contexts, then it needs to be able to demonstrate its practicality and effectiveness in a range of instructional settings. Starts have been made in this direction (see, for example, the articles in the special issue 'Complementary theoretical perspectives on task-based classroom realities', *TESOL Quarterly*, 51, 3) and in Shintani (2016). However, much more research is needed. Advocates of TBLT agree on this but differences exist in the directions they think this research should take.

Issue 2: What Types of Tasks Should Figure in a Task-Based Course?

One issue where there is a clear divergence of opinion among TBLT advocates concerns the types of tasks that should figure in a task-based course. Differences exist regarding whether they should be real-world tasks or pedagogic tasks (a distinction originally made by Nunan, 1989) and also whether focused (as opposed to unfocused tasks) have a role to play in a TBLT programme.

In Long's version of TBLT (Long, 1985), a needs analysis is first conducted to establish the target tasks that a particular group of learners need to master. These then serve as a basis for developing the tasks in a syllabus. Long (2015) has continued to maintain this position, which is clearly the ideal way to proceed for those groups of learners who have well-defined target needs, such the US Border Patrol Agency students in González-Lloret and Nielson's (2015) study (see

Chapters 10 and 11). But for many learners – for example, those in state schools learning a foreign language – there are no immediate target needs and a needs analysis would have to be based on putative future requirements. Lambert (2012) attempted this with a group of Japanese university students only to find that the tasks he identified and designed did not motivate the students (see Chapter 7). For many students, a better approach is surely to build a course around pedagogic tasks that engage them.

The use of focused tasks is another point of controversy among TBLT advocates. Both Long (2016) and Skehan (1998) see no need for them in TBLT. Long dismisses focused tasks on the grounds that they belong to a focus-on-forms approach. Skehan sees the aim in TBLT as ensuring a balanced development in terms of complexity, accuracy and fluency, which can be achieved through the adroit selection of tasks to induce a variable focus on these aspects of language production. Skehan argued that only unfocused tasks are needed to achieve this. Ellis (2003), however, proposed that focused tasks do have a place in both a language programme and in research designed to inform pedagogy. Learners are likely to experience problems with certain linguistic features (e.g. subject–verb agreement and complex structures such as hypothetical conditionals) even at an advanced stage of development. The selective use of focused tasks directed at these structures can help learners overcome their learning problems. Focused tasks are useful in research because they make it possible to pre- and post-test learners in order to investigate whether performing tasks results in the learning of the targeted features. Investigating the learning that might result from unfocused tasks is much more problematic because pre-testing is not possible.[3]

A particular type of focused task is a consciousness-raising (CR) task (Fotos and Ellis, 1991; Ellis, 1993). This makes a linguistic feature (typically grammatical or pragmatic) the topic of the task and aims to help learners achieve a metalinguistic understanding of a rule or regularity by guiding them through an analysis of data that illustrates the forms and uses of the target feature. Long (2016) dismisses CR tasks on the grounds that they are 'components in the delivery of a traditional linguistic syllabus' (p. 6). Ellis (2018b) responded to Long's critique of CR tasks by pointing out that his idea was not that they should comprise the entire syllabus but rather that they could provide the means for developing explicit knowledge to help learners overcome specific and persistent learning problems. Thus CR tasks would only figure at a stage in learners' development when they were able to communicate reasonably effectively in the L2 but with restricted accuracy. Ellis also pointed to another advantage of CR tasks. He suggested that they can provide opportunities for communicating if learners work collaboratively to solve the linguistic problems they pose. It is in for this reason that they can still be called 'tasks'. In a CR task, language becomes the topic of talk and for serious-minded learners language is surely a relevant topic. An interesting example of the use of CR tasks can be found in Williams (2008), who drew on Concept-based Language Teaching (Lantolf and Thorne, 2006) to enable learners to develop a scientific concept for choice of auxiliaries in L2 French (a persistent problem for learners), which they then applied in a task that required them to verbalize their grammatical choices.

Issue 3: What Makes a Task Complex and How Can Tasks Be Sequenced Effectively?

Ahmadian and Mayo (2018), in their introduction to a book examining recent trends in task-based language teaching, observed that little attention has been paid to how tasks can be used as the basic units of language teaching syllabi even though Van den Branden (2006) had pointed to this as a major problem many years previously. Central to this issue is the question of how to determine the complexity of tasks in order to ensure a progression from 'simple' to 'complex' tasks. Long (2016) saw this as a 'real issue'. He noted that while 'much good work has been published on task complexity ... the overall yield has been disappointing' (p. 27). He saw the solution as more research to 'help make findings cumulative, encourage replication studies, increase productivity, and generally speed up progress on this issue'.

In the case of input-based tasks, however, the problem is less 'real' as there are established ways of determining the complexity of input – for example, standard measures of readability such as the Dale and Chall formula (1948). These measures were developed to measure the readability of written texts but they may also be relevant for oral texts as research has shown that the cognitive processes involved in reading and listening are quite similar (Jobard, Crivello and Tzourio-Mazoyer, 2006). Word-frequency lists derived from corpora also provide a basis for grading the oral and written texts used in input-based tasks. The extensive work on simplifying input to make it comprehensible to learners can also help (see Ellis, 2008, chapter 6). Long and Ross (1993), for example, pointed to the advantage of what they called 'elaborative simplification', which involves the restructuring of the propositional content rather than the language of a text.

Determining the complexity of output tasks is, however, much more challenging, as was noted in Chapter 1. This is what Long (2016) was referring to when he considered the overall results disappointing. The most developed framework for sequencing tasks from simple to complex – and the one that has attracted the most research – is Robinson's (2001, 2011) Cognition Hypothesis. This was discussed in Chapters 3 and 7 where we noted some obvious problems. It cannot be assumed that a task designated as 'complex' in terms of Robinson's framework actually entails a greater cognitive load when it is performed. However, this can be addressed by obtaining independent measures of the cognitive load posed by a task – for example, by utilizing a dual-task methodology or by collecting ratings from learners who perform the task, as in Sasayama (2016). However, this may not solve the fundamental problem of determining the complexity of production tasks. As noted in Chapter 3, tasks are holistic and involve conglomerates of factors. Research that investigates just one or two design variables hypothesized to affect task complexity (e.g. +/− reasoning; +/− familiar topic) may succeed in showing how these variables affect complexity in these tasks but there is no guarantee that they will work in the same way in a set of tasks that involve different clusters of features. There is currently no theory of how the myriad design variables interact to affect task complexity. The problem is exacerbated by the fact that the complexity of any single task depends not just on its design but also on how the task is implemented. Whether learners have the opportunity to plan before or during the performance of a task, for example, will affect the cognitive load that the task places on the learner. Thus, the impact that design variables have on task complexity cannot be determined independently of implementation conditions. Skehan (2016), while not rejecting the importance of design variables, felt that the research that has focused on them has failed to 'generate consistency or robust generalizations' (p. 37) and went on to suggest that studies that have investigated the effect of task conditions – such as pre-task planning – have proved more insightful. In short, we believe that we should not be optimistic that a research agenda directed at identifying the design factors that determine task complexity will bear much fruit.

The way forward is for course designers to make use of what research has shown about task complexity but also to draw on their own experience and intuition about what constitutes the right type and level of task for a particular group of learners. The fact that this may result in a less than precise sequencing of tasks in terms of their intrinsic difficulty may matter less if due regard is given to how a task is implemented with a particular group of learners. In other words, methodology may help to overcome the problems of grading and sequencing tasks in a syllabus.

Issue 4: What Is the Role of Explicit Instruction?

TBLT advocates agree that explicit instruction has a role to play in the post-task stage of a lesson. There is some disagreement about whether it has a role in the main task phase. Willis and Willis (2007) argue that it will subvert the purpose of the task by causing learners to focus-on-form rather than meaning. In contrast, Long (1991b) and Ellis (2003) point to the need for drawing learners' attention to form during the performance of a task. This often involves corrective feedback but can also include explicit instruction directed at linguistic problems if these arise. A good example of how this can be carried out can be found in the lesson based on the Things in Pocket Task reported in Samuda (2001). The main point of disagreement, however, lies in whether explicit instruction has a place in the pre-task stage. In task-supported language instruction (TSLT) it clearly does. TSLT draws on an inventory of linguistic forms which are first taught explicitly and then practised in 'real operating conditions' using tasks in accordance with skill-learning theory (DeKeyser, 1998). However, in the kind of 'pure' TBLT that Long (2015) promotes, it does not. Long argues that there is no room for explicit instruction preceding the performance of a task as this would constitute a return to 'focus-on-forms', which he sees as antithetical to the principle that 'learners, not teachers, have most control over their development' (p. 24).

In pitting 'focus-on-form' against 'focus-on-forms' some obvious questions need to be asked. One such question is whether focus-on-forms cannot result in true implicit knowledge, as Long claims. This question is notoriously difficult to address given the difficulty in devising tests that afford separate measures of explicit and implicit knowledge It is now clear, however, that TSLT can result in the ability to deploy the target of instruction in free production (see Norris and Ortega's, 2000, meta-analysis of form-focused studies). However, TSLT studies that report a positive effect for functional grammar teaching (e.g. Harley, 1989; Day and Shapson, 1991), typically involve massive amounts of practice directed at the target feature and, as Long points out, this is not feasible if teachers have to cover all the linguistic features listed in the syllabus. But this does not justify the wholesale rejection of TSLT, as it may still be of value in helping learners acquire those linguistic features that are not learned 'naturally', such as the target structures that figured in the studies of Day and Shapson and Harley. In other words, while TSLT cannot replace TBLT, it might usefully complement it (Ellis, 2018b).

There is, however, a possible drawback to providing explicit instruction prior to the performance of a task. As Willis and Willis

(2007) suggested, it may interfere with how learners perform a task by leading them to treat the task as a practice exercise rather than as opportunity to communicate naturally. There has been surprisingly little research that has addressed this question. Mochizuki and Ortega (2008) reported that a group that received a handout providing explicit information about English relative clauses produced more than twice as many relative clauses when they performed the focused task than a group that did not receive the handout. They also found that there was no difference in the global complexity and fluency of the production of the two groups. In the second study, Li et al. (2017), also found that learners who had received explicit instruction in the target structure (past passive) were more likely to try to use it when they performed the tasks than learners who did not receive this instruction. In this study, however, the explicit instruction resulted in production that was less complex and fluent and tended to be less accurate overall. Whether and to what extent explicit instruction 'interferes' in the way a task is performed is an important issue for TSLT. If it does interfere, then clearly tasks are not functioning in the same way as in TBLT. Even if they result in better learning of the target structure, they will not provide the same opportunities for natural language use and thus, in the long term, may be less successful in developing all-round proficiency in the L2. Clearly, though, this is an issue in need of further investigation.

Issue 5: Teachers and Students' Negative Perceptions about TBLT

The final issue concerns how teachers and students perceive TBLT. Where perceptions are negative it is unlikely that TBLT will work effectively. The outsider critics' critiques of TBLT derive from their own negative perceptions about TBLT. But there is also plenty of research evidence to point to the concerns that teachers and students have about TBLT. East (2018) reported on this via his interviews with teachers and teacher-educators in New Zealand. He found that they were uncertain about the extent to which they needed to 'let go' in TBLT, noting that a tension arose when 'teachers struggled to reconcile the primary emphasis on communication with the supporting requirement to develop language knowledge' (p. 224). The teachers felt a need for explicit instruction as a complement to TBLT. East concluded that the 'teachers' practices are most aligned with a task-supported form of TBLT' (p. 229). East (2012) also found that the teachers were concerned about the amount of planning that TBLT required of them, as there were few existing task-based resources.

Students can also have negative perceptions of TBLT if they are wedded to an approach that treats language as a set of linguistic objects to be mastered and so they therefore resist performing tasks or just treat them as fun activities rather than as serious activities that help them learn the language (Foster, 1998).

The literature on TBLT is in fact replete with the problems that teachers have experienced in attempting to introduce TBLT into their classrooms (see Chapter 11). These include structural problems that arise from classroom-level and societal–institutional level constraints (Butler, 2011) – for example large class sizes that make small group difficult to manage (Li, 1998; Samimy and Kobayashi, 2004). Other constraints include the structural syllabus that teachers may still be required to teach to and discrete item tests emphasizing linguistic accuracy that their students need to pass. Several commentators (Littlewood, 2007, 2014; Butler, 2011) pointed to the conflicts that exist in Asia between TBLT and culturally embedded traditional teaching approaches although Lai (2015) warned against 'essentialist statements about cultural inappropriateness of TBLT in Asia' (p. 14).

The problems that teachers face shape their perceptions of the desirability and viability of TBLT. When students lack an understanding of how tasks can help them develop proficiency in an L2 they will resist performing them. Long (2016) rightly points out that many of the problems associated with TBLT are also evident in structurally based language teaching. But some are new, and, in any case, it is much easier for teachers to tackle problems from the standpoint of a teaching approach they are familiar with than from one that is new to them.

Conclusion

In this chapter we have discussed a number of critiques of TBLT – some derived from outsider critics who view TBLT as an inadequate replacement for traditional mainstream approaches where language is taught directly and explicitly, and others arising from what we have called insider critics who advocate for TBLT but also see issues that need to be addressed. Table 12.2 summarizes the various issues. We have presented arguments to show that many of the outsider critics' issues (points 1, 2, 3, 4, 5 and 6) are in fact non-issues arising from a misunderstanding of the nature of TBLT (in particular its diversity) and/or ignorance or rejection of the relevant research that gives support to TBLT. However, we have also acknowledged that some of the issues they raise (points 7, 8 and 9) do need to be addressed. Of the issues raised by insider critics, some derive from differences in their

Table 12.2 Critiques of TBLT

Outsider critics	Insider critics
1. Tasks cannot serve as the units of a syllabus.	1. Task-based research is limited in a number of respects.
2. TBLT does not help learners learn 'new' language.	2. What types of tasks should figure in a task-based course?
3. There is no grammar in TBLT.	3. What makes a task complex and how can tasks be sequenced effectively?
4. Performing tasks encourages indexical and minimal use of the L2.	4. What is the role of explicit instruction in TBLT?
5. TBLT is not suited to low-proficiency learners.	5. Teachers' and students' negative perceptions about TBLT.
6. TBLT assigns the teacher a very limited role.	
7. 'Task' is an ill-defined construct.	
8. Learners will resort to using their L1 when performing tasks.	
9. TBLT is not suited to 'acquisition-poor' environments.	

views about what TBLT is (e.g. points 2, 3 and 4), while others are generally acknowledged (e.g. points 1 and 5).

There is the obvious danger that focusing on problems and difficulties will lead readers to the conclusion that TBLT is not worth the effort. However, we believe that it is essential to look critically at TBLT and to distinguish the non-issues from the real issues. In doing this, we can identify the problems that need to be looked at. In particular, we see the need to consider what additional research is still needed, what role task-based and task-supported teaching play in a language curriculum and how the constraints that affect the introduction of TBLT in many instructional contexts can be addressed.

13 Questions, Challenges and the Future

The final chapter is in three sections. The first returns to the questions which were posed at the end of Chapter 1, and attempts answers to each of them. The second section identifies a set of challenges facing task-based learning and teaching, and outlines responses to these challenges. The conclusion then offers brief suggestions for the future.

Section 1: Questions

The ten questions which ended Chapter 1 are wide-ranging in nature, and set out the major areas which this book seeks to address. This section tries to explore where the discussions in the various chapters of the book have taken us. In some cases, the answers which can be provided are fairly comprehensive, while in others it is clear there is still scope for greater progress to be made (and hence the Challenges section which follows).

Question 1: How should the central unit of task-based teaching – the task – be defined?
Although Chapter 1 included this question in the set of ten questions, in fact, that very same chapter had already offered a response: that tasks are activities which make meaning primary, which include some kind of gap which needs to be addressed and hopefully resolved, which require learners to rely on their own language resources and which have a clearly defined outcome. We feel this definition is still operative after the coverage from the book. Its purpose was to distinguish tasks from exercises, and we feel that it does that. It is noteworthy that the definition does not include explicit reference to the real world (although other approaches might well make this a very important component of the definition). We feel that the existing components of the definition ensure that there will be a real-world relationship in the way a task is carried out, and it will be sufficiently authentic in the way language is used.

Question 2: What kinds of tasks are appropriate for different groups of learners? Is a needs-based approach for identifying target tasks appropriate for all learners? Question 4: How can task-based teaching be made to work for beginner-level learners who have no or very little knowledge of the L2?

Here we are bundling two questions from Chapter 1 because, essentially, we can consider Question 4 to be a special case within Question 2. There are a number of parts to the answer to this question. First of all, while there is still room for progress, we have learned a great deal about the factors which influence task difficulty, and so we have a basis for finding tasks which are appropriate for different proficiency levels, and different ages. Similarly, the importance of task conditions has emerged very clearly and this also provides a way to increase the pressure within a task, or more likely, to reduce it, for example, through planning time provision, visual support and so on. Then it is very important to stress that not all tasks are speaking tasks. Shintani (2016) shows that input-based tasks with an emphasis on listening work very effectively with young, beginner Japanese learners. There are many options with tasks and how they are used, and this openness has to be exploited to ensure the relevance and practicality of tasks in different situations. Question 2 also raised the issue of whether needs-based tasks are always appropriate. Here we have seen different perspectives. Long (2015) advocates the use of needs analyses followed by the development of associated pedagogic tasks. Throughout this book, though, there has been a slightly different emphasis in task definition. There does need to be a real-world relationship in a task, to some degree, and learners have to use their own linguistic resources. But the starting point for task design is not seen as inevitably based on needs analyses. Pedagogic issues, previous experience and learner interests are all likely to be independent motivators for task design. The central issue is how the task fits into a task-based approach to pedagogy and whether it will realize appropriate pedagogic goals. Needs analysis-based tasks are fine, and often totally appropriate, but they are not the only way to identify desirable tasks.

Question 3: How can the problems of determining the complexity of tasks be resolved to ensure that learners of different levels of proficiency are faced with tasks that pose a reasonable challenge?

The response to this question has to be that progress has been made, but that the future looks even more promising. As discussed at various points (Chapters 2, 3 and 9) a great deal of research has been conducted into task complexity, with mixed results. There is some degree of agreement, and a range of task features have been identified which do have some consistency in the way they are used, in practical settings, to organize task sequences (see Chapter 7). But there is also a degree of unpredictability with tasks, as discussed in Chapter 3. This is perhaps less evident with task conditions, although such conditions do not relate to task complexity in the same direct way. There is, though, still no convincing and unified theoretical account of task complexity that is empirically grounded, only a range of (very interesting) generalizations about particular task characteristics. The greatest hope for the future has to come from two related areas. First, relating task complexity to cognitive load, and in turn, to an examination of this construct through the use of secondary measures (time estimation, secondary tasks, etc.) may well enable an independent account of complexity to emerge. Second, there may be a shift in the future from predominantly quantitative approaches to research to the use of qualitative methods. Each of these is taken up in the Challenges section. A point repeated at several points in the book, however, is that it is the conditions under which a task is performed, rather than the complexity of the task-as-workplan, that has the greatest impact on the resulting activity.

Question 5: Is there a role for focused as well as unfocused tasks, and if so, how should focused tasks be incorporated into a task-based syllabus?
In general, it would seem a reasonable claim that tasks will be predominantly unfocused in nature. Such tasks are more typical of research, certainly, and of much pedagogy. But we have seen that there are powerful arguments for the use, at least some of the time, of focused tasks. Chapters 2, 4 and 7 all discussed focused tasks in one way or another. Samuda (2001, 2015) examines how tasks can create pedagogic spaces and shows, through clever task design, how this can be achieved. Ellis (2003) has argued that consciousness-raising tasks, where the task itself concerns language, can be effective as tasks by motivating learners to reflect upon aspects of language itself. Swain (2006), through her concept of languaging, has also suggested that tasks can elicit talk about language leading to greater understanding of language itself. Then, in Chapter 7, we have seen how such tasks can be incorporated into a syllabus. In addition, one would have to say, that tasks which incorporate an integral focus on language also have their convenience since they may enable more conventional syllabus planning to be accomplished, resulting in greater systematicity in what is covered. The key point is that what is done does not compromise the 'taskiness' of the activity.

Question 6: Is there merit in a modular curriculum that includes both a task-based component and a traditional structural component? How should such a curriculum be organized?

Any answer to this question has to have strong connections to other questions, such as Questions 2 and 4 (covered together) and Question 5. The issue was discussed in Chapters 7 and 12. The major point is that one needs to relate a task-based syllabus to context, and recognize the challenge that might arise in certain circumstances, with contexts such as beginners, low-proficiency learners, acquisition-poor environments and culturally challenging contexts. A modular approach then enables the unfamiliarity and potentially threatening nature of a complete task-based approach to be mitigated flexibly. As was described in Chapter 7, this approach has many advantages, and might enable a task-based approach to be acceptable where otherwise it might never be used. The proposal is that there would need to be clear separation in time between the two co-existing approaches (e.g. different days) and that a decision would need to be made whether to start off with a more conventional approach at earlier levels and move towards a task-based approach as proficiency increases or vice-versa, where the aim would be to establish basic proficiency with a task-based approach first and introduce a structural component with focused tasks later on (see Ellis, 2018b).

Question 7: What alternatives are there for the organization of a task-based lesson? Is the lesson format proposed by Willis (1996), which has proved very influential, the only way?
The Willis approach contains pre-task, during-task and post-task phases. Of these, only the during-task phase is required. As a starting point here, it is clear that three phases of this sort have to be considered the norm for task-based and many other sorts of learning. Using three phases strongly suggests that tasks need to be prepared for and contextualized, and that simply completing a task is not enough without some sort of reflection, extension or evaluation. The Willis model, though, is specific in what is likely to happen at each of these stages. For one thing, particular suggestions are proposed for the pre-task and post-task phases, and it is inevitable that individual teachers will make their own decisions at each of these stages, may not follow Willis-type suggestions or may prefer to replace them. But the essential point is that good task-based teaching is likely to prepare the ground (with some form of input, model, topic preparation, vocabulary), and the post-task phase is likely to take language made salient by the task itself, and then do something with that language. Chapter 8 discusses these issues at some length, and provides an example teaching sequence. So broadly (if not in total detail) there is agreement between the Willis approach and general practice.

The major area of potential difference concerns what happens during the task phase itself. Willis advocates doing the task, then building on what has been learned through planning and then completion of a linked, non-identical task. In addition, she rejects a focus-on-form in the main task phase, arguing that learners should be entirely focused on meaning. In contrast, most task research has emphasized other factors that might be operative at the task phase, including a focus-on-form (see Chapter 2) and explored other options like time pressure (and opportunity for online planning), effect of support material available, provision of feedback and so on (see Chapter 8). This contrast brings out the central response to this question – teaching means decision making – and embraces infinite variety. It is likely that teachers will tread their own path, and approaches such as that of Willis, or any other set of proposals in task-based teaching, will have influence but will be adapted in any particular teaching encounter.

Question 8: How can a focus-on-form be best incorporated into a task-based lesson?
The basic point, covered at several places within the book, but especially in Chapters 2, 4 and 8, is that tasks (in which meaning has to be primary) provide an arena within which it is essential that form does not lose focus (while a task is being transacted) but that engineering such a focus-on-form (FonF) is not always easy. Much research and pedagogic innovation has been directed towards achieving such a FonF. Clearest in this regard, and a significant success within task-based research, is our greater understanding of the range and variety of feedback that can be provided and of the comparative effectiveness of these different types of feedback (see Chapters 2 and 8). It is clear that while a task is running, there are opportunities to provide FonF without disturbing the interaction or compromising the primacy of meaning. Focused tasks, as well as approaches such as languaging, also show how form can come into focus. In addition, pre- and post-work can also be relevant. In the first case, pre-task work can make aspects of form salient (Mochizuki and Ortega, 2008). In the latter, post-task activities such as public performance or transcription of one's performance (Foster and Skehan, 2013; Li, 2014) can change how attention was allocated when the task was done and make form more salient. Post-task activities can also exploit the form which has emerged during task completion and consolidate and develop it.

Question 9: How can teachers carry out formative assessments of task-based lessons to gather evidence of whether learning is taking place and what changes may be needed to the task?
We would like to see a wider range of possibilities in answer to this question, and it connects with the need to develop more achievement

tests (see the next section). But the activity in this area has not been so extensive. Chapter 11 discusses issues connected with programme evaluation, and formative assessment certainly fits in with this. But there are some other initiatives which are worth mentioning. Two, interestingly, involve self-assessment. Harrison (1982), covered in Chapter 9, used a system of task-cards, each containing ten mini-tasks. Each learner then worked through the mini-tasks by asking a classmate to 'sign off' when a task was completed satisfactorily, and the student only approached the teacher for the tenth and final task. In this way, important formative feedback was obtained about progress. Winke (2014), with a CALL-based course, also had provision for learners to self-assess, and, interestingly, these self-assessments showed high agreement with teacher-based assessments. In this way learners were engaging in assessment that provided them with fairly direct information about their own progress. One other example that has an element of formative assessment comes from the discussion in Chapter 4 of dynamic assessment – this, by its nature, with scaffolding being provided as an integral part of the assessment, is necessarily formative in nature.

Question 10: What problems do teachers face in implementing task-based teaching and how can these be addressed?
The problems here are numerous. They range across uncertainly as to what 'task' actually means, whether grammatical development might be neglected, how different learner types and contexts might be inappropriate for a task-based approach, a general lack of resources, the challenge of the different teacher role a task-based approach introduces, whether external pressures (institutional or assessment-linked) will render such an approach impossible or at least very difficult, excessive workload and even whether this approach may lead to excessive noise! We have looked at some of these already, and will revisit them in the Challenges section. There have been successes, for example, with regard to different types of learners (Chapters 7 and 8); with the options available to ensure that grammatical development is not neglected (covered in Chapters 2 and 8); and with assessment, to a limited degree (in Chapter 9).

These responses are very important. But at a more general level, three sorts of response hold some promise. First, very clearly, is the dissemination of good practice. All the problems mentioned in this section have been solved somewhere. The challenge is to convey to other prospective task-based teachers what has been achieved in sufficient detail that the success has a chance of being replicated. Second, and connected to this, there is the development of international organizations, such as the International Association of Task-Based Language Teaching (http://www.tblt.org/about/), which can act as a clearinghouses for such good practice. Third, there is the need to develop teacher training so that it prepares teachers for the challenges that are likely to occur when task-based teaching is used. Taken together, these three responses have a great deal to offer. We will return to them in the next section particularly when we discuss teacher training.

Section Two: Challenges for Task-Based Approaches

The previous section tried to address the questions from Chapter 1. But arising from them, and also from the various chapters in the book more generally, a number of challenges can be identified for task-based learning and teaching. This section explores these challenges. In some cases, the outline of a response is clear. In others it is not, and that is part of the excitement of this approach – we have to wait and see how the field develops.

Broadly speaking, three types of challenge are identified: theoretical, research and practical. The categories are not mutually exclusive but represent tendencies, and follow from different sections of the book.

Theoretical Challenges

1. COMPLEXITY AND COGNITIVE LOAD

Task complexity has had a considerable impact on task research, not least because it is so important to two of the accounts (the Cognition Hypothesis and the Limited Attention Capacity approach) that have been proposed in this area. It is also important in more general research terms. Any proposals for choosing tasks need to be grounded on a clear view of complexity and the demands that will be placed on the learner, and so it is relevant to any research study which uses tasks, to language testing and to pedagogic decision making. As we have touched upon, research findings in this area have had mixed success. There have been achievements, but there are many examples of research results not turning out as expected. Clearly a first reaction here would be to hope that future research will overcome these problems and deliver more consistent and even predicted results. We have learned through the problems which have already been identified, such as participants in studies finding certain factors confusing and making unforeseen interpretations (Inoue, 2013; Sasayama, 2015). The key question is whether tasks are inherently unpredictable, or if it is simply the case that research designs need to be improved. There are a couple of developments which give grounds for optimism, and may pave the way for generalizations to emerge more clearly. First, there are the insights emerging from the use of qualitative research methods. These provide a window to understand interpretations of task demands more deeply (Pang and Skehan, 2014; Sasayama, 2015). Second, there is the general area of using independent measures to establish cognitive load, referred to earlier. In the past, claims have been made about task complexity simply on the basis of researcher analysis. Such analyses may be limited in effectiveness – excellent starting points but needing to be supplemented by more objective measures. The range of possibilities that we are now seeing in the field, increasingly on a routine basis, may be a crucial development. This knowledge will enable more focused research designs which can (a) explore the relationship between complexity and dimensions of performance and (b) provide a sounder basis for theorizing, which includes tasks themselves and also task conditions.

2. TASKS AND ACQUISITION

The emphasis in much task research is on performance itself. There are suggestions within the Cognition Hypothesis and the Limited Attention Capacity approach which do speak to acquisition (more in the former than the latter) but they are limited. Of course, nurturing performance is important, and so all this research is relevant to the ways changes in underlying language systems can be transformed into effective real-time language use. But accounting for acquisition itself has not been a major component of most task-based work. The Interaction Hypothesis and the Cognition Hypothesis are stronger on the *process* of change (through feedback) rather than on the course of development or any account of underlying system change. Coupled with this, task-research is often quite short-term in nature, and one can make the oft-repeated (yet totally justified) critique that more longitudinal research is needed. So one would hope to see, within task research, longer-term research designs, and evidence that sustained task work leads to development and increased proficiency. The chapters on evaluation are encouraging in this regard. It would be nice, though, to see connections between task research and underlying processes, to clarify whether we are dealing with explicit or implicit processes (or, of course, most likely both); whether the focus is automaticity and access, or alternatively underlying system change. A model to account for these issues, specifically in the context of task-based approaches, would be of enormous value. Chapter 2 raised these issues. There is still a need for progress.

Research Challenges

The challenges in this section do not have strong theoretical underpinning but are included simply because research gaps are evident. Existing research is often suggestive as to where additional data would be worth collecting to flesh out a broader picture. Theory is not unimportant, but the focus is more on research gaps which have been identified.

1. MEASUREMENT: CALF AND BEYOND

Complexity, accuracy and fluency have been used in many of the psycholinguistic studies covered in Chapter 3. More recently lexical performance (diversity and sophistication) has been added to this basic set of measures. In addition, Interaction Hypothesis studies have tended to use the sorts of feedback types covered in Chapters 2 and 8. Finally, sociocultural theory approaches have tended to use a different approach, emphasizing patterns of interaction and particularly language-related episodes (LREs), as well as evidence of dynamic assessment. These various measures have served us well, and have had a major impact on our understanding of performance. But in a sense, they capture what has been learned from what might be termed the first phase of task research. We now have additional possibilities we need to consider. Chapter 3, for example, discussed the greater understanding we now have of sub-dimensions of CALF, and how this knowledge needs to be reflected in more sophisticated performance measures. In addition, there is clearly an urgent need, following Révész, Ekiert and Torgersen (2016), to incorporate indices of outcome and of acquisition. Other areas, relating to interaction, can also explore new measures that might be used, of contingency, for example. Such developments will be important. Task effects and condition effects have already been detected with the measures we have available. It is to be hoped that in the future newer, subtler, more valid measures may do an even better job at detecting the impacts that are hypothesized in task research designs.

2. TASKS AND INDIVIDUAL DIFFERENCES

Chapter 5 used Robinson's Cognition Hypothesis and its triarchic structure to locate the relevance of individual differences for task research, particularly regarding claims about task difficulty. The fundamental point to make is that the model effectively provides a list, only, of possible influences on task performance and task difficulty. But the research base relevant to this is not very extensive, and so currently, proposals are often speculative. One can wonder whether different aspects of aptitude have greater or lesser influence on performance with different sorts of task, as well as different (e.g. explicit vs. implicit) types of learning. We need to know more about working memory and its connection with different types of planning. Motivation (and see also the discussion of involvement in Chapter 6) may link importantly with the use of different types of task, and possibly in different learning environments. There is also a case to include additional ID variables, such as personality. Tasks involve interaction, and it could be that different personality profiles respond differently to various sorts of tasks. Even beyond this, there may be potential for aptitude-treatment interaction studies which probe the ways particular types of task, or task-driven syllabuses, for example, interact with different sorts of ID. Much fundamental research in this area needs to be done if we are to better understand how tasks function with different learners and how we can gain greater understanding of task difficulty.

3. LONGITUDINAL RESEARCH

Pedagogy takes place over an extended time period. Research, very frequently, takes place over a shorter time span, probably lasting between as little as thirty minutes and rarely longer than two to four weeks. The TBLT field has many findings and generalizations, and these have been covered extensively in this book. But as mentioned elsewhere, a major challenge is to forge greater connections between theory-motivated research, on the one hand, and the practice of TBLT, on the other. There is considerable scope to explore research designs which last longer than two to four weeks, and come to resemble more the lengths of contact that teachers typically have with their students. What would be the consequences, for example, of researching planning, or post-task interventions or repetition over something like a fifteen-week period? Would planning lose or gain effectiveness, for example? Could learners be trained to exploit planning more effectively? Could planning be selectively directed at performance, or alternatively and more challenging, to promote acquisition? Similarly, one can ask additional questions about a task feature such as structure, given the positive findings which have been accumulated. Would learners, with regular exposure to this variable, come to realize that imposing their own structure is beneficial for performance? Again, there is considerable scope here. A solid database of such longer-term findings would enable more straightforward connections to be made with pedagogy.

Pedagogic Challenges

1. THE TASK CYCLE AND HOW BEST TO SET UP (PRE-TASK WORK) AND THEN CONSOLIDATE (POST-TASK WORK)

This issue was raised as Question 7, at the end of Chapter 1. Broadly, as we saw, it is uncontroversial to suggest a three-part structure for teaching (pre-, during-, post-), and this links nicely with much task research. Researchers try to manipulate and control, in an attempt to identify the effects of particular variables. But the real challenge is to identify optimal environments for teaching, and this means judicious combinations of pre-, during and post- activities which go well beyond the confines of particular, focused research studies. The alternatives for pre-task work were set out in Chapter 8, and we need to learn more about their practical effectiveness in classrooms. Similarly, the during-task options are extensive, and so we need to learn more about useful advice for teachers regarding, for example, feedback options, timing options and so on. Finally, the post-task stage may be the most complex of all. Tasks make language salient, and so the post-task stage may be ideal to capitalize upon this. How this is best done becomes a major challenge in task work. But all along there is a tension between maximizing the chances that there will be a focus on language, and most ambitiously, conditions where new language becomes salient, and then developing more automatized skills with that new language. With pre-, during- and post-task phases, the tension is essentially the same: Should the general aim be to push for change and development or should it be to achieve greater levels of control? The challenge is to find optimal ways of achieving this. We have learned a great deal about the different options available – now we need to learn how they can be combined.

2. TASKS AND EXTENDED TEACHING: ARE THERE OPTIMAL SYLLABUSES?

Educational contexts vary. Elsewhere in this book we have discussed ways that tasks can be shown to be relevant for a variety of learners (young, in acquisition-poor contexts and so on). We have also seen that there are circumstances where a needs-based approach to syllabus design is appropriate. But the general educational context is a challenge, and in many parts of the world, even though using tasks may be seen as desirable, there are also countervailing forces which argue for more traditional methods. In such circumstances to move to a fully fledged TBLT approach may be impractical, and so a modular approach may be more realistic as an option. It is important to say that the goal of a TBLT approach is not lost, but by taking a more nuanced approach, greater practicality is achieved to work towards the same general aim. We also need to move on and consider whether different versions of a task-based approach are better than others, particularly when we relate different approaches to different contexts. This, too, is a considerable and important challenge for the future.

3. THE NEED FOR TEACHERS TO FIND AND/OR TO GENERATE TASKS

Tasks need to be appropriate to particular groups of learners and this means that teachers are less likely to be able to simply rely on course book tasks (and see answer to Question 10 in the previous section). Their choices are either to find suitable tasks, or to generate the tasks themselves. That is not to say that course book series do not have useful tasks. It is more that since task-based courses are generally learner-centred, it is likely that there will be a need for tasks which are suitable for particular groups, and this may go beyond textbooks (and be necessary in situations where there are no textbooks). If the choices are finding or generating, then with the first of these, there is considerable merit in 'task banks' and it is likely that, through the aegis of bodies like IATBLT, these will grow in number and in organization so that it may be possible to search databases of tasks to find ones that are appropriate for particular groups of learners, of particular ages and proficiency levels, in particular locations and so on. Regarding the generation of tasks, in Chapter 1 the approach taken by Jane Willis was described illustrating a number of pedagogic task types: listing, ordering and sorting, comparing and classifying, problem solving, sharing personal experiences, creative tasks. These options could be applied to endless topics. Imagine, for example, trying to produce six tasks, following each of the possible options, for dating, and for pets. This is a practical method of generating tasks and undoubtedly there are others. Below we discuss the issue of teacher training, and it is clear that in the context of task-based work, a teacher training component needs to focus on methods such as Willis's in order to help teachers to meet this challenge during their professional careers.

4. HOW CAN TASKS WORK IN DIFFERENT CONTEXTS AND WITH DIFFERENT LEARNERS

We have explored this issue at different points during the book, and indeed this was the focus for Questions 2 and 4 at the end of Chapter 1. We have seen several ways in which problems can be addressed, with respect to young learners, beginners and also in difficult contexts such as acquisition-poor settings and culturally challenging contexts. In general, these initiatives have shown that these educational settings do not preclude the use of tasks, but at the same time, it is not as if there is a profusion of examples of how the various problems have been overcome. Perhaps young learners and beginners have been the most successful in this regard. Creative teachers (see the previous section on generating tasks) and creative textbook writers have produced relevant materials in each case. In addition, by interpreting tasks more broadly, and not exclusively focusing on speaking, it is clear that judicious use of contextual support can provide interesting and challenging educational environments. In addition, the use of a modular approach to syllabus design can go some way to reducing the scale of these problems.

Acquisition-poor environments are indeed an issue but, as was pointed out earlier, this problem is not exclusive to task-based approaches – it is general, and only disguised in 'organized' and teacher-dominated classrooms. Two approaches to addressing this problem are, in fact, more available with a task-based context. First, there is a natural connection between task-based approaches and project work. In other words, it is natural, within a task-based context, to transcend the limits of the classroom and to plan how additional language opportunities that do exist can be exploited (Fried-Booth, 1986). This links with a second response to this same problem – the potential of technology to provide language use opportunities even in acquisition-poor environments. The internet (and see the section on CALL) provides a wealth of resources, with audio as well as print materials. If projects are designed to use such materials, there will be many opportunities for listening and reading tasks, and even writing tasks also. Task-based approaches, with the autonomy they foster, can enable learners of many ages and proficiencies, provided they are stimulated with appropriate tasks, to go well beyond the limitations of their own particular learning context.

A related worry is that a task-based approach is inappropriate because of a mismatch between the processes and procedures of using tasks and cultural expectations regarding the role of the teacher and the nature of learning. We saw discussion of this earlier in relation, for example, to some Asian cultures where it has been argued that the authoritative role of the teacher and a view of learning as transmissible knowledge is seen as provoking difficulty (Littlewood, 2007). Indeed there are accounts of difficulties when task-based approaches have been tried in such contexts (e.g. Carless, 2004). But first of all, we need to consider whether other issues were at play, not simply cultural mismatch. Lack of appropriate teacher training (and see the section

'Teacher Roles and Training') might be one such factor, as would a mismatch between task-based teaching and the nature of the examination system, or indeed, an unrealistic expectation about the speed with which an innovation can be introduced.

We would argue that these are early days regarding the impact of any cultural mismatch, and that there are grounds for optimism, provided that realism and some willingness for persistence are involved. In this book we have seen examples of task-based approaches being successfully implemented in Japan, for example. In China, too, there are important initiatives. Yafu Gong (2014) has published a major task-based coursebook series, following extensive research into the sorts of tasks that are appropriate for mainland China school-age learners. He has also provided a book-length rationale for this work (Gong, 2015) and this shows that task-based insights are relevant even in what might be considered to be the most challenging of circumstances.

Even so, these are serious challenges for a task-based approach. To be able to point to impressive examples of how these challenges have been responded to by committed teachers and educational groups is one thing; for the approach to gain general currency is quite another. The real challenge here is the dissemination of good practice so that those who might not otherwise consider using a task-based approach become more enthusiastic about doing so.

5. CALL AND THE USE OF TECHNOLOGY

The major issue here is that technology is pervasive, and so not to exploit the possibilities it enables would probably be regarded as very odd by most students! The possibilities themselves are endless. There is scope to access text, audio and video sources on the web or through social media; there are opportunities to contact native L2 speakers directly, and in real-time; it will also undoubtedly become commonplace to access artificial intelligence-driven resources, for information and for interaction. All these are changing language learning possibilities rapidly (not simply in relation to tasks), and recasting what an acquisition-poor environment means. Teachers and learners focusing on listening skills can access huge quantities of ever-changing materials, speaking can be facilitated by international interactions, reading has the resources of the entire web available and writing can be enhanced by massive access to relevant input material as well as support software for the process of writing itself. Tasks, clearly, have to be alert to all these possibilities, and the evidence is that they are, for research and, more relevantly here, for pedagogy.

The use of technology as a source of input and support is exemplified by Oskoz and Elola (2014), who were concerned with students learning to write expository and argumentative texts. They show how technology was used to scaffold learners through the stages of writing (planning, drafting, getting feedback and revising). They also show how the use of computer chats and wikis had a major role in driving the content of what was written. As a contrast to this, several researchers report on initiatives to develop virtual worlds which enable learners to interact with the locations and the characters in these worlds to develop their language abilities. Learners are given tasks that structure the way they can develop language, and it is interesting to see how task theorizing and research can impact on the design of these encounters. For example, in a task-based context, Sykes (2014) explored the untiring nature of the virtual world to enable learners to restart encounters intended to develop ability with the speech acts of apologizing and requesting. Restarting was seen as highly useful in automatizing the speech act skills concerned. Sykes also reported that if one takes such a technological path, the real-world norms of gaming have to be respected – encounters need to be player – rather than learning-driven, for example, even if the real intention is that learning should occur. Canto, De Graaf and Jauregi (2014) also uses a virtual world, but theirs is intended to enhance capacity to handle intercultural meanings, and show that tasks and technology can work together in areas beyond simply language code. Gutierrez (2014) shows the potential of the virtual world approach by basing its design in her research on sociocultural theory – yet another twist on linking tasks, technology and applied linguistic theory.

The web also contains incredible quantities of unstructured resources. The relevance for linguistic input is very great, but one of the major challenges will be how to organize the ways language learners access this wealth of material. It is clear that the structure provided by task-driven learning is likely to be the major way that this happens, but that the value of doing so will depend on how effectively this potential is curated – another major challenge for the future.

6. TEACHER ROLES AND TEACHER TRAINING

One of the criticisms made of tasks (covered in Chapter 12) is that the approach leaves the teacher with nothing to do. As indicated earlier, we find this a curious claim. In some ways we would find it easier to understand the opposite critique, namely that a task-based approach is very demanding of teachers! The central issue, of course, is that a task-based approach necessarily encourages a greater degree of learner autonomy, and then the question concerns the ways a teacher continues to exert control, to monitor what is happening and to design future work (and keep in mind institutional pressures such as examination systems) while learners function relatively independently within tasks. Added to this, teachers may need to design tasks on a regular basis, or at least adapt existing ones. Then they need to deal with alternatives at the post-task stage, where choices of extending, analysing, consolidating and automatizing all come into play. Taking a slightly longer timescale, there may be a need to design effective formative assessments. The set of challenges is forbidding!

A major issue we then have to consider is the way teachers are prepared for such challenges, and in that respect the focus switches towards the procedures within pre-service or in-service teacher education. Much current teacher education attempts to develop sets of skills which will serve teachers well during their careers. But the emphasis, generally, is towards teachers as deliverers of materials within conventional educational systems. The wider range of challenges that a task-based approach requires does not have a corresponding emphasis. As a consequence, a major issue for the future will be the development of changes within teacher training systems to equip teachers for such a contrasting approach. Until that is done, there will be a considerable impediment to the wider use of tasks. Task-based teachers have to be knowledgeable, resourceful and flexible, and teacher training needs to provide them with the beginnings of the skills they will need to develop further.

7. ACHIEVEMENT TESTING

This is certainly the area where a magic wand is most needed. Long's (2015) claim, as we saw, is that progress with task-based achievement testing would be the single most effective advance for the widespread use of task-based approaches. It was also clear in Chapter 9 that while there have been interesting initiatives in this area, progress is limited. To develop a point made there, the way forward would seem to be the establishment of collaboration and networks of teachers. Testing is time-consuming and requires unavoidable standards, e.g. for reliability and validity. In addition, unlike testing in other areas where a set of test questions can be devised and reused, it is inherent with task-based approaches that developing achievement tests based on tasks-as-workplans is not sufficient. What happens in classrooms may have a relationship to tasks-as-workplans, but it is going to go well beyond it, and achievement testing will necessarily need to reflect this. Therefore, this is going to be a serious challenge for the field, so there is a need to find frameworks to promote and to catalyse collaboration. We briefly saw two examples. Colpin and Gysen (2006) report on the development of a series of achievement tests for several groups of quite different learners. Harrison (1982) was associated with the development of achievement tests for French with secondary (high) school-age children in the UK. Interestingly Colpin and Gysen worked in a university education department and Harrison worked for an examination board, with all these authors working *with* teachers in the development of the achievement tests. This may be an important approach for achievement testing – initiatives bringing together people with general testing expertise and actual teachers able to shape tests that are appropriate to particular local circumstances. Obviously there needs to be compromise here. The tests which are developed in these cases have to have some generality, but at the same time they should address the detail and variation in the different teaching contexts.

Section Three: Theory and Praxis

It is said that responses to innovations go through three stages, as a marker of acceptability:

1 This innovation will never work.
2 This innovation will work but it is unimportant, marginal, minor!
3 That's not an innovation. I've been doing it for a long, long time!

We think it reasonable to place task-based approaches between numbers 2) and 3) on this 'scale', and realistically, closer to 2)! This, of course, means that such approaches are taken seriously and have some importance, but are far from mainstream. One can wonder, therefore, what will happen next.

It is our contention that the vitality represented in this book, the research, the practical applications and the variety of approaches will all contribute to the continuing importance of a task-based approach. There is the fundamental advantage that this approach aims at developing the capacity to use language effectively, and that this is what will characterize language education in the twenty-first century. The capacity to be effective in languages is likely to be even more important in a future characterized by increasing internationalization. Task-based approaches are appropriate to the challenge this represents.

The book has shown that task-based approaches have certainly come of age. Significant progress has been made in the area of theory, with alternative accounts each offering interesting interpretations of what happens when tasks are used, and how these relate to underlying disciplines like linguistics, psycholinguistics, sociolinguistics, education and so on. A considerable amount of relevant research has been completed, and even more important, research methods have been refined and have evolved as greater understanding of issues like task complexity and performance measurement has been reached. There have also been impressive accounts of syllabus and methodology, as well as examples of task-based approaches in operation in a variety of circumstances. Comparative evaluations have been published (with encouraging results) –see Chapter 10 – and increasingly task practitioners have developed methods of critiquing and examining what they have done in class. In addition, the formation of the IATBLT group – which organizes a biennial international conference, has a growing website and provides an important source of contact for task-based researchers and teachers alike – is a major development. Its growth is a testament to the vitality of the field. Local TBLT organizations, such as those in Japan, have also flourished.

A slight worry one might mention is the relationship between theory and practice. Both have been covered in the book, but it has to be said that in the field more generally, there has been something of a separation between the two. In an ideal world a closer and clearer connection between theory and practice would have been better. But it is possible to state the opposite argument. Both areas have developed strongly, and rather independently, but have been aware of the other's existence, and frequently bridges have been built between them. It may be, in fact, that it has been better to have a degree of separation as each of them has developed through important stages. Now, with each in a position of some strength, the way they can come together may lead to greater synergies and progress both theoretical and practical.

Endnotes

1 The Pedagogic Background to Task-Based Language Teaching

1. Prabhu's Communicational Teaching Project actually started in 1979. Another early programme that could lay claim to be being task-based was in Malaysia. The Malaysian Language Syllabus (see Richards, 1984) specified objectives in task-like terms and suggested 'procedures' for realizing them.
2. As a result of experience with the Communicational Teaching Project, Prabhu did offer some quite concrete suggestions for grading and sequencing tasks. Beginning tasks needed to be input- rather than output-based. Information-gap tasks were easier than reasoning-gap tasks, which in turn were easier than opinion-gap tasks.
3. Loschky and Bley-Vroman (1993) acknowledged that it is very difficult to design a structure-based task that makes the production of a predetermined linguistic feature essential given that the choice of what linguistic resources to use when performing the task is still left to the learner. Achieving task essentialness is much easier with input-based tasks that learners can only perform successfully if they are able to process the target structure.
4. The conviction that in TBLT the traditional distinction between syllabus and methodology is no longer relevant dies hard, however. Van den Branden (2006) continued to claim that the 'what' and the 'how' are blurred in TBLT (see p. 6).
5. Long (2005), however, claimed that 'every language course should be considered a course for specific purposes, varying only (and considerably, to be sure) in the precision with which learner needs can be specified' (p. 1).
6. Richards and Rodgers (2014) also concluded that TBLT was unlikely to provide a basis for national teaching programmes but suggested it could constitute a 'partial approach' alongside a traditional language-based syllabus.

2 Cognitive-Interactionist Perspectives

1. Lyster and Ranta's list is not exhaustive. Nassaji and Fu (2016) identified twelve types of CF in ten hours of classroom interactions in an adult Chinese-as-a-foreign-language classroom – recasts, delayed recasts, clarification

requests, translation, metalinguistic feedback, elicitation, explicit correction, asking a direct question, repetition, directing a question to other students, re-asks and using L1 English.
2. Long (2015) repeatedly links incidental and implicit learning.
3. Long considers it still an open question whether explicit learning is necessary for L2 adults. He accepts, however, that 'intentional and explicit learning are likely to speed up acquisition and so becomes a legitimate component of a theory of ISLA (instructed language acquisition)' (2015, p. 65).
4. In fact, though, input-based tasks can still allow for two-way interaction as learners may elect to speak even though the task does not require them to do so.
5. There is, of course, also non-interactive input – for example, when someone reads a text, listens to a tape or the radio or watches TV. Tasks can provide non-interactive input but this is not the focus of this chapter.
6. Ellis et al. (2001) proposed a similar construct to LREs – *FFEs*. By and large studies of small group interactions have preferred LREs while studies of whole classroom interaction have investigated form-focused episodes.
7. Robinson (2007b) also argued that task complexity affects the CAF of L2 production. This is considered in Chapter 3.
8. Uptake-with-repair certainly indicates that learners have noticed but may not constitute evidence of deep processing if the learners have just echoed the corrected utterance.
9. Learners need multiple exposures to lexical items to learn them but extensive exposure is even more necessary for grammatical features. The learners in Shintani (2016) demonstrated better productive knowledge of the target feature than did the learners in Erlam and Ellis (2018), reflecting the greater exposure in her study (nine as opposed to two lessons).
10. In fact, one reading of the CF experimental research is that what it shows is not that CF is effective but that explicit instruction + CF is effective.

4 Sociocultural Perspectives

1. 'Tasks' here refers to any stimulus for talk given to a learner. It includes tasks in the technical sense of the term in this book but it also includes what would qualify as 'exercises' (see Chapter 1 for this distinction).
2. Wertsch, Minick and Arns (1984) pointed out that the motives of the teachers and rural mothers were culturally determined. Rural mothers, for example, were socialized to engage in activities (e.g. producing and selling artefacts such as clothes and pottery) that necessitated the avoidance of error.
3. The use of the L1 is not restricted to establishing shared goals for a task. Storch and Wigglesworth (2003), reported that six pairs of students (each with a shared L1) in a task used their L1 for four functions: (1) task management, (2) task clarification, (3) discussing vocabulary and meaning, and (4) deliberating about grammar points.
4. Dynamic assessment studies have typically investigated grammar. However, van Compernolle et al. (2016) and Qin and van Compernolle (in press) also applied dynamic assessment to socio-pragmatic aspects of language.

5. In fact, for Lantolf, SCT does not provide a rationale for TBLT because TBLT does not aim to develop the learner's scientific concepts of language.

11 Evaluating Task-Based Language Teaching

1. This list of the kinds of issues that can be addressed in micro-evaluations comes from the collection of practitioner research studies reported in Edwards and Willis (2005).
2. Prabhu (1990) pointed out a number of problems with Beretta's interpretation of the project.
3. Other examples of de facto action research studies of TBLT can be found in Edwards and Willis (2005), where teachers focused on some specific aspect of TBT that interested them and then investigated this in the context of their own classrooms.

12 Responding to the Critics of Task-Based Language Teaching

1. TBLT is not just informed by SLA research. It is also supported by the principles of sound education – see Chapter 6.
2. Despite his doubts about TBLT, Seedhouse (2017) has been closely involved in one of the most innovatory task-based projects in recent years where learners participate in a digital kitchen to carry out instructions about how to prepare different food dishes in a foreign language.
3. Skehan (1998) did suggest that tasks could be designed that would involve clusters of specific linguistic features. Such tasks could be considered semi-focused. It might be possible to pre-test in this case.

References

Abbs, B. & Freebairn, I. (1982). *Opening Strategies*. Harlow: Longman.

Ableeva, R. & Lantolf, J. (2011). Mediated dialogue and microgenesis of second language listening comprehension. *Assessment in Education: Principles, Policy and Practice* 18, 133–49.

Adams, R., Nuevo, A. & Egi, T. (2011). Explicit and implicit feedback, modified output, and SLA: Does explicit and implicit feedback promote learning and learner-learner interaction? *Modern Language Journal* 95, 42–63.

Ahmadian, M. J. (2012). The relationship between working memory capacity and L2 oral performance under task-based careful online planning condition. *TESOL Quarterly* 46, 165–75.

Ahmadian, M. J. & Mayo, M. (2018). Introduction recent trends in task-based language teaching and learning. In Ahmadian, M. & Mayo, M. (eds.), *Recent Perspectives on Task-Based Language Teaching* (pp. 1–8). Boston/Berlin: Mouton de Gruyter.

Ahmadian, M. J. & Tavakoli, M. (2011). The effects of simultaneous use of careful online planning and task repetition on accuracy, complexity, and fluency in EFL learners' oral production. *Language Teaching Research* 15, 35–59.

Aida, Y. (1994). Examination of Horwitz, Horwitz, and Cope's construct of foreign language anxiety: The case of students of Japanese. *The Modern Language Journal* 78(2), 155–68.

Al Khalil, M. (2011). Second language motivation: Its relationship to noticing, affect, and production in task-based interaction. PhD dissertation, Georgetown University.

Alderson, J. & Beretta, A. (eds.) (1992). *Evaluating Second Language Education*. Cambridge: Cambridge University Press.

Alderson, J., Clapham, C. & Steel, D. (1997). Metalinguistic knowledge, language aptitude and language proficiency. *Language Teaching Research* 1, 93–121.

Alderson, J. & Scott, M. (1992). Insiders, outsiders and participatory evaluation. In Alderson, J. & Beretta, A. (eds.), *Evaluating Second Language Education* (pp. 25–58). Cambridge: Cambridge University Press.

Aljaafreh, A. & Lantolf, J. (1994). Negative feedback as regulation and second language learning in the Zone of Proximal Development. *The Modern Language Journal* 78, 465–83.

Allwright, D. (2003). Exploratory practice: Rethinking practitioner research in language teaching. *Language Teaching Research* 7, 113–41.

Allwright, D. (2005). Developing principles for practitioner research: The case for exploratory practice. *Modern Language Journal* 89, 353–66.

Allwright, D. & Hanks, J. (2009). *The Developing Learner: An Introduction to Exploratory Practice*. Basingstoke: Palgrave Macmillan.

Ammar, A. & Spada, N. (2006). One size fits all? Recasts, prompts, and L2 learning. *Studies in Second Language Acquisition* 28, 543–74.

Aoki, M. (2016). English heads for elementary school in 2020 but hurdles abound. *Japan Times*, 5 September.

Appel, C. & Gilabert, R. (2002). Motivation and task performance in a task-based web-based tandem project. *ReCALL* 14, 16–31.

Arslanyilmaz, A. (2013). Computer-assisted foreign language instruction: Task based vs. form focused. *Journal of Computer Assisted Learning* 29, 303–18.

Aubrey, S. (2017a). Inter-cultural contact and flow in a task-based Japanese EFL classroom. *Language Teaching Research* 21, 717–34.

Aubrey, S. (2017b). Measuring flow in the EFL classroom: Learners' perceptions of inter-cultural and intra-cultural task-based interactions. *TESOL Quarterly* 51, 661–92.

Avermaet, P. & Gysen, S. (2006). From needs to tasks: Language learning needs in a task-based approach. In Van den Branbden, K. (ed.), *Task-Based Language Education: From Theory to Practice* (pp. 17–46). Cambridge: Cambridge University Press.

Bachman, L. F. (1990). *Fundamental Considerations in Language Testing*. Oxford: Oxford University Press.

Bachman, L. F. (2002). Some reflections on task-based language performance assessment. *Language Testing* 19, 453–76.

Bachman, L. F. & Palmer, A. S. (1996). *Language Testing in Practice*. Oxford: Oxford University Press.

Bachman, L. F. & Palmer, A. S. (2010). *Language Testing in Practice*, second edition. Oxford: Oxford University Press.

Baddeley, A. (2007). *Working Memory, Thought, and Action*. Oxford: Oxford University Press.

Bao, R. & Kirkebaek, M. (2013). Danish students' perceptions of task-based teaching in Chinese. In Kirkebæk, M., Du X.-Y. & Jensen A. (eds.), *Teaching and Learning Culture* (pp. 61–78). Rotterdam: Sense Publishers.

Baralt, M. (2014). Task complexity and task sequencing in traditional versus online language classes. In Baralt, M., Gilabert, R. & Robinson, P. (eds.), *Task Sequencing and Instructed Second Language Learning* (pp. 59–122). New York: Bloomsbury Academic.

Baralt, M. & Gurzynski-Weiss, L. (2011). Comparing learners' state anxiety during task-based interaction in computer-mediated and face-to-face communication. *Language Teaching Research* 15(2), 201–29.

Baralt, M., Gurzynski-Weiss, L. & Kim, Y. (2016). Engagement with language: How examining learners' affective and social engagement explains successful learner-generated attention to form. In Sato, M. & Ballinger, S. (eds.), *Peer*

Interaction and Second Language Learning: Pedagogical Potential and Research Agenda (pp. 209–40). Amsterdam: John Benjamins.

Bax, S. (2003). The end of CLT: A context approach to language teaching. *ELT Journal* 57, 278–87.

Benevides, M. & Valvona, C. (2008). *Widgets: A Task-Based Course in Practical English.* Hong Kong: Pearson Longman Asia ELT.

Beretta, A. (1989). Attention to form or meaning? Error treatment in the Bangalore project. *TESOL Quarterly* 23, 283–303.

Beretta, A. (1990). Implementation of the Bangalore project. *Applied Linguistics* 11, 321–37.

Beretta, A. & Davies, A. (1985). Evaluation of the Bangalore project. *ELT Journal* 39, 121–7.

Berwick, R. (1990). *Task Variation and Repair in English as a Foreign Language.* Kobe: Kobe University of Commerce/Institute of Economic Research.

Bialystok, E. (1994). Analysis and control in the development of second language proficiency. *Studies in Second Language Acquisition,* 16, 157–68.

Blake, R. (2000). Computer-mediated communication: A window on L2 Spanish interlanguage. *Language Learning & Technology* 4, 120–36.

Block, D. (2003). *The Social Turn in Second Language Acquisition.* Edinburgh: Edinburgh University Press.

Breen, M. (1984). Processes in syllabus design. In Brumfit, C. (ed.), *General English Syllabus Design* (pp. 47–60). Oxford: Pergamon.

Breen, M. (1989). The evaluation cycle for language learning tasks. In Johnson, R. K. (ed.), *The Second Language Curriculum* (pp. 187–206). Cambridge: Cambridge University Press.

Brindley, G. (2013). Task-based assessment. In Chapelle, C. A. (ed.), *The Encyclopedia of Applied Linguistics (online).* Oxford: Blackwell.

Brooks, F. & Donato, R. (1994). Vygotskyan approaches to understanding foreign language learner discourse during communicative tasks. *Hispania* 77, 262–74.

Brooks, L. & Swain, M. (2014). Contextualizing performances: Comparing performances during TOEFL iBTTM and real-life academic speaking activities. *Language Assessment Quarterly,* 11, 353–73.

Brown, G. & Yule, G. (1983). *Teaching the Spoken Language: An Approach Based on the Analysis of Conversational English.* Cambridge: Cambridge University Press.

Brown, G., Andersen, Shilcock & Yule, G. (1984). *Teaching Talk: Strategies for Production and Assessment.* Cambridge: Cambridge University Press.

Brown, J. D., Hudson, T., Norris, J. & Bonk, W. J. (2002). *An Investigation of Second Language Task-Based Performance Assessments.* Honolulu, HI: University of Hawai'i Press.

Bruner, J. S. (1960). *The Process of Education.* Cambridge, MA: Harvard University Press.

Bruton, A. (2002a). From tasking purposes to purposing tasks. *ELT Journal* 56, 280–8.

Bruton, A. (2002b). When and how language development in TBI? *ELT Journal* 56, 296–7.

Burns, A. (2010). *Doing Action Research for English Language Teachers: A Guide for Practitioners*. New York: Routledge.

Butler, Y. (2004). What level of English proficiency do elementary school teachers need to attain to teach EFL? Case studies from Korea, Taiwan, and Japan. *TESOL Quarterly* 38, 245–78.

Butler, Y. (2011). The implementation of communicative and task-based teaching in the Asia-Pacific region. *Annual Review of Applied Linguistics* 31, 36–57.

Butler, Y. (2017a). Young learners' rationales for self-assessing their performance with and without tasks. Unpublished paper in 7th International Conference on Task-Based Language Teaching, Barcelona.

Butler, Y. (2017b). Motivational elements of digital instructional games: A study of young L2 learners game designs. *Language Teaching Research* 21, 735–50.

Bygate, M. (2001). Effects of task repetition on the structure and control of oral language. In Bygate, M., Skehan, P. & Swain, M. (eds.), *Researching Pedagogic Tasks: Second Language Learning, Teaching and Testing* (pp. 23–48). Harlow: Longman.

Bygate, M. (2018). Dynamic systems: Theory and the issue of predictability in task-based language: Some implications for research and practice in TBLT. In Ahmadian, M. & Mayo, M. (eds.), *Recent Perspectives on Task-Based Language Teaching* (pp. 146–66). Boston/Berlin: Mouton de Gruyter.

Calvert, M. & Sheen, Y. (2015). Task-based language learning and teaching: An action-research study. *Language Teaching Research* 19, 226–44.

Cambridge English. (n.d.). Available at: www.cambridgeenglish.org.

Cameron, L. (2001). *Teaching Languages to Young Children*. Cambridge: Cambridge University Press.

Canale, M. (1983). On some dimensions of language proficiency. In Oller, J. (ed.), *Issues in Language Testing Research* (pp. 333–42). Rowley, MA: Newbury House.

Canale, M. & Swain, M. (1980). Theoretical bases of communicative approaches to second language teaching and testing. *Applied Linguistics* 1, 1–47.

Cancino, H., Rosansky, E. & Schumann, J. (1978). The acquisition of English negatives and interrogatives by native Spanish speakers. In Hatch, E. (ed.), *Second Language Acquisition*. Rowley, MA: Newbury House.

Candlin, C. (1987). Towards task-based language learning. In Candlin, C. & Murphy, D. (eds.), *Language Learning Tasks*. Englewood Cliffs, NJ: Prentice Hall International.

Canto, S., De Graaf, R. & Jauregi, K. (2014). Collaborative tasks for negotiation of intercultural meaning in virtual worlds and video-web communication. In González-Lloret, M. & Ortega, L. (eds.), *Technology-Mediated TBLT: Researching Technology and Tasks* (pp. 183–212). Amsterdam: John Benjamins.

Carless, D. (2003). Student use of the mother tongue in the task-based classroom. *ELT Journal* 62, 331–8.

Carless, D. (2004). Issues in teachers' reinterpretation of a task-based innovation in primary schools. *TESOL Quarterly* 38, 639–62.

Carr, W. & Kemmis, S. (1986). *Becoming Critical: Education, Knowledge and Action Research*. London: The Falmer Press.

Carroll, J. (1961). Fundamental considerations in testing for English language proficiency of foreign students. In Center for Applied Linguistics (ed.), *Testing the English Proficiency of Foreign Students* (pp. 30–40). Washington, DC: Center for Applied Linguistics.

Carroll, J. (1981). Twenty-five years of research on foreign language aptitude. In Diller, K. (ed.), *Individual Differences and Universals in Language Learning Aptitude*. Rowley, MA: Newbury House.

Carroll, J. & Sapon, S. (1959). *Modern Language Aptitude Test*. New York: The Psychological Corporation/Harcourt Brace Jovanovich.

Catani, M., Dell'Acqua, F. & De Schotten, M. (2013). A revised limbic system model for memory, emotion and behaviour. *Neuroscience and Biobehavioral Reviews* 37, 1724–37.

Cheng, Y., Horwitz, E. K. & Schallert, D. L. (1999). Language anxiety: Differentiating writing and speaking components. *Language Learning* 49(3), 417–46.

Colpin, M. & Gysen, S. (2006). Developing and introducing task-based language tests. In Van den Branden, K. (ed.), *Task-Based Language Education: From Theory to Practice* (pp. 151–74). Cambridge: Cambridge University Press.

Conway, A., Kane, M., Bunting, M., Hambrick, D. & Engle, R. (2005). Working memory span tasks: A methodological review and user's guide. *Psychonomic Bulletin & Review* 12, 769–86.

Cook, V. (2001). Using the first language in the classroom. *Canadian Modern Language Review* 57, 402–23.

Corder, S. P. (1967). The significance of learners' errors. *International Review of Applied Linguistics* 5, 161–9.

Côté, S. & Gaffney, C. (2018). The effect of synchronous computer-mediated communication on beginner L2 learners' foreign language anxiety and participation. *The Language Learning Journal* First view: 1–12.

Coughlan, P. & Duff, P. (1994). Same task, different activities: Analysis of a SLA task from an activity theory perspective. In Lantolf, J. & Appel, G. (eds.), *Vygotskyan Approaches to Second Language Research* (pp. 173–93). Norwood, NJ: Ablex.

Council of Europe. (2001). *Common European Framework of Reference for Language Learning, Teaching, and Assessment*. Cambridge: Cambridge University Press and Council of Europe.

Council of Europe. (2008). *Relating Language Examinations to the Common European Framework of Reference for Language Learning, Teaching, Assessment*. Available online at: www.coe.int/t/dg4/portfolio/documents/exampleswriting.pdg.

Cowan, N. (2015). Second-language use, theories of working memory, and the Vennian mind. In Wen, Z., Mota, M. B. & McNeill, A. (eds.), *Working Memory in Second Language Acquisition and Processing: Theories, Research, and Commentaries* (pp. 29–40). Clevedon: Multilingual Matters.

Cox, D. (2005). Can we predict language items for open tasks? In Edwards, C. & Willis, J. (eds.), *Teachers Exploring Tasks in English Language Teaching* (pp. 171–86). Basingstoke: Palgrave Macmillan.

Crespo, M. (2011). The effects of task complexity on L2 oral production as mediated by differences in working memory capacity. MA thesis, University of Barcelona.
Crookes, G. (1989). Planning and interlanguage variation. *Studies in Second Language Acquisition* 55, 367–83.
Crookes, G. & Schmidt, R. (1991). Motivation: Reopening the research agenda. *Language Learning* 41, 469–512.
Csikszentmihalyi, M. (1975). *Beyond Boredom and Anxiety.* San Francisco: Jossey-Bass.
Csikszentmihalyi, M. (1990). *Flow: The Psychology of Optimal Experience.* New York: Harper Perennial.
Cutrone, P. & Beh, S. (2014). *Welcome to Kyushu: A Task-Based Approach to EFL Learning Using Authentic Dialogues.* Tokyo: Shohakusha.
Dale, E. & Chall, J. (1948). A formula for predicting readability: Instructions. *Educational Research Bulletin* 27, 37–54.
Day, E. & Shapson, S. (1991). Integrating formal and functional approaches to language teaching in French immersion: An experimental study. *Language Learning* 41, 25–58.
De Bot, K. (1992). A bilingual production model: Levelt's 'Speaking' model adapted. *Applied Linguistics* 13, 1–24.
De Bot, K. & Larsen-Freeman, D. (2011). Researching second language development from a dynamic systems theory perspective. In Verspoor, M., de Bot, K. & Lowie, W. (eds.), *A Dynamic Approach to Second Language Development.* Amsterdam: John Benjamins.
De Graaf. (1997). *Effects of Explicit Instruction on Second Language Acquisition.* Netherlands: Holland Institute of Generative Linguistics.
De Jong, N. H., Groenhout, R., Schoonen, R. & Hulstijin, J. (2013). L2 fluency: Speaking style or proficiency? Correcting measures of L2 fluency for L1 behaviour. *Applied Psycholinguistics* 36, 1–23.
De la Fuente, M. J. (2006). Classroom L2 vocabulary acquisition: Investigating the role of pedagogical tasks and form-focused instruction. *Language Teaching Research* 10, 263–95.
DeKeyser, R. (1998). Beyond focus on form: Cognitive perspectives on learning and practicing second language grammar. In Doughty, C. & Williams, J. (eds.), *Focus on Form in Classroom Second Language Acquisition* (pp. 42–63). Cambridge: Cambridge University Press.
DeKeyser, R. (2007). Skill acquisition theory. In VanPatten, B. & Williams, J. (eds.), *Theories of Second Language Acquisition: An Introduction* (pp. 94–112). New York: Routledge.
Dembovskaya, S. (2009). Task-based instruction: The effect of motivational and cognitive pre-tasks on second language oral production. PhD thesis, University of Iowa.
De Ridder, I., Vangehuchten, L. & Gomez, M. (2007). Enhancing automaticity through task-based language learning. *Applied Linguistics* 28, 309–15.
Dewey, J. (1913). *Interest and Effort in Education.* Boston: Houghton Mifflin.
Dewey, J. (1938). *Experience and Education.* New York: Simon and Schuster.

Donato, R. (1994). Collective scaffolding in second language earning. In Lantolf, J. & Appel, G. (eds.), *Vygotskian Approaches to Second Language Research* (pp. 33–56). Norwood, NJ: Ablex.

Donato, R. (2000). Sociocultural contributions to understanding the foreign and second language classroom. In Lantolf, J. (ed.), *Sociocultural Theory and Second Language Learning* (pp. 27–50). Oxford: Oxford University Press.

Dörnyei, Z. (2002). The motivational basis of language learning tasks. In Robinson, P. (ed.), *Individual Differences and Instructed Language Learning*. Amsterdam: John Benjamins.

Dörnyei, Z. (2005). *The Psychology of the Language Learner: Individual Differences in Second Language Acquisition*. Mahwah, NJ: Lawrence Erlbaum Associates.

Dörnyei, Z. & Kormos, J. (2000). The role of individual and social variables in oral task performance. *Language Teaching Research* 4, 275–300.

Dörnyei, Z. & Ottó, I. (1998). Motivation in action: A process model of L2 motivation. *Working Papers in Applied Linguistics (Thames Valley University, London)* 4, 43–69.

Dörnyei, Z. & Ushioda, E. (eds.). (2009). *Motivation, Language Identity and the L2 Self*. Clevedon: Multilingual Matters.

Doughty, C. (2001). Cognitive underpinnings of focus on form. In Robinson, P. (ed.), *Cognition and Second Language Instruction*. Cambridge: Cambridge University Press.

Doughty, C. (2003). Instructed SLA: Constraints, compensation, and enhancement. In Doughty, C. & Long, M. (eds.), *Handbook of Second Language Acquisition* (pp. 256–310). New York: Blackwell.

Douglas, D. (2000). *Assessing Languages for Specific Purposes*. Cambridge: Cambridge University Press.

Dulay, H. & Burt, M. (1973). Should we teach children syntax? *Language Learning* 23, 245–58.

Dunn, W. & Lantolf, J. (1998). Vygotsky's zone of proximal development and Krashen's *i* +1: Incommensurable constructs; incommensurable theories. *Language Learning* 48, 411–42.

Duran, G. & Ramaut, G. (2006). Tasks for absolute beginners and beyond: Developing and sequencing tasks at basic proficiency levels. In Van den Branden, K. (ed.), *Task-Based Language Education: From Theory to Practice* (pp. 47–75). Cambridge: Cambridge University Press.

East, M. (2012). *Task-Based Language Teaching from the Teachers' Perspective: Insights from New Zealand*. Amsterdam: John Benjamins.

East, M. (2014). Encouraging innovation in a modern foreign language initial teacher education programme: What do beginning teachers make of task-based language teaching? *The Language Learning Journal* 42, 261–74.

East, M. (2018). 'If it is all about tasks, will they learn anything?' Perspectives on grammar instruction in the task-oriented classroom. In Ahmadian, M. & Mayo, M. (eds.), *Recent Perspectives on Task-Based Language Teaching* (pp. 217–31). Boston/Berlin: Mouton de Gruyter.

Eckerth, J. (2008). Task-based language learning and teaching – Old wine in new bottlers? In Eckerth, J. & Siekmann, S. (eds.), *Task-Based Language Learning and Teaching: Theoretical, Methodological, and Pedagogical Perspectives* (pp. 13–46). Frankfurt am Main: Peter Lang.

Edwards, C. & Willis, J. (eds.). (2005). *Teachers Exploring Tasks in English Language Teaching*. Basingstoke: Palgrave Macmillan.

Egbert, J. (2003). A study of flow theory in the foreign language classroom. *Modern Language Journal* 87, 499–518.

Egi, T. (2007). Interpreting recasts as linguistic evidence: The roles of linguistic target, length, and degree of change. *Studies in Second Language Acquisition* 29, 511–37.

Ehrman, M. E. & Oxford, R. L. (1995). Cognition plus: Correlates of language learning success. *The Modern Language Journal* 79, 67–89.

Eisenstein, M. (1980). Childhood bilingualism and adult language learning aptitude. *Applied Psychology* 29, 159–72.

Ekiert, M., Lampropoulou, S., Révész, A. & Torgerson, E. (2018). The effects of task-type and L2 proficiency on discourse appropriacy in oral task performance. In Taguchi, N. & Kim, Y. (eds.), *Task-Based Approaches to Teaching and Assessing Pragmatics* (pp. 247–64). Amsterdam: John Benjamins.

Elkhafaifi, H. (2005). Listening comprehension and anxiety in the Arabic language classroom. *The Modern Language Journal* 89(2), 206–20.

Ellis, D. (2011). The role of task complexity in the linguistic complexity of native-speaker output. Qualifying paper, PhD in Second Language Acquisition Program, College, Park, MD: University of Maryland.

Ellis, N. (2005). At the interface: Dynamic interactions of explicit and implicit language knowledge. *Studies in Second Language Acquisition* 27, 305–52.

Ellis, N. & Robinson, P. (2008). An introduction to cognitive linguistics and second language acquisition. In Robinson, P. & Ellis, N. (eds.), *Handbook of Cognitive Linguistics and Second Language Acquisition* (pp. 3–24). London: Routledge.

Ellis, R. (1984). *Classroom Second Language Development*. Oxford: Pergamon.

Ellis, R. (1987). Interlanguage variability in narrative discourse: Style shifting in the past tense. *Studies in Second Language Acquisition* 9, 1–19.

Ellis, R. (1993). Second language acquisition and the structural syllabus. *TESOL Quarterly* 27, 91–113.

Ellis, R. (1994). A theory of instructed second language acquisition. In Ellis, N. (ed.), *Implicit and Explicit Learning of Languages* (pp. 79–114). San Diego, CA: Academic Press

Ellis, R. (1997). *SLA Research and Language Teaching*. Oxford: Oxford University Press.

Ellis, R. (1999). *Learning a Second Language through Interaction*. Amsterdam: John Benjamins.

Ellis, R. (2000). Task-based research and language pedagogy. *Language Teaching Research* 4, 193–220.

Ellis, R. (2001). Non-reciprocal tasks, comprehension and second language acquisition. In Bygate, M., Skehan, P. & Swain, M. (eds.), *Researching Pedagogic Tasks: Second Language Learning, Teaching, and Testing* (pp. 49–74). Harlow: Longman.
Ellis, R. (2003). *Task-Based Language Learning and Teaching*. Oxford: Oxford University Press.
Ellis, R. (2005). Planning and task-based research: Theory and research. In Ellis, R. (ed.), *Planning and Task Performance in a Second Language*. Philadelphia: John Benjamins Publishing Company.
Ellis, R. (2007). The differential effects of corrective feedback on two grammatical structures. In Mackey, A. (ed.), *Conversational Interaction and Second Language Acquisition: A Series of Empirical Studies*. Oxford: Oxford University Press.
Ellis, R. (2008). Evaluating and researching grammar consciousness-raising tasks. In Rea-Dickens, P. & Germaine, K. (eds.), *Managing Evaluation and Innovation in Language Teaching* (pp. 220–52). London: Longman.
Ellis, R. (2009a). Task-based language teaching: Sorting out the misunderstandings. *International Journal of Applied Linguistics* 16, 221–46.
Ellis, R. (2009b). The differential effects of three types of task planning on the fluency, complexity, and accuracy in L2 oral production. *Applied Linguistics* 30, 474–509.
Ellis, R. (2010). Cognitive, social, and psychological dimensions of corrective feedback. In Batstone, R. (ed.), *Sociocognitive Perspectives on Language Use and Language Learning* (pp. 151–65). Oxford: Oxford University Press.
Ellis, R. (2011). Macro- and micro-evaluations of task-based teaching. In Tomlinson, B. (ed.), *Materials Development in Language Teaching*, second edition (pp. 212–35). Cambridge: Cambridge University Press.
Ellis, R. (2012). *Language Teaching Research and Language Pedagogy*. Malden, MA: Wiley-Blackwell.
Ellis, R. (2015a). Teachers evaluating tasks. In Bygate, M. (ed.), *Domains and Directions in the Development of TBLT* (pp. 247–70). Amsterdam: John Benjamins.
Ellis, R. (2015b). *Understanding Second Language Acquisition*, second edition. Oxford: Oxford University Press.
Ellis, R. (2016). Focus on form: A critical review. *Language Teaching Research* 20, 405–28.
Ellis, R. (2017a). Moving task-based language teaching forward. *Language Teaching* 50, 441–82.
Ellis, R. (2017b). The case for introducing task-based language teaching in Asian primary schools. Invited talk at Kansai University, Japan (4 July).
Ellis, R. (2018a). *Reflections on Task-Based Language Teaching*. Clevedon: Multilingual Matters.
Ellis, R. (2018b). Towards a modular curriculum for using tasks. Language Teaching Research. First view: https://doi.org/10.1177/1362168818 765315.

Ellis, R. (2019). Explicit versus implicit oral corrective feedback. In Hossein, N. & Kartchava, E. (eds.), *Cambridge Handbook on Corrective Feedback*. Cambridge: Cambridge University Press.
Ellis, R., Basturkmen, H. & Loewen, S. (2001). Pre-emptive focus on form in the ESL classroom. *TESOL Quarterly* 35, 407–32.
Ellis, R., Basturkmen, H. & Loewen, S. (2002). Doing focus-on-form. *System* 30, 419–32.
Ellis, R. & He, X. (1999). The roles of modified input and output in the incidental acquisition of word meanings. *Studies in Second Language Acquisition* 21, 285–301.
Ellis, R. & Heimbach, R. (1997). Bugs and birds: Children's acquisition of second language vocabulary through interaction. *System* 25, 247–59.
Ellis, R., Li, S. & Zhu, Y. (2018). The effects of pre-task explicit instruction on the performance of a focused task. *System* 80, 38–47.
Ellis, R., Loewen, S. & R. Erlam. (2006). Implicit and explicit corrective feedback and the acquisition of L2 grammar. *Studies in Second Language Acquisition* 28, 339–68.
Ellis, R. & Mifka-Provozic, N. (2013). Recasts, uptake and noticing. In Bergsleitner, J., Frota, S. & Yoshioka, J. (eds.), *Noticing and Second Language Acquisition: Studies in Honor of Richard Schmidt* (pp. 61–79). Honolulu, HI: University of Hawai'i at Manoa, National Foreign Language Center.
Ellis, R. & Shintani, N. (2014). *Exploring Language Pedagogy through Second Language Acquisition Research*. New York: Routledge.
Ellis, R., Tanaka, Y. & Yamazaki, A. (1994). Classroom interaction, comprehension, and the acquisition of L2 word meanings. *Language Learning* 44, 449–91.
Ellis, R. & Yuan, Y. (2004). The effects of planning on fluency, complexity, and accuracy in second language narrative writing. *Studies in Second Language Acquisition* 26, 59–84.
Engeström, Y. (1999). Activity theory and individual and social transformation. In Engeström, Y., Miettinen, R. & Punmäki, R.-L. (eds.), *Perspectives on Activity Theory* (pp. 19–38). Cambridge: Cambridge University Press.
Erlam, R. (2006). Elicited imitation as a measure of L2 implicit knowledge: An empirical validation study. *Applied Linguistics* 27, 464–91.
Erlam, R. (2016). I'm still not sure what a task is: Teachers designing language tasks. *Language Teaching Research* 20, 275–99.
Erlam, R. & Ellis, R. (2018). Task-based language teaching for beginner-level learners of L2 French: An exploratory study. *Canadian Modern Language Review* 74(1), 1–26.
Erlam, R., Ellis, R. & Batstone, R. (2013). Oral corrective feedback on L2 writing: Two approaches compared. *System* 41, 257–68.
Estaire, S. & Zanon. J. (1994). *Planning Classwork: A Task-Based Approach*. Oxford: Heinemann.
Ewald, J. D. (2007). Foreign language learning anxiety in upper-level classes: Involving students as researchers. *Foreign Language Annals* 40(1), 122–42.
Feuerstein, R., Falik, L. & Rynders, J. E. (1988). *Don't Accept Me as I Am. Helping Retarded Performers Excel*. New York: Plenum.

Foster, P. (1998). A classroom perspective on the negotiation of meaning. *Applied Linguistics* 19, 1–23.

Foster, P. (2001). Rules and routines: A consideration of their role in the task-based language production of native and non-native speakers. In Bygate, M., Skehan, P. & Swain, M. (eds.), *Researching Pedagogic Tasks: Second Language Learning, Teaching, and Testing* (pp. 75–93). Harlow: Longman.

Foster, P. & Skehan, P. (1996). The influence of planning on performance in task-based learning. *Studies in Second Language Acquisition* 18, 299–324.

Foster, P. & Skehan, P. (1999). The influence of source of planning and focus of planning on task-based performance. *Language Teaching Research* 3, 185–214.

Foster, P. & Skehan, P. (2012). Complexity, accuracy, fluency and lexis in task-based performance: A synthesis of the Ealing research. In Housen, A., Kuiken, F. & Vedder, I. (eds.), *Dimensions of L2 Performance and Proficiency: Complexity, Accuracy, and Fluency in SLA* (pp. 199–220). Amsterdam: John Benjamins.

Foster, P. & Skehan, P. (2013). The effects of post-task activities on the accuracy of language during task performance. *Canadian Modern Language Review* 69, 249–73.

Foster, P. & Tavakoli, P. (2009). Lexical diversity and lexical selection: A comparison of native and non-native speaker performance. *Language Learning* 59, 866–96.

Foster, P. & Wigglesworth, G. (2016). Capturing accuracy in second language performance: The case for a weighted clause ratio. In Mackey, A. (ed.), *Annual Review of Applied Linguistics* 36, 98–116.

Foster, P., Tonkyn, A. & Wigglesworth, G. (2000). Measuring spoken language: A unit for all reasons. *Applied Linguistics* 21, 354–75.

Fotos, S. & R. Ellis. (1991). Communicating about grammar: A task-based approach. *TESOL Quarterly* 25, 605–28.

Fredricks, J., Blumenfeld, P. & Paris, A. (2004). School engagement: Potential of the concept, state of evidence. *Review of Educational Research* 74, 59–105.

Fried-Booth, D. (1986). *Project Work*. Oxford: Oxford University Press.

Fried-Booth, D. (1989). *COLLINS COBUILD English Course Tests*. London: Collins.

Fu, M. & Li, S. (2017). The associations between the cognitive processes of task performance and working memory. *Modern Foreign Languages* 40, 114–24.

Fulcher, G. (1996). Does thick description lead to smart tests? A data-based approach to rating scale construction. *Language Testing* 13, 208–28.

Gal'perin, P. I. (1989). Mental actions as a basis for the formation of thoughts and images. *Soviet Psychology* 27, 45–64.

Galaczi, E. (2008). Peer–peer interaction in a speaking test: The case of the first certificate in English examination. *Language Assessment Quarterly* 5, 89–119.

Galaczi, E. & ffrench, A. (2010). Context validity. In Taylor, L. (ed.), *Examining Speaking: Studies in Language Testing 30* (pp. 112–70). Cambridge: Cambridge University Press.

Gardner, R. C. (1985). *Social Psychology and Second Language Learning: The Role of Attitudes and Motivation*. London: Edward Arnold.

Gardner, R. C. & Lambert, W. E. (1965). Language aptitude, intelligence, and second-language achievement. *Journal of Educational Psychology* 56, 191–9.

Gass, S. (1997). *Input, Interaction, and the Development of Second Languages*. Mahwah, NJ: Erlbaum.

Gass, S. (1998). Apples and oranges: Or why apples are not oranges and don't need to be. A response to Firth and Wagner. *Modern Language Journal* 82, 83–90.

Gass, S. & Mackey, A. (2000). *Stimulated Recall Methodology in Second Language Research*. Mahwah, NJ: Erlbaum

Gass, S. & Mackey, A. (2007). Input, interaction, and output in second language acquisition. In VanPatten, B. & Williams, J. (eds.), *Theories in Second Language Acquisition* (pp. 175–200). London: LEA.

Gass, S. & Mackey, A. (2015). Input, interaction, and output in second language acquisition. In VanPatten, B. & Williams, J. (eds.), *Theories in Second Language Acquisition* (pp. 180–206). New York: Routledge.

Gass, S. & Varonis, E. (1985). Task variation and nonnative/nonnative negotiation of meaning. In Gass, S. & Madden, C. (eds.), *Input in Second Language Acquisition*. Rowley, MA: Newbury House.

Gass, S. & Varonis, E. (1994). Input, interaction and second language production. *Studies in Second Language Acquisition* 16, 283–302.

Gass, S. & Varonis, M. (1984). The effect of familiarity on the comprehension of nonnative speech. *Language Learning* 34, 65–89.

Gass, S., Mackey, A., Alvarez-Torres, M. & Fernandez-Garcia, M. (1999). The effects of task repetition on linguistic output. *Language Learning* 49, 549–81.

Gilabert, R. & Barón, J. (2013). The impact of increasing task complexity on L2 pragmatic moves. In Mackey, A. & McDonough, K. (eds.), *Second Language Interaction in Diverse Educational Settings* (pp. 45–69). Amsterdam: John Benjamins.

Gilabert, R. & Munoz, C. (2010). Differences in attainment and performance in a foreign language: The role of working memory capacity. *The International Journal of Engineering and Science* 10, 19–42.

Gilabert, R., Baron, J. & Levkina, M. (2011). Manipulating task complexity across task types and modes. In Robinson, P. (ed.), *Second Language Task Complexity* (pp. 105–40). Amsterdam: John Benjamins.

Gilabert, R., Baron, J. & Llanes, A. (2009). Manipulating cognitive complexity across task types and its impact on learners' interaction during oral performance. *IRAL* 47, 367–95.

Gilabert, R., Manchón, R. & Vasylets, O. (2016). Mode in theoretical and empirical TBLT research: Advancing research agendas. *Annual Review of Applied Linguistics* 36, 117–35.

Givon, T. (1985). Function, structure, and language acquisition. In Slobin, D. (ed.), *The Crosslinguistic Study of Language Acquisition, Vol. 1* (pp. 1008–25). Hillsdale, NJ: Lawrence Erlbaum Associates.

Gong, Y. (2014). *New Notion English*. Beijing: Foreign Language Teaching and Research Press.
Gong, Y. (2015). *Reconceptualising English Education: A Multi-Goal Approach to English Curriculum Design for School-Age Learners*. Beijing: CIP.
González-Lloret, M. & Nielson, K. (2015). Evaluating TBLT: The case of a task-based Spanish program. *Language Teaching Research* 19, 525–49.
González-Lloret, M. & Ortega, L. (eds). (2015). *Technology-Mediated TBLT: Researching Technology and Tasks*. Amsterdam: John Benjamins.
Goo, J. (2012). Corrective feedback and working memory capacity in interaction-driven learning. *Studies in Second Language Acquisition* 31, 445–74.
Goo, J., Granema, G., Novella, M. & Yilmaz, Y. (2015). Implicit and explicit instruction in L2 learning; Norris & Ortega (2000) revisited and updated. In Rebuschat, P. (ed.), *Implicit and Explicit Learning of Languages* (pp. 443–82). Amsterdam: John Benjamins.
Goo, J. & Mackey, A. (2013). The case against the case against recasts. *Studies in Second Language Acquisition* 35, 127–65.
Granena, G. (2013). Individual differences in sequence learning ability and second language acquisition in early childhood and adulthood. *Language Learning* 63, 665–704.
Granena, G. (2015). Cognitive aptitudes for implicit and explicit learning and information-processing styles: An individual differences study. *Applied Psycholinguistics* 37(3), 577–600.
Granena, G. (2016). Individual versus interactive task-based performance through voice-based computer mediated interaction. *Language Learning and Technology* 30, 40–59.
Grice, P. (1975). Logic and conversation. In Cole, P. & Morgan, J. (eds.), *Syntax and Semantics. 3: Speech Acts* (pp. 41–58). New York: Academic Press.
Guará Tavares, M. (2011). Pre-task planning, working memory capacity, and L2 speech performance. *Organon* 51, 245–66.
Gurzynski-Weiss, L. & Baralt, M. (2014). Exploring learner perception and use of task-based interactional feedback in FTF and CMC modes. *Studies in Second Language Acquisition* 35, 1–28.
Gutierrez, G. A. G. (2014). The third dimension: A sociocultural theory approach to the design and evaluation of 3D virtual worlds tasks. In González-Lloret, M. & Ortega, L. (eds.), *Technology-Mediated TBLT: Researching Technology and Tasks* (pp. 213–238). Amsterdam: John Benjamins.
Hadley. G. (2013). Review of task-based language teaching from the teacher's perspective. *System* 41, 194–6.
Hall, G. & Cook, G. (2012). Own-language use in language teaching and learning. *Language Teaching* 45, 271–308.
Halliday, M. (1973). *Explorations in the Functions of Language*. London: Arnold.
Han, Z.-H., Park, E. & Combs, C. (2008). Textual enhancement of input: Issues and possibilities. *Applied Linguistics* 29, 597–618.
Harley, B. (1989). Functional grammar in French immersion: A classroom experiment. *Applied Linguistics* 19, 331–59.

Harley, B. & Hart, D. (1997). Language aptitude and second language proficiency in classroom learners of different starting ages. *Studies in Second Language Acquisition* 19, 379–400.

Harley, B. & Hart, D. (2002). Age, aptitude and second language learning on a bilingual exchange. In Robinson, P. (ed.), *Individual Differences and Instructed Language Learning*. Amsterdam: John Benjamins.

Harley, B., Allen, J. P. B., Cummins, J. & Swain, M. (1990). *The Development of Second Language Proficiency*. Cambridge: Cambridge University Press.

Harris, J. & Leeming, P. (2016). *On Task 2*. Tokyo: Abax.

Harrison, A. (1982). Student-centered testing: Assessing communication in progress. *Levende Talen* 372, 401–10.

Hedge, T. (2000). *Teaching and Learning in the Language Classroom*. Oxford: Oxford University Press.

Henzl, V. (1979). Foreigner talk in the classroom. *International Review of Applied Linguistics* 17, 159–67.

Hoey, M. (1983). *On the Surface of Discourse*. London: George Allen and Unwin.

Horwitz, E., Horwitz, M. & Cope, J. (1986). Foreign language classroom anxiety. *Modern Language Journal* 70(2), 125–32.

Housen, A. & Kuiken, F. (2009). Complexity, accuracy, and fluency in second language acquisition. *Applied Linguistics* 30(4), 461–73.

Howatt, A. P. R. (1984). *A History of English Language Teaching*. Oxford: Oxford University Press.

Hu, R. (2013). Task-based language teaching: Responses from Chinese teachers of English. *The Electronic Journal for English as a Second Language* 16(4), n.p.

Hulstijn, J. (2015). *Language Proficiency in Native and Non-Native Speakers*. Amsterdam: John Benjamins.

Hwu, F., Wei, P. & Sun, S. (2014). Aptitude-treatment interaction effects on explicit rule learning: A latent growth curve analysis. *Language Teaching Research* 18, 294–319.

Hyland, F. (2003). Focusing on form: Student engagement with teacher feedback. *System* 31, 217–30.

Hymes, D. (1971). *On Communicative Competence*. Philadelphia: University of Pennsylvania Press.

Inoue, C. (2013). *Task Equivalence in Speaking Tests*. Bern: Peter Lang.

Inoue, C. (2016). A comparative study of the variables used to measure syntactic complexity and accuracy in task-based research. *The Language Learning Journal* 1, 1–18.

Ishikawa, T. (2007). The effect of manipulating task complexity along the +/- here-and-now dimension on L2 written narrative discourse. In Garcia Mayo, M. del P. (ed.), *Investigating Tasks in Formal Language Learning* (pp. 136–56). Clevedon: Multilingual Matters.

Iwashita, N., McNamara. T. & Elder, C. (2001). Can we predict task difficulty in an oral proficiency test? Exploring the potential of an information-processing approach to task design. *Language Learning* 51, 401–36.

Jackson, D. O. & Suethanapornkul, S. (2013). The cognition hypothesis: A synthesis and meta-analysis of research on second language task complexity. *Language Learning* 63, 330–67.

Jauregi, K., de Graaff, R., van den Bergh, H. & Kriz, M. (2012). Native/non-native speaker interactions through video-web communication: A clue for enhancing motivation? *Computer Assisted Language Learning* 25(1), 1–19.

Jeon, I.-J. & Hahn, J.-W. (2006). Exploring EFL teachers' perceptions of task-based language teaching: A case study of Korean secondary school classroom practice. *Asian EFL Journal* 8, 123–43.

Jepson, K. (2005). Conversation and negotiated interactions in text and voice chat rooms. *Learning & Technology* 9, 79–98.

Jobard G., Crivello F. & Tzourio-Mazoyer N. (2003). Evaluation of the dual route theory of reading: A meta-analysis of 35 neuroimaging studies. *Neuroimage* 20, 693–712.

Johnson, K. (1982). *Communicative Syllabus Design and Methodology*. Oxford: Pergamon.

Johnson, K. (2000). What task designers do. *Language Teaching Research* 4, 301–21.

Johnson, K. (2005). Fighting fossilization: Language at different stages in the task cycle. In Edwards, C. & Willis, J. (eds.), *Teachers Exploring Tasks in English Language Teaching* (pp. 191–200). Basingstoke: Palgrave Macmillan.

Juffs, A. & Harrington, M. (2012). Aspects of working memory in L2 learning. *Language Teaching* 44, 137–66.

Kahnemann, D. (2011). *Thinking, Fast and Slow*. London: Penguin.

Kahng, J. (2014). Exploring utterance and cognitive fluency of L1 and L2 English speakers: Temporal measures and stimulated recall. *Language Learning* 64, 809–54.

Keenan, J., MacWhinney, B. & Mayhew, D. (1977). Pragmatics in memory: A study of natural conversation. *Journal of Verbal Learning and Verbal Behavior* 16, 549–60.

Kelly, C. & Kelly, E. (1996). *The Snoop Detective School Conversation Book*. Tokyo: Macmillan Language House.

Khabbazbashi, N. (2017). Topic and background knowledge effects on performance in speaking assessment. *Language Testing* 34, 23–48.

Kiele, R. & Rea-Dickens, P. (2005). *Program Evaluation in Language Education*. Basingstoke: Palgrave Macmillan.

Kim, Y. (2009). The effects of task complexity on learner-learner interactions. *System* 37, 254–68.

Kim, Y. (2012). Task complexity, learning opportunities, and Korean EFL learners' question development. *Studies in Second Language Acquisition* 34, 627–58.

Kim, Y. (2013). Effects of pre-task modelling on attention to form and question development. *TESOL Quarterly* 47, 8–35.

Kim, J. & Lantolf, J. (2018). Developing understanding of sarcasm in L2 English through explicit instruction. *Language Teaching Research* 22, 209–29.

Kim, Y., Payant, C. & Pearson, P. (2015). The intersection of task-based interaction, task complexity, and working memory. *Studies in Second Language Acquisition* 37, 549–81.

Kim, Y. & Taguchi, N. (2015). Promoting task-based pragmatics instruction in EFL classroom context: The role of task complexity. *Modern Language Journal* 99, 656–77.

Kim, Y. & Tracy-Ventura, N. (2011). Task complexity, language anxiety, and the development of the simple past. In Robinson, P. (ed.), *Second Language Task Complexity: Researching the Cognition Hypothesis of Language Learning and Performance* (pp. 287–306). Amsterdam: John Benjamins.

Kim, Y. & Tracy-Ventura, N. (2013). The role of task repetition in L2 performance development: What needs to be repeated during task-based interaction? *System* 41, 829–40.

Klein, W. & Perdue, C. (1997). The basic variety (or: couldn't natural languages be much simpler?). *Second Language Research* 13, 301–47.

Kormos, J. (2006). *Speech Production and Second Language Acquisition*. Mahwah, NJ: Lawrence Erlbaum.

Kormos, J. (2011). Speech production and the cognition hypothesis. In Robinson, P. (ed.), *L2 Task Complexity: Researching the Cognition Hypothesis of Language Learning and Performance* (pp. 39–60). Amsterdam: John Benjamins.

Kormos, J. & Dörnyei Z. (2004). The interaction of linguistic and motivational variables in second language task performance. *Zeitschrift für interkulturellen Fremdsprachenunterricht* 9, 1–19.

Kormos, J., Kiddle, T. & Csizer, K. (2011). Systems of goals, attitudes, and self-related beliefs in second-language learning motivation. *Applied Linguistics* 32, 495–516.

Kormos, J. & Trebits, A. (2011). Working memory capacity and narrative task performance. In Robinson, P. (ed.), *Second Language Task Complexity: Researching the Cognition Hypothesis of Language Learning and Performance* (pp. 267–86). Amsterdam: John Benjamins.

Krashen, S. (1981a). Aptitude and attitude in relation to second language acquisition and learning. In Diller, K. (ed.), *Individual Differences and Universals in Language Learning Aptitude*. Rowley, MA: Newbury House.

Krashen, S. (1981b). *Second Language Acquisition and Second Language Learning*. Oxford: Pergamon.

Krashen, S. (1985). *The Input Hypothesis: Issues and Implications*. London: Longman.

Krashen, S. & Terrell, T. (1983). *The Natural Approach: Language Acquisition in the Classroom*. Oxford: Pergamon.

Kuiken, F. & Vedder, I. (2008). Cognitive tasks complexity and written output in Italian and French as a foreign language. *Journal of Second Language Writing* 17, 48–60.

Kumaravadivelu, B. (2001). Toward a postmethod pedagogy. *TESOL Quarterly* 35, 537–60.

Lai, C. (2015). Task-based language teaching in the Asian context: Where are we now and where are we going? In Thomas, M. & Reinders, H. (eds.), *Contemporary Task-Based Teaching in Asia* (pp. 12–29). London: Bloomsbury.

Lai, C. & Li, G. (2011). Technology and task–based teaching: A critical review. *CALICO Journal* 28, 498–521.

Lam, D. M. K. (2018). What counts as 'responding'? Contingency on previous speaker contribution as a feature of interactional competence. *Language Testing* 35, 377–401.

Lambert, C. (1997). Motivation and personal investment in the learning process. *Journal of Nanzan Junior College* 24, 55–88.

Lambert, C. (1998). The role of the learner in classroom task performance. *Journal of Nanzan Junior College* 26, 85–101.

Lambert, C. (2002). Task sequencing and affective performance variables. *Kitakyushu University Faculty of Foreign Studies Bulletin* 103, 97–175.

Lambert, C. (2004). Reverse-engineering communication tasks. *ELT Journal* 58, 18–27.

Lambert, C. (2010). Task-based needs analysis: Putting principles into practice. *Language Teaching Research* 14, 99–112.

Lambert, C. (2017). Tasks, affect and second language performance. *Language Teaching Research* 21(6), 657–64.

Lambert, C., Gong, Q. & Zhang, G. (in press). Learner-generated content and the lexical recall of beginning-level learners of Chinese as a Foreign Language. Available at: www.academia.edu/39149761/_2019_Learner-generated_content_and_the_lexical_recall_of_beginning-level_learners_of_Chinese_as_a_Foreign_Language.

Lambert, C. & Hailes, A. (2002). *Simulations: A Task-Based Approach to Conversational English*. Kitakyushu: The University of Kitakyushu, Faculty of Foreign Studies.

Lambert, C., Kormos, J. & Minn, D. (2016). Task repetition and second language speech processing. *Studies in Second Language Acquisition* 38, 1–30.

Lambert, C. & Minn, D. (2007). Personal investment in L2 task design and learning: A case study of two Japanese learners of English. *ELIA: Estudios de Lingüística Inglesa Aplicada* 7, 127–48.

Lambert, C., Philp, J. & Nakamura, S. (2017). Learner-generated content and engagement in L2 task performance. *Language Teaching Research* 21, 665–80.

Lambert, C. & Robinson, P. (2014). Learning to perform narrative task: A semester long study of task sequencing effects. In Baralt, M., Gilabert, R. & Robinson, P. (eds.), *Task Sequencing and Instructed Second Language Learning* (pp. 207–30). London: Bloomsbury.

Lambert, C. & Zhang, G. (2019). Engagement in the use of English and Chinese as second languages: The roles of learner-generated and teacher-generated content. *Modern Language Journal* 103(2), 391–411.

Lamendella, J. T. (1977). The limbic system in human communication. In Whitaker, H. & Whitaker, H. A. (eds.), *Studies in Neurolinguistics, Volume 3* (pp. 154–222). New York: Academic Press.
Lantolf, J. (2000). Introducing sociocultural theory. In Lantolf, J. (ed.), *Sociocultural Theory and Second Language Learning* (pp. 1–26). Oxford: Oxford University Press.
Lantolf, J. (2007). Conceptual knowledge and instructed second language learning: A sociocultural perspective. In Fotos, S. & Nassaji, H. (eds.), *Form-Focused Instruction and Teacher Education: Studies in Honour of Rod Ellis* (pp. 35–54). Oxford: Oxford University Press.
Lantolf, J. (2009). Dynamic assessment: The dialectic integration of instruction and assessment. *Language Teaching* 42, 355–68.
Lantolf, J., Kurtz, L. & Kisselev, O. (2016). Understanding the revolutionary character of L2 development in the ZPD: Why levels of mediation matter. *Language and Social Cultural Theory* 3, 153–71.
Lantolf, J. P. & Poehner, M. E. (2014). *Sociocultural Theory and the Pedagogical Imperative in L2 Education: Vygotskian Praxis and the Theory/Practice Divide*. New York: Routledge.
Lantolf, J. & Thorne, S. (2006). *Sociocultural Theory and the Genesis of Second Language Development*. Oxford: Oxford University Press.
Lantolf, J., Thorne, S. & Poehner, M. (2015). Sociocultural theory and second language acquisition. In VanPatten, B. & Williams, J. (eds.), *Theories in Second Language Acquisition* (pp. 207–26). New York: Routledge.
Lantolf, J. & Zhang, X. (2017). Concept-based language instruction. In Loewen, S. & Sato, M. (eds.), *The Routledge Handbook of Instructed Language Acquisition* (pp. 146–65). New York: Routledge.
Larsen-Freeman, D. (2000). *Techniques and Principles in Language Teaching*, second edition. New York: Oxford University Press.
Laufer, B. & Hulstijn, J. (2001). Incidental vocabulary acquisition in a second language: The construct of task-induced involvement. *Applied Linguistics* 22, 1–26.
Leaver, B. & J. Willis. (2004). *Task-Based Instruction in Foreign Language Education*. Washington, DC: Georgetown University Press.
Lee, A. & Lyster, R. (2016). The effects of corrective feedback on instructed L2 speech production. *Studies in Second Language Acquisition* 38, 35–64.
Lee, L. (2005). Using web-based instruction to promote active learning: Learners' perspectives. *CALICO Journal* 23, 139–56.
Lee, S. & Huang, S. (2008). Visual input enhancement and grammar learning. A meta-analytic review. *Studies in Second Language Acquisition* 30, 307–31.
Leontiev, A. (1978). *Activity, Consciousness, and Personality*. Englewood Cliffs, NJ: Prentice Hall.
Leontiev, A. (1981). *Psychology and the Language Learning Process*. London: Pergamon.
Leow, R. (2015). Explicit and implicit learning in the L2 classroom: Processes and products. In Rebuschat, P. (ed.), *Implicit and Explicit Learning of Languages* (pp. 47–68). Amderdam: John Benjamins.

Leung, J. H. C. & Williams, J. N. (2011). The implicit learning of mappings between forms and contextually derived meanings. *Studies in Second Language Acquisition* 33, 33–55.

Levelt, W. J. (1989). *Speaking: From Intention to Articulation*. Cambridge, MA: The MIT Press.

Levelt, W. J. (1999). Producing spoken language: A blueprint of the speaker. In Brown, C. & Hagoort, P. (eds.), *Neurocognition of Language* (pp. 83–122). Oxford: Oxford University Press.

Lewis, M. (1993). *The Lexical Approach*. Hove: Language Teaching Publications.

Li, D. (1998). It's always more difficult than you planned: Teachers' perceived difficulties in introducing the communicative approach in South Korea. *TESOL Quarterly* 32, 677–703.

Li, L., Chen, J. & L. Sun. (2015). The effects of different lengths of pre-task planning time on L2 learners' oral test performance. *TESOL Quarterly* 49, 38–66.

Li, Q. (2014). Get it right in the end: The effects of post-task transcribing on learners' oral performance. In Skehan, P. (ed.), *Processing Perspectives on Task Performance* (pp. 129–54). Amsterdam: John Benjamins.

Li, S. (2010). The effectiveness of corrective feedback in SLA: A meta-analysis. *Language Learning* 60, 309–65.

Li, S. (2013a). The interactions between the effects of implicit and explicit feedback and individual differences in language analytic ability and working memory. *Modern Language Journal* 97, 634–54.

Li, S. (2013b). The differential roles of language analytic ability and working memory in mediating the effects of two types of feedback on the acquisition of an opaque linguistic structure. In Sanz, C. & Lado, B. (eds.), *Individual Differences, L2 Development & Language Program Administration: From Theory to Application*. Boston: Cengage Learning.

Li, S. (2015). The associations between language aptitude and second language grammar acquisition: A meta-analytic review of five decades of research. *Applied Linguistics* 36, 385–408.

Li, S. (2016). The construct validity of language aptitude. *Studies in Second Language Acquisition* 38, 801–42.

Li, S. (2017). Teacher and learner beliefs about corrective feedback. In Nassaji, H. & Kartchava, E. (eds.), *Corrective Feedback in Second Language Teaching and Learning* (pp. 143–57). New York: Routledge.

Li, S., Ellis, R. & Zhu, Y. (2016). Task-based versus task-supported language instruction: An experimental study. *Annual Review of Applied Linguistics* 36, 205–29.

Li, S., Ellis, R. & Zhu, Y. (2017). The influence of pre-task grammar instruction on task performance and L2 learning in task-supported language instruction: A process-product study.

Li, S. & Fu, M. (2017). Strategic and unpressured within-task planning and their associations with working memory. *Language Teaching Research* 22, 230–53.

Li, S., Zhu, Y. & Ellis, R. (2016). The effects of the timing of corrective feedback on the acquisition of a new linguistic structure. *Modern Language Journal* 100, 276–95.

Lin, T.-B. & Wu, C.-W. (2012). Teachers' perceptions of task-based language teaching in English classrooms in Taiwanese high schools. *TESOL Journal* 3, 586–609.

Linck, J., Osthus, P., Koeth, J. & Bunting, M. (2014). Working memory and second language comprehension and production: A meta-analysis. *Psychonomic Bulletin & Review* 21, 861–83.

Littlewood, W. (2007). Communicative and task-based language teaching in East Asian classrooms. *Language Teaching* 40, 243–9.

Littlewood, W. (2014). Communication-oriented teaching: Where are we now? Where do we go from here? *Language Teaching* 47, 249–362.

Loewen, S. (2005). Incidental focus on form and language learning. *Studies in Second Language Acquisition* 27, 361–86.

Loewen, S., Erlam, R. & Ellis, R. (2009). The incidental acquisition of 3rd person –s as implicit and explicit knowledge. In Ellis, R., Loewen, S., Elder, C., Erlam, R., Philp, J. & Reinders, H. (eds.), *Implicit and Explicit Knowledge in Second Language Learning, Testing and Teaching* (pp. 262–80). Bristol: Multilingual Matters.

Loewen, S. & Nabei, T. (2007). The effect of oral corrective feedback on implicit and explicit L2 knowledge. In Mackey, A. (ed.), *Conversational Interaction and Second Language Acquisition: A Series of Empirical Studies* (pp. 361–78). Oxford: Oxford University Press.

Long, M. (1980). Input, interaction and second language acquisition. Unpublished PhD dissertation, University of California at Los Angeles.

Long, M. (1983). Native-speaker/non-native speaker conversation and the negotiation of comprehensible input. *Applied Linguistics* 4, 126–41.

Long, M. (1985). A role for instruction in second language acquisition: Task-based language teaching. In Hyltenstam, K. & Pienemann, M. (eds.), *Modelling and Assessing Second Language Acquisition*. Clevedon: Multilingual Matters.

Long, M. (1989). Task, group, and task-group interactions. *University of Hawaii Working Papers in ESL* 8, 1–26.

Long, M. (1990). Maturation constraints on language development. *Studies in Second Language Acquisition* 12, 251–85.

Long, M. (1991a). Focus on form in task-based language teaching. In Lambert, R. & Shohamy, E. (eds.), *Language Policy and Pedagogy: Essays in Honour of A. Ronald Walton* (pp. 179–92). Amsterdam: John Benjamins.

Long, M. (1991b). Focus on form: A design feature in language teaching methodology. In de Bot, K., Ginsberg, R. & Kramsch, C. (eds.), *Foreign Language Research in Cross-Cultural Perspective* (pp. 39–52). Amsterdam/Philadelphia: John Benjamins.

Long, M. (1996). The role of the linguistic environment in second language acquisition. In Ritchie, W. & Bhatia, T. (eds.), *Handbook of Second Language Acquisition* (pp. 121–58).) San Diego, CA: Academic Press.

Long, M. (1998). SLA breaking the siege. *University of Hawaii Working Papers in ESL* 17, 79–129.

Long, M. (2005). Methodological issues in learner needs analysis. In Long, M. (ed.), *Second Language Needs Analysis* (pp. 19–76). Cambridge: Cambridge University Press.

Long, M. (2006). *Problems in SLA*. Mahwah, NJ: Lawrence Erlbaum.
Long, M. (2015). *Second Language Acquisition and Task-Based Language Teaching*. Oxford: Wiley-Blackwell.
Long, M. (2016). In defence of tasks and TBLT: Nonissues and real issues. *Annual Review of Applied Linguistics* 36, 5–33.
Long, M. H., Adams, L., McLean, M. & Castaños, F. (1976). Doing things with words: Verbal interaction in lockstep and small group classroom situations. In Fanselow, J. & Crymes, R. (eds.), *On TESOL '76* (pp. 137–53). Washington, DC: TESOL.
Long, M. & Norris, J. (2000). Task-based teaching and assessment. In Byram, M. (ed.), *Encyclopedia of Language Teaching* (pp. 597–603). London: Routledge.
Long, M. & Porter, P. (1985). Group work, interlanguage talk, and second language acquisition. *TESOL Quarterly* 19, 207–28.
Long, M. & Ross, S. (1993). Modifications that preserve language and content. In Tickoo, M. (ed.), *Simplification: Theory and Application* (pp. 29–52). Singapore: SEAMEO Regional Language Centre.
Loschky, L. (1994). Comprehensible input and second language acquisition: What is the relationship. *Studies in Second Language Acquisition* 16, 303–23.
Loschky, L. & Bley-Vroman, R. (1993). Grammar and task-based methodology. In Crookes, G. & Gass, S. (eds.), *Tasks and Language Learning: Integrating Theory and Practice* (pp. 123–67). Clevedon: Multilingual Matters.
Loumpourdi, L. (2005). Developing from PPP to TBL: A focused grammar task. In Edwards, C. & Willis, J. (eds.), *Teachers Exploring Tasks in English Language Teaching* (pp. 33–9). Basingstoke: Palgrave Macmillan.
Lovblad, K., Schaller, K. & Vargas, M. (2013). The fornix and limbic system. *Seminars in Ultrasound, CT and MRI* 35, 459–73.
Lynch, T. (2009). Responding to learners' perceptions of feedback: The use of comparators in second language speaking courses. *Innovation in Language Learning and Teaching* 3, 191–203.
Lyster, R. (1998). Recasts, repetition, and ambiguity in L2 classroom discourse. *Studies in Second Language Acquisition* 20, 51–81.
Lyster, R. (2001). Negotiation of form, recasts, and explicit correction in relation to error types and learner repair in immersion classrooms. *Language Learning* 51, 265–301.
Lyster, R. (2004). Differential effects of prompts and recasts in form-focused instruction. *Studies in Second Language Acquisition* 26, 399–432.
Lyster, R. (2007). *Learning and Teaching Languages through Content: A Counterbalanced Approach*. Amsterdam/Philadelphia: John Benjamins.
Lyster, R. & Mori, H. (2006). Interactional feedback and instructional counterbalance. *Studies in Second Language Acquisition* 28, 269–300.
Lyster, R. & Ranta, L. (1997). Corrective feedback and learner uptake. *Studies in Second Language Acquisition* 19, 37–66.
Lyster, R. & Ranta, L. (2013). Counterpoint piece: The case for variety in corrective feedback research. *Studies in Second Language Acquisition* 35, 167–84.
Lyster, R. & Saito, K. (2010). Oral feedback in classroom SLA: A meta-analysis. *Studies in Second Language Acquisition* 32, 265–302.

Macaro, E. (2001). Analysing student teachers' codeswitching in foreign language classrooms: Theories and decision making. *The Modern Language Journal* 85, 531–48.

MacIntyre, P. D. & Gardner, R. C. (1994). The subtle effects of language anxiety on cognitive processing in the second language. *Language Learning* 44(2), 283–305.

Mackey, A. (1999). Input, interaction and second language development: An empirical study of question formation in ESL. *Studies in Second Language Acquisition* 21, 557–87.

Mackey, A. (2006). Feedback, noticing and second language learning. *Applied Linguistics* 27, 405–430.

Mackey, A. & Philp, J. (1998). Conversational interaction and second language development: Recasts, responses and red herrings. *The Modern Language Journal* 82, 338–56.

Mackey, A., Philp, J., Egi, T., Fujii, A. & Tatsumi, T. (2002). Individual differences in working memory, noticing of interactional feedback, and L2 development. In Robinson. P. (ed.), *Individual Differences and Instructed Language Learning*. Philadelphia: John Benjamins.

MacWhinney, B. (2000). *The CHILDES Project: Tools for Analysing Talk: Volume 1: Transcription Format and Programs*, third edition. Mahwah, NJ: Lawrence Erlbaum.

MacWhinney, B., Keenan, J. & Reinke, P. (1982). The role of arousal in memory for conversation. *Memory and Cognition* 10, 308–17.

Maehr, M. (1984). Meaning and motivation: Toward a theory of personal investment. In Ames, R. & Ames, C. (eds.), *Motivation in Education: Student Motivation*, vol. 1 (pp. 115–44). San Diego, CA: Academic Press.

Mak, B. (2011). An exploration of speaking-in-class anxiety with Chinese ESL learners. *System* 39, 202–14.

Malicka, A. & Levkina, M. (2012). Measuring task complexity: Does L2 proficiency matter? In Shehadeh, A. & Coombe, C. (eds.), *Task-Based Language Teaching in Foreign Language Contexts: Research and Implementation* (pp. 43–66). Amsterdam: John Benjamins.

Malicka, A. & Sasayama, S. (2017). The importance of learning from the accumulated knowledge: Findings from a research synthesis on task complexity. Paper presented at the 7th Biennial International Conference on Task-Based Language Teaching, Barcelona, Spain, April.

McDonough, K. (2015). Perceived benefits and challenges with the use of collaborative tasks in EFL contexts. In Bygate, M. (ed.), *Domains and Direction in the Development of TBLT* (pp. 225–45). Amsterdam: John Benjamins.

McDonough, K. & Chaikitmongkol, W. (2007). Teachers' and learners' reactions to a task-based EFL course in Thailand. *TESOL Quarterly* 41, 107–32.

McNamara, T. (1996). *Measuring Second Language Performance*. London: Longman.

Mehnert, U. (1998). The effects of different lengths of time for planning on second language performance. *Studies in Second Language Acquisition* 20, 52–83.

Mercer, S., Ryan, S. & Williams, M. (2012). Introduction. In Mercer, S., Ryan, S. & Williams, M. (eds.), *Psychology for Language Learning: Insights from Research, Theory, and Practice* (pp. 10–25). New York: Palgrave.

Mesulam, M. (2000). Behavioural neuroanatomy: Large-scale networks, association cortex, frontal syndromes, the limbic system, and the hemispheric specializations. In Mesulam, M. (ed.), *Principles of Behavioural and Cognitive Neurology*, second edition (pp. 1–120). Oxford: Oxford University Press.

Michel, M. (2011). Effects of task complexity and interaction on L2 performance. In Robinson, P. (ed.), *Second Language Task Complexity: Researching the Cognition Hypothesis of Language Learning and Performance* (pp. 141–74). Amsterdam: John Benjamins.

Mifka-Profozic, N. (2013). *The Effectiveness of Corrective Feedback and the Role of Individual Differences in Language Learning*. Frankfurt am Main: Peter Lang.

Miyake, A. & Friedman, N. (1998). Individual differences in second language proficiency: Working memory as language aptitude. In Healy, A. & Bourne, L. (eds.), *Foreign Language Learning: Psycholinguistic Studies on Training and Retention*. Mahwah, NJ: Erlbaum.

Mochizuki, N. (2017). Contingent need analysis for task implementation: An activity systems analysis of group writing conferences. *TESOL Quarterly* 51, 607–31.

Mochizuki, N. & Ortega, L. (2008). Balancing communication and grammar in beginning-level foreign language classrooms: A study of guided planning and relativization. *Language Teaching Research* 12, 11–37.

Muller, T. (2005). Adding tasks to textbooks for beginning learners. In Edwards, C. & Willis, J. (eds.), *Teachers Exploring Tasks in English Language Teaching* (pp. 69–77). Basingstoke: Palgrave Macmillan.

Nabei, T. & Swain, M. (2001). Learner awareness of recasts in classroom interaction: A case study of an adult EFL student. *Language Awareness* 11, 43–63.

Nakatsukasa, K. (2016). Efficacy of requests and gestures on the acquisition of locative prepositions. *Studies in Second Language Acquisition* 38, 771–99.

Nassaji, H. (2009). Effects of recasts and elicitations in dyadic interaction and the role of feedback explicitness. *Language Learning* 59, 411–52.

Nassaji, H. (2016). Interactional feedback in second language teaching and learning: A synthesis and analysis of current research. *Language Teaching Research* 20, 535–62.

Nassaji, H. (2017). The effectiveness of extensive versus intensive recasts for L2 learning of grammar. *Modern Language Review* 101, 353–68.

Nassaji, H. & Fu, T. (2016). Corrective feedback, learner uptake, and feedback perception in a Chinese as a foreign language classroom. *Studies in Second Language Learning and Teaching* 1, 159–81.

Nassaji, H. & Swain, M. (2000). A Vygotskian perspective on corrective feedback in L2: The effect of random versus negotiated help in the learning of English articles. *Language Awareness* 9, 34–51.

Negueruela, E. J. & Lantolf, J. P. (2006). A concept-based approach to teaching Spanish grammar. In Salaberry, R. & Lafford, B. (eds.), *Spanish Second Language Acquisition: State of the Art* (pp. 79–102). Washington, DC: Georgetown University Press.

Neumann, O. (1987). Beyond capacity: A functional view of attention. In Heuer, H. & Sanders, A. (eds.), *Perspectives on Perception and Action* (pp. 361–94). Berlin: Springer.

Nielson, K. (2014). Evaluation of online, task-based Chinese course. In González-Lloret, M. & Ortega, L. (eds.), *Technology-Mediated TBLT: Researching Technology and Tasks* (pp. 295–321). Amsterdam: John Benjamins.

Nitta, R. & Nakatsuhara, F. (2014). A multifaceted approach to investigating pre-task planning effects on paired oral test performance. *Language Testing* 31, 147–75.

Niwa, Y. (2000). Reasoning demands of L2 tasks and L2 narrative production: Effects of individual differences in working memory, intelligence, and aptitude. Unpublished master's thesis, Aoyama Gakuin University, Tokyo.

Norris, J. (2009a). Task-based teaching and *testing*. In Long M. & Doughty C. (eds.), *The Handbook of Language Teaching* (pp. 578–94). Malden: MA: Blackwell.

Norris, J. (2009b). Understanding and improving language education through program evaluation: Introduction to the special issue. *Language Teaching Research* 13, 7–13.

Norris, J. (2015). Thinking and acting programmatically in task-based language teaching. In Bygate, M. (ed.), *Domains and Directions in the Development of TBLT* (pp. 27–57). Amsterdam: John Benjamins.

Norris, J. (2016). Current uses for task-based language assessment. *Annual Review of Applied Linguistics* 36, 230–44.

Norris, J., Brown, J. D., Hudson, T. & Yoshioka, J. (1998). *Designing Second Language Performance Assessments*. Honolulu, HI: University of Hawai'i Press.

Norris, J. & Ortega, L. (2000). Effectiveness of L2 instruction: A research synthesis and quantitative meta-analysis. *Language Learning* 50, 417–528.

Norris, J. & Ortega, L. (2009). Towards an organic approach to investigating CAF in instructed SLA: The case of complexity. *Applied Linguistics* 30, 555–78.

Norton, J. (2013). Performing identities in speaking tests: Co-construction revisited. *Language Assessment Quarterly* 10, 309–30.

Nunan, D. (1989). *Designing Tasks for the Communicative Classroom*. Cambridge: Cambridge University Press.

Nunan, D. (1990). The teacher as researcher. In Brumfit, C. & Mitchell, R. (eds.), *Research in the Language Classroom. ELT Documents 133*. Modern English Publications.

O'Grady, S. (2019). The impact of pre-task planning on speaking test performance for English-medium university admission. *Language Testing*.

Oga-Baldwin, W. & Nakata, Y. (2017). Engagement, gender, and motivation: A predictive model for Japanese young language learners. *System* 65, 151–63.

Ohta, A. (2001). *Second Language Acquisition Processes in the Classroom: Learning Japanese*. Mahwah, NJ: Lawrence Erlbaum Associates.

Ortega, L. (1999). Planning and focus on form in L2 oral performance. *Studies in Second Language Acquisition* 21, 109–48.

Ortega, L. (2005). What do learners plan? Learner-driven attention to form during pre-task planning. In Ellis, R. (ed.), *Planning and Task Performance in a Second Language* (pp. 77–110). Amsterdam: John Benjamins.

Ortega, L. (2009). Interaction and attention to form in L2 text-based computer-mediated communication. In Mackey, A. & Polio, C. (eds.), *Multiple Perspectives on Interaction in SLA: Research in Honor of Susan M. Gass* (pp. 226–53). New York: Routledge.

Ortega, L. (2015). Researching CLIL and TBLT interfaces. *System* 54, 103–9.

Oskoz, A. & Elola, I. (2014). Promoting foreign language collaborative writing through the use of Web 2.0 tools and tasks. In González-Lloret, M. & Ortega, L. (eds.), *Technology-Mediated TBLT: Researching Technology and Tasks* (pp. 115–48). Amsterdam: John Benjamins.

Pang, F. & Skehan, P. (2014). Self-reported planning behaviour and second language performance in narrative retelling. In Skehan, P. (ed.), *Processing Perspectives on Task Performance* (pp. 95–128). Amsterdam: John Benjamins.

Paradis, M. (1994). Neurolinguistic aspects of implicit and explicit memory: Implications for bilingualism and SLA. In Ellis, N. (ed.), *Implicit and Explicit Learning of Languages* (pp. 393–419). New York: Academic Press.

Paradis, M. (2004). *A Neurolinguistic Theory of Bilingualism*. Amsterdam: John Benjamins.

Park, M. (2015). Development and validation of virtual interactive tasks for an aviation English assessment. Unpublished doctoral dissertation, Iowa State University, Ames, IA.

Park, S. (2010). The influence of pre-task instructions and pre-task planning on focus on form during Korean EFL task-based interaction. *Language Teaching Research* 14, 9–26.

Patanasorn, C. (2010). Effects of procedural, content, and task repetition on accuracy and fluency in an EFL context. Unpublished PhD dissertation, Northern Arizona University.

Phillips, E. M. (1992). The effects of language anxiety on students' oral test performance and attitudes. *The Modern Language Journal* 76(1), 14–26.

Philp, J. & Duchesne, S. (2016). Exploring engagement in tasks in the language classroom. *Annual Review of Applied Linguistics* 36, 50–72.

Philp, J., Oliver, R. & Mackey, A. (2006). The impact of planning time on children's task–based interactions. *System* 34, 547–65.

Phung, L. (2017). Task preference, affective response, and engagement in L2 use in a US university context. *Language Teaching Research* 21, 751–66.

Pica, T. (1987). Second language acquisition, social interaction, and the classroom. *Applied Linguistics* 8, 3–21.

Pica, T. (1996). Second language learning through interaction: Multiple perspectives. *Working Papers in Educational Linguistics* 12, 1–22.

Pica, T. (1997). Second language teaching and research relationships: A North American view. *Language Teaching Research* 1, 48–72.

Pica, T. & C. Doughty. (1985a). Input and interaction in the communicative language classroom: A comparison of teacher-fronted and group activities. In Gass, S. & Madden, C. (eds.), *Input in Second Language Acquisition*. Rowley, MA: Newbury House.

Pica, T. & C. Doughty. (1985b). The role of group work in classroom second language acquisition. *Studies in Second Language Acquisition* 7, 233–48.

Pica, T., Kanagy, R. & Falodun, J. (1993). Choosing and using communication tasks for second language research and instruction. In Crookes, G. & Gass, S. (eds.), *Task-Based Learning in a Second Language* (pp. 9–34). Clevedon: Multilingual Matters.

Pienemann, M. (1985). Learnability and syllabus construction. In Hyltenstam, K. & Pienemann, M. (eds.), *Modelling and Assessing Second Language Acquisition* (pp. 23–75). Clevedon: Multilingual Matters.

Plonsky, L. & Gass, S. (2011). Quantitative research methods, study quality, and outcomes: The case of interaction research. *Language Learning* 61, 325–66.

Plonsky, L. & Kim, J. (2016). Task-based learner production: A substantive review. *Annual Review of Applied Linguistics* 36, 73–97.

Plough, I. & Gass, S. (1993). Interlocutor and task familiarity: Effects on interactional structure. In Crookes, G. & Gass, S. (eds.), *Tasks and Language Learning: Integrating Theory and Practice*. Clevedon: Multilingual Matters.

Poehner, M. (2008). *Dynamic Assessment: A Vygostkian Approach to Understanding and Promoting L2 Development*. Berlin: Springer.

Poehner, M. & Infante, P. (2017). Mediated development: A Vygotskian approach to transforming second language learner abilities. *TESOL Quarterly* 51, 332–57.

Poehner, M. & Lantolf, J. (2005). Dynamic assessment in the language classroom. *Language Teaching Research* 9, 233–65.

Pollitt, A. (1991). Giving students a sporting chance: Assessment by counting and judging. In Alderson, J. C. & North, B. (eds.), *Language Testing in the 1990s* (pp. 46–59). London: Macmillan.

Prabhu, N. (1987). *Second Language Pedagogy*. Oxford: Oxford University Press.

Prabhu, V. (1990). Comments on Alan Beretta's 'Attention to form or meaning? Error treatment in the Bangalore project'. *TESOL Quarterly* 24, 112–15.

Pulido, D. (2007). The effects of topic familiarity and passage sight vocabulary on L2 lexical inferencing and retention through reading. *Applied Linguistics* 28, 66–86.

Qin, T. & van Compernolle, R. (forthcoming). Computerized dynamic assessment of implicature comprehension in L2 Chinese. *Language Learning and Technology*.

Quinn, P. (2014). Delayed versus immediate corrective feedback on orally produced past passive errors in English. Unpublished PhD thesis, University of Toronto, Canada.

Rainey, S. (2000). Action research and the English as a foreign language practitioner: Time to take stock. *Educational Action Research* 8, 165–91.

Ranta, L. (2002). The role of learners' language analytic ability in the communicative classroom. In Robinson, P. (ed.), *Individual Differences and Instructed Language Learning*. Amsterdam: John Benjamins.

Rassaei, E. (2015). Oral corrective feedback, foreign language anxiety and L2 development. *System* 49, 98–109.

Rebuschat, P. & Williams, J. N. (2009). Implicit learning of word order. In Taatgen, N. & van Rijn, H. (eds.), *Proceedings of the 31st Annual Conference of the Cognitive Science Society* (pp. 425–30). Austin, TX: Cognitive Science Society.

Reese, C. & Wells, T. (2007). Teaching academic discussion skills with a card game. *Simulation and Gaming* 38, 546–55.

Reeve, J. & Lee, W. (2014). Students' classroom engagement produces longitudinal changes in classroom motivation. *Journal of Educational Psychology* 106, 527–40.

Révész, A. (2009). Task complexity, focus on form, and second language development. *Studies in Second Language Acquisition* 31, 437–70.

Révész, A. (2011). Task complexity, focus on L2 constructions, and individual differences: A classroom-based study. *Modern Language Journal* 95, 162–81.

Révész, A. (2012). Working memory and the observed effectiveness of recasts on different L2 outcome measures. *Language Learning* 62, 93–132.

Révész, A. (2017). Replication in task-based language teaching research: Kim (2012) and Shintani (2012). First view: *Language Teaching*, 1–11.

Révész, A., Ekiert, M. & Torgersen, E. N. (2016). The effects of complexity, accuracy and fluency on communicative adequacy in oral task performance. *Applied Linguistics* 37(6), 828–48.

Révész, A., Michel, M. & Gilabert, R. (2016). Measuring cognitive task demands using dual-task methodology, subjective self-ratings, and expert judgments: A validation study. *Studies in Second Language Acquisition* 38, 703–37.

Richards, J. (1984). Language curriculum development. *RELC Journal* 15, 1–29.

Richards, J. & Rodgers, T. (1986). *Approaches and Methods in Language Teaching*, second edition. Cambridge: Cambridge University Press.

Richards, J. & Rodgers, T. (2014). *Approaches and Methods in Language Teaching*, third edition. Cambridge: Cambridge University Press.

Robinson, P. (2001). Task complexity, cognitive resources, and syllabus design: A triadic framework for examining task influences on SLA. In Robinson, P. (ed.), *Cognition and Second Language Instruction* (pp. 287–318). Cambridge: Cambridge University Press.

Robinson, P. (2002). Learning conditions, aptitude complexes and SLA: A framework for research and pedagogy. In Robinson, P. (ed.), *Individual Differences and Instructed Language Learning*. Amsterdam: John Benjamins.

Robinson, P. (2007a). Aptitudes, abilities, contexts, and practice. In DeKeyser, R. M. (ed.), *Practice in Second Language: Perspectives from Applied Linguistics and Cognitive Psychology* (pp. 256–86). New York/Cambridge: Cambridge University Press.

Robinson, P. (2007b). Re-thinking-for-speaking and L2 task demands: The Cognition Hypothesis, task classification, and sequencing. Plenary address at the

Second International Conference on Task-based Language Teaching, Hawaii, 20–22 September.

Robinson, P. (2007c). Task complexity, theory of mind, and intentional reasoning: Effects on L2 speech production, interaction, uptake and perceptions of task Difficulty. *International Review of Applied Linguistics* 45, 193–214.

Robinson, P. (2010). Situating and distributing cognition across task demands: The SSARC model of pedagogic task sequencing. In Putz, M. & Sicola, L. (eds.), *Cognitive Processing in Second Language Acquisition: Inside the Learner's Mind* (pp. 243–68). Amsterdam: John Benjamins.

Robinson, P. (2011). Second language task complexity, the cognition hypothesis, language learning, and performance. In Robinson P. (ed.), *Second Language Task Complexity: Researching the Cognition Hypothesis of Language Learning and Performance* (pp. 3–38). Amsterdam: John Benjamins.

Robinson, P. (2015). The cognition hypothesis, second language task demands, and the SSARC model of pedagogic task sequencing. In Bygate, M. (ed.), *Domains and Directions in the Development of TBLT* (pp. 87–122). Amsterdam: John Benjamins.

Roever, C. (2011). Testing of second language pragmatics: Past and future. *Language Testing* 28, 463–81.

Roever, C. & Kasper, G. (2018). Speaking in turns and sequences: Interactional competence as a target construct in testing speaking. *Language Testing* 35, 331–55.

Rolin-Ianziti, J. (2010). The organization of delayed second language correction. *Language Teaching Research* 14, 183–206.

Romanova, N. (2010). Planning, recasts, and learning of L2 morphology. *The Canadian Modern Language Review* 66, 843–75.

Rulon, K. & McCreary, J. (1986). Negotiation of content: Teacher-fronted and small-group interaction. In Day, R. R. (ed.), *Talking to Learn: Conversation in Second Language Acquisition* (pp. 182–99). Rowley, MA: Newbury House.

Sabet, P. & Zhang, G. (2015). *Communicating through Vague Language: A Comparative Study of L1 and L2 Speakers*. Basingstoke: Palgrave Macmillan.

Sachs, R. (2010). Individual differences and the effectiveness of visual feedback of reflexive binding in L2 Japanese. PhD dissertation, Georgetown University.

Saito, K. & Akiyama, Y. (2017). Video-based interaction, negotiation for comprehensibility, and second language learning: A longitudinal study. *Language Learning* 67, 43–74.

Saito, Y., Horwitz, E. K. & Garza, T. J. (1999). Foreign language reading anxiety. *The Modern Language Journal* 83(2), 202–18.

Samimy, K. & Kobayashi, C. (2004). Toward the development of intercultural competence: Theoretical and pedagogical implications for Japanese English teachers. *JALT Journal* 26, 245–61.

Samuda, V. (2001). Guiding relationships between form and meaning during task performance: The role of the teacher. In Bygate, M., Skehan, P. & Swain, M.

(eds.), *Researching Pedagogic Tasks: Second Language Learning, Teaching and Testing* (pp. 119–40). Harlow: Longman.

Samuda, V. (2015). Tasks, design, and the architecture of pedagogical spaces. In Bygate, M. (ed.), *Domains and Directions in the Development of TBLT* (pp. 271–301). Amsterdam: John Benjamins.

Samuda, V. & Bygate, M. (2008). *Tasks in Second Language Learning*. Basingstoke: Palgrave Macmillan.

Sanders, A. (1998). *Elements of Human Performance*. Mahwah, NJ: Lawrence Erlbaum.

Sangarun, J. (2005). The effects of focusing on meaning and form in strategic planning. In Ellis, R. (ed.), *Planning and Task Performance in a Second Language*. Philadelphia: John Benjamins.

Sasayama, S. (2015). Validating the assumed relationship between task design, cognitive complexity, and second language task performance. Unpublished PhD dissertation, Georgetown University.

Sasayama, S. (2016). Is a 'complex' task really complex? Validating the assumption of task complexity. *Modern Language Journal* 100, 231–54.

Satar, H. & Ozdener, N. (2008). The effects of synchronous CMC on speaking proficiency and anxiety: Text versus voice chat. *The Modern Language Journal* 92, 595–613.

Sato, M. (2017). Interaction mindsets, interactional behaviors, and L2 development: An affective-social-cognitive model. *Language Learning* 67, 249–83.

Sato, M. & Loewen, S. (2018). Metacognitive instruction enhances the effectiveness of corrective feedback: Variable effects of feedback types and linguistic targets. *Language Learning* 68, 507–45.

Sato, M. & Lyster, R. (2012). Peer interaction and corrective feedback for accuracy and fluency development: Monitoring, practice, and proceduralization. *Studies in Second Language Acquisition* 34, 591–626.

Schmidt, R. (1990). The role of consciousness in second language learning. *Applied Linguistics* 11, 129–58.

Schmidt, R. (1994). Deconstructing consciousness: In search of useful definitions for applied linguistics. *AILA Review* 11, 11–26.

Schmidt, R. (2001). Attention. In Robinson, P. (ed.), *Cognition and Second Language Instruction* (pp. 3–32). Cambridge: Cambridge University Press.

Schmidt, R. & Frota, S. (1986). Developing basic conversation ability in a second language: A case-study of an adult learner. In Day, R. (ed.), *Talking to Learn: Conversation in Second Language Acquisition*. Rowley, MA: Newbury House.

Schumann, J. (2001). Appraisal psychology, neurobiology, and language. *Annual Review of Applied Linguistics* 21, 23–42.

Schwartz, B. D. (1993). On explicit and negative data effecting and affecting competence and linguistic behavior. *Studies in Second Language Acquisition* 15, 147–63.

Seedhouse, P. (1999). Task-based interaction. *ELT Journal* 53, 149–56.

Seedhouse, P. (2005a). 'Task' as research construct. *Language Learning* 55, 533–70.

Seedhouse, P. (2005b). Conversation analysis and language learning. *Language Teaching* 38, 165–87.
Seedhouse, P. (ed.). (2017). *Task-Based Language Learning in a Real-World Digital Environment: The European Digital Kitchen*. London: Bloomsbury.
Seipp, B. (1991). Anxiety and academic performance: A meta-analysis of findings. *Anxiety Research* 4(1), 27–41.
Sfard, A. (1998). On two metaphors for learning and the dangers of choosing just one. *Educational Researcher* 27, 4–13.
Sheen, R. (1994). A critical analysis of the advocacy of the task-based syllabus. *TESOL Quarterly* 28, 127–51.
Sheen, R. (2003). Focus on form–a myth in the making? *ELT journal* 57, 225–33.
Sheen, R. (2004). Corrective feedback and learner uptake in communicative classrooms across instructional settings. *Language Teaching Research* 8, 263–300.
Sheen, R. (2005). Focus on forms as a means of improving accurate oral production. In Housen, A. & Pierrard, M. (eds.), *Investigations in Instructed Language Acquisition* (pp. 270–310). Berlin: Mouton de Gruyter.
Sheen, R. (2006). Focus on forms as a means of improving accurate oral production. In Housen, A. & Pierrard, M. (eds.), *Investigations in Instructed Second Language Acquisition* (pp. 271–310). Berlin: Mouton de Gruyter.
Sheen, R. (2006). Exploring the relationship between characteristics of recasts and learner uptake. *Language Teaching Research* 10, 361–92.
Sheen, R. (2007). The effects of corrective feedback, language aptitude, and learner attitudes on the acquisition of English articles. In Mackey, A. (ed.), *Conversational Interaction in Second Language Acquisition*. Oxford: Oxford University Press.
Sheen, R. (2008). Recasts, language anxiety, modified output, and L2 learning. *Language Learning* 58(4), 835–74.
Sheen, R. (2010). Differential effects of oral and written corrective feedback in the ESL classroom. *Studies in Second Language Acquisition* 32, 203–34.
Shehadeh, A. (2005). Task-based learning and teaching: Theories and applications. In Edwards, C. & Willis, L. (eds.), *Teachers Exploring Tasks* (pp. 13–30). Basingstoke: Palgrave Macmillan.
Shehadeh, A. (2012). Broadening the perspective of task-based language teaching scholarship: The contribution of research in foreign language contexts. In Shehadeh A. & Coombe, C. A. (eds.), *Task-Based Language Teaching in Foreign Language Contexts: Research and Implementation* (pp. 1–20). Philadelphia: John Benjamins.
Shintani, N. (2011). A comparison of the effects of comprehension-based and production-based instruction on the acquisition of vocabulary and grammar by young Japanese learners of English. Unpublished PhD thesis, the University of Auckland.
Shintani, N. (2012). Repeating input-based tasks with young beginner learners. *RELC Journal* 43, 39–51.
Shintani, N. (2013). The effect of focus on form and focus on forms instruction on the acquisition of productive knowledge of L2 vocabulary by young beginning-level learners. *TESOL Quarterly* 47, 36–62.

Shintani, N. (2015). The incidental grammar acquisition in focus on form and focus on forms instruction for young beginner Learners. *TESOL Quarterly* 49, 115–40.
Shintani, N. (2016). *Input-Based Tasks in Foreign Language Instruction for Young Learners*. Amsterdam: John Benjamins.
Shintani, N. & Ellis, R. (2010). The incidental acquisition of English plural –*s* by Japanese children in comprehension-based lessons: A process–product study. *Studies in Second Language Acquisition* 32, 607–37.
Skehan, P. (1984). Issues in the testing of English for specific purposes. *Language Testing* 1/2, 202–20.
Skehan, P. (1996). A framework for the implementation of task-based learning. *Applied Linguistics* 17, 38–62.
Skehan, P. (1998). *A Cognitive Approach to Language Learning*. Oxford: Oxford University Press.
Skehan, P. (2001). Tasks and language performance assessment. In Bygate, M., Skehan, P. & Swain, M. (eds.), *Researching Pedagogic Tasks, Second Language Learning, Teaching and Testing* (pp. 167–85). Harlow: Longman.
Skehan, P. (2002). Theorizing and updating aptitude. In Robinson, P. (ed.), *Individual Differences and Instructed Language Learning* (pp. 69–94). Amsterdam: John Benjamins.
Skehan, P. (2003). Task-based instruction. *Language Teaching* 36, 1–14.
Skehan, P. (2007). Task research and language teaching: Reciprocal relationships. In Fotos, S. (ed.), *Form-Meaning Relationships in Language Pedagogy: Essays in Honour of Rod Ellis*. Oxford: Oxford University Press.
Skehan, P. (2009a). Modelling second language performance: Integrating complexity, accuracy, fluency and lexis. *Applied Linguistics* 30, 510–32.
Skehan, P. (2009b). Lexical performance by native and non-native speakers on language-learning tasks. In Richards, B., Daller, H., Malvern, D. D. & Meara, P. (eds.), *Vocabulary Studies in First and Second Language Acquisition: The Interface Between Theory and Application* (pp. 107–24). London: Palgrave Macmillan.
Skehan, P. (2009c). Models of speaking and the assessment of second language proficiency. In Benati, A. G. (ed.), *Issues in Second Language Proficiency* (pp. 202–15). London: Continuum International Pub Group.
Skehan, P. (2012). *Researching Tasks: Performance, Assessment, Pedagogy*. Shanghai/Amsterdam: Shanghai Foreign Language Education Press/De Gruyter.
Skehan, P. (2013). Nurturing noticing. In Bergsleithner, J. M., Frota, S. N. & Yoshioka, J. K. (eds.), *Noticing and Second Language Acquisition: Studies in Honor of Richard Schmidt* (pp. 169–80). Honolulu, HI: University of Hawai'i, National Foreign Language Resource Center.
Skehan, P. (2014a). *Processing Perspectives on Task Performance*. Amsterdam: John Benjamins.
Skehan, P. (2014b). Introduction: Coordinated research into task-based performance. In Skehan, P. (ed.), *Processing Perspectives on Task Performance* (pp. 1–26). Amsterdam: John Benjamins.

Skehan, P. (2014c). Synthesising and applying task research. In Skehan, P. (ed.), *Processing Perspectives on Task Performance* (pp. 211–60). Amsterdam: John Benjamins.

Skehan, P. (2015). Limited attentional capacity and cognition: Two hypotheses regarding second language performance on tasks. In Bygate, M. (ed.), *Domains and Directions in the Development of TBLT: A Decade of Plenaries from the International Conference* (pp. 123–55). Amsterdam: John Benjamins.

Skehan, P. (2016). Tasks vs. conditions: Two perspectives on task research and its implications for pedagogy. *Annual Review of Applied Linguistics* 36, 34–49.

Skehan, P. (2018). *Second Language Task-Based Performance: Theory, Research, and Assessment*. New York: Routledge.

Skehan, P. & Foster, P. (1997). The influence of planning and post-task activities on accuracy and complexity in task-based learning. *Language Teaching Research* 1, 185–211.

Skehan, P. & Foster, P. (1999). Task structure and processing conditions in narrative retellings. *Language Learning* 49(1), 93–120.

Skehan, P. & Foster, P. (2001). Cognition and tasks. In Robinson P. (ed.), *Cognition and Second Language Learning* (pp. 183–205). New York: Cambridge University Press.

Skehan, P. & Foster, P. (2005). Strategic and on-line planning: The influence of surprise information and task time on second language performance. In Ellis, R. (ed.), *Planning and Task Performance in a Second Language* (pp. 193–216). Philadelphia: John Benjamins Publishing Company

Skehan, P. & Foster, P. (2007). Complexity, accuracy, fluency and lexis in task-based performance: A meta-analysis of the Ealing research. In Van Daele, S., Housen, A., Kuiken, F., Pierrard, M. & Vedder I. (eds.), *Complexity, Accuracy, and Fluency in Second Language Use, Learning, and Teaching* (pp. 207–26). Brussels: University of Brussels Press.

Skehan, P. & Shum, S. (2017). What influences performance? Personal style or the task being done? In Wong, L. L. C. & Hyland, K. (eds.), *Faces of English Education: Students, Teachers, and Pedagogy* (pp. 28–43). London: Routledge.

Skehan, P., Xiaoyue, B., Qian, L. & Wang, Z. (2012). The task is not enough: Processing approaches to task-based performance. *Language Teaching Research* 16, 170–87.

Slimani-Rolls, A. (2005). Rethinking task-based language learning: What we can learn from the learners. *Language Teaching Research* 9, 195–218.

Smith, B. (2003). Computer-mediated negotiated interaction: An expanded model. *Modern Language Journal* 26, 365–98.

Smith, B. (2012). Eye-tracking as a measure of noticing: A study of explicit recasts in SCMC. *Language Learning and Technology* 16, 53–18.

Snow, R. E. (1991). Aptitude-treatment interaction as a framework for research on individual differences in psychotherapy. *Journal of Consulting and Clinical Psychology* 59, 205–16.

Solon, M., Long, A. & Gurzynska-Weiss, L. (2017). Task complexity, language related episodes, and production of L2 Spanish vowels. *Studies in Second Language Acquisition* 39, 347–80.

Spada, N., Jessop, L., Tomita, Y., Suzuki, W. & Valeo, A. (2014). Isolated and integrated form-focused instruction: Effects on different types of L2 knowledge. *Language Teaching Research* 18, 453–73.

Spada, N. & Lightbown, P. (1999). Instruction, first language influence, and developmental readiness in second language acquisition. *Modern Language Journal* 83, 1–22.

Sparks, R. L. & Patton, J. (2013). Relationship of L1 skills and L2 aptitude to L2 anxiety on the foreign language classroom anxiety scale. *Language Learning* 63(4), 870–95.

Storch, N. (2002). Patterns of interaction in ESL pair work. *Language Learning* 52, 119–58.

Storch, N. (2007). Investigating the merits of pair work on a text-editing task in ESL classes. *Language Teaching Research* 11, 143–59.

Storch, N. (2008). Metatalk in a pair work activity: Level of engagement and implications for language development. *Language Awareness* 17, 95–114.

Storch, N. (2017). Sociocultural theory in the L2 classroom. In Loewen, S. & Sato, M. (eds.), *The Routledge Handbook of Instructed Second Language Acquisition* (pp. 69–84). New York: Routledge.

Storch, N. & Wigglesworth, G. (2003). Is there a role for the use of the L1 in an L2 setting? *TESOL Quarterly* 37, 760–70.

Stroud, R. (2017). The impact of task performance scoring and tracking on second language engagement. *System* 69, 121–32.

Svalberg, A. (2009). Engagement with language: Developing a construct. *Language Awareness* 18, 242–58.

Swain, M. (1995). Three functions of output in second language Learning. In Cook, G. & Seidhofer, B. (eds.), *Principles and Practice in the Study of Language: Studies in Honour of H. G. Widdowson* (pp. 125–44). Oxford: Oxford University Press.

Swain, M. (2000). The output hypothesis and beyond: Mediating acquisition through collaborative dialogue. In Lantolf, J. (ed.), *Sociocultural Theory and Second Language Learning* (pp. 97–114). Oxford: Oxford University Press.

Swain, M. (2006). Languaging, agency and collaboration in advanced second language learning. In Byrnes, H. (ed.), *Advanced Language Learning: The Contributions of Halliday and Vygotsky* (pp. 95–108). London: Continuum.

Swain, M. (2013). The inseparability of cognition and emotion in second language learning. *Language Teaching* 46, 195–207.

Swain, M., Kinnear, P. & Steinman, L. (2011). *Sociocultural Theory in Second Language Education: An Introduction through Narratives*. Bristol: Multilingual Matters.

Swain, M. & Lapkin, S. (1998). Interaction and second language learning: Two adolescent French immersion students working together. *Modern Language Journal* 82, 320–37.

Swain, M. & Lapkin, S. (2001). Focus on form through collaborative dialogue: Exploring task effects. In Bygate, M., Skehan, P. & Swain, M. (eds.),

Researching Pedagogic Tasks, Second Language Learning, Teaching and Testing (pp. 99–118). Harlow: Longman.

Swain, M. & Lapkin, S. (2002). Talking it through: Two French immersion learners' response to reformulation. *International Journal of Educational Research* 37, 285–304.

Swain, M. & Lapkin, S. (2007). The distributed nature of second language learning: A case study. In Fotos, S. & Nassaji, H. (eds.), *Focus on Form and Teacher Education: Studies in Honour of Rod Ellis* (pp. 73–86). Oxford: Oxford University Press.

Swain, M., Lapkin, S., Knouzi, I., Suzuki, W. & Brooks, L. (2009). Languaging: University students learn the grammatical concept of voice in French. *Modern Language Journal* 93, 5–29.

Swan, M. (2005a). Legislation by hypothesis: The case of task-based instruction. *Applied Linguistics* 26, 376–401.

Swan, M. (2005b). Review of Rod Ellis' task-based language learning and teaching. *IJAL* 15, 251–9.

Sweller, J. (1988). Cognitive load during problem solving: Effects on learning. *Cognitive Science* 12, 257–85.

Sweller, J. (1994). Cognitive load theory, learning difficulty, and instructional design. *Learning and Instruction* 4, 295–312.

Sykes, J. M. (2014). TBLT and synthetic immersive environments: What can in-game task restarts tell us about design and implementation? In González-Lloret, M. & Ortega, L. (eds.), *Technology-Mediated TBLT: Researching Technology and Tasks* (pp. 149–82). Amsterdam: John Benjamins.

Tavakoli, P. (2018). A *detailed* analysis of oral fluency at different levels of proficiency. Paper presented at the L-SLARF Annual Conference. Birkbeck College, London, 2 June.

Tavakoli, P. & Foster, P. (2008). Task design and second language performance: The effect of narrative type on learner output. *Language Learning* 58(2), 439–73.

Tavakoli, P. & Skehan, P. (2005). Planning, task structure, and performance testing. In Ellis, R. (ed.), *Planning and Task Performance in a Second Language* (pp. 239–76). Amsterdam: John Benjamins.

Thai, C. & Boers, F. (2015). Repeating a monologue under increasing time pressure: Effects on fluency, complexity, and accuracy. *TESOL Quarterly* 50, 369–93.

Thomas, M. & Reinders, H. (eds.). (2010). *Task-Based Learning and Teaching with Technology*. London: Continuum.

Thomas, M. & Reinders, H. (eds.). (2015). *Contemporary Task-Based Teaching in Asia*. London: Continuum.

Timpe-Laughlin, V. (2018). Pragmatics in task-based language assessment: Opportunities and challenges. In Taguchi, N. & Kim, Y. (eds.), *Task-Based Approaches to Teaching and Assessing Pragmatics* (pp. 287–304). Amsterdam: John Benjamins.

Tobias, S. (1985). Test anxiety: Interference, defective skills, and cognitive capacity. *Educational Psychologist* 20(3), 135–42.

Tomlin, R. & Villa, V. (1994). Attention in cognitive science and second language acquisition. *Studies in Second Language Acquisition* 16, 183–203.
Tomlinson, B. (2015). TBLT and materials and curricula: From theory to practice. In Thomas, M. & Reinders, H. (eds.), *Contemporary Task-Based Teaching in Asia* (pp. 328–339). London: Bloomsbury.
Toth, P. (2008). Teacher- and learner-led discourse in task-based grammar instruction: Providing procedural assistance for L2 morphosyntactic development. *Language Learning* 58, 237–83.
Trebits, A. (2014). Sources of individual differences in L2 narrative production: The contribution of input, processing, and output anxiety. *Applied Linguistics* 37(2), 155–74.
Trofimovich, P., Ammar, A. & Gatbonton, E. (2007). How effective are recasts? The role of attention, memory, and analytical ability. In Mackey, A. (ed.), *Conversational Interaction in Second Language Acquisition*. Oxford: Oxford University Press.
Trondheim, L. (2007). *Mr. I*. New York: Nantier, Beall & Minoustchine.
Van Avermmaat, P. & Gysen, S. (2006). From needs to tasks: Language learning needs in a task-based approach. In Van den Branden, K. (ed.), *Task-Based Language Education: From Theory to Practice* (pp. 17–46). Cambridge: Cambridge University Press.
Van Compernolle, R. & Zhang, H. (2014). Dynamic assessment of elicited imitation: A case analysis of an advanced L2 English speaker. *Language Testing* 31, 395–412.
Van Compernolle, R., Weber, A. & Gomez-Laich, M. (2016). Teaching L2 Spanish sociopragmatics through concepts: A classroom-based study. *Modern Language Journal* 100, 341–61.
Van de Guchte, M., Rijlaarsdam, G., Braaksma, M. & Bimmel, P. (2015). Learning new grammatical structures in task-based language learning: The effects of recasts and prompts. *The Modern Language Journal* 99, 246–62.
Van de Guchte, M., Rijlaarsdam, G., Braaksma, M. & Bimmel, P. (2017). Focus on language versus content in the pre-task: Effects of guided peer-video model observations on task performance. *Language Teaching Research* 23(3), 310–29.
Van den Branden, K. (2009). Diffusion and implementation of innovations. In Long, M. & Doughty, C. (eds.), *The Handbook of Language Teaching* (pp. 659–72). Malden, MA: Wiley-Blackwell.
Van den Branden, K. (ed.). (2006). *Task-Based Language Education: From Theory to Practice*. Cambridge: Cambridge University Press.
Van den Branden, K., Bygate, M. & Norris, J. M. (2009). *Task-Based Language Teaching: A Reader*. Amsterdam: John Benjamins.
Van den Branden, K., Van Gorp, K. & Verhelst, M. (2007). Introduction. In Van den Branden, K. et al. (eds.), *Tasks in Action: Task-Based Language Education from a Classroom-Based Perspective* (pp. 1–6). Newcastle: Cambridge Scholars Publishing.
Van Gorp, K. & Deygers, B. (2014). Task-based language assessment. In Kunnan, A. (ed.), *The Companion to Language Assessment*, vol. 2 (pp. 271–87). Malden, MA: John Wiley & Son.

Van Lier, L. (1996). *Interaction in the Language Curriculum: Awareness, Autonomy and Authenticity*. London: Longman.
VanPatten, B. (2015). Input processing in adult SLA. In VanPatten, B. & Williams, J. (eds.), *Theories in Second Language Acquisition*. New York: Routledge.
Varnosfadrani, A. & Basturkmen, H. (2009). The effectiveness of implicit and explicit error correction on learners' performance. *System* 37, 82–98.
Varonis, E. & Gass, S. (1985). Non-native/non-native conversations: A model for negotiation of meaning. *Applied Linguistics* 6, 71–90.
Vygotsky, L. (1978). *Mind in Society: The Development of Higher Psychological Processes*, Cole, M., John-Steiner, V., Scribner, S. & Souberman, E. (eds.). Cambridge, MA: Harvard University Press.
Vygotsky, L. (1986). *Thought and Language*. Cambridge, MA: MIT Press.
Vygotsky, L. (1987). The Collected Works of L. S. Vygotsky, *Volume 1: The Problems of General Psychology*. R. W. Rieber & A. S. Carton (eds.). New York: Plenum Press.
Vygotsky, L. (2000). *Thought and Language*. Cambridge, MA: MIT Press.
Wang Q. (2007). The national curriculum changes and their effects on english language teaching in the People's Republic of China. In Cummins, J. & Davison C. (eds.), *International Handbook of English Language Teaching*. Springer International Handbooks of Education, vol. 15 (pp. 87–105). Boston: Springer.
Wang, Z. (2009). Modelling speech production and performance: Evidence from five types of planning and two task structures. Unpublished PhD thesis, Chinese University of Hong Kong.
Wang, Z. (2014). On-line time pressure manipulations: L2 speaking performance under five types of planning and repetition conditions. In Skehan, P. (ed.), *Processing Perspectives on Task Performance* (pp. 27–62). Amsterdam: John Benjamins.
Wang, Z. & Skehan P. (2014). Task structure, time perspective and lexical demands during video-based narrative retellings. In Skehan, P. (ed.), *Processing Perspectives on Task Performance* (pp. 155–86). Amsterdam: John Benjamins.
Watanabe, Y. & Swain, M. (2007). Effects of proficiency differences and patterns of pair interaction on second language learning: Collaborative dialogue between adult ESL learners. *Language Teaching Research* 11, 121–42.
Watson-Todd, R. (2006). Continuing change after innovation. *System* 34, 1–14.
Weaver, C. (2012). Incorporating a formative assessment cycle into task-based language teaching in a university setting in Japan. In Shehadeh, A. & Coombe, C. (eds.), *Task-Based Language Teaching in Foreign Language Contexts* (pp. 287–312). Amsterdam: John Benjamins.
Weir, C. (2005). *Language Testing and Validation: An Evidence-Based Approach*. Basingstoke: Palgrave Macmillan.
Weir, C. & Roberts, J. (1994). *Evaluation in ELT*. Oxford: Blackwell.
Weir, C., Vidakovic, I. & Galaczi, E. (2014). *Measured Constructs: A History of Cambridge English Language Examinations, 1913–2012: Studies in Language Testing 37*. Cambridge: Cambridge University Press.
Wen, Z. (2016). *Working Memory and Second Language Learning: Towards an Integrated Approach*. Clevedon, Avon: Multilingual Matters.

Wen, Z., Skehan, P., Biedroń, A., Li, S. & Sparks, R. (eds.) (in press). *Rethinking Language Aptitude: Multiple Perspectives and Emerging Trends*. New York: Routledge.

Wertsch, J. V. (1985). *Vygotsky and the Social Formation of Mind*. Cambridge, MA: Harvard University.

Wertsch, J. V., Minick, N. & Arns, F. J. (1984). The creation of context in joint problem-solving. In Rogoff, B. & Lave, J. (eds.), *Everyday Cognition: Its Development in Social Context* (pp. 151–71). Cambridge, MA: Harvard University Press.

White, L. (1987). Against comprehensible input: The input hypothesis and the development of L2 competence. *Applied Linguistics* 8, 95–110.

Wickens, C. D. (2007). Attention to the second language. *International Review of Applied Linguistics* 45, 177–91.

Widdowson, H. (2003). *Defining Issues in English Language Teaching*. Oxford: Oxford University Press.

Wigglesworth, G. & Elder, C. (2010). An investigation of the effectiveness and validity of planning time in speaking test tasks. *Language Assessment Quarterly* 7(1), 1–24.

Wigglesworth, G. & Frost, K. (2017). Task and performance-based assessment. In Shohamy E., Or, I. & May, S. (eds.), *Language Testing and Assessment: Encyclopedia of Language and Education*, third edition. Cham: Springer.

Wilkins, D. (1976). *Notional Syllabuses*. Oxford: Oxford University Press.

Williams, J. (1999). Learner-generated attention to form. *Language Learning* 49, 583–625.

Williams, J. (2013). Attention, awareness, and noticing in language processing and learning. In Bergsleithner, J., Frota, M., Nagem, S. & Yoshioka, Jim Kei (eds.), *Noticing and Second Language Acquisition: Studies in Honor of Richard Schmidt* (pp. 39–57). Honolulu, HI: University of Hawai'i, National Foreign Language Resource Center

Williams, L. (2018). Task-based teaching and concept-based instruction. In Ahmadian, M. & Mayo, M. (eds.), *Recent Perspectives on Task-Based Language Teaching* (pp. 121–41). Boston/Berlin: Mouton de Gruyter.

Willis, D. & Willis, J. (2007). *Doing Task-Based Teaching*. Oxford: Oxford University Press.

Willis, J. (1996). *A Framework for Task-Based Language Teaching*. New York: Longman.

Willis, J. & Willis, D. (1988). *Collins COBUILD English Course: Book 1*. London: Collins.

Winke, P. (2014). Formative, task-based oral assessments in an advanced Chinese language class. In González-Lloret, M. & Ortega, L. (eds.), *Technology-Mediated TBLT: Researching Technology and Tasks* (pp. 264–93). Amsterdam: John Benjamins.

Winter, E. (1976). *Fundamentals of Information Structure: A Pilot Manual for Further Development According to Student Need*. Hatfield: Hatfield Polytechnic, English Department.

Xi, X. (2005). Do visual chunks and planning impact the overall quality of oral descriptions of graphs? *Language Testing* 22(4), 463–508.

Yang, Y. & Lyster, R. (2010). Effects of form-focused practice and feedback on Chinese EFL learners' acquisition of regular and irregular past-tense forms. *Studies in Second Language Acquisition* 32, 235–63.

Yilmaz, Y. (2013a). Relative effects of explicit and implicit feedback: The role of working memory capacity and language analytic ability. *Applied Linguistics* 34, 344–68.

Yilmaz, Y. (2013b). The relative effectiveness of mixed, explicit and implicit feedback in the acquisition of English articles. *System* 41, 691–705.

Youn, S. J. (2018). Task design and validity evidence for assessment of L2 pragmatics in interaction. In Taguchi, N. & Kim, Y. (eds.), *Task-Based Approaches to Teaching and Assessing Pragmatics* (pp. 217–46). Amsterdam: John Benjamins.

Yuan, F. & R. Ellis. (2003). The effects of pre-task and on-line planning on fluency, complexity and accuracy in L2 monologic oral production. *Applied Linguistics* 24, 1–27.

Yuksal, D. & Inan, B. (2014). The effects of communication mode on negotiation and its noticing. *ReCALL* 26, 333–54.

Yule, G. (1997). *Referential Communication Tasks*. Hillsdale, NJ: Lawrence Erlbaum.

Yule, G. & McDonald, D. (1990). Resolving referential conflicts in L2 interaction: The effect of proficiency and interactive role. *Language Learning* 40, 539–56.

Zhang, J. & Rahimi, M. (2014). EFL learners' anxiety level and their beliefs about corrective feedback in oral communication classes. *System* 42, 429–39.

Zhang, X. & Lantolf, J. (2015). Natural or artificial: Is the route of L2 development teachable? *Language Learning* 65, 152–80.

Zhao, Y. (2015). The effects of explicit and implicit recasts on the acquisition of two grammatical structures and the mediating role of working memory. Unpublished PhD thesis, University of Auckland.

Ziegler, N. (2016). Taking technology to task: Technology-mediated TBLT, performance and production. *Annual Review of Applied Linguistics* 36, 136–63.

Zuengler, J. & Miller, E. (2006). Cognitive and social perspectives: Two parallel SLA worlds. *TESOL Quarterly* 40, 35–58.

Index

ability analysis, 190
ability for use, 241, 245–6, 249, 254–6, 259, 261, 265, 274
accountability, 181, 186, 189, 199, 223, 303, 307
accuracy, 16, 23, 28, 53, 58, 60, 65–6, 68–9, 72–5, 78, 80, 82–3, 85, 87–8, 90–3, 98–100, 113, 117, 120, 122, 125, 136, 138, 140, 144, 149, 191, 194, 210, 212, 214, 218, 220–1, 226, 231, 247–9, 256, 260, 262–4, 288, 296, 299, 301, 321, 328, 334, 336, 338–9, 346, 351, 361
achievement testing, 259, 266–8, 368
acquisition poor environments, 344, 356, 365
acquisition/acquisitional sequence, 338
action research, 308, 317–18, 373
Activity Theory, 109–11, 113, 115–16
affective profiles, 192
anxiety, 81, 129–30, 147–54, 156, 161, 193, 212, 217, 225
aptitude, 70, 81, 129, 131–5, 148, 153, 156, 190, 192, 196, 198, 204–6, 362
   language analytic ability, 131, 133–5
   MLAT, 131–2, 134
   working memory, 46, 51, 70, 76, 79, 81, 87, 90, 116, 129, 135–41, 149, 153, 192–3, 227, 255, 261, 265, 362
aptitude profiles, 192, 196
articulation, 68, 71, 97, 136
attention, 9, 13, 15–17, 29, 38–9, 43, 45, 48–9, 52, 54, 56, 63, 70, 72, 76–8, 80, 82, 87, 94, 98, 109, 111, 129, 136, 139, 147, 150, 152, 156, 158, 160, 162, 176, 185, 193, 200, 202, 206, 212, 217–19, 221–2, 224, 226, 228, 247, 250, 255, 285, 289, 303, 314, 339, 343–4, 349, 357, 359–60
attentional limitation, 71–2, 77, 89
automatize, 82, 112, 121, 194, 200, 202, 204, 218, 363

Bangalore Project (Communicational Language Teaching Project), 175, 184, 221, 285, 310

co-construction, 105, 114, 118, 251, 253, 265
Cognition Hypothesis, 41, 64, 69, 73–4, 82, 87, 93, 129–30, 148, 190, 212, 247, 348, 359–60
   ability analysis, 190
   behavioral analysis, 190
   information-theoretic analysis, 190, 192
   resource-dispersing task factors, 194
cognitive load, 99, 113, 206, 216, 292, 348, 355, 359
cognitive-interactionist perspective, 29, 105, 109
collaborative dialogue, 116–21
common European framework of reference (CEFR), 257, 271, 273
communicative language teaching (CLT), 3–4, 9, 18, 21, 24, 134–5, 208, 325, 328–9, 338
comparative method studies, 23, 281, 299, 302, 330
compensation ability, 255
complexity, 7, 14, 28, 39–40, 42, 47, 58, 62, 65–6, 69, 73–5, 78, 80–3, 85, 87–9, 91–2, 97–9, 113–14, 136, 143, 168, 188, 192, 194, 211–14, 220–1, 226, 231, 247–9, 252, 257, 262–4, 269, 273, 288, 296, 299, 301, 305, 336, 339, 346–7, 350, 354, 359, 361, 372
complexity-accuracy-fluency (CAF), 58, 65, 79, 87, 91, 214, 216, 218, 220, 227, 231, 263
complexity-accuracy-lexis-fluency (CALF), 65, 70–2, 74, 87–8, 90, 247–9, 264, 361
lexical complexity, 65, 67, 72, 84, 98, 101, 138, 214, 288, 296
lexical density, 83

lexical sophistication, 67, 102, 258
lexical variety, 213
syntactic complexity, 148–9, 213–14, 288, 296
comprehensible input, 33
comprehensible output, 32
pushed output, 32
computer-mediated (CM) tasks, 42, 46
concept-based language teaching, 112, 347
consciousness-raising tasks, 321, 346, 355
content-based language teaching/CLIL, 17–18
contingency, 253, 361
corrective feedback, 34–6, 39, 45, 50–1, 55, 60, 62, 116–17, 132–3, 137, 140, 148, 151, 153, 171, 208, 215, 222–3, 232, 235, 237, 239, 290, 338–9, 341, 349
  clarification request, 36, 46, 53, 57, 224, 322, 372
  delayed feedback, 55, 232
  elicitation, 37, 53, 224, 241, 372
  explicit correction, 37, 54, 61, 117, 133, 141, 224, 372
  explicit feedback, 54, 60, 62, 116, 135, 140, 153, 224, 226
  focus on form, 16–17, 32, 35, 39, 44, 47, 51, 60, 62, 98, 133–4, 153, 176, 211, 217, 219, 222–3, 232, 235, 237, 286, 293, 314, 334–5, 338
  immediate feedback, 56, 232
  implicit feedback, 54, 62, 116, 133, 135, 140, 226, 237
  intensive corrective feedback, 51
  metalinguistic clue/feedback, 36–7, 54, 133, 140, 152, 224, 372
  prompts, 45, 52, 55–7, 61, 117, 123, 143, 224, 226, 228
  recasts, 16, 35, 44, 46, 52, 54, 56, 61, 117, 133, 140, 144, 152–3, 224, 226–7, 371
  repetition, 36, 40, 49, 68, 73–4, 91–3, 96–7, 102, 140, 176, 224, 228, 230, 232, 237, 247–8, 264, 362, 372
  uptake, 21, 23, 38, 44, 46–7, 62, 87, 304, 332, 372
course book, 16, 267–8, 275–6, 278, 364
criterion-referencing, 242, 279
critics of TBLT, 335, 344
critiques/criticisms of TBLT, 23–4, 331, 335, 350, 352

definition of task, 38, 190, 196
delayed CF, 55
discourse competence, 243
discourse repair, 34
dynamic assessment, 108, 114, 116, 121–4, 127, 358, 361, 372

engagement, 63, 80, 88–9, 119, 143–4, 146, 153, 160, 165, 171, 182, 295, 322, 326
engagement in language use (ELU), 171, 182
everyday concepts, 105, 107, 112, 114
experiential learning, 155, 157, 170, 172, 325
explicit correction, 37, 54, 61, 117, 133, 140, 224, 372
  corrective feedback, 34–6, 39, 45, 50–1, 55, 60, 62, 116, 132, 171, 208, 290, 338–9, 341, 349
explicit instruction, 31, 44, 57–8, 62–3, 111–12, 125, 223, 234, 291, 303, 311, 325, 328, 341, 349–50, 352
explicit learning, 30, 111, 133, 153, 334, 372
exploratory practice, 308, 317–19
extensive CF, 52
Extensive CF, 52

familiarity, 8, 40, 75, 80, 92, 113, 163–4, 191, 194, 197, 215, 221, 248, 252, 317
filled pauses, 68, 258
flow theory, 171
fluency, 4, 16, 23, 50, 58, 65, 68, 72–5, 78, 83–4, 88, 92–3, 97, 101–2, 113, 136, 138, 144, 168, 191–2, 199, 201, 211, 213–14, 220–1, 227, 231, 247–8, 250, 257, 263, 287, 296, 299, 301, 316, 336, 338–9, 346, 350, 361, 372
focus on form (FonF), 16–17, 32, 35, 39, 44, 47, 51, 60, 98, 111, 133–4, 153, 176, 189, 211, 217, 219, 222–3, 232, 235, 237, 286, 293, 314, 334–5, 338, 349
  corrective feedback, 34–6, 39, 45, 50–1, 55, 60, 62, 116–17, 132–3, 137, 140, 148, 151, 153, 171, 208, 215, 222–3, 232, 235, 237, 239, 290, 338–9, 341, 349
focus on forms (FonFs), 21, 111, 127, 229, 232, 286, 338

formative, 21, 25, 176, 242, 279, 309, 318, 357, 368
formative evluation, 308, 318

general programme comparisons, 281, 285–6, 295
goal-tracking, 169, 205
Grading and sequencing tasks, 7–8, 14, 197, 348, 371
grammar in TBLT, 338, 344, 352

here-and-now, 42, 66, 76, 80, 83, 85, 88, 95

IATBLT, 364, 370
imitation, 56, 105–9, 111
immediate corrective feedback (CF), 56
   immediate feedback, 56, 232
immersion, 45, 55, 132, 134–5
implementation variables, 40, 43, 345
implementing TBLT, 22, 146, 282, 304, 306, 318, 324–30
implicit language learning, 51, 111
incidental language learning, 170, 337
individual differences, 90, 130, 133, 156, 169, 190, 192, 195–6, 361
information-gap task, 11, 40, 339, 341, 371
information-theoretic analysis, 190, 192
initiation-response-feedback (IRF), 292
innovation, 22, 282, 285, 303–7, 314, 324, 329, 357, 366, 369
input-enhancement, 43
insider critics, 336, 344–51
intensive corrective feedback, 51
interaction approach, 29, 35, 40
Interaction Hypothesis, 29, 82, 136, 360
interactional authenticity, 12, 21, 244, 250, 260
interactionally modified input, 43, 48
interactive ability, 243–4, 259, 261, 266, 268, 274, 280
interactive tasks, 43, 63, 75, 98, 156, 215, 338
International Association of Task-Based Language Teaching (IATBLT), 359

LAC, 64, 72, 74, 76–8, 83, 86, 89, 98, 100
language aptitude, 129, 131–5
   language analytic ability, 131, 133–5
   MLAT, 131–2, 134
   psychological perspectives, 129
   working memory, 46, 51, 70, 76, 79, 81, 87, 90, 116, 129, 135–41, 149, 153, 192–3, 227, 255, 261, 265, 362
language related episodes (LREs), 108, 219, 361
languaging, 105–9
language related epispdes (LREs)
   languaging, 105, 108, 120–1, 125, 355, 357
learner-generated content, 162–3
lemma, 71, 89, 97, 255
lexical variety, 213
lexis, 65, 75, 84, 91–2, 97, 179, 247–8, 344
   lexical complexity, 65, 67, 72, 84, 98, 101, 138, 214, 288, 296
   lexical density, 83
   lexical sophistication, 67, 102, 258
limbic system, 170
Limited Attention Capacity Hypothesis, 136
listen-and-do task, 48, 340
longitudinal research, 360, 362

macro evaluation, 307–9, 316
macrostructure, 78, 98
main task, 15, 143, 161, 176, 200, 206, 209, 212–13, 221, 228, 234, 237, 239, 322, 339, 349, 357
measurement, 8, 64, 67–8, 91, 122, 153, 249, 256, 259, 267, 287, 296, 298, 301, 361, 370
measuring task-based performance, 64–9
mediation, 105–7, 109, 111, 114, 116–17, 120, 122, 126–7
meta-analyses/meta-analysis, 39, 43, 51–2, 83–5, 90–3, 99, 131, 147, 225, 247–8, 253, 263, 338, 349
metacognition, 256
metalinguistic feedback, 54, 133, 140, 152, 372
   corrective feedback, 34–6, 39, 45, 50–1, 55, 60, 62, 116, 132, 171, 208, 290, 338–9, 341, 349
micro processes, 98
micro-evaluation, 282, 307–8, 316–23, 328, 330
modality, 89, 91, 148, 150–2, 230
Modern Language Aptitude Test (MLAT), 131–2, 134
   aptitude, 81, 129, 131–5, 148, 153, 362
   language aptitude, 129, 131–5

modular curriculum/syllabus, 25, 33, 199, 335, 355
modular syllabus, 204
motivation, 81, 90, 94, 129, 131, 142–7, 153, 156, 160, 162, 170–1, 181, 192, 196, 199, 203, 205–6, 208, 210, 221, 223, 225, 308, 320–2, 362

narrative tasks, 148, 152, 165
native-speaker, 66, 101–2, 316
needs analysis, 20, 115, 163–4, 186, 188, 190, 197, 200, 244, 269, 312, 316, 318, 345–6, 354
negotiation of form, 35, 47, 61, 168–9
negotiation of meaning, 35, 39–40, 42, 47, 60–1, 82, 168, 191, 294, 319, 322
non-understanding routines, 34–5
norm-referencing, 242
noticing, 29–30, 32, 39, 43–4, 46–7, 51, 61, 63, 80, 82, 87–8, 108, 140–1, 144, 153, 169, 227, 233, 334–5, 345

on-line planning, 73, 90, 97, 247, 255, 264, 357
opinion gap task, 40
outcome, 4, 10, 12, 21, 40, 48, 80, 109, 113–14, 133–4, 139–40, 142, 144, 147, 151–2, 157, 164, 169, 172, 175, 182, 184, 189, 191, 196, 198, 203, 205, 207, 210, 222, 228, 231, 235, 245, 262, 273, 284, 287, 289–90, 295, 300, 308, 314, 317, 319, 322, 339, 342–3, 345, 353, 361
output prompting corrective feedback (CF), 52
output-based task, 33, 47, 50, 169, 338, 341
output-prompting corrective feedback (CF) prompts, 45, 52, 55–7, 61, 117, 123, 143, 224, 226, 228
outsider critics, 335–44, 350, 352

participation variables, 79–80
participatory structure, 59–60, 146, 209, 224, 235–7, 239, 335, 341
pedagogic tasks, 7, 12–13, 18, 89, 159, 164, 167, 172, 175, 182, 186–7, 191, 195, 197, 200, 206, 336, 345–6, 354
performance measurement, 370
personal investment theory, 160–2, 169, 172
phonological short-term memory, 139

planning, 17, 19, 58, 69, 72–3, 75–7, 80, 85, 90–1, 93, 96–7, 101, 130, 137, 139, 141, 150, 154, 176, 202–3, 211–13, 215–16, 223, 226, 236, 244, 247–50, 254–5, 263–4, 269, 273, 326–7, 334, 336, 339, 343, 348, 354–5, 357, 362, 367
  pre-task planning, 138, 141, 211
  strategic planning, 73, 90, 97, 137, 212, 227, 247, 255
  within-task planning, 137, 139, 141, 213, 223, 226
post-task activities, 228, 322, 334, 357
post-task condition, 73, 75–6, 93, 247
post-task feedback, 229, 232
  delayed feedback, 55, 232
post-task options, 161, 228–35, 237
practitioner research, 235–6, 373
pragmatic ability/abilities, 251–3, 265
pragmatic competence, 42, 196, 244
pre-emptive focus on form, 44, 222
pre-modified input, 43, 48, 62
pre-task focus on form, 217
  pre-task grammar instruction, 211, 217–18, 239
pre-task modelling, 211, 217, 234, 237
pre-task options/work, 161, 209
pre-task planning, 17, 137, 139, 141, 176, 212–13, 215, 217, 227, 236, 250, 264, 327, 339, 343, 348
  planning, 17, 19, 58, 69, 72–3, 75–7, 80, 85, 90–1, 93, 96–7, 102, 130, 137, 139, 141, 150, 154, 176, 202–3, 211–13, 215–16, 223, 226, 236, 244, 247–50, 254–5, 263–4, 269, 273, 326–7, 334, 336, 339, 343, 348, 354–5, 357, 362, 367
pre-verbal message, 71, 254
private speech, 105–6, 108, 111, 120
problem-solution structure, 76, 85
procedural syllabus, 198
proficiency level, 57, 66, 79–80, 89, 138, 156, 169, 191, 252, 271, 275, 354, 364
proficiency tests, 260, 266, 304
project work, 365
prompts, 45, 52, 55–7, 61, 117, 123, 143, 224, 226, 228
  corrective feedback, 34–6, 39, 45, 50–1, 55, 60, 62, 116, 132, 171, 208, 290, 338–9, 341, 349
  output-prompting feedback, 61–2, 137
pushed output, 32, 171

416   Index

qualitative methods/research, 85, 248, 355, 360
quantitative methods/research, 320

range, 23, 52, 60, 65, 70, 73, 77, 84, 89–91, 93, 95, 99–100, 119, 169, 206, 209, 242, 245, 247, 250–1, 254–5, 257, 260, 262, 267, 269, 271, 274, 276–8, 344, 354, 357, 360, 368
raters, 245–6, 252, 256–8
rating scales, 245–6, 256, 258, 271
reactive focus on form, 36, 39, 44, 51, 222, 339
   corrective feedback, 34–6, 39, 45, 50–1, 55, 60, 62, 116–17, 132–3, 137, 140, 148, 151, 153, 171, 208, 215, 222–3, 232, 235, 237, 239, 290, 338, 341, 349
real-world tasks/real-life tasks, 7, 12, 20, 184–6, 190, 192, 197, 259–60, 269, 276, 345
reasoning, 8, 41–2, 80–1, 83, 85, 88, 91–2, 113, 129, 139, 148, 175, 183–4, 192–3, 197–8, 263, 274, 348
   reasoning demands, 84
reasoning gap tasks, 183
recasts, 16, 35, 44, 46, 52, 54, 56, 61, 117, 133, 140, 144, 152–3, 224, 226–7, 372
   corrective feedback, 34–6, 39, 45, 50–1, 55, 60, 62, 116, 132, 171, 208, 290, 338–9, 341, 349
   focus on form, 16–17, 32, 35, 39, 44, 47, 51, 133–4, 153, 176, 189, 211, 217, 219, 222–3, 232, 235, 237, 286, 293, 314, 334–6, 338
reflection, 77, 80, 171, 186, 229, 235, 250, 309, 317, 322
reliability, 56, 241, 266–7, 270–1, 278, 329, 368
repair fluency/repair-linked fluency, 68
   fluency, 50, 58, 65, 68, 72–5, 78, 83, 88, 91–3, 97, 101–2, 113, 136, 138, 144, 211, 213–14, 218, 220–1, 227, 231, 247–8, 250, 257, 263, 287, 296, 299, 301, 336, 339, 346, 350, 361, 372
repetition, 36, 40, 49, 68, 73–4, 91–3, 96–7, 102, 140, 176, 224, 228, 230–1, 237–8, 247–8, 264, 341, 343, 362, 372
   corrective feedback, 34–6, 39, 45, 50–1, 55, 60, 62, 116–17, 132–3, 137, 140, 148, 151, 153, 171, 208, 215, 222–3, 232, 235, 237, 239, 290, 338–9, 341, 349

resource pools, 79, 87
resource-directing task factors, 193
resource-dispersing task factors, 193
restructure, 82, 86, 188, 202–3

scaffolding, 105–9, 117, 119, 211, 221, 317, 358
scientific concepts, 105, 107, 109, 111, 114, 124, 127, 373
second language mental lexicon, 71, 255
sequencing, 7–8, 11, 14, 79, 81, 89, 113, 175, 179, 187, 191, 322, 337, 371
sequencing tasks, 322
skill-learning theory, 30, 328, 349
SLML, 72, 74, 78
small group work, 15, 29, 59–60, 120, 327, 341
sociocultural theory, 56, 103, 105, 108–9, 113, 126, 221, 322, 336, 361, 367
   scaffolding, 105–9, 117, 119, 211, 221, 317, 358
   zone of proximal development, 106–7
specific purposes, 287, 371
SSARC, 64, 69, 79, 81–2, 84, 86, 88–9, 98, 100, 188, 194, 200
stabilise, 83, 86
stimulated recall, 45–6
strategic competence, 243–4, 254, 260
strategic planning, 73, 90, 97, 137, 212, 227, 247, 255
   pre-task planning, 17, 138, 141, 176, 211–13, 215, 217, 227, 236, 250, 264, 327, 339, 343, 348
structural complexity, 65, 67–9, 74, 78, 83, 91, 102
Structural Oral-Situational Method/Model, 6, 285–6
structural syllabus, 3, 24, 180, 199, 204, 303, 328, 351
structured/unstructured tasks, 66, 73, 77, 98, 138, 247, 249
subordination, 65, 94, 102, 138, 201, 213, 220, 257
   syntactic complexity, 148–9, 213–14, 288, 296
summative assessment, 21
summative evaluation, 308
support material, 269, 357
syllabus design, 180–4, 195–6
System 1, 94
System 2, 94

task characteristics, 70–2, 75, 78, 89, 93, 96, 192, 211, 247–8, 250, 254, 259, 261, 263–4, 271, 355
task complexity, 14, 41, 79–83, 87–8, 90, 98–101, 115, 130, 137, 139, 146, 148–9, 152, 168, 217, 263–4, 347, 354, 359, 370, 372
task conditions, 70–2, 75, 78, 80, 89, 93, 96, 101, 130, 139, 141, 149–50, 152, 154, 191, 247–8, 250, 253–4, 261, 263–4, 348, 354–5, 360
task design, 11, 39–41, 43, 58, 62, 73, 94, 96, 113, 116, 127, 173, 188, 193, 319, 345, 354
task difficulty, 14, 74, 79, 81, 90, 99–100, 130, 259, 262, 270, 278, 354, 361
task fulfilment, 257, 262
task implementation, 40, 116–17, 127, 169, 173, 175, 208
task repetition, 40, 73, 228, 231–2, 237, 343
   posttask options, 229
task selection, 13, 42, 113–15, 163, 175, 179, 187, 191–2, 197
task sequencing, 79, 81, 180, 182–3, 188, 191, 193–5, 197, 200, 206, 348
syllabus design, 79, 82, 87, 98, 179, 363, 365
task support, 93, 248
task types, 7, 11, 42, 70, 77, 151, 163, 165, 186–7, 204, 247, 316, 319, 364
task-as-process, 7, 10, 196, 198
task-as-workplan, 7, 10, 115, 143, 196, 198, 336, 355
task-based (language) assessment, 20–1, 169, 266, 278–9, 329, 332
task-based lesson, 15, 25, 55, 175, 209, 219, 236, 309, 326, 334, 356–7
task-based research, 39, 47, 66, 97, 139, 212, 279, 308, 319, 331, 343–4, 352, 357

TBLT as innovation, 304–7
technology mediated tasks/TBLT, 18–20
there-and-then, 66, 76, 80, 83, 85, 88, 91, 95
time perspective, 76, 80, 84, 86, 88, 91, 96, 247
time pressure, 74, 160, 202, 204, 215, 226, 256, 264, 272, 278, 357
topic preparation, 211, 356
trade-off, 69, 75, 77, 79

underlying competence, 243–5, 249, 254–5, 260–1
unplanned, 83, 101, 250
uptake, 21, 23, 38, 44, 46–7, 62, 87, 194, 304, 307, 372
   corrective feedback, 34–6, 39, 45, 50–1, 55, 60, 62, 116–17, 132–3, 137, 140, 148, 151, 153, 176, 208, 215, 222, 232, 235, 237, 239, 290, 338–9, 341, 349
use of first language (L1), 310

validity, 67, 100, 124, 131, 151, 208, 242, 266–7, 270–1, 273, 276, 278, 284–5, 300, 329, 337, 368
virtual worlds, 367

washback, 176, 242, 266, 268, 275–6, 278
   task-based assessment, 20–1, 74, 169, 266, 277–9, 329
within-task planning, 137, 139, 141, 213, 223, 226
words per clause, 66
   syntactic complexity, 148–9, 213–14, 288, 296
working memory, 46, 51, 70, 76, 79, 81, 87, 90, 116, 129, 135–41, 149, 153, 192–3, 227, 255, 261, 265, 362
www.tblt.org, 359

Zone of Proximal Development, 106–7, 127

Made in the USA
Monee, IL
06 April 2023

31448050R00243